Belmore

The Lowry Corrys of Castle Coole
1646–1913

PETER MARSON

Virtus semper viridis

Belmore

The Lowry Corrys of Castle Coole
1646–1913

PETER MARSON

ULSTER HISTORICAL FOUNDATION

Ulster Historical Foundation is pleased to acknowledge support for this publication
provided by the Belfast Natural History and Philosophical Society and
the Esme Mitchell Trust.

First published 2007
by Ulster Historical Foundation
Cotton Court, Waring Street, Belfast BT1 2ED
www.ancestryireland.com
www.booksireland.org.uk

© Peter Marson
ISBN 978 1 903688 64 9

Printed by Bath Press
Design by Cheah Design

CONTENTS

Part Four

A Practical Man: Somerset Richard, Fourth Earl Belmore, 1835–1913

PREFACE AND ACKNOWLEDGEMENTS

This story of the families at Castle Coole ends with the death of the fourth Earl of Belmore in 1913, because by this time the society in which the first four earls lived had itself passed away. The recollections of Brigadier Eden in the final chapter suggest that the next 25 years were a coda, perhaps a rather melancholy one, lasting until after the Second World War – when, as Lord Belmore's foreword shows, the family's circumstances at Castle Coole changed quite markedly and the house itself received a new lease of life under the arrangements with the National Trust.

I am indebted to the many students of the past, professional and amateur, who have always been ready to help in and discuss with me the making of this story. Many are the professional staff of the record offices and libraries, too numerous to mention, without whose help historical research would be difficult indeed. The Public Record Office of Northern Ireland has, of course, been a major source of material for this work. All of its staff have been unfailingly courteous and supportive.

All who visit Castle Coole or take an interest in it must be grateful to the National Trust for its impeccable restoration work in the 1980s and for its continuing care and conservation of the Castle. I am privileged to count former colleagues, the house staff, guides and wardens at Castle Coole among my friends.

My very special thanks are due to Lord Belmore for his unstinting support and encouragement which itself represents but a fraction of his personal and total commitment to Castle Coole, its history and its people. He and Lady Belmore, through many challenges and changes, have kept the faith with that most important element of any house – the life of its family. My thanks are due to Lady Anthea Forde, Lord Belmore's sister, for permission to quote from the memoir specially written for her by her cousin, Lady Winifred Lowry Corry.

I gratefully acknowledge the following for their interest, advice and support and have only myself to blame for any faults which have resulted in failing to heed them: Frances Bailey, the staff and wardens at Blickling Hall, Irene Burrowes, Jim Cooke, Patricia Donald, Chris Donegan, Joan Hill, Sarah Emily Horrocks, Roger de Keersmaeker, Dr Anthony Malcomson, Deborah Manley and her sister Peta Rée, Dr Edward McParland, Commander George S. Pearson OBE Royal Navy (retd), the Poore family, Olwen Purdue, William Roulston, Bryan Rutledge, the Earl of Sandwich, Peter Towell, Patricia Usick and Nigel Strudwick of the Department of Egypt and Sudan at the British Museum and Sophie Wright.

My heartfelt thanks are due to my wife Ellen who did so much to enhance our work at Castle Coole and continued her unfailing support and practical help when the unavoidably lonely business of research and writing tended, at times, to become obsessive and an interfering presence.

PETER MARSON

ILLUSTRATIONS (ACKNOWLEDGEMENTS)

Page 17 perspective drawing by Stephen Conlin courtesy of the National Trust Northern Ireland Region

Page 32 John Hobart, 2nd Earl of Buckinghamshire and his wife, Lady Caroline (Conolly) by Gainsborough ©NTPL/John Hammond

Page 36 The Irish House of Commons by Francis Wheatley 1780 Henry Grattan 'urging the Claims of Irish Rights, 8 June 1780'. Armar Lowry Corry on the left ©Leeds Museums and Galleries (Lotherton Hall)

Pages 50 and 51 maps from Thomas McErlean Historic Development of the Park at Castle Coole 1984 ©The National Trust Northern Ireland

Pages 74 The Library ©NTPL Patrick Prendergast; page 78 mason's marks ©The National Trust Northern Ireland; page 116 the Bow room ©NTPL Patrick Prendergast; page 166 the State bedroom ©NTPL Christopher Hill; and 245 Lady Belmore's bedroom ©NTPL Northern Ireland Region and cover photograph ©NTPL/Matthew Antrobus

Page 83 John James Hamilton, 1st Marquess of Abercorn KG PC (Ireland) from a Private Collection in Fermanagh

Page 94 Photograph of Mount Juliet, Thomastown, Kilkenny by courtesy of Conrad Hotels

Page 140 Graffiti of two *Osprey* sailors courtesy of Roger O De Keersmaecker *Graffito Graffiti*

Page 145 View of Grand Cairo by Henry Salt 1809 ©Queen's Printer and Controller of HMSO 2007. UK Government Art Collection

Pages 143 and 147 Temple of Dendur, details showing graffiti of Captain A.L. Corry, the 2 seamen carvers and 2nd Earl Belmore ©The Metropolitan Museum of Art, given to the United States by Egypt in 1965, awarded to the Metropolitan Museum of Art in 1967, and installed in the Sackler Wing in 1978 (68.154)

Page 180 and 181 Images taken from the website of *The Atlantic Slave Trade and Slave Life in the Americas: A Visual Record* Jerome S. Handler and Michael L. Tuite Jr.

Page 200 Admiral Armar Lowry Corry and his children at Ballinacourt, their home near Dublin courtesy of the Poore family

Page 222 The Derby Cabinet, 1867, including Henry Corry, by Henry Gales, 1868 ©National Portrait Gallery London

Page 233 Throsby Park homestead from west, Moss Vale Robert Deane 1996 nla.pic-an12002893–22 ©National Library of Australia

Page 238 Montagu William Lowry Corry, Baron Rowton after Marion Margaret Violet Manners, Duchess of Rutland lithograph, 1888 NPG D23372 ©National Portrait Gallery London

Page iv and xii photographs by Patrick Prendergast

NOTES

Money

Amounts of money appearing in the text are all as originally stated, sometimes in Irish pounds, shillings and pence and sometimes in English sterling. The discount in the Irish pound fluctuated but seems to have been about 8%. A figure in sterling can be multiplied by 60 to arrive at a very approximate modern figure but, because of changes in lifestyle, it may not accurately represent equivalence in the value of things (i.e., the commodities themselves might now be different in kind or not considered to be of such relative importance).[1]

Names

The earl current to any given passage is always referred to as 'Belmore' and his eldest son, whose title is viscount, as 'Corry'. The first Earl, before he was raised to the peerage, was Armar Lowry, subsequently Armar Lowry Corry, and is referred to in the text as 'Armar' until the point where he became a peer.

FOREWORD BY LORD BELMORE

With Cecil Lowry Corry's death in 1949 and the arrival of my parents and my sisters Anthea and Wendy at Castle Coole later that year, it was clear that changes were required to secure the future of the house.

Plans were quickly drawn up to transfer the house and 70 acres of land to the National Trust, and by 1955 parts of the house were open to the public, electricity having been installed in most of the building after 1951.

Our father took the land in hand and planted a good number of commercial woods: it must have seemed that a new age had dawned on the property. A nine-hole golf course was opened which was later extended to 18 holes.

By 1960, the year our father, sadly, died at age 47, there was a feeling that we had finally redirected the house and demesne onto a sound footing, both for the benefit of the public and for our family. Unfortunately, another tranche of death duties had to be met and my trustees felt they had no choice but to close my father's farming business down, as a result of which the land was let to a variety of neighbours, amongst them Colonel Crichton, Jason Graham and, more recently, Cecil Cooke, George Black and Billy Johnston.

I came back to live at Castle Coole in the early 1970s and soon the National Trust were busy refacing the house with Portland stone and carrying out general repairs which cost several million pounds. In order to preserve the landscape between the house and Enniskillen, now only a mile away, I sold a further 340 acres to them in 1982.

There are exciting plans to create new footpaths for the public and, by 2008, some of these should be in place.

In September 1984 Mary and I were married and we now live in the walled garden with Monty (born in 1989) and Martha (born in 1992). Our eldest son, John (born in 1985), has moved back into Castle Coole, where he briefly lived as a young boy.

The present Lord Belmore's father, mother and sisters on the steps of Castle Coole after their arrival in 1949

Part One

Lord of the Mountains: Armar, First Earl Belmore

Chapter One

Origins I

Two new arrivals in Ireland in the early seventeenth century were at the root of the eventual link between the Lowry and the Corry families.

In 1641, John Corry from Dumfries in Scotland settled in Belfast as a merchant, along with his wife Blanch and their eight-year-old son James. Family tradition has it that, somewhat earlier, James Lowry from Maxwelton, also in Dumfries, joined Sir George Hamilton's plantation settlement in Ballymagorry, near Strabane, County Tyrone. Although their experience of life in Ireland was very different, a common factor in establishing themselves and in the opportunities they took was the availability of land, cheap for Protestant purchasers and the most secure large investment that could be made. It brought steady income and influence, and could readily be used as collateral for further purchases.

John Corry and James, who almost certainly worked with his father, must have been a successful combination because, on 1 July 1654, John was elected a merchant of the staple, giving him entry into a closed circle of merchants who monopolised the trade in basic or staple goods, such as wool and hides. The financial advantages he enjoyed as a result would have enabled him to amass a fortune.[1] Conditions in Belfast were unsettled by bitter civil war, economic problems and pestilence. That, and the fact that he was getting on in years, may have encouraged him to move his family away to Fermanagh in the north-west.

At Michaelmas in 1655 he purchased an estate called Manor Coole, including the Castle of Coole (alias Castle Atkinson) for £860. It came with a history of troubles: a previous owner had been murdered and his successor in England was probably keen to dispose of it. It certainly was a bargain, for it had been sold ten years earlier by Atkinson, the original owner, for £1,650, and in the almost half century since Atkinson had first developed the estate there had obviously been a great deal of value added to it.[2]

Shortly after they arrived, John's wife died and James, now aged 23, began to play a larger part in their affairs. His marriage in 1663 to Sarah Anketill of Anketill Grove, Monaghan added land near Castle Coole at Magherastephana, Tirkennedy to the family holdings – but of their four children, only one (John, born at Enniskillen in 1667) was a son and heir. One daughter, Sarah, died in infancy; two others, Rebecca and Elizabeth, survived. Rebecca would eventually marry James Moutray of Favour Royal, County Tyrone and Elizabeth would marry James Auchinleck of Enniskillen, who lived at Thomastown near Castle Coole.

While John Corry continued to live in Castle Coole, James and his family took a house in Enniskillen, on the site of the present Town Hall.

His acquisition of Castle Coole did bring John recognition: he was a justice of the peace for Fermanagh, a commissioner for levying subsidies in 1662, the High Sheriff in 1666 and also a justice of the peace for Cavan. However, his chief concern was the succession to Castle Coole which, in view of the birth of only one son, had to be formally secured.

John Corry's signature and drawing of the copper merchant's one penny token in Benn's History of the Town of Belfast no 68 'John. Corry of Bellfast, Marchant, 1656'

In April 1679 father and son agreed on a settlement of John's property on James for life and then on James's son John, provided that he married 'a wife of equivalent birth and fortune'. As it happened, John did so in 1701 when he married Sarah Leslie, the co-heiress of William Leslie of Prospect, County Antrim. In practice, the family wealth was also protected by the simple fact that marriages were not usually made with outsiders – cousins tended to marry cousins and thus maintained a degree of closeness and mutual understanding of what was required of them.

John Corry lived on as a substantial landowner for 30 years after moving to Castle Coole, dying in his eighties some time between 1683 and 1685.

During his father's time, James had already begun to consolidate the Corry family's fortunes. He had money to spend and he spent it very actively. He acquired further land in Clabby, Longford, Dublin and Monaghan. He was a survivor, a proud, tough man who became a significant figure in the government of Fermanagh – in 1666, as captain of the Fermanagh Foot Militia; in 1671, as high sheriff of Fermanagh and in 1677 as high sheriff of Monaghan.

He was to face further difficulties during his own long tenure of the demesne. He had, for example, little luck in starting a new family. By 1683 Sarah had died and in that year James married Lucy Mervyn, daughter of Henry Mervyn of Trillick, County Tyrone. Sadly, it was a short marriage which produced only one child, Sarah, who died young.

Arms and Alimony

In February 1688, James II became king and there began the series of events that led, later in the same year, to an invitation being issued to William of Orange to assume the throne.

The defence of Enniskillen against the Catholic army by a handful of determined Protestants has become one of the enduring stories of Protestant history, allied to the story of the Siege of Derry. James Corry was closely, and controversially, involved in the Enniskillen story – perhaps inevitably so, given his position and the strategic importance of Castle Coole. He was accused of supporting King James, running away from Ireland

Colonel James Corry by James Pooley

to avoid the troubles and, after it was all over, claiming compensation for the burning of Castle Coole during the Siege of Enniskillen in July 1689.

It is true that in December 1688 he had ordered the townspeople of Enniskillen to find housing and supplies for two companies of King James's infantry, but at that time, as a local magistrate, he was simply upholding the authority of the existing government. Resistance would have been futile and would have amounted to treason. It is also true that James left Castle Coole with his wife and children and went to England. However, this was not until the townspeople refused to accept his appointment as colonel of foot and governor of Enniskillen: his position was then such that he had no say in how any defence was to be conducted. In spite of this, before he left, he made careful arrangements to provide a garrison and provisions at Castle Coole for the defence of Enniskillen.

On 13 July, an army under the command of the Duke of Berwick, illegitimate son of King James, approached Castle Coole in order to occupy it for their attack on Enniskillen. But, to increase the security of the town, Castle Coole and its dependent houses had already been burned and its garrison, with all its provisions, ordered into the town. There was a serious skirmish and only its artillery on Fort Hill, which forced Berwick to retreat, saved the town. On 31 July, at the Battle of Newtownbutler, Berwick's army was defeated.

The negative account of James Corry's actions was expressly repudiated later by a certificate of the leading townspeople of Enniskillen themselves, who declared that he:

> 'was verry Industrouse and Deligent in Raiseing and Arming men for his late Majestie's service, and for ye support and defence of the Protestant interest of this Kingdom, that he raised a very good troope of horse and foot company, and mount'd and armed many of them at his own expense'.

James supplied Enniskillen with materials for its defence and substantial amounts of food. Furthermore, he suffered serious loss:

> 'his house of Castle Coole, which is about a mile out of ye towne, was burn'd by ye Governor's order, upon ye approach of ye Duke of Barwick and by ye advice of ye chief officers, to prevent ye said Duke's Posteing himself there'.[3]

James did apply for compensation – which, after protracted legal proceedings, was granted – but it did not amount in all to more than £1,000 (his losses being estimated at over £3,000). The certificate of the townspeople also noted that James Corry's son John, now aged 20, fought for William in Ireland and Flanders. There is no evidence that James and his son differed over the question of which side to support. In fact, James was specifically named in the Act of Attainder passed by King James's parliament in May 1689, and in July 1689 he and his son John joined in an address to King William saying that they, with others, had proclaimed their allegiance to him on 11 March 1689. His loyalty to the Protestant interest was therefore confirmed.

Troubles never come singly, and James's departure for England compounded them. Shortly after they arrived there his second wife died, and in 1691, aged 58, he decided to marry for the third time. He had not received any income from Ireland for three years so he was facing money problems. The marriage may well have eased these, for his bride, Miss Elizabeth Harryman of St Clement's Dane, London, belonged to a prosperous family of tradespeople and had a property in what is now Crown Passage, King Street, St James (then newly built) and a piece of land in Spring Gardens, off Trafalgar Square.

Sadly, the marriage and any financial gain from it did not last long. He was back in Ireland less than a year later, in late 1692, and was elected a knight of the shire for Fermanagh County. In 1694 he was elected a burgess of the Corporation of Enniskillen. He rose high in the government of Enniskillen, becoming provost and a freeman of the town in 1697 and deputy governor of Fermanagh.

James's new wife did not accompany him to Ireland but, instead, sued him for alimony in 1695. In August 1696 the matter was settled and they formally separated, James paying Mrs Corry £20 a year and securing the agreement with a bond of £300. In return, she released him from all other claims she may have had upon him and his properties.

James Corry continued to sit in successive parliaments in Ireland, a strong supporter of government, for over 25 years until his death. He took a great interest in trade and, in 1703, carried a bill through the House of Commons to reduce the general commercial rate of interest to eight per cent.

Since 1692 James had been commissioned as colonel of horse militia but, in 1702, he took his military involvement further by forming the Fermanagh Regiment of Foot Militia under the guidance of a Swiss noble and military expert, Rudolf Wattenwyl. The Fermanagh Militia were claimed to be the best in Ireland, locally known as the 'Blue Sogers' because of their uniform, which was blue faced with red, with silver buttons and lace, topped by cocked hats. Their arms were firelocks and pikes and they were drilled by Wattenwyl, their 'exercising officer', once every two weeks during the year on a parade ground at Castle Coole. Wattenwyl died in 1710 after falling from some builder's scaffolding, during the building of James's new house. At Wattenwyl's own request he was buried on that parade ground.[4] In 1705 James, appointed governor of Fermanagh, raised a completely new corps of militia under warrant of 7 November 1705.

In 1708 he purchased more property in Oxmantown Green, Dublin and in Longford.

James's son John joined him in parliament by successfully contesting a by-election for Enniskillen in 1711. When Queen Anne died in 1714 James was on a 'black list' of Tories. Those who featured on the 'black list' were seen as more favourably inclined towards

Letter from James Corry to Denny Muschamp secretary to Michael Boyle,
Archbishop of Armagh (1678–1702) and to the Lords Justices

Catholics (who often voted for Tory MPs as the lesser of two evils) and looked upon the removal of King James as a regrettable necessity rather than a revolutionary triumph. James continued to sit for Fermanagh until his death in 1718.

'Of great advantage as well as ornament': The Second Castle Coole

The old Castle of Coole had been established in 1611 as a defensive structure, part of the Plantation of Ulster, by Captain Roger Atkinson, an Englishman who had served as a captain of foot stationed on Lough Foyle and had briefly been provost marshal of the forces in Ulster. He was granted, as a retired soldier or 'servitor', a thousand good, profitable acres, to be known forever as the Manor of Coole. Under the rules of the plantation he paid a low rent of only eight pounds a year provided that he undertook to build 'a strong bawne of lime and stone, sixty feet square, with three flankers … a strong stone house … two watermills, one for corn, and another, a tucking mill'. A bawn was a fortified courtyard containing a principal house, sometimes built into a corner of the wall, sometimes separate from it inside the walls. A tucking mill cleaned and processed cloth.

To secure their mutual defence his tenants were required to build their houses in a group near the Castle and 'not in a scattered manner or by themselves'. Atkinson was also required to store specified numbers and types of weapon in his house at all times. After five years, but not before, he could sell the Castle and its demesne as long as it was not

Architect John Curle's drawing of Castle Coole built for James Corry in 1709

transferred to the 'Meer Irish' or to anyone who would not take the oath of supremacy. When it was acquired by James Corry's father it had grown into an estate of 4,575 acres including, besides the old castle, a mansion house, 200 houses with their own gardens, 200 cottages, two water mills, one dower house, three orchards and other land. However, as previously described, the old castle had been all but destroyed in the conflict of 1688. James had returned to live in the house in Enniskillen and his son John lived on a farm at Bonnybrook, Castle Coole.

Towards the end of the seventeenth century, times had begun to change and a period of peace and prosperity prompted some landowners to build anew, some simply extending existing castles, some using the latest Anglo-Dutch style, as at Eyrecourt in Galway, Kilmacurragh in Wicklow, Beaulieu in Louth and Stackallen House in Meath. James probably had it in mind to build a house in that style when, in 1707, he exchanged four acres of Agherenagh for four acres of Lackaboy, of excellent quality and watered by three streams. He added these acres to some of his own land to make a new 132-acre deer park at Killyvilly, on the demesne. Then, in 1709, even though he was already 76 years old, he had plans drawn up for a new house. The style, a blend of Dutch and Classical design in red brick, was fashionable at the time. John Curle was the architect and his design, though more modest, is similar to that which he made for Beaulieu, built about the same time.

The house was large enough, as it needed to be, to accommodate the extended Corry family and their servants. It had five principal bedrooms on the first and second floors and two principal and two subsidiary bedrooms in the attic. There were two parlours and a drawing room. However, according to the typical layout of those times, there were many passages with access to the main rooms with their closets. It must have been difficult to maintain privacy amongst all the comings and goings.

Between 1709 and 1716 James settled all his property with the usual pious hope that he would be called to a much better life and be buried with his ancestors, to whom he directed his son to erect a monument in the old church of Derryvullen. He died on 1 May 1718. The Manor of Coole and other estates acquired by James Corry had already been settled on John by the arrangements of 1679, but James proudly went on to record his personal achievement in putting together more, namely:

> 'my estate that is of my own purchasing, being near six hundred pounds per annum of land of inheritance, in the counties of Fermanagh, Longford, Dublin and Monaghan, besides several considerable leases, and a personal estate of horses, cattle, sheep, mares and colts, household furniture, plate and several debts due to me together with great improvements of building and planting, as well of houses, gardens, orchards, as a large deer park, all well walled, and of great advantage as well as ornament'.[5]

The Last of the Corrys: Colonel John Corry and his Son Leslie Corry

John Corry was already 51 when he inherited his father's properties and he lived for just another eight years. During his father's life John Corry and his family had lived in a house on the Castle Coole demesne at Bonnybrook.

Colonel John Corry by Thomas Pooley

Martha Corry, circle of Charles Jervas

John had been born in 1667, educated at Kilkenny, and had entered Trinity College in 1685. He and his wife Sarah had eight children – four sons, only one of whom survived (Leslie, born in 1712) and four daughters (Martha, Sarah, Mary and Elizabeth).

After the death of his father in 1718 John succeeded to the representation of Fermanagh. In 1721, he voted twice for a national bank.

After his family moved into Castle Coole itself he reslated it and made improvements to the demesne by adding Largy to the area between Ballyreagh and Toppid Mountain. In 1723 he had a map of the demesne made by William Starrat, entitled 'An exact map of Manor Coole'. In fact, it was not exact, since it included more than just Manor Coole – namely, Largy, Glasdrumman, Toppid Mountain and other lands. The Loughside estate is shown in the wrong place but nevertheless the fourth Earl commented, 'It is made to scale, and is tolerably accurate'.

John died in 1726. His only son, Leslie, was aged just 14 at the time and seems to have suffered from poor health, so John appointed his nephew Margetson Armar, who was himself only 25, as guardian to manage Leslie's affairs. Ten years later in 1736, Margetson married his first cousin, John Corry's daughter, Mary. Margetson continued to look after Leslie's business (in Leslie's own words, with 'ability, honesty and affection') and to live at Castle Coole with him, his mother Sarah and his cousins Elizabeth and Mary until Leslie's death.

Leslie Corry was educated by a private tutor and entered Trinity College in 1728. He graduated as BA in 1732. In 1739 he was elected MP for the Conyngham borough of Killybegs, Donegal. He served for only two and a half years but in that time was nominated for six committees. In 1740 the Lord Lieutenant appointed him in place of

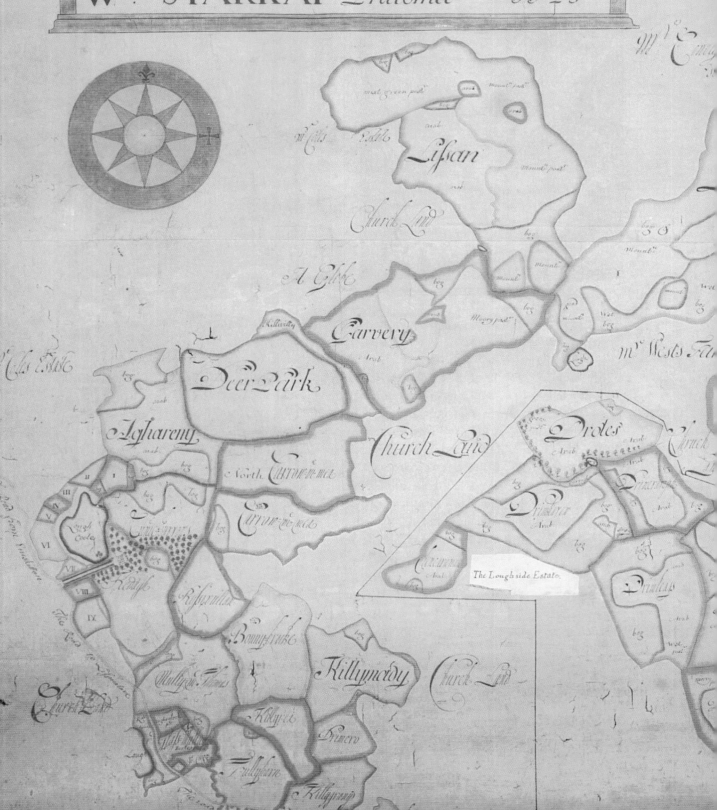

AN Exact MAP of MANNOR COOLE

Belonging to COll. IOHN CORRY by

Wm. STARRAT Philomath 1723

Lisan

Church Land

A Globe

Carvery

Killivitty

Deer Park

Agharemy

North Carrow-m-ned

Carrow-m-ned

Gortgomet

Bush Coole

Rendall

Richarditan

Bonnybrook

Mully in Flian

Killyre

Tullyhone

Killynnoy

Killymoidy

Church Land

Church Land

Church Land

Droles

Drumdran

Drumlea

The Loughside Estate

Mr Wests Farm

Mount

bog

Mr Cox Curris Estate

Far Bettyreagh

near Bettyreagh

Arab

Mount

Mr Cox Curris Estate

Arab

Mount

Arab

Mr Coles Estate

Arab

mount

bog

Arab & green

Mully Kerdro Toped Mountain

Arab & green poll

Mount

the Drool

Lough bog

Sr Ralph Gores Estate

Teehattan

Mount poll

bog

bog

Arab

Arab

Arab

A Scale of perches Forty to the Inch

Th Glebe

Sr Ralph Gores Estate

Arab

Arab

Drumbetty

Church Ld

bog

Modenagh

Mullanabrack

Drumenroe

Gartan

Tullynaskine

Arab

Arab

Sr Ralph Gores estate

his father as colonel of a militia regiment of foot and captain of a company of foot in Fermanagh. Later in the same year he was appointed a deputy governor of Fermanagh. His death in February 1741 resulted in the extinction of the male line of Corrys at Castle Coole.

To secure his daughter, Mary, John left most of the Castle Coole estate to Margetson but the Magherastephana lands, part of the Castle Coole estate, the Longford property and the Dublin property went to his daughter Martha for life. She had married another cousin, Edmund Leslie, in 1738 and under a condition of John's will they took the name Corry to become Mr and Mrs Leslie Corry. Her sister Elizabeth married (firstly) Archibald Hamilton and (secondly) her cousin James Leslie. All three families would die without children surviving them. Martha would pass away in 1764, Mary in 1774 and Margetson in 1776, so that in over little more than a decade John's remaining daughter Sarah would become the last of the Corrys and inherit their estates. Her family would be the future for Castle Coole in the person of her only son, Armar Lowry – who, as Armar Lowry Corry, would become the first Earl Belmore. In the meantime, however, the estate passed into the hands of Margetson and Mary Armar.

Chapter Two

Interregnum: A Man of Ability, Honesty and Affection – Margetson Armar

Margetson Armar was the uncle of Armar, the first Earl Belmore, and his closest male relation, next to his father. Margetson's long-term management of Castle Coole meant that Leslie Corry's life and death had little effect on the development of the demesne. Margetson managed the estate from 1726 until his death in 1773, a continuous period of 47 years. He also inherited Leslie's estates in Clabby and Antrim. The Clabby estate included Toppid Mountain and Tyralton. Even though the next in the direct line of the Corrys was the eldest daughter Martha, it was Margetson who inherited, and he was not required to adopt the name Corry.

On the face of it, had Margetson Armar and his wife had a son of their own they might have passed their property on to him rather than to Armar, Margetson's nephew. However, Leslie, having had no children upon whom he could settle the Castle Coole estate and his other settled land, had done the next best thing. He had made a special arrangement with Margetson, his cousin and trusted close friend, relying on him to pass on the inheritance through his aunts Mary and Sarah to Armar. The circumstances under which Margetson inherited are a special example of the ambience of mutual trust and understanding that existed in this family and that ensured the survival of the Corry name.

In his own words, Margetson asked his wife Mary:

> 'as his most ardent expression towards her … to accept of his acknowledgements of the honour she did him in accepting him for a husband, and for her frank and unsuspecting reliance upon him to make such a settlement afterwards upon her, as the honour she conferred upon him, independent of her own merit deserved. In return for such unmerited and unbounded confidence he has considered her and her peculiar [i.e., particular] relations in his will, in the amplest manner he could, by conferring on her and them, all or most of his acquisitions'.

In this way the Corry estates would be certain to pass to the one person who, since Leslie Corry's death in 1741, could carry on the family name – Armar Lowry Corry. Armar's aunt Mary and his mother would succeed to the Castle Coole demesne, but only for their own lifetimes.

Armar was a year old when Margetson inherited Castle Coole and must have been named after his uncle, no doubt out of respect and affection for the man who was at the centre of family life there.

'He makes his Riches, like his Waters, flow / In many copious channels'

Margetson Armar was born in 1700 in the County of Antrim and educated in Enniskillen School, under its master, Mr Grattan. He entered Trinity College at the age of 16 as a fellow commoner and graduated in 1720. His father, William Armar, Archdeacon of Connor, had died when Margetson was only seven and, as a result, Margetson had been brought up at Castle Coole. He had two surviving sisters, Mary, who married a member of the Gordon family, and Elizabeth, who married Hugh Montgomery of Derrygonnelly, County Fermanagh.

He made improvements to the estate and demesne, which he considerably enlarged. The fourth Earl observed:

> 'at a period when under drainage was unknown, and artificial plantations few, the works which he executed in the way of large double fences, with trees planted on top of the banks, must have been very judicious and useful, as they certainly were substantial, in an unsheltered country such as Fermanagh must have been; when all, or nearly all, the cattle had probably to winter in the fields; and it must moreover have been the means of giving a vast amount of employment to the poor people of the neighbourhood'.[1]

Mrs Armar by Francis Bindon

In 1747 Margetson also refurbished the house for some extra comfort and a little luxury: two new grates were put in the parlour and drawing room and expensive marble was used on the fireplaces, which were fitted with carved mantelpieces; a brass curb was mended and basket fire screens provided. Floors were covered with Scotch and 'Kidiermaster' (i.e., Kidderminster) carpeting and walls with flock paper. Damask stuff curtains were put up at the windows. For decoration there were 'flower pieces', Indian pictures, a collection of framed Hogarth prints; other prints were glazed and pictures framed. A portrait of Mrs Armar was painted by Francis Bindon; old furniture was repaired and new furniture installed; a weather glass and a new clock were purchased.[2]

China, plate and other household items were bought, long china dishes, a tea tray, a

Margetson Armar

Mary Corry, circle of Charles Jervas

chest and a china service and silver plate. The gardens were improved by the addition of new blowhouses (heated greenhouses) and new stone stairs at the back of the house gave access *à la mode* down to the garden.

Margetson was a friendly, hospitable man with a circle of friends who had literary pretensions. One of them, the Reverend Joseph Finlay, eager to record Margetson's charitable disposition, wrote:

'An epigram on the Waterworks at Castlecool, which gave bread to a number of the
Poor employed there in a time of scarcity

'The Bread cast on the Water, Scripture says
And thou shalt find it after many days.
Armar obedient to the Text appears,
And may he find it after many years[.]

'He makes his Riches, like his Waters, flow
In many copious channels, that conduce
At once to Public ornament and Use
Foe to the vagrant weed's destructive growth,
Sustaining Want, he exercises Sloth
In splendid Labours, where his seeming Waste
Is only Beauty in the dress of Taste'.

This poem, written in the late 1750s, suggests that that was the time when Margetson had the formal garden laid out for the Queen Anne house and a fish pond and canal made between the house and Coneyburrow wood. Many fine beech trees were planted in the wood and wide terraces laid out to curve around and through it for driving or walking.

In addition to the improvements at Castle Coole, Margetson organised public works in Enniskillen on roads and bridges, including long-overdue repairs to the church roof, if an anonymous poet is to be believed:

> 'The Pews disjoynted totter, half destroyed,
> The Pulpit, screaming to the hoarse alarms
> Of babling echo, through the vocal void,
> Defeats the Preacher's oratorical Arms;

> 'The fractur'd ceilings, as by subtil Threads
> Dreadful, dependant with what cumbrous weight;
> To praying crowds full o'er their subject Heads,
> In act to tumble, threaten instant Fate'.

Margetson was the High Sheriff of Fermanagh in 1742 and a colonel of the Fermanagh Militia from 1743 onwards:

> 'When mad Rebellion standards durst display
> And mandates from the Throne came to array,
> Armar, among th'appointed Leaders nam'd
> At higher honour than the title aim'd.
> He soon habiliments of War prepar'd'.

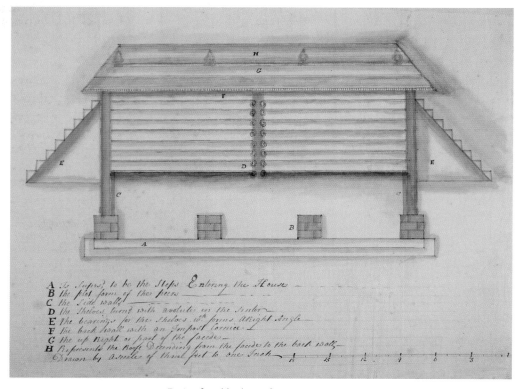

Design for a blowhouse for Margetson Armar

Artist's impression of Castle Coole, canal and formal gardens in Margetson and Mary Armar's time

On 8 May 1756 he was appointed one of the governors of Fermanagh, 'to command and govern all the Militia forces of Horse, Foot and Dragoons'. That he was active in this role is shown by a letter from Sir Arthur Brooke who was at Castle Coole on 30 November 1756. The government had ordered an urgent turnout of the Fermanagh Militia and Sir Arthur commented:

> 'Mr Armar, at whose house I now am, is of opinion, with me, that there ought to be a meeting of the several Governors now in the Country to consult in what manner those commands are to be obeyed'.[3]

In the early 1750s Margetson had acquired a leasehold estate, called the Churchlands, belonging to the See of Clogher, which had previously been held by the Corry family as subtenants only. The purchase made them direct tenants of the head landlord, the Bishop of Clogher. This not only secured land essential to the Castle Coole demesne itself, including, as it did, part of the main oak avenue leading from the old Dublin Road to the door of the Queen Anne house itself, but also added generally to the family holdings. However, most of the land acquired was at some distance from the demesne, and included Breandrum, Rossory, Killyhevlin, Derryvullen, Derrychara and Tamlagh. The total was almost 12,000 English acres, for which Margetson paid £8,000 – just 3 years' purchase

John Corry by Thomas Pooley

Leslie Corry by Thomas Pooley

for the annual rental value of just over £2,400 paid by some 22 tenants, including Margetson himself.

Margetson also acquired a large estate called Blessingbourne, which included Fivemiletown. This he left in his will to his nephew Alexander Gordon. In 1736 he began to rebuild Fivemiletown Church.

Margetson was trusted in business affairs not only by his immediate family but also by others outside it. He held power of attorney from Lady Gore, the widow of Sir Ralph Gore, fourth Baronet of Bellisle, Lisbellaw, to manage their estate during the minority of her son. He was also for some years also a trustee, with Sir Arthur Brooke, of part of the estate of the Coles of Florence Court, charged with the business of clearing the debts to which it was subject.

Margetson and his wife were known for their charity to the poor – for example, for bringing in food from afar when famine struck:

> 'Remember, O Fermanagh, when he fed
> Thy famished children once with Distant Bread,
> With foreign Food as friendly hands supply,
> The Infant when his Mother's breast is dry'.

Although they were a very affectionate couple they were childless and did not enjoy good health. Margetson was very deaf. By the 1750s their health had declined:

'Philander (Margetson) and Aspasia (Mary)
A Poem
'Weighed with the leaden hand of Sickness, down,
She pines without a murmur or a frown:
Her melancholy never turns severe,
Nor casts a shadow on the objects near
O! You with her, the Blessing of the Swain!
The Partner of her Patience, as her Pain …
But spare thy poor remains of precious health,
Opprest with other cares, behold, he bends!'

In spite of her poor health Mary Armar was a skilled and productive gardener whose work made the gardens at Castle Coole famous. The same poem appears to paraphrase the Lowry Corry motto, *virtus semper viridis*, paying tribute to her:

'Thy hand, Aspasia, rears each lovely flow'r;
Instructs them how to scape the dang'rous hour,
To fence their tender breasts from nightly harms
And by their union multiply their charms:
Preserve their sweetness, when their bloom is past,
And by their fragrant *virtues always last*'.

Margetson wrote from Castle Coole to Sir James Caldwell on 25 January 1769, 'I have not been in my garden these many years, and do not know how it is furnished but refer you to Mrs Armar's card'.[4] The card was probably a trade card, the usual way of advertising, for roses, trees, fruit and vegetables. There always seems to have been a trade in plants from the Castle Coole demesne, which at that time Mrs Armar must have run.

In a codicil to his will, made when he was 73, shortly before he died, Margetson refers to 'the infirmities which for a long time I have been labouring under'. In accordance with the promise he had made to Leslie Corry he left Castle Coole to his wife for the duration of her life, to Sarah Lowry Corry for the duration of her life after Mary's death and, after Sarah's death, to Armar for life, with remainder to his male heirs. Margetson did, as a matter of principle, leave the property to his own children, but there were never likely to be any. Had Armar Lowry Corry not succeeded, and had the Corry family died out, then Castle Coole was to have gone to the future Earls of Enniskillen, the Mountflorence family of Florence Court, into which Armar's sister Anna had married. Margetson died in 1773 and Mary survived him by only a year, dying in 1774.

Chapter Three

Origins II

Virtue Always Flourishes: The Lowrys of Aghenis

The Lowry ancestor of the Earls of Belmore was James Lowry of Ballymagorry, near Strabane, County Tyrone. He may originally have gone to Ireland in the early seventeenth century to join Sir George Hamilton's settlement in Ballymagorry.[1] His only son, John, who is said to have been present at the Siege of Derry and was attainted by King James's parliament in 1689, had two sons, John and Robert, by his first marriage to Mary Buchanan. The elder brother, John, died childless in 1698. The younger brother, Robert, Armar Lowry Corry's grandfather, began in 1692 to put together the estates in Tyrone that were to be Armar's principal inheritance. It was well worth raising loans at that time, when land was cheap and society had become more settled after the revolution. He started with a lease of land in the Barony of Dungannon, which he later converted to a freehold. By 1700 his acquisitions included land at Aghenis, near Caledon, upon which he built what was to be the Lowry family seat. In 1705 he purchased, from Lord and Lady Dungannon, the Manor of Finagh, Tyrone, which alone extended to thousands of acres.

Robert had married Anna Sinclair of Holyhill, Tyrone, in 1698. They had four sons – John, Robert, Galbraith and James – and a daughter, Isabella. John died before his father. Galbraith, as the second surviving son, inherited Finagh, the major part of the family estates in Tyrone. By his father's marriage settlement Robert came into lands at Six Mile Cross; by his father's will James inherited land in Dungannon. Eventually, death, the eighteenth-century scourge of family arrangements, left Galbraith Lowry as the successor to the properties of both his brothers. Born in 1706, he was set to be a wealthy country gentleman, an establishment figure.

The two most outstanding years in Galbraith's life were 1733 and 1764. In 1733, aged 27, qualified by his landholdings in Tyrone and his considerable means, he became the leading man in the county and chief administrator of the legal system, when he was appointed high sheriff. But perhaps more significantly from a personal point of view, in that same year he married Sarah, the daughter of John Corry of Castle Coole, Enniskillen. Sarah (Sally to the family) lived until her marriage at Castle Coole with her mother (also Sarah), her brother Leslie, her sisters Martha, (Matty), Mary (Molly) and Elizabeth (Betty), born between 1704 and 1715. Two of John's sons, William and John, had died in infancy. An aunt, Miss Elizabeth Leslie, also lived with them. The only men in the house were Leslie, a minor and the last surviving male Corry, and their cousin Margetson

Galbraith Lowry Corry by Robert Hunter   Sarah Lowry Corry, circle of Charles Jervas

Armar. Several servants and frequent visitors must have kept the house fairly crowded and busy.

Galbraith (Gilly) and Sarah might well have met in the usual county social round – Aghenis is not far from Castle Coole and they would have moved in the same Fermanagh and Tyrone circles. However, they might have met in Dublin, to which all families of the gentry usually went for the sessions of parliament, for the social round and (gentry ladies in particular) for shopping. Sarah and her sisters were given regular allowances for trips to Dublin and, during 1732 and 1733, in the run up to her marriage, her visits were more frequent and more expensive.

Galbraith and Sarah were married at Castle Coole on 26 July 1733. This was more than a personal union, for it signified the joining of forces between the Lowrys and the larger Corry family, mostly female, with its own formidable history and its own demesne 'of great advantage as well as ornament'. They were to become very close – the accounts show the ladies Corry, in the years following the marriage, making frequent visits to Mr and Mrs Lowry at Aghenis.

The Lowrys become Lowry Corrys

By 1740 the Lowrys, in attempting to establish their own family, had suffered an eighteenth-century disaster – the loss of two infant sons, Robert and John, and a daughter, Sarah. They must both have been thankful, and and at the same time apprehensive, when in April of that year a son, Armar, was born. They later lost another daughter, Mary, born in 1748, who died aged 26 in 1774. Anna, their only surviving daughter, born in 1738, would marry William Willoughby Cole in 1763, later first Earl of Enniskillen, who was a neighbour of the Corrys at Florence Court. Soon after Armar's birth, Galbraith Lowry inherited the Corry estates in Monaghan when Armar's uncle, Leslie Corry, died.

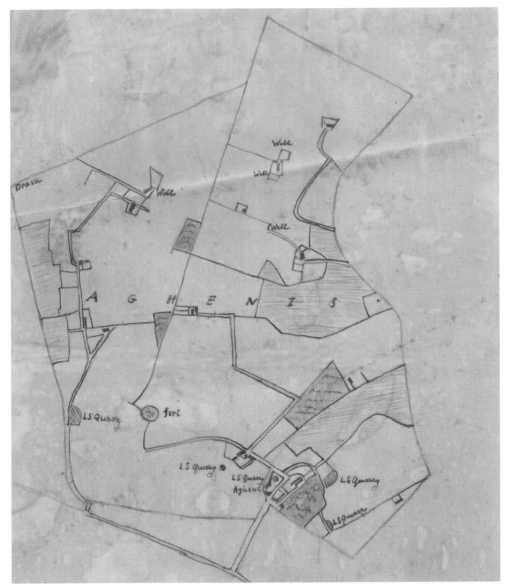

Plan of Aghenis, Tyrone the old Lowry property

With large estates in Tyrone and elsewhere it was not surprising that Galbraith stood for election to the Irish parliament in Dublin. He was elected MP for Tyrone in 1748, aged 42.

Galbraith remained the member for Tyrone for 20 years. His career covered ten sessions, each session usually starting in October and ending in the following April or May but, probably due to his poor health, he did not attend the House of Commons very regularly – he was more than once recorded as being 'absent, in the country', causing the the freeholders of Fintona to register 'our unhappy situation in being deprived by sickness, of the attendance of our worthy Knight of the Shire, Galbraith Lowry Esq., of whose candour and patriot worth we are all convinced'.[2]

Even so, Galbraith was nominated for 29 committees between 1755 and 1760.

The reference to 'Patriot worth' reveals a developing brand of politics, a brand which was handed down to his son and grandchildren. While land was the basis, Parliament was the means, by which the Protestant gentry could exercise power and influence in Ireland. In parliamentary business, they were especially sensitive to revenue matters, the use and, as they often saw it, the abuse, by government of its income and expenditure. During the early part of the eighteenth century, Galbraith's class, the landed gentry, particularly those who became especially identified as 'Patriots', could not be relied upon to support government and worked at exerting their influence over government expenditure. However, their opposition to English policies in his time was no more than embryonic. It would have been usual for Galbraith to support government as he did in 1757 over a major issue, their deliberate use of grants of pensions to secure influence. He voted in support of the government against resolutions declaring such grants to be 'an alienation of the public revenue and an injury to the crown and to this kingdom'. As the century progressed, pressure to establish legislative and commercial independence from England intensified. Armar was only ten at this time but grew up against the background of these developing themes in the politics of his class. The full flowering of Patriot policies, when his class had come to be known as the Protestant Ascendancy, did not occur until the 1770s onwards.

1764 proved to be as eventful a year for Galbraith and his family as had the year of their marriage. His brother Robert died childless, so that he inherited Six Mile Cross, Tyrone, 45 acres of land at Drummin, Armagh and a half share of an advowson – a commercially valuable right of patronage – of the rectory and vicarage of Clogherny. In 1732, Galbraith's brother Robert had given the living at Clogherny to his younger brother, then the Reverend James Lowry, from whom the Lowrys of Pomeroy and Rockdale are descended. Galbraith himself had already added further to the Lowry family estates by acquiring, in 1750, an interest in an estate of some 11,000 acres in Donaghadee and Monterloney.

In that same year, Galbraith's sister-in-law Martha Leslie Corry died. She had married her cousin, Edmund Leslie, in 1738, and had inherited the Longford estate and property in Fermanagh and Dublin under her father's and grandfather's wills, with the condition that she and her husband adopt the name Corry. Yet again, in 1743, death had intervened in the family line when they too had lost their only child, John, who was just two years old.

After Martha's death her property in Longford and Dublin passed, under their father's will, to Armar's mother, Sarah. The Dublin house in Queen Street, Oxmantown, was by then an inn, the Black Lyon, which they let in 1766 to an innkeeper, John Lynch. They already had a house of their own in what became Upper Sackville Street, Dublin. To inherit these properties the Lowrys were also required to assume the name and arms of Corry, which they did in 1765. Armar Lowry Corry was now heir to a large fortune in land.

Armar Lowry Corry: Early Life

'I was born on the 7th of April 1740 – so I do not add or diminish to my age, New Style make [*sic*] my birth day fall on the 18th inst'.[3]

Arms of Lowry Corry, Earls of Belmore

Armar's father Galbraith had had a fairly typical education for a man of his class. He had been privately tutored by a Dr Knowles in the family home at Aghenis, and then sent on to Trinity College, Dublin – where, in 1728, he had graduated as BA at the age of 22. He had also spent some time at the Middle Temple in London, no doubt acquiring some education in basic legal principles. Armar did not go to Trinity like his father, but was educated privately at home by a tutor named Roger Dodd.

Dodd was not Armar's favourite person: in one of his school books, an English/Latin grammar, which he signed 'Armar Lowry', he wrote, 'bad luck to Roger Dodd'. Dodd, however, either because he liked his young pupil or because he liked the job, gave Armar a book entitled *The Gentleman's Recreations* for his sixteenth birthday, inscribed, 'The gift of Roger Dodd to his dear pupil Armar Lowry Esq, April 9th, 1756'. It contained treatises on several branches of science but, much more to the liking of the 'dear pupil', more on outdoor recreations and occupations, especially horsemanship. Armar's other school books reflected his conventional education: works on history, the Roman authors and Latin cribs (in one of which he doodled, 'Gee up my Blossom', thinking about his horse rather than the Latin, and adding geometrical shapes and scribbles). There was also French, the compulsory modern language for a gentleman, represented by *Monsieur A. Boyer, the Compleat French Master for Ladies and Gentlemen*.

Armar was not sent on the grand tour. The probability is that Galbraith, being very much a down-to-earth man of business, was one of the many parents who looked with disfavour on the grand tour as a waste of time and money, and who also harboured little enthusiasm for local schools, which were often thought to be a bad influence and to be run badly. There was already an example of this attitude in the family. Armar's maternal grandfather, John Corry, had expressed the anxious wish that his son Leslie should not be permitted to travel during his minority, but should be 'soberly and virtuously educated in Ireland or Great Britain'. Sobriety and virtue, then, were not thought to be found abroad or at school.

Galbraith did not enjoy the best of health so, because he was the only surviving son and heir, Armar was kept close to home and thoroughly trained by his father in the family business of estate management. This is indicated by an old parchment rent roll, which Galbraith, known as a 'precise' businessman, endorsed as worthy of his son's attention. There are also leases and memoranda, endorsed sometimes by Armar and his father jointly, and sometimes by Armar alone.

Most of all, Armar enjoyed the outdoor life. Fishing was a favourite, especially sea fishing. An old pocket book still exists in which there is a collection of feathers, marked by him as 'cod bate': a length of line with five or six feathered hooks on it which would have been a fairly standard way of fishing for cod. The colours are 'Green Drake' (feathers from the head of a mallard drake), black and orange breast, and other feathers – brown, black, ginger, green, pink and red. Not surprisingly, he also had a great interest in horses and dogs. In his own signed copy of *The Gentleman's Farriery, Dublin 1765*, by surgeon J. Bartlett, he wrote out his own prescriptions for horse ailments and for preventing mange in dogs.[4]

Throughout his life he hunted and raced horses; he enjoyed shooting and, for the fishing, frequently rented a house in Bundoran, County Donegal.

Whatever Dr Dodd thought of him, Galbraith was more than satisfied with his pupil and genuinely thought well of his ability: in a codicil to his will, he not only appointed Armar his sole executor and successor, but expressly made the point that he had been impressed by his experience of his son's ability and integrity.

Another part of Armar's upbringing, of the greatest importance to the family tradition and an inevitable consequence of the Lowrys' importance as major landowners in Tyrone, was preparation for the political life he would take over from his father. Tyrone politics had occupied his father's life greatly and would occupy much of his.

In his second parliament, ending in May 1768, in the only division list in which he is noted, Galbraith was again recorded as absent – in the country, no doubt, once again, because of his poor health. He died on 28 December 1769.

A North Country Gentleman: Politics and Marriage

Land was the foundation on which the life of the Lowry Corrys was based and a life in politics was the activity that their extensive land ownership inevitably involved. In the House of Commons and later in the House of Lords, Armar might on any given occasion have been a supporter of government – but, if government policies challenged the security he experienced within the Protestant Ascendancy, he might equally have been against it. He inherited the political instincts of his father and the Corrys in good measure.

The electoral system under which the Lowry and Corry families were chosen for parliament was very circumscribed, not least by the Penal code. Candidates would stand either for a borough or a county, and if, as could happen, they were elected for both, they would usually choose the county representation. Furthermore:

> 'as regards the county, the members have always been chosen from amongst the landlords or their immediate relatives … the great majority of the principal resident families have had at least one turn in the representation … between county and borough elections Fermanagh has, in nine successive generations (1661–1880), sent 16 members of the Cole family to the House of Commons'.[5]

In Tyrone, the Lowrys and Corrys were also almost continuously in the House of Commons or, later, the House of Lords.

Ireland's executive government was conducted by the Lord Lieutenant, representative of the King of England, or, in his absence, the Lords Justices, advised by the Privy Council. The legislature – the Irish parliament in Dublin – seemed similar to the parliament at Westminster in that there was a House of Lords, consisting of Anglican bishops and the lay peerage, and a House of Commons, elected by the freeholders of the 32 counties, by those entitled to vote in boroughs and by the University of Dublin. However, the reality of county and borough elections can be gauged from the remarks of the fourth Earl above, although borough elections could be expensive to contest.

Parliament was the means by which the mainly Protestant landed gentry could exercise power. During the long eighteenth century that class worked at intensifying its legislative and commercial independence from England, a process which more or less coincided with Armar Lowry Corry's parliamentary career. Armar's political views are revealed by his voting record: he was in favour of financial restraint, but opposed to heavy taxation or other revenue-raising methods that bit into a country gentleman's income and interest. He was against Catholic emancipation, even of a limited kind, and for control of Irish affairs by the Irish parliament, free from undue interference from London.

Armar followed in his father's footsteps when he was elected (on a show of hands by the voters, and at great expense) member for Tyrone in the parliament of 1769. His election expenses came to no less than £6,048, equally divided between himself and his colleague James Stewart. £4,429 went on public houses in Omagh.[6]

He entered parliament at a time when a rethinking of the constitutional relationship of Ireland and Britain was being sought to a greater and greater degree. Between 1779 and 1783 politicians of his persuasion successfully pressed for measures that they believed would establish a constitution for Ireland, distinct from that of Great Britain. In parliament Armar was, not surprisingly, noted first and foremost as 'a man of large fortune'. A large fortune might explain his reputation for having an independent attitude: it was considered that he 'favoured opposition'. This probably meant no more than that, like those other members of his class, he voted 'no' whenever the administration's proposals or actions ran counter to their vision of an Ireland free to trade, free to enact its own legislation, master of its own house and keenly aware of its liberties. Paradoxically, in spite of their insistence on Irish liberties, Patriot gentlemen set great store on the connection with Great Britain, and were well aware of their reliance on it for protection in any emergency.

Some two years after his election, on 8 October 1771, Armar married Lady Margaret Butler, elder daughter of Somerset Hamilton, Earl of Carrick.

She came with a reasonable fortune of £5,000 and with an impressive pedigree, descended as she was (on her mother's side) from Henry VII; her grandfather was Henry Boyle, first Earl of Shannon. This marriage created a close and long-lasting relationship between the Belmore family and the Butlers of Kilkenny. They had three children: Galbraith, who was born and baptised in Dublin in 1772, but died there after only seven months; Somerset, born on 11 July 1774, who succeeded as the second Earl Belmore; and Juliana, who died an infant.

It was said to be a happy marriage but it certainly did not interfere with Armar's political life – for, the day after his wedding, he was back in the House of Commons, where he voted against the address to the Lord Lieutenant, because it contained resolutions supporting policies which were intensely disliked by Armar and those of his persuasion. The address was, in effect, the House of Commons's reply to the government's prospective programme.

The Lord Lieutenant, Townshend, had decided to strengthen the control of the Dublin Castle administration over what he and the British government saw as Ireland's corrupt and expensive political life, with its patronage monopolised by a few (such as John Ponsonby and Armar's new relation by marriage, the Earl of Shannon) and to bring revenues and control of patronage back into the direct control of the Castle. Shannon, Ponsonby and others of similar views were removed from their positions. Independent country gentlemen like Armar probably felt threatened by these dismissals, fearing what they always feared – that the Castle would begin to exercise more control over their parliamentary interests on behalf of the English government.

In the same parliament Armar also voted for Sir Lucius O'Brien's motion for 'retrenchment'. O'Brien was a Patriot and, like Armar, an independent country gentlemen. He was a believer in economic improvement and in constitutional reforms which would tend towards curbing the power of the executive. From 1770 onwards the Irish economy had been facing difficulties, including a growing budget deficit, a crisis in the linen trade and a financial crisis in Dublin. Patriots in such circumstances preferred economies or retrenchment to the usual government alternatives of extra taxation or money-raising schemes like lotteries.

In 1772, descriptions of Armar ranged from 'a north country gentleman who seeks popularity' to 'a supporter of government'. However, in the same year he voted for a short money bill, which showed that he would not hesitate to vote against government if he thought it was acting against his interests. The House of Commons formally inspected the public accounts before a money bill was introduced, and that bill was the means by which government raised the revenue it needed. By voting for a short bill the Commons was not only challenging the government's accounts, but also asserting their right to control the government. Certainly, in this sense, Armar was often 'against' the government in parliamentary votes. Even though the opposition list of 1774 described him as 'generally absent', he turned up to vote against a measure of Catholic relief.

He was 'against' again in 1775 when he voted for the pro-American amendment to the speech from the throne. He shared the sympathy that many Protestant gentlemen felt for the rebel colonists, faced with a threat to their constitutional independence. Being dictated to was no more welcome in Ireland than it was proving to be in America. Their sympathy was misplaced. The disastrous American war created one of the pressures that led to a rethinking by the government in England of what its relationship with Ireland should be.

In 1776 Armar faced another election – one that threatened to be even more expensive than his first in 1768. This was because there were serious differences between his own unswerving support of the Established Church and his colleague James Stewart's equally strong support of the large Presbyterian population in Tyrone. Such a difference could threaten their joint approach to the election, encourage their opponents and lead to additional and costly explanations to the electorate. James Gledstanes, a friend to both men, wrote to Stewart on 9 March:

Juliana Countess of Carrick and her daughters, on the left, Lady Margaret Butler,
first wife of Armar Lowry Corry, mezzotint by J R Smith after Richard Cosway *c.* 1773

'with pain I observe there is no junction between you and Mr Corry. You should
remember that an earlier one upon the last occasion would have saved some thousands
… I therefore recommend an immediate junction and advertisement together'.[7]

Those political differences, however, were not as serious as Armar's personal suffering.
After only five years of marriage he had lost his wife, who had died in February, leaving
him with an infant son. In the same letter Gledstanes added that Armar was 'in great
affliction – and to add to his distress his mother lays in a most dangerous way, being given
over by all her physicians'.[8] Armar's notebook, previously referred to, contains the last
shopping account of Lady Margaret with Henrietta Boswell of Dublin for dresses, flowers
and trimmings. She died after recovering from measles – as a result, it was said, of a cold
she caught by taking off one of her own garments to give to a poor woman. *Walker's
Hibernian Magazine* for February 1776 described Armar in the conventional language of
the time as 'the tenderest and most afflicted of husbands'. Conventional though the
language was, there is no reason to doubt it that it was true. Any prospect Armar had of
establishing his own family at Castle Coole had received a severe setback.

After Lady Margaret's death, Armar was more often absent from the House of
Commons. He reorganised his life and continued to manage the Corry estates for his
ailing mother. Even so, he is mentioned in parliamentary lists for 1776, 1777 and 1779
yet again as a man who 'seeks popularity … very independent … always against'. This view

is supported by his vote in the session of 1778 against the Popery Bill, which was intended to allow Catholics who took the oath to acquire leasehold property for up to 999 years.

Armar made sure that it was very much business as usual at Castle Coole. He had grown to full manhood during Margetson Armar's tenure and, owing to Margetson's ill health, had been very much involved in administering the affairs of the Castle Coole demesne while his aunt, Mrs Armar and his mother were nominally its owners (they, too, suffered health problems). An account book, in which they settled personal money transactions between themselves, runs from 1773 to 1779, and shows him taking the lead in financial and estate business.[9] The only transaction his mother carried out herself was to grant a lease of a house, a garden and cow's grass to one of her servants, Robert Armstrong (probably the father of William Armstrong, who later became steward at Castle Coole).

Armar, on the other hand, supervised the business of selling produce from the demesne. Writing to his neighbour, Sir James Caldwell, in April 1778, he said:

> 'I return you many thanks for the sale, & send you Twenty Rose Trees, you should have got more of them, but I am at present but weak in them'.[10]

He occupied himself in family life as a country gentleman and dutiful son, but changing circumstances were soon to bring him out into the limelight.

Chapter Four

Supreme Felicity

The death of Armar's mother in 1779 made him not simply possessor of three proud family names – Armar, Lowry and Corry – but sole possessor of all the Lowry and Corry estates, amounting to some 70,000 acres in Counties Tyrone, Fermanagh, Longford, Monaghan, Armagh and Dublin. As a consequence, this very wealthy country gentleman and rich widower became worthy of the most serious consideration in high places. The Earl of Shannon, the great fixer of Irish political life, who considered himself 'with respect to my influence, steadiness and abilities as the first object of government', not only thought so but did something about it.[1] He proposed Armar for a peerage. This in itself was not unusual, but Shannon went further – he negotiated for the marriage of the rich widower to Henrietta, the eldest daughter of John Hobart, Earl of Buckinghamshire – the Lord Lieutenant himself:[2] 'it was Lord Shannon who made the proposal for the marriage: he is the relation and friend of Lord Belmore'.*

The marriage and the peerage were, no doubt, intended as a package, not only to benefit Armar but also to secure his political support for Buckinghamshire's administration. Buckinghamshire needed all the help he could get at this time. His daughters were a constant, heavy expense and a good marriage was the obvious and customary solution. Politically, things were already far from easy for him in 1778, and in 1779 they got worse, with increasing pressure for Irish trade to be freed from British restrictions as well as rumours of a French invasion. It was known that if the French had appeared, Buckinghamshire would not have had enough money in the treasury to call out the militia. This led to a growing body of volunteers, which was gaining influence but was outside his control. Armar joined with fellow members of the House of Commons, each writing to the government in London to press for free trade and to warn of the danger arising from the 'martial spirits' that the rumoured prospect of invasion stirred up in the people.[3]

In November 1779 Shannon had a letter from Lady Charlotte Boyle Walsingham in England, expressing a society opinion about the situation:

*John Hobart, Earl of Buckinghamshire, whose title was usually shortened to Buckingham, is not to be confused with George Nugent-Temple-Grenville, first Marquess Buckingham (1753–1813), whose title was not created until 1784. Confusion is made easier because the latter was himself twice lord lieutenant of Ireland, firstly from 1782 to 1783 and secondly from 1787 to 1789.

Armar Lowry Corry and his first wife Lady Margaret (Butler) by Robert Hunter

'I hear government here is much dissatisfied with your Governor, who is said to have quite forgot this Country, and to affect to be the patriot on your side the water. His Secretary is also much blamed for not dividing the House and that *I know* to be true. You know most likely whether it is true that Lord B. has toasted a free trade at his own table'.[4]

The English were mistaken if they thought Buckinghamshire had gone native, but he was persuaded by Shannon that his daughter should.

Buckinghamshire was a man who could never resist a joke, particularly a scurrilous one. His early experience in Dublin had encouraged him in a cynical view:

'most Irish gentlemen enter my closet with a P in their mouths (place, peerage, pension or Privy Council) as naturally as they would enter a lady's closet with a P in their hands'.[5]

He could not have anticipated the delight and relief he would feel when, on 1 February 1780, he announced that his eldest daughter, Henrietta, had consented to receive the addresses of a Mr Armar Lowry Corry:

'... member for the County of Tyrone ... the best match in this Kingdom ... his property is immense. He is universally esteemed, acknowledged to be generous without profusion, honourable upon the most correct line. He is rather well in his figure. His age is 32, and in addition to these capital points his nose resembles mine'.[6]

It was Buckinghamshire's manner to use a joke to mask a serious point, which it might have been bad taste to make seriously. The reference to Armar's nose, which might well in different circumstances (especially in Ireland at that time) have provoked a request for satisfaction, in fact hid the enormous satisfaction that Buckinghamshire felt at the

John Hobart, 2nd Earl of Buckinghamshire and his wife, Lady Caroline (Conolly) by Gainsborough

prospect of such a match. Armar was as far removed from his caricature of an Irish gentleman as could be imagined. A portrait by Robert Hunter, painted a few years earlier, shows him elegantly posed – 'rather well in his figure', but with the nose, as far as possible, redesigned on classical lines.

In two respects, Buckinghamshire was mistaken about Armar and his daughter. At his true age of 40 Armar was nearly 23 years older than Henrietta and during the marriage negotiations conducted by the Earl of Shannon she was not consulted, nor did she meet Armar. For such a dynastic treaty between families it was not essential to consult the lady, but it was often done – if not out of an affectionate regard for her feelings, then as a matter of prudence.

On this occasion it may have been only human for the brilliance of the match to blind the gentlemen to the need for attending to such detail. In addition to its material advantages for him, Armar could once again look forward to the prospect of establishing his family on a secure footing with a well-endowed and beautiful wife who would bring him money and children. Buckinghamshire's motives for the match were obvious. He had already revealed his priorities in advice he had given to a young lady less than a year earlier: 'never listen to any man, whatever he may offer with one hand, unless he brings his rental with the other'.[7]

Henrietta had arrived in Dublin in 1776, at the age of 15, with her father, her stepmother, and her younger sisters, Caroline, Sophia and Emily. Her mother had been dead for many years, leaving £20,000 as Henrietta's prospective fortune. Caroline, Lady Buckinghamshire was a sister-in-law of that most responsible member of the Conolly family of Castletown, Lady Louisa Conolly, who took charge:

> 'Lady Hariet Hobart is only 15, and on the footing of a child, so that there is nothing to be done with her but taking her to the play, which I did last night, to poor old Crow Street, where we had a very full house'.[8]

Henrietta continued to enjoy the elegance and variety of social life in Georgian Dublin and, in the words of Lady Charlotte Boyle Walsingham, 'had grown into a beautiful young woman'.[9] She was well connected and had a manner that encouraged friendship and affection. 'You shall hear from me very soon,' wrote Lady Moira to Henrietta in 1779, some time before the engagement, 'on a more minute scale to tell you what some people say of your beauty, & others of your understanding'.[10]

The order in which Buckinghamshire set out Armar's qualities is significant, for entry into the peerage and promotion once in it were not available unless the applicant was attractive to the government. The peerage could be likened to an exclusive club with the government as a selection committee. Members had ready access to other members and were therefore in close proximity to power and influence. The King as the 'senior member' was a strong influence. Buckinghamshire, therefore, mentioned first that Armar was the member of parliament for Tyrone.

It was useless looking for a peerage without a 'parliamentary interest', which itself was best underpinned by the wealth and the patronage that came with landed estates.[11] This fact was all too obvious to Armar's contemporaries. Sir John Irvine wrote to Lord George Germain on 20 February 1780, 'Lady Harriot Hobart is to be married immediately to a Mr Corry, a man of great estate and wealth'.[12] Henrietta Hobart herself realised that the peerage was part of the inducement for the marriage. When, in September, Buckinghamshire recommended Armar for a peerage, having admitted his personal interest as prospective father-in-law, he urged the advantages of estate and wealth, but added another – that Armar would give the government his vote:

> 'My private wish would certainly influence in favour of Mr Armar Lowry Corry; but his extensive property, his having supported the government … may give him some claim to his Majesty's favour'.

Armar had supplied an account of his wealth and estates for the marriage treaty itself. This showed that his annual income at the time was about £11,000 a year and was expected to rise to about £17,000 a year when leases were renewed in the course of the next few years. His net indebtedness at that time was shown as £15,400, the interest on which could readily be met from his income. Although these figures presented Armar's wealth to the best advantage they were not, at the time, in any sense misleading.

Buckinghamshire's own home was at Blickling Hall in Norfolk. He had a house in Bond Street, London and he also owned Marble Hill, the famous Palladian villa at Twickenham, which came from his aunt, Henrietta, Countess of Suffolk. Buckinghamshire had lost an infant son at the end of 1778, so Armar would not have discounted the possibility that Henrietta (named for her great aunt), as the eldest of Buckinghamshire's three daughters, might well inherit Blickling Hall itself, thus securing him and his family a significant estate in England.

Lady Henrietta Hobart

Without question, Armar had achieved something of a coup in winning Henrietta's hand and allying himself with a noble English family. Even though a peerage was in sight as part of the deal, and Armar's wealth compared very favourably with some of the richest men in Ireland, he was still simply 'a Mr Corry,' a country gentleman and an Irish one at that. Even peers of Ireland were generally unlikely to secure matches with highly placed English heiresses, because an Irish peerage was not held in very high regard. Only about one in ten of Irish peers got to marry into English families. Armar had some sterling qualities but was essentially a practical man.[13]

Walker's Hibernian Magazine for March 1780, describing Armar's bride as 'a young lady possessed of youth, beauty, elegance of manners, and a fortune of £30,000' showed that society would be only too well aware of his good fortune by adding, 'It affords a pleasing reflection that a native of this country has been destined to enjoy such supreme felicity'. Henrietta and Armar were married in Dublin Castle on Saturday 11 March 1780 by Thomas Barnard, Bishop of Killaloe. Present were Armar's sister and brother-in-law, the Earl and Countess of Enniskillen.

From a personal point of view, Buckinghamshire might well have seen the match as his greatest achievement during his troubled time as lord lieutenant. His official acts were not viewed by anyone on either side of the Irish Sea with great enthusiasm. By the time of his abrupt recall in December 1780, he had given Armar his first step up. Armar was now Baron Belmore, a title that his young wife had chosen for him from the mountain of that name near Castle Coole. He took the name to please her, but his choice also suggests that he had already decided to make Castle Coole his principal home. This possibility is supported by the fact that he wanted to take 'Fermanagh' as his title, but it was not available. In the meantime, to make his new bride's reception a happy and comfortable one at Castle Coole, he had the old house expensively refurbished. It failed to please her.

The teenage girl, who had enjoyed the spirited social life of Dublin, did not much like the house or the gardens, which were both old-fashioned and could not compare with her home at Blickling. Fermanagh must have seemed remote to her. Brought up in an English Whig family, Irish politics (especially Armar's narrow Patriot brand) must have seemed alien, if they interested her at all. For his part, Armar almost immediately plunged himself into electioneering for the new parliamentary session.

Two weeks after their marriage, on 24 March, the source of Armar's power – the gentlemen, clergy and freeholders of Tyrone – thanked him and his colleague James Stewart for their support of popular measures in the previous session and urged them to support measures to free Ireland's constitution and reduce public expenditure.[14] They had previously urged Armar and Stewart to 'take particular care that the Protestant part of this kingdom be not endangered by any bill that may be brought into Parliament for the enlargement of Roman Catholic privileges'. These were heady times for the Protestant Ascendancy.

Economic depression, failure to achieve an American peace and paramilitary activity by the volunteers created an unsettled atmosphere in which pressure grew for an independent Irish parliament – which, it was claimed, could best improve things. On 19 April 1780 Grattan spoke in the House of Commons, urging that the Irish parliament be solely empowered to make laws for Ireland. In the painting of the occasion by Francis Wheatley, Armar can be seen in his seat, listening to Grattan's oratory:

> 'England now smarts under the lessons of the American war … you are the only nation in Europe that is not her enemy … But Liberty, the foundation of Trade, the independency of parliament … are yet to come. Ireland is a colony … and you are a provincial synod without the privileges of a parliament … combined by the ties of common interest, equal trade and equal liberty, the Constitution of both countries may become immortal, a new and milder empire may arise from the errors of the old'.[15]

Armar may have enjoyed the oratory but, to the extent that it implied any threat to the ties with Britain, he would have found it unacceptable. Amongst his increasing political difficulties, Buckinghamshire managed to get some relief from lighter moments:

> 'The ball upon the Queen's birthday (19th May) was brilliant beyond measure and did not suggest the most distant idea of Ireland being undone. The scene was so particularly striking that I could not forbear wishing my master [the King] had been seated in my place'.[16]

Armar was probably there, although Buckinghamshire, knowing that he (if not Ireland) was undone, wished to be gone. A particular crisis engulfed him when his private secretary Sir Richard Heron failed to manage parliament over the Perpetual Mutiny Bill:

> 'Several gentlemen who had formerly pledged themselves to support Government voted in the minority last Wednesday which, together with the circumstances of many individuals concealing their sentiments, makes it difficult for me … How can a Lord Lieutenant speak with confidence upon any point at a period when no fix'd principle

The Irish House of Commons in 1776 by Francis Wheatley 1780 showing Armar Lowry Corry on the left
©Leeds Museums and Galleries (Lotherton Hall)

directs, no obligations attach and no assurances can bind. Every inconvenience must necessarily be increased from the distracted state of the Mother country'.[17]

The vote on the Perpetual Mutiny Bill was to be Armar's last in the House of Commons. He voted for it, probably because it was an Irish bill replacing the Mutiny Law – which was, in Foster's words, 'the law of another country'.[18] But, in voting for it, he also stayed on side for his father-in-law, a fact which may have influenced his vote as much as his own inclination to support the Bill. By the time the official warrant creating him Baron Belmore passed the privy seal in England on 15 December 1780, Buckinghamshire had gone, remarking 'It is feminine to complain, but in truth my lot has been a hard one'.[19] To add to his grievances, his replacement was carried out with unseemly haste. Unhappily for Buckinghamshire, bad news from Ireland was not long in following him to England.

Chapter Five

An Unhappy Affair

Belmore and Henrietta had been married for just a year on the day in March 1781 when Belmore, upset, angry and smarting under the disgust that Henrietta constantly and publicly showed at the sight of him, called on Buckinghamshire's private secretary, Sir Richard Heron. He intended to announce 'his determined resolution of being separated from Lady Belmore so soon as she shall be recovered from her lying in'.[1]

Heron was so alarmed by the strength of Belmore's feelings that he immediately wrote to Tom and Louisa Conolly, Buckinghamshire's relations in Ireland, to seek their help in calming the storm and to try to bring about some sort of compromise. In the meantime, he tried to soften Belmore's approach by suggesting that he should wait until Henrietta had recovered from childbirth before telling Buckinghamshire – for:

> 'if any accident should happen to her he would be sorry to have made Lord Buckinghamshire unhappy by an unnecessary communication of their disagreement'.

This was realistic advice in an age when many women died after childbirth. Heron also expressed the hope that 'the affections which will naturally arise for their child may lead to a disposition more agreeable to him'.

Belmore, unmoved by appeals for compromise, expressed his 'unalterable determination' to conclude a formal separation which, as far as he was concerned, would be a complete divorce. Heron was shocked to discover that Belmore had not told Henrietta anything about his intentions, but Belmore dismissed his concern, angrily asserting that she knew before her father left Ireland at the end of 1780 that he wanted a separation, and that it had only been her entreaties that had prevented it then:

> 'The consciousness of my own rectitude throughout the whole of this unhappy affair both supports me and determines me – indeed it is the only support I have left from which I can derive comfort – Had I not been prevented by the entreaty of Lady Belmore, and by tenderness to that entreaty I would have brought this matter to a conclusion when Lord Buckingham was in the Kingdom'.

It was not until the second week of May that Henrietta, who was in Belmore's Sackville Street house, received the news in a letter from Belmore whose tone shocked her. She looked for forgiveness and reconciliation:

'Blameable though my past behaviour has undoubtedly been, yet love for my poor little child and my sincere and unalterable wish of convincing Lord Belmore of my gratitude towards him will enable me for the future to fulfill that duty which till the birth of my little girl all my efforts could not accomplish'.

Unknown to Henrietta, it had already been arranged that she should be warned of the harsh truth of her situation 'by a lady as dignified by her conduct, as from her exalted rank'. This was, of course, her first chaperone in Ireland, Lady Louisa Conolly. Lady Louisa made it clear to Henrietta that a separation could not take place without her consent. This consent Henrietta was not ready to give. Instead, 'being averse to becoming the subject of public conversation and exceedingly anxious to avoid the uneasiness this measure would give her father', she gave her authority for anything to be done that might persuade Belmore to alter his resolution.

Belmore knew that since there was no infidelity or improper conduct on her part he must have her consent, and hinted 'at Lady Belmore's residing at Castle Coole' if she refused. He was well aware that the last thing Henrietta would want was to be confined and committed to spending her life in that remote, old-fashioned house. Actually, Belmore was so angry that he was 'very averse' to Buckinghamshire's wish that she should remain in Ireland.

It seems that both Belmore and Henrietta were victims of Buckinghamshire's careless arrangements for the match. Having failed as lord lieutenant he could not face this added personal failure and throughout the dissolution of the marriage wanted to be bothered by the business as little as possible. No doubt he was angered and shamed by the breakdown of what he had imagined was to be a rewarding union. Knowing of the threat of a breakdown before he left Ireland at the end of 1780, he must have been bitterly disappointed that the problems had not gone away by the following spring.

Lady Louisa then hit upon the notion that Belmore should keep his determination secret for a year at least – but, in the meantime:

'*Let it be supposed* that *she* goes to England to see her father & that *he* stops here on account of his own private affairs. That would give time for her to reflect and to get over the aversion which she had for him, and for him to find it easier to relent and take her back'.

It was no good. Belmore's 'mind was absolutely made up and his determination of parting irrevocable'. He had only agreed to call on the Conollys 'to communicate and not to consult'. They were left with nothing to do 'but to lament the melancholy prospect of a young woman'.

Henrietta was taken to Castletown where Louisa Conolly told her that the separation was inevitable, news which she received:

'with a becoming concern, not *affectedly* so but in a manner such as I expected from a person of her very good understanding and I must add, good heart, and she did not attempt justifying herself in any degree; on the contrary, she justified Lord Belmore's conduct towards her in this instance which she acknowledges has ever been in every respect that of an honourable, generous and worthy man, but that she was so unfortunate as not to have it in her power either to make *him* or *herself* happy; and she had tried in vain; what answer could I make to so generous a confession?'

What could be said from her perspective? In a statement she made, Henrietta revealed that 'When Lord Belmore was first proposed to Lady Belmore, she did not even know him by sight'. She had been overlooked or ignored both by her father and by Belmore in the treaty for the marriage and had not had any opportunity to object. It was worse:

> 'from the commencement of the treaty for this marriage Lord Belmore had reason to believe that Lady Belmore had a very great dislike to it, which he trusted he should be able to overcome by his obliging conduct, and it is certain, no man could be more attentive or indulgent than Lord Belmore was, from the day of his marriage until the resolution to separate. The truth is that Lady Belmore, who was under eighteen, shewed so evident a dislike to marrying Mr Corry that he proposed to her the taking upon himself to break it off; but the match being agreeable to her father & considering the time in which she ought to have been consulted as past, she unfortunately desired it might proceed'.

Questioned by Louisa Conolly about her dislike to the marriage, Henrietta admitted 'she had not been compelled to this match, for neither [her father] nor Lady Buckingham knew of her dislike to it as she had never *owned* it'.

Once Henrietta had consented to the principle of a separation, custody of the baby, Louisa, and maintenance had to be agreed. Henrietta wanted to keep her baby with her but Belmore would only agree to let her have Louisa for five years, at the end of which he wanted her to live with him – 'as it is the only comfort he looks for at home, as his son will be at school'. Louisa Conolly thought this was so reasonable that she could not but agree to it, although she acknowledged that it would be heartbreaking for Henrietta to hand her child over at the age of five. In the event, Belmore took the child immediately after the separation and kept her with him to be brought up at Castle Coole.

Belmore's sister, Lady Enniskillen, who did her best to maintain an interest in Louisa's well-being, thoroughly disapproved of Belmore's action and fell out with him, losing contact with Louisa as a result.

Henrietta thanked her for her kindness:

> 'to my poor little girl, she needs it so much, and what you mention of the dispute between you and Lord Belmore, completes my grief at not having her with me as she is now deprived in a great measure of what alone could compensate for the care of her mother – tell me, my dearest Lady Enniskillen, is there no method in the world by which I could obtain her? Lord Belmore had promised Lady Louisa Conolly that she should remain with me, and it was not till after I left Ireland that he revoked it'.

The bitterness Henrietta felt at losing her little girl never left her: 'I make no comments on her ever having been kept from me, it needs none for everybody must consider it in the same light'.[14] Belmore, however, did not consider it in that light at all. In a letter he wrote over a decade later (after Henrietta had become Lady Ancram) to his niece, Lady Florence Balfour (*née* Cole) – the Enniskillens' daughter and wife of Blaney Townley Balfour of Townley Hall, Drogheda, County Louth – he commented:

> 'I am sure your own good sense would not approve with my consenting that she should have any intercourse with her unfortunate mother during the time she is under my care … you would not recommend it to me to employ a woman to educate my daughter whose want of principle was so strongly stamped as that of Lady A'.

Money questions, not unsurprisingly, caused friction, too. There were three issues. The first was a maintenance payment, agreed at a total of £1,000 a year (£500 a year with a further £500 a year for pin money), to be paid in Irish pounds at a discount of about eight per cent against sterling. As Henrietta would be required to live outside Ireland that seemed to her unfair, so her lawyer asked for payment in sterling. Belmore rejected this. Secondly, he was asked to increase the maintenance if Buckinghamshire died, as he would then be paid the balance of £15,000 in sterling agreed under the marriage settlement. He rejected this too. Thirdly, he was asked if he would give up any rights he might have to any money or property acquired by Henrietta in her own right after the separation. He absolutely rejected this. Marriage at that time gave a husband the right to any property coming to the wife and Belmore would not forgo the possibility of inheriting at least part of Buckinghamshire's estates.

As things turned out, when Buckinghamshire died in 1793, although he made generous financial provision for Henrietta and her son, he left Blickling Hall to her sister Caroline for her life. This turned out to be an interim measure, for Caroline died childless, and Henrietta's husband, by then seventh Marquess of Lothian, inherited Blickling Hall. Had the Belmore marriage survived, Blickling might have passed to the Lowry Corry family. Louisa Conolly was particularly troubled by this possibility:

> 'Lord Belmore's having any future advantage by Lady Belmore does not, in *my humble* opinion seem reasonable but 'tis a consideration that certainly should be well weigh'd by proper persons … How hard it would be if Lord Belmore's family or even her own little girl (that is now so well provided for) should entirely swallow up (what she may have) to the prejudice of other children of hers by another husband? (and that possibly may want it)'.

Belmore, who thought his proposals perfectly fair, was impatient to see the matter completed:

> 'I conceived it impossible that any delay could arise but from the base mechanical part of the business – I have wished only to expedite a business of so awkward a nature that I supposed every party concerned would have been pleased with bringing it to a speedy

conclusion – My ideas in regard to it are fair plain and simple, and have neither been complicated by me nor will be departed from by me – The consciousness of my own rectitude throughout the whole of this unhappy affair both supports me and determines me – indeed it is the only support I have left from which I can derive comfort'.

Louisa Conolly commented that 'poor Lord Belmore's distracted state of mind makes him *sore* at every trifle'. Henrietta Belmore, on the other hand, though delighted that the separation was to proceed at last, was angered by a sense that Belmore was ungenerous, and had simply used her to get his title and her property. Louisa Conolly observed, 'she continues to *behave* very properly, tho' I see her fist ready to *break* out whenever Lord Belmore is named in regard to this money business' and, in a footnote, added, 'Lady Belmore cannot bear the idea of Lord Belmore's *getting any thing* more by her'.

Buckinghamshire, while critical of Belmore's stance, was not prepared to take Henrietta's part or to intervene in any way and shrugged the problem aside:

'Lady Belmore must determine for herself either to accept the terms or abide the consequence of declining them. The first will probably be her choice, but no consideration should induce me to advise'.

The separation deed was completed and signed on 15 June 1781. Henrietta remained in Dublin for a short while and for one last time was to be seen at a ball, enjoying herself, if a letter written by her father is to be believed: 'Lady Buckingham, Lady Harriet Corry and Lady Emilia Hobart are all subdued by the naked hocks of Lord Strathaven, a blooming Highlander'.[2] The attraction to a Scot was to prove almost prophetic. Shortly afterwards she had to leave Ireland for Paris where, accompanied by her younger sister, Lady Sophia, she was taken into L'Abbaye Royale de Panthemont, a convent in St Germain. She passed through London on her way but was not allowed to visit Blickling. The Abbaye was in what is now the Rue Bellechasse and was, effectively, a convent finishing school for aristocratic young ladies. Boarding fees were £250 a quarter, the whole of her yearly maintenance.

'My honor, my peace of mind, and the reputation of my daughter called for a divorce'
Henrietta remained in Paris for five years as Baroness and subsequently Viscountess Belmore, until her return to England in 1786. Two years later her life took another dramatic turn when, at a party in Scotland, she met Lord Ancram. They fell in love and wanted to marry, but without a divorce she was not free even to consider it. Her adultery with Ancram prevented her from bringing divorce proceedings herself. Then she became pregnant. She knew only too well that Belmore had considered the separation as final, effectively as a divorce – which was not an unusual view in those days, but it meant that he would not take proceedings of his own accord. As a result, she had to find some way of forcing Belmore into divorcing her. The fact that by this time he himself had three illegitimate children was not a problem, for a man's adultery did not bar him from initiating divorce proceedings. But what was she to do in order to induce him to do so?

At the beginning of August 1791 Henrietta left the house in Welbeck Street where she had lived since her return from Paris and, accompanied by Ancram, began a succession of hurried travels – planned and acknowledged in her own words as 'a very violent step', intended to provoke a scandal. She must have been heavily pregnant because it was in this month that she gave birth to their illegitimate son, William John Anderson. They started with a furnished house in Broadstairs in Kent for three months, left for two weeks in Calais, returned to England for a short while but then went back to Calais where they stayed publicly as Lord and Lady Ancram for a week at L'Hotel d'Angleterre. They moved to a furnished house near Calais and stayed there as man and wife for six weeks. They returned in a hurry to England as 'Mr Anderson and Mrs Smith', travelling to Edinburgh, where they took private lodgings for about a fortnight. Next, they took a furnished house a few miles from Edinburgh and finally, in February, they travelled as Mr and Mrs Anderson to London, taking a house as man and wife in Queen Street, Edgware Road.

By the end of 1791 the provocation had worked. A few days after he heard of Henrietta's movements and her pregnancy, he wrote to Buckinghamshire saying that, even though he was 'deep in mortar' at Castle Coole, he was so scandalised by the conduct of the woman who still carried his name that he was forced to seek a divorce. It was, he said, also for the sake of his daughter Louisa and her reputation. This was the daughter who, because of the poor health of his son, Somerset, would probably soon be his only child.

The matrimonial affairs of the Belmores, the elopement and the forthcoming divorce were the talk of Dublin at the time. A rumour that Belmore would return Henrietta's fortune of £20,000 to her was already the gossip of a dinner party there. Ancram's financial position, it was said, was desperate. He depended entirely on an allowance from his father, Lord Lothian, who was himself deep in debt.

Buckinghamshire, who had at first wanted as little as possible to do with the affair, was finally stirred into action by the prospect of having to support Henrietta himself, wrote to Belmore in an affectionate way, as a family connection, and appealed directly to his honour, a quality crucial to Belmore's view of himself:

> 'the forms of law are little known to me, but I conceive from recollection of several instances that my child is not to be left destitute. A proper confidence in your Lordship's noble nature would have prevented my touching upon the subject had it not seemed that you might be desirous of learning my wishes in that instance, which go no further than the continuation of her present annuity'.

Belmore had Captain Cole, his man of business, reply. He avoided committing himself in other than the most general terms to the financial support of Henrietta but later he attempted to use Buckinghamshire's letter as establishing an agreement that he should only pay Henrietta's £1,000 a year during his life and no jointure – that is, nothing after his death. The jointure or widow's annuity was no less than £2,000 a year. Belmore was still bitterly upset: 'the daughter clinging to my heart would have brought to my remembrance that she once had a mother'.

Eventually, he had to concede Henrietta's right to her jointure and on Tuesday 12 February 1793, Belmore presented his petition to the Irish parliament for the divorce on terms fully agreed. On 6 and 7 March the Divorce Bill passed through the Irish parliament and, on 19 March, became a completed act. It cost Belmore slightly over £4,187 Irish.

Henrietta Belmore married Ancram immediately after the divorce on 16 April 1793 in St Marylebone. She died in 1805.

Chapter Six

Building and Rebuilding: A New Wife and a New House in a New Demesne

One way of coping with disappointment is to work and for Belmore, as always, this meant politics. As he was now a member of the House of Lords he could no longer sit for Tyrone in the Commons, and this led to a by-election in May 1781. Belmore had as yet no son or relation to support for the seat so the candidate was Montgomery Moore. It must have given Belmore some relief to be able to busy himself with something he understood well and something which was usually pretty animated. He entertained the voters in the usual handsome fashion, providing dinner for 158 followers at £1 6s each, with 47 gallons of ale, 11 gallons of spirits, punch and two bottles of wine. There was drink for the drum and fife band, servants and two horses.[1]

In another sense the business of politics was not quite as usual. Attitudes towards Catholics and Dissenters were changing in the direction of measures of accommodation. Belmore was not in favour of change. On 3 May 1782 the House of Lords debated and passed the Protestant Dissenters' Relief Bill to allow marriages to be conducted by ministers who were not of the Established Church. Belmore, as before and always, a staunch member of the Established Church, voted with the minority against the Bill on the grounds that it gave dissenting ministers the rights given to ministers of the Established Church but not the restrictions imposed on them.

On 22 July 1782 he opposed a proposal to disqualify government revenue officers from voting in elections, once again opposing change and on this occasion supporting government, which had always sought to maintain a basis of support as a result of its officials voting with it.

Belmore's next move was to increase his clout by purchasing the borough of Belturbet from the Earl of Lanesborough for 8,000 guineas. This gave him control of Belturbet's two seats for the rest of the parliament and was thought to cost him 'a clear four thousand more'. On 16 March 1784 Belmore, with others (including Lord Farnham), was permitted to sign a memorial to the House of Commons. The subject is unknown but it may, perhaps, have been connected with Flood's proposals for parliamentary reform, which had been introduced in that month: some support for this view may be lent by the record in the Journals of the House of Commons for 13 March 1784 of an unsigned petition from the gentlemen of Fermanagh offering a plan of parliamentary reform. Lord

Farnham was considered 'an advocate for Mr Flood's doctrines', which were in favour of reforming parliament procedurally but without making inroads in any way into Ascendancy domination. Belmore could certainly have gone along with that, and he would go along with Farnham again on more than one occasion.

On 23 February 1785 Belmore was absent by leave from the House of Lords but he was back in Dublin by April. During that year Pitt's proposals for a comprehensive resolution of the economic differences between England and Ireland – known as the Commercial Propositions – were debated in both the English and Irish parliaments. The proposal put to the Irish parliament in August was that it should automatically enact, without modification, all existing British legislation relating to Ireland's external trade. Although the Irish parliament had long wanted such a settlement ensuring economic equality with England, the necessary constitutional implication was that the Westminster parliament was the prime mover. That was going dangerously close to allowing that the Westminster parliament was supreme.

As a good Patriot, Belmore inevitably voted against the Commercial Propositions on 6 September in a formal protest, in which he and others stated their 'utmost abhorrence' to a bill that struck at their fundamental constitutional and commercial rights. The scheme was abandoned, but even though they accepted they had been 'happily rescued from its baleful effects' they registered their protest against any proposal for a repeat measure in the future.

By 1788 it was known and remarked that Baron Belmore 'asks promotion in the peerage' to viscount and he was, it is said, given much encouragement. The information must have been correct because, on 23 December 1789 Belmore was created Viscount Belmore of the County of Fermanagh and introduced into the House of Lords as such on 3 February 1790.

He had been made to wait for this further step because during the previous two years he had sided with a group opposing the government over the regency crisis. The King (George III) had been disabled by one of his attacks of porphyria. The Irish opposition supported Charles James Fox's plan to appoint the Prince of Wales as regent and a group of Patriot gentlemen, normally supportive of the government, joined them – possibly supposing that they would gain influence if the Prince were to replace the King. This group included, besides Belmore, Lords Shannon, Loftus, Leinster and Clifden. They were basically brought to heel by the Lord Lieutenant, Buckingham,* so that Shannon (described by Buckingham as 'frightened') and Belmore (described by Buckingham as 'penitent') changed sides and thereafter supported the government. It was understood that in return for the grant of his viscountcy, Belmore would commit one of his parliamentary seats to the government side. This was the usual practice.

Buckingham recorded that one of his *absolute engagements* was:

> 'to one Viscountcy, in favour of Lord Belmore, a penitent Baron, who had Orde's [Chief Secretary to the Lord Lieutenant] solemn promise for the first batch, and is now to wait, and to purchase his promotion with one seat which he gives me'.

*George Nugent-Temple-Grenville, first Marquess Buckingham (see note, page 30 ante).

Lady Moira, Henrietta Belmore's old friend, abreast as ever of the latest intelligence, jokingly predicted that as 'he has chose his title from the name of some mountain near Bail Môr (which is your present one in Irish orthography). I conclude that his Earldom will be that of the Lord of the Mountains'.[2] Belmore sold his other Belturbet seat to John McClintock, a government supporter, but even though he got his step up there was still an irritation typical of the extreme sensitivities of newly created peers: his actual precedence in the peerage was challenged by Lord Conyngham. However, Major Robert Hobart, Henrietta Belmore's cousin and now the Chief Secretary, concluded that:

> 'the King's letter for Lord Belmore's barony is dated five days prior to Lord Conyngham's and therefore I apprehend we cannot accede to Lord Conyngham's claim without great offence to Lord Belmore, which ought to be avoided … Lord Belmore, who is I believe in England, and to whom I have written to desire he would call upon you respecting his title, has desired to be Viscount Fermanagh but I find that *your friend*, Earl Verney, is also Viscount Fermanagh, and I do not conceive he has consented to Lord Belmore's taking that title; indeed, I am certain he has not been spoken to about it. I have therefore left a blank in the official letter for Lord Belmore's title, which you will be so good as to have filled up'.[3]

The fact that Belmore had got his step up in the peerage did not, by any means, provide him with much relief from the other pressures in his life. Before the 1790 election Belmore was politicking – not for himself, but in an attempt to get his 16-year-old son elected to the House of Commons. The fact that Somerset was under age and a sickly child did not prevent Belmore arranging with Thomas Knox, by that time Lord Welles, for both their sons to be elected, even though the fathers were well known as 'old and obstinate opponents'. Somerset, 'an amiable young man', was obviously ineligible. And even worse was the general view that he 'will not live to carry on the contest but, should he, it is by no means clear that the men of Tyrone are much disposed to gratify his father's wishes'.

But politics did not occupy the whole of Belmore's time. He spent more time at Castle Coole away from gossiping society, no doubt hunting, shooting and fishing on the demesne. He also bought more land in Tyrone at Mullaghmore, Balnahatty and Tallykeal.

In the absence of a wife, Belmore had relationships with two women on the estate who produced three children between them. The first of these relationships was with Margaret Begby, who lived in Derryvullen. She was the mother of his first illegitimate child, Emily Maria Lowry Corry, born in 1784. The liaison continued for some while, because she was also mother of Belmore's second illegitimate child, John Corry, who was born in November 1787.

In 1793, Belmore was to have another illegitimate child – a son, who was named Armar after him. This Armar's mother was the daughter of Thomas Bowen, the coachman at Castle Coole. The tradition of the Poore family of New Zealand, who are descendants of that Armar Lowry Corry, is that he was the son of the first Earl and 'the Lodge Keeper's daughter'. Miss Bowen lived in the gatehouse at the back of Standingstone. Presumably she lived with her father, who was the coachman rather than the lodge keeper (although

Marianne (Caldwell), Countess of Belmore by Hugh Douglas Hamilton

it is perfectly possible that she, in fact, was the lodge keeper). These relationships, from 1783 to 1793, filled the years between his separation from Henrietta and his third marriage in 1794.[4]

However, politics and affairs were not enough for the expression of Belmore's sense of his achievements: the embarrassment of his failed marriage, his need to establish his family securely in society and his own contentment called for more. Belmore had no grounds for optimism in marrying again, but he was determined to try.

About 12 months after the divorce from Henrietta was finalised, he married Mary Anne Caldwell, the daughter of his friend Sir John Caldwell of Castle Caldwell, on 11 March 1794 at Bath. She had an extensive acquaintance – among whom, especially, were the Enniskillens (whose finances she seemed to be very familiar with) and the O'Neills, with whom she often stayed at Shane's Castle. She was an inveterate visitor. Her early correspondence reveals her as very money-conscious but also as a very dutiful and affectionate daughter. Perhaps, not surprisingly, it was those very qualities of loyalty and affection which drew Belmore to her. She was also a lively, even comic, person – which, no doubt, brought some enjoyment back into Belmore's life. Her dowry of £2,100 was a decent, but not outstanding, sum for those days. The settlement as a whole was a poor financial deal for Belmore, in that the jointure she was to be provided with on his death was no less than £1,000 a year, as well as a legacy of £300. These amounted to a considerably larger percentage of her dowry than customary deals provided.[5]

She was no great beauty and at the time of their marriage was 39 years old. Belmore was 54. The marriage settlement provided sums for children and, even though children may have seemed an unlikely outcome, they obviously tried. In December 1798 Mary Anne gave birth to a child but, unhappily, it was either stillborn or died almost immediately (see page 87 *post*).

Preparations for a New Demesne Landscape

From the early 1780s onwards Belmore threw himself into developing a new demesne that would be suitable for his new house. His relationship with Buckinghamshire, which remained friendly even after the breakdown of his marriage to Henrietta – 'there is no man living has a higher respect esteem and affection for him than I have', he wrote in May 1781[6] – might have influenced his thinking about what kind of demesne and house he would aim for. Buckinghamshire invited him to Blickling Hall for the summer of 1792 and, although he did not go then, he may have been there before.[7]

Buckinghamshire had already had the park at Blickling redesigned to make a fashionable, naturalistic landscape, with the lake as the main focal point of the vista. For his alterations to the jumbled Tudor interior of the house, Buckinghamshire's original architects were the Ivory brothers. However, in 1779, they were replaced at their own suggestion by 'Mr Wyat at London'. This was not James Wyatt, but his brother Samuel, who was one of the leading exponents of neoclassicism at that time. The Peter the Great room, the state bedroom and the orangery were completed to his designs in 1782. In their times together between 1779 and 1781, Belmore and Buckinghamshire must surely have discussed each of their projects for Blickling and for Castle Coole.

Belmore, understandably, immersed himself in his plans. He had, he said in a letter to his agent, no time to express a view about the state of Tyrone politics. Of more immediate concern to him was his great disappointment at getting only half the income he thought he had been sure of from estate and garden sales. He intended to pay for most of the building work out of income, but he did raise over £7,000 of the capital he would need for landscaping work by mortgages and bonds. In May 1783 he secured the income of the Churchlands by paying off the mortgage of £8,000 with which Margetson Armar had originally bought them.

He also had to attend to the daily round of estate business. It included the sale of trees and advice about planting them; a proposal to provide a market house and store in Sixmiletown to hold stores safe for his 'own people' in times of distress; and cautionary advice to his agent to ensure that an agreement was put into writing in order to avoid disputes with tenants. He advised Samuel Galbraith about planting new trees – which he 'will supply with pleasure' (but he needed to know the kind) – and warned against having them moved until they were quite ready to be put into the ground. From the estate he sold 50 spruce firs, 50 scotch firs, 50 oak and 100 sycamore trees and was more than willing to supply more. There was, he commented, little time left before the spring planting would be over, if the season continued so dry.

By September 1787 Belmore had 10,000 slates delivered to Castle Coole for roofing heated greenhouses in the new garden, and he was also making improvements to the Queen Anne house, where life continued as usual. In the late summer of that year he entertained the Lord Lieutenant, the Duke of Rutland, who came to stay during his tour of the great houses of Ireland. The house accounts show that in August there were 'bought at sundry times fresh turkey and hen eggs for the use of Lord Belmore during the delay of the Lord Lieutenant at Castle Cool'. In a ceremony there at the time Rutland knighted a local worthy, Walter Hudson of Enniskillen.

Belmore had the quality of his lands in Tyrone surveyed and described by Henry Hood, a well-known local surveyor, possibly to ensure that he would have sufficient rental income to support the expense of the work at Castle Coole. The land taken in hand to create the new demesne required a great deal of alteration and improvement by removing buildings, fences and signs of occupation and by draining and ditching – changes which would inevitably involve a loss of income.[8] For example, two farms in Standingstone and Derrymacken, which were tenanted by house servants (the Martin and Magennis families) were removed by 1783, and the sites were made into two large fields. On the north side of the demesne, Flaxfield and Killenure Hill were added to it by the removal of farms in Killenure and Agherainy, and tree screening was continued towards Agherainy. By 1788, more farms had been removed from Thomastown, Derrymacken and Rossyvullen.

From what is now the back exit at Castle Coole he diverted the then-public road to Dublin to create a new thoroughfare, using part of the road around Lough Coole. It continued along the near side of Lough Yoan and the foot of Standing Stone Hill to join the old Dublin Road again in Glassmullagh. He also had the twin gatehouses built, which are now the oldest houses on the demesne. This change enlarged the demesne by including in it the whole of Gortgonnell Hill, Standing Stone Hill and parts of Killenure. Standing Stone Hill is named after a large piece of sandstone on its crest. Tradition has it that a giant, moving from Toppid Mountain to Cuilcagh Mountain, used the stone as a stepping-stone.

The levels of both Lough Yoan and Lough Coole were lowered to secure a road through the new demesne to the site of the new house.

The new demesne boundary was marked by a double ditch and a line of beech trees, some of which can still be seen. Further work on the south side brought in a strip of Thomastown, Bonnybrook and Ballylucas, which extended the demesne as far as the road to Toppid Mountain. That road was itself thus connected to the new Dublin Road. A screen of trees was planted on the east side of Carrowmacmea to include the horse parks. All these clearances added a substantial band of parkland all around the old demesne.[9]

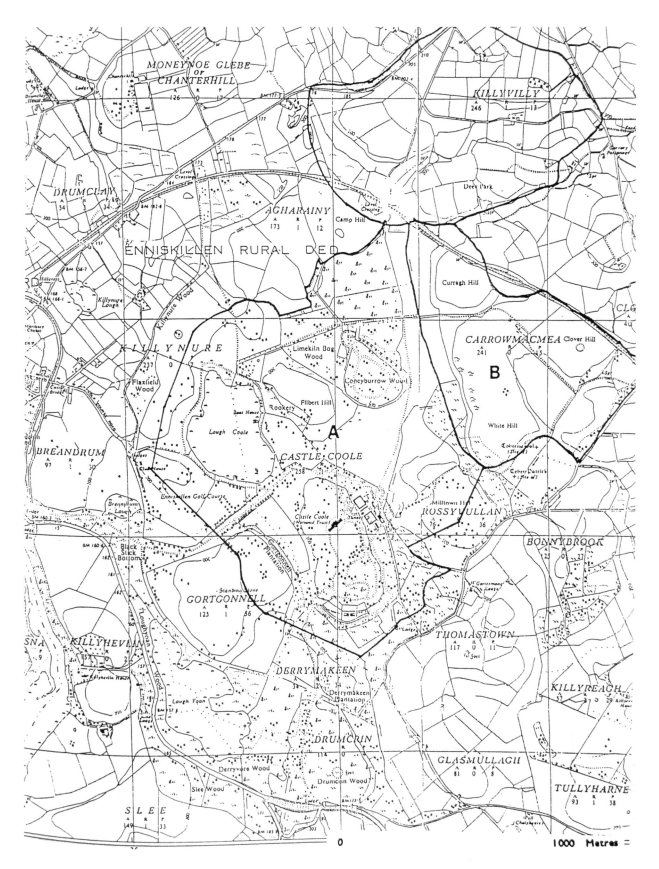

The Pre-1783 Demesne

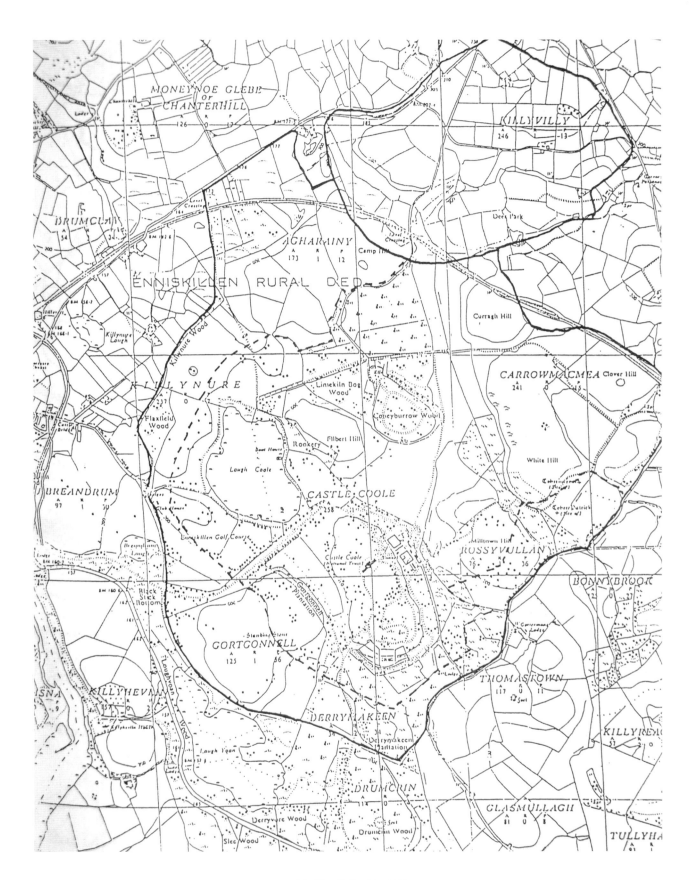

The New Park 1783–1813

Chapter Seven

'My Lord's intentions in the building line … I study it and nothing else night and day': Alexander Stewart, Architect

In May 1788, after some years creating the landscape and the walled garden, Alexander Stewart (Belmore's clerk of works) began the groundwork for the new house.[1] There was a hierarchy of control and a system of accounting, all of which ended with Belmore. He was not just the client, his was the controlling influence at all times, and Stewart saw him as a commander in chief:

> 'we are like a numerous family depending entirely on the market day for all we want & my Admiral must look very sharp more so than ever he has done yet by far'.

Stewart and Joseph Rose, the plasterwork designer, were both plagued by Belmore's changes of mind. Stewart complained that 'no man living could tell where it might end'. Rose tried to steer clear of argument with his client, telling Belmore 'to please yourself as to what you chuse to have done as I do declare that I have no wish about it, only that you should be pleased'. Rose points out that Belmore made significant changes:

> 'the staircase was then intended to be plain, but I have your *Lordship's letter from Bath ordering me to make designs for it* … the basement story was was then intended *to be finished in common plastering* but order was given for it to be done in the best manner – also *door cornices and friezes*. I could mention more but I shall not tire your Lordship by enumerating them'.

Even though William Armstrong (Belmore's land steward) checked the workmen's and suppliers' bills and Captain Cole (Belmore's man of business) checked Stewart's estimates, Belmore himself double-checked them all, witnessed by his note on one of Stewart's letters – 'He is mistaken in his calculations'.

Belmore's choice of the Castle Coole demesne for his new house was explained to the fourth Earl by a son of Belmore's Tyrone agent, Samuel Galbraith. The Earl recorded:

> 'My great grandfather had some idea of building his new house near Omagh, and forming a demesne, between the rivers which flow by Crevenagh and Campsey, uniting

at Omagh. One is called the Camowan river. Over this river there is a bridge, called the Bloody Bridge, in consequence of some skirmish during the wars, probably in King James II's time. Lord Belmore, however, finally decided upon building at Castlecoole, which is a better site, owing to the formation of the ground, the lakes, and the superior mountain views, in addition to the fact, that there was already a certain amount of timber, for which the soil is better suited than that of the other site'.

The Dublin Chronicle for 4 November 1790, in what might almost have been a press release, was very clear about Belmore's choice of site:

> 'Lord Belmore is at present building a magnificent mansion-house at Castle Coole in the county of Fermanagh, on a large scale indeed; the principal front extending near 300 feet, and the computed expence not less than sixty thousand pounds. The gardens have long been celebrated for their extent and beauty; the situation is princely and there will now be a residence there adequate to the demesne'.[2]

Their calculation of the cost of building is uncannily accurate, far more so than Stewart's original estimate. There is a family tradition that Belmore chose to build on the hill away from the lake to avoid dampness, which exacerbated the rheumatism from which he increasingly suffered. The existence of a learned medical dissertation in Belmore's library by Adrian Kluit (*Dissertatio Medica Inauguralis de Rheumatismo, Leiden, Holland 1783*) may support this theory. Neurological problems also beset him, if that was the significance of the fact that his copy of *Dissertatio Medica de Phrenitide Idiopathica, Edinburgh, 1786*, by Thomas Burnside contained a personal dedication to him. However, it is certain that the stress caused him by the building work and its cost affected his health.

The choice of site having been made, Belmore had to select an architect to design the house itself. His first choice was an Irishman, Richard Johnston (1759–1806), who worked with his brother Francis from Eccles Street, Dublin. Belmore would certainly have known Johnston's reputation, if only from the Rotunda Assembly Rooms in the same area of Dublin. Very little is known about him now, however. Dr Edward McParland describes him as 'clearly a fashionable and fashion-conscious designer in the 1790's: Daly's Club House, beside the Parliament House in Dublin, was a very prominent commission'.

Johnston's drawings for Castle Coole were not available until October 1789 but, at some time towards the end of 1789, his designs were abandoned in favour of new designs by James Wyatt (1746–1813), an even more fashionable London architect celebrated for his 1772 design for the Pantheon in Oxford Street. It was, perhaps, no coincidence that Belmore was in England in November 1789. Did Johnston recommend him to Wyatt then?

Dr McParland suggests that there was an aristocratic clique in Dublin in favour of Wyatt and Cooley and against Gandon. This clique included particular friends of Belmore's, such as his frequent political ally, Lord Farnham of Farnham House, Cavan.[3] It has been suggested that Johnston's drawing may have been too old fashioned – too much, for example, like Florence Court, which was then already some 20 years old. It has been thought that Belmore wished to outdo Florence Court in a spirit of rivalry with his sister, Anna Enniskillen.[4]

Although it is true that the pair had fallen out in 1784, they had been reconciled by 1785 and their normal friendly relations had been restored. If there was a rival establishment to outdo it was Baronscourt, Irish home of the Marquess of Abercorn, Belmore's great political adversary. Abercorn's predecessor had built a villa to the designs of George Steuart, the Scottish architect. The work must have attracted notice for, in 1779, Steuart arrived with 17 masons, six carpenters and two plasterers from London. The house was completed in 1782, when Belmore's ideas were developing. One of the masons was none other than Alexander Stewart, who also worked for Wyatt at Slane and would be working for Belmore at Castle Coole.[5]

In 1790, Alexander Stewart was faced with instructions that Belmore wanted the house finished in three years. He must have had working drawings supplied by Wyatt in 1789, when the foundations were already dug. The majority of Wyatt's drawings were done by 1792 – except some ceiling-plaster designs, which were completed later, in 1793. Alexander Stewart struggled unsuccessfully to stick to Belmore's timetable.

Site clearance and excavation for the foundations had already begun in 1788 following the ground plan designed by Johnston. Fortunately, Wyatt's ground-floor design increased the width of the central block of the house very little. His major change was in the design of the wings and pavilions, which were lengthened and widened, and it is probable that their foundations were not far advanced when it became necessary to extend them to accommodate Wyatt's design. Stewart's building returns show that, in April, the workforce was still 'removing the ground and sinking the foundation' along with other preparatory work. It was in the middle of June 1790 that the accounts show the workforce building up, and on Monday 14 June the carpenters were fitting up the roll-call office, to which all workers would report. On the same day, John Brett, described as 'architect', drew up plans for buildings. These were probably the working buildings that were going to be needed for the many tradesmen who would work and sleep on the site. By Tuesday 3 July, the stonecutters were working to make the main plinth of the house. All in all, therefore, it would seem that Wyatt's drawings of May 1790 were delivered in time for the architects and workmen to make the adjustments resulting from the change of design.

A comparison of Johnston's and Wyatt's ground-floor plans immediately reveals how much more elegant are the proportions chosen by Wyatt. This elegance is carried over into his designs for the elevations and principal floors which Dr McParland describes as 'far more sophisticated and of an altogether higher quality' than Johnston's. The changes proposed by Wyatt emphasise the imposing simplicity of the completed house, which Dr McParland says:

> 'is seen to be severe, almost bleak, and shaved of all unnecessary ornament. The great pedimented portico gains impact from being set close against the sheer unrelieved face of the main block … Form contrasts with form; light and shade are exploited to heighten the contrast; and all is worked out with the precision of impeccable stonework'.[6]

Elevation of South West Front

Elevation of South East Front

South East Elevation of Castle Coole The Seat of The Right Hon.ble The Earl of Belmore in the County of Fermanagh in Ireland
James Wyatt Architect

North West Elevation of Castle Coole The Seat of The R.t Hon.ble The Earl of Belmore in the County of Fermanagh in Ireland
James Wyatt Architect

Johnston's elevations (top) and Wyatt's

Frieze in the hall showing rose and chalice design

This restrained simplicity, 'classical' according to the architectural ideas of the time, was perhaps not within Johnston's experience or imagination. 'Severe, bleak and impeccable' are the kinds of words which were used by some to describe Belmore himself.

Wyatt's designs and the completed house have been the subject of many commentaries. These verdicts of posterity are principally directed at the two most obvious aspects of Castle Coole, its architectural and political significance. But Belmore's essential motive was to 'eternize the family name'.[7] De la Tocnaye's tart comments about Castle Coole are often quoted. They reflected his ill humour at having been put up in the attic, in one of the rooms intended for visitors, which he says are 'like cellars', adding, 'my taste is perhaps odd, but I confess that a house that is comfortable appears to me preferable to a palace which is not'. His visit must have been in the summer of 1796, because he noticed an inscription to 'the glorious memory of the first of July' on a gate in Enniskillen 'recently'. At that time Castle Coole was not finished and the family had not moved in. Comfort was unlikely with workmen still around. He concludes, 'Temples should be left to the gods'.[8] The part of Belmore's plan that aimed to 'eternize' his family name, seeking immortality perhaps, is reflected in the design of the frieze in the great hall. Carried all around above the visitor's eye is a pattern made from the rose and a chalice with branches coming out of it. The rose was in the old Corry arms and the chalice was in those of the Lowry family.

At this point in the story, however, the issue is more earthy: the site had to be prepared. Digging the foundations and lowering the hill by some 12 feet in front of the house to replace it with a lawn involved the removal of mountains of earth; the orchard on the hill had to be cut down, cabins and workplaces prepared and men assembled. This began in May 1788 and the building work then continued for nearly ten years, during which time Stewart or his assistants signed weekly accounts of the work done for the approval of Belmore or Captain Cole, including comments on the weather and working conditions. In the eighteenth century a person experienced in any branch of practical building – for example, a carpenter or a stonemason – might be put in charge of a whole project and become a mixture of clerk of works, foreman and architect. Stewart made estimates of the mounting costs as work proceeded, the first of which, signed by him in 1790, came to £33,663 7s 8d Irish.[9] He supervised the work and the workmen but, other than the odd sketch that may be by him, there is no evidence he was an overall designer. In fact, in June 1790, another man, John Brett, drew plans for the farm buildings and for the 'subterraneous tunnel' leading from the area below the house up to the kitchen. He also took over from Alexander Stewart when Stewart was otherwise occupied. Brett was a carpenter by trade. Another man who occasionally supervised work and signed the weekly returns was William Kane, a stonecutter.

Nothing more is known about Alexander Stewart. He made his will at Castle Coole in 1796 and died in 1805 in Scotland, from where he probably came.

Stewart worked closely with William King, probably the same King who had done some landscaping at Florence Court and Mount Stewart. The rivalry between Abercorn's Baronscourt house and Belmore's new house was reflected in the description of King as 'a common manufacturer of lawns and plantations' by his professional rival, William Hudson, who had designed the gardens at Baronscourt. King was head gardener. He was in charge of the work on the new walled garden and greenhouses and, together, Stewart and King supervised the tree and shrub planting, the rearranging of roads and other work to relate the demesne to the new house. Although William King is thought by some to have been influenced by Capability Brown, there is no evidence for this. It is perfectly possible that Belmore, well aware of the fashion for a naturalistic style of landscaping, had such trees removed or planted as would enhance the drumlin landscape and relate the house to the lake below. At any rate, he spent such a great deal on the house that it is not surprising the accounts do not show any great sum of money spent on the layout of the park. It lent itself naturally to the required style. In fact, until the early nineteenth century, the landscape was left quite bare around the house itself.

The gardens were another matter. In the days of Margetson Armar and his wife, Mary Corry, the formal garden and greenhouses had been famous. Therefore it was to be expected that Belmore would have new gardens made to carry on the tradition. Gardens, of course, supplied both the house and the locality with plants, vegetables and fruit. King and Stewart created the new garden between 1788 and 1795. There was an east and west grapery, an east and west peachery, a melon house, a cherry house, an orangery and a greenhouse. There were 'blow houses' – that is, heated greenhouses; just outside the garden an ice house was built. James Croker, the gardener in the new walled garden, supervised several gardeners and labourers. They planted larch, 'thornquicks' and 11 myrtles and supervised work on hotbeds and the maintenance of stoves. 375 penny, tuppenny and threepenny garden pots were bought. Dung was brought in to manure the garden beds; flower boxes were painted and beehives set up. Masons built the sundial. In January shrubs were clipped and, for work in the ice house, candles, salt and whiskey were bought. Later in the year sash cords were fitted to the greenhouses and leaf tobacco was purchased in March: whether it was for making a fumigant or for the personal use of Croker and his men (or perhaps a bit of both) is not clear. The sashes and frames of greenhouses and lanthorns were painted green and Fitzwilliam Corry (one of the Corrys of Carrowmacmea), glass-worker, supplied and fitted glass to the orangery. The list of vegetable seeds shows that a great variety of vegetables was grown: six varieties of cabbage, mustard and cress, asparagus, five onion varieties and five varieties of bean, cauliflower, broccoli, lettuce, kale, celeriac, celery, turnip, chervil, salsify, spinach, beet, leeks, savory and carrots.[10]

'The weekly accounts of Labourers and Mechanics imployed at Castle Coole by A. Stewart 1788 onwards'

The weekly accounts were meticulously kept, wind and weather notwithstanding, and they give a complete picture of the immense logistical undertaking that was the building of Castle Coole. The scale of the operation was worthy of a Roman invasion force under Julius Caesar: men, animals and materials had to be brought to the site by boat, carriage and ox cart; a cherry orchard at the site was cut down, its timber trimmed and used to build cabins for workmen; huge quantities of earth were removed by gangs of labourers to lower Forth Hill around the site of the house by some 12 feet; foundations were dug for the house and the servants' tunnel; a brig, *Martha*, 'my Lord's boat', was used to carry the Portland stone from Dorset to Ballyshannon. From there it was brought up by several boats on Lough Erne to a quay specially built at Enniskillen and, finally, by ox cart to the site. Bricks and ironwork were made on site. Stone was dug from places in the demesne, such as the old deer park. Boatloads of sand and gravel were brought in from sites around Lough Erne.

Summaries of selected entries in the accounts show how this immense undertaking must have put Belmore under pressure, making inroads on his time and energy, even as he was also provoked by his wife's notorious conduct, the divorce and the pressures of politics.

Rt. Honble. Lord Visct. Belmore ~~~ Seed Bill ~~~
1794.

				£	s	d
Jany. 1	10 qts. Early pea	£0.	6	8		
	6 Do. Mazagan Bean		2	6		
	6 Do. Lisbon Do.		2	6		
	8 oz York Cabbage		7	4		
	8 oz Sugar Loaf Do.		4			
	1½ lb Flat Dutch		8	8		
	4 oz Red Do.		4			
	4 oz Batterrea		2			
	8 oz Early Turnep		2			
	½ lb White Spanish Onion		2	8		
	½ lb Deptford Do.		1	4		
	4 lb Strasburgh Do.		10	10		
	4 oz Welsh Onion		1	8		
	8 qts. Speckled Bean		16			
	8 Do. Forcing Do.		16			
	4 Do. Yellow Do.		2			
	2 Black Do.		4			
	1 Bushel Windsor		16	3		
	2 Do. Longpod Do.	1	10	6		
	4 qts. Genoa Bean		2	1		
	1 pk Sandwich Do.		4	2		
	2 qts. Scarlet Runners		4			
	8 oz Radish Turnep		1	4		
	8 oz Salmon Do.		1	4		

£ 6 . 12 . 10

Seed list for the new garden

1788

February – 'from the Barrack Co', four tons of timber and three hundredweight of best red deal are brought to the Right Honourable Lord Belmore.

2 May – the preparatory groundwork begins: labourers level the hill, called Forth Hill, that overlooks the lake and the Queen Anne house, and chop down the cherry orchard that grows there. Wood from the cherry trees and from apple trees, which are also removed, is used to build cabins for workmen.

1 July – in the old farmyard, the office and ridge at the rear of the steward's house at the end of the workhorse stable are thatched. The office is probably for Captain Cole.

November – Alexander Stewart signs a receipt 'for 14 horses drawing timber from the deer park to erect a stage in Enniskillen for landing the stone'.

1789

'7th January 1789 – Hatchet Men Neale and Barney McGuire cutting down apple trees and Cherry trees and squaring Cherry Trees for sawyers'.

There is a lot of preliminary stone moving; hand barrows are made for the gardener and for building work.

Three stonecutters and one boy face ashlars for the building; a path is made out of the yard to the four-acre park; labourers rub Portland stone in the shades; work in the deer park consists of making a new road and putting in new stone pipes to drain it; also drainage pipes are installed on Long Hill.

Labourers Barney McGirr, Geo Doughertey, John Scott, Barney McAleer, Terrance McManus, Sam'l Breden and John McCafrey and stonecutter William Shane cut and square apple trees, make shades for the bullocks and move stone into place; apple and cherry trees are cut, timber and stone are sorted, horses drag trees away for trimming and the stonecutters' shade is cut around to run off water. Ash and elm are cut.

Alex Stewart pays for whiskey for the men loading from the stage at Enniskillen.

Bales are made for John Moor and sewers constructed.

In February stonecutters make ashlars for the building.

6 April – roads have to be repaired after flooding.

'To John Maguire at building and weatherboarding the shades in the four-acre park'. The shades are shelters for stonecutters and others in the park, the principal work space adjacent to the yard of the old house.

Wheelbarrows, carts etc are made and a plough is mended.

The quay at Enniskillen is cleared for the reception of the stone and later the stage, which had been overloaded, is cleared.

August – Forth Hill is levelled and workers are engaged 'Bearing ground to be laid up for manure at sundry places'.

Labourers work at drawing hay for Mr Forsyth and the carpenters make wheelbarrows and a cider press for 'Mr Crocker' (Croker, the gardener).

Wednesday 23 September – labourers build a fence around the foundations to prevent cows from falling in.

September and October – subsidence while digging the foundations causes problems. Throughout September, October and November, during the building of the mill, the weather continues to be a problem – '31 September Last night a most tremendous storm of wind and rain, the flood is within a foot of the top of the [mill] rampart this morning'.

Friday and Saturday 1 and 2 October – the floods continue and are predicted to reach the level of the rampart before night.

Tuesday 6 and Wednesday 7 October – 'rainey [sic] weather' and 'the weather continues shocking bad. The mill mason is obliged to stop and brick maker have his break and go home after 15 days raining continually'.

Wednesday 18 November – 'a very stormy day'. The 'subterraneous road' has been under construction since October. This was for the servants' tunnel from the yard up into the kitchen basement. Through November and December regular payments for a gallon of whiskey appear in the accounts: it was usual to give the labourers whiskey to help the work along.

Four brick kilns and a covering for the old kiln are put up by Owen Mullen and partner. In December 50,000 bricks are produced out of two kilns.

December – sand is thrown up at the quay in Enniskillen for fear of the water.
The first recorded injury to a workman occurs: on Friday 4 December, labourer McCaffrey is hurt by a young bullock. After that he is only able to hold the wagon while others gather hay for the bullocks.

December 1789–January 1790 – William Kane signs a return for work on the 'blow houses'.

Working relationships were not always easy. Alexander Stewart and William Armstrong were constantly getting on each other's nerves. Armstrong had worked at Castle Coole since he was a boy, more or less following in his father's footsteps. He had risen to be land steward but he had an alcohol problem – a problem that got no better as the years went on. No doubt because of it, he was not attending carefully to his work. In January 1790, to Stewart's disgust, he allowed the labourers to damage Stewart's vouchers when they signed them:

'N.B. I request the favour of Mr Armstrong not to make the labourers sign their ugly scrawling names on the face of my vouchers as I endeavour and wish to keep them clear for inspection'.

Stewart seems to imply that Armstrong was deliberately spoiling his vouchers. (Perhaps he was.)

1790
Tuesday 7 February – a rainy day. There is also snow.

Saturday 6 March – a boat sinks in the lough and has to be hauled up, on the first of many such occasions.

Tuesday 5 April – Lady Louisa's piano needs repairing and on 27 April the carpenter prepares to make a stool for her to sit at her music.

April 1790 – large stones are brought from the deer park. These may have been used for the foundations: 'removing the ground and sinking the foundation' was in progress. An oar is made from an ash tree for my Lord's boat, one carpenter attending. The boats are: my Lord's boat, Dr Owens's and Mr Graydon's boats and the sand boats of Irwin and Jones from Meath; the *Royale Oak*, a stone boat and the Castle Hume boat. Sand is transported to the quay from Ballyshannon and then to the building site by bullock cart or horses.

Saturday 15 May–Saturday 22 May – accounts show that the workforce is building up and on Monday 14 June the carpenters fit up the roll-call office. The weather continues to play fast and loose with work. On Saturday 14 August Stewart notes, 'This day getting remarkably wet, at 10 o'clock obliged the masons to trail off'.

9 October – the carpenters are engaged with making moulds for the saloon. Later in the month another injured workman, Alex Nolden, hurt by a bank falling on him, is paid while sick.

24 November – six carpenters are engaged with making 'girders' for the bedchamber floor.

During the weeks ending 11 and 18 December, 13 men travel 263 miles with seven chests from Edinburgh to Castle Coole, costing £36 19s 4d. The following week's return notes, 'Scotch stonecutters Mistake of exchange between English and Irish mony & carriage of boxes from Belfast'.

Monday 20 December – labourers put stones on the quay to prevent the flood.

Christmas brings hard work: during the week ending 25 Dec 1790 workers are engaged in drawing stones from the bog road; carpenters work on basement-storey windows. Labourers again pile stones at the quay to stop it being washed away by floods.

Turf vaults are constructed in the tunnel.

1791

1 January – 'carpenter drawing of architecture'. This refers to John Brett, described as 'architect' previously. The work at this time is mainly on the 'subterraneous passage'. Perhaps this needed to be drawn up on site, not being a feature covered by Wyatt's brief. This kind of tunnel is very much a practical, Irish feature to arrange the passage of goods and servants from the yard into the kitchen area without being seen from the house. Carpenters make 'centres' for the subterranean passage. The tunnel when built was longer than it is now and was probably shortened when the grand yard was made in the early nineteenth century.

The weather, wind this time, is difficult again: Tuesday 1 and Wednesday 2 February – workers cover the sand to prevent it being blown away.

Labourers help a thatcher in February, when a new forge is being made and thatched.

March and April – there is some difficulty keeping labour. Stewart refers to 'borrowing labourers', sending an express to Donegal for masons. In the week ending 23 April a sick man, John Thorbes, is given money to travel home. In August, the wages of a mason, John Doherty, are stopped for absenting himself without leave on Friday 19 August.

Thursday 19 May – one boy is kept busy 'minding the Greyhound' (a wagon).

Monday 23 May – 14 boys are at work at the quay raising a boat.

Tuesday 24 May – three boys mind the 'Greyhound'.

Week ending 25 June – 'flaggs' (flagstones) arrive at Bow Island.

First week of July – carpenters make a room in the office of Mr Andrews, the head stonemason.

1 September – carpenters are at work putting down the floors in the eastern side of the house.

September – 'flaggs' and stone are transported from Bow ('Boa') Island and Monea and from 'Slea Bea'.

October – Lord Belmore's boat brings lead and slates.

Thursday 24 October – one carpenter spends a few days making a 'leaping rail' for horses.

November – the basement offices are being attended to and workers pave the ground floor.

Work is in progress on the house of Maitland, the stonemason, including glazing.

Week ending 3 December – workers raise Portland stone sunk in Lough Erne.

Week ending 17 December – the labourers are given whiskey.

Example of Stewart's weekly building accounts

Brooding over the previous year's work and the likely progress that could be made in the year to come, and under pressure from Belmore to complete in 1793, Alexander Stewart was also worried about costs. On 12 January 1791 he wrote to Belmore:

'Since you left Castle Coole I have, in the course of my musing about next year's operation, turn'd over in my mind the serious sum of money necessary to put it into effect and thought it my duty to lay it before your lordship in time'.

The original time scale for completion of the building itself seems to have been five years, based on two years' site preparation from the starting date in May 1788 plus three years' building work. Stewart's estimates in this letter, for which 1793 is the last year, confirm this. But he warned:

'if we mean to cover one wing in this season and have the house up to the string [cornice] which I think we can do if supply'd properly, then of course the supply is the serious side of the business and no time is to be lost to think of it, namely stone, lead and slates'.

He estimated the cost to 1793 as £28,180 – 'the total amount to finish with that already expended if frugally gone about'. Frugality, however, was scarcely the watchword needed to achieve what Belmore wanted and, whether because of supply difficulties, changes instigated by Belmore himself or other reasons, it was optimistic to expect to complete by 1793. The weather itself, as is not unusual in Fermanagh, made itself felt:

'Your Lordship was pleased to allow me a few turfs to burn in this office. I had one parcel in a carr while my Lord was here & yesterday I wanted a few more & could not get them unless I would carry them out of the barge on my back and really it is so cold that I can not hold the pen and makes my paper so damp that my pen goes through it like a cobweb. I believe we shall have never a stone on this ground or a cill up until the first of March. I wish I may be mistaken for once but it will not be easy to put us in again'.

To cap it all, Stewart and William Armstrong were at loggerheads again:

'I have got the timber out of the grove yesterday and I had a great deal to do to stop Will from continuing to draw a parcel of trees there belonging to George. I wrote him while I was almost sick but could not make him sensible but by T-rs he would draw them all. The bullock boy attempted to make him sensible and he beat him on the spot nor would look at last to any paper. This is one of the most cruel days of wind and rain I ever saw and he has the poor animals out. I leave it to your Lordship what will be the consequence. I think it will be that they cannot do their business on a better day properly with all the corn in the world'.

Belmore was not impressed by Stewart's complaints. He was certainly less than happy about the mounting cost of the building work. On 2 January 1791 he wrote to Stewart to ask why, when the building was then covered against the weather, there should be so much expense. Stewart was confident that Belmore's house could be finished by the early summer of 1794, with one important proviso: 'my Lord suffering any material alteration to be made in his present design otherwise no man living could tell where it might end'. That has always been the stumbling block in the path of builder and client alike. Stewart fell back on the obvious let-out: 'What I advanced was not any more than a probable conjecture of the yearly expenditure my Lord finishing in three years'. In any case, he pointed out, there was an insuperable barrier to the reduction of expense:

> 'with regard to labour there is no diminishing it while all is finished unless it be the work of horses and perhaps a few labourers, and as you dismiss one set you take on another, though not so numerous, yet more expensive, which keeps the expense to the very last, especially in buildings that must get on & finish in a given time'.

Stewart's estimates had already produced differing figures, from £28,180 at the beginning of January to £33,175 at the end of the month. If this irked Belmore he must have been positively infuriated by subsequent increases. By May 1793, after exactly five years' work, the actual cost had risen to £38,779. Worse was yet to come: two years later the cost had risen again to reach £51,666.[10] It was to rise even further, for there was another three years' work to be done on furniture and carpentry, as well as continuing outside work. Belmore was himself responsible for much of the increase by making 'material alterations' in his designs.

In spite of all the vexation, by the summer of 1792, Belmore's new house, now described by Stewart as 'the Castle', was taking shape.

1792

A limestone quarry at Connagrany and a quarry at Cavancross supply lime and stone.

Week ending 18 February – the stonecutters work at the 'great columns' for the house portico; by the end of April they are busy 'setting balustrade over west wing'. It is difficult work, the weather being 'squally, high wind out with showers' – with, on one particular night, 'great showers of hail and a great fall of snow'.

Week ending 19 May – joiners are at work – two on sash frames, two on moulding, one at the skirting for the attic rooms and one at the door for the 'green house' (not a greenhouse as understood nowadays, but the portico area in front of the doors in each wing – possibly intended to allow for glass partitions between the columns, catching sunlight and making a shelter for plants and a pleasant area for sitting in).

The flooring goes in, attics are constructed, beds are made and a plasterer begins work for the first time. 'Plaister of Paris' arrives in Lord Belmore's boat at the end of June. During that summer plaster and stucco are delivered regularly and Joseph Rose's man, the specialist for fine work, is there in August.

In September, the labourers, who have worked hard in difficult conditions, carrying cut stone to the setters and turf to various workplaces, are again rewarded with whiskey. The men are still available for other work: on Friday 19 July a carpenter repairs a sports chaise for Lord Belmore and on Thursday 15 November one man and a horse repair the 'sluicing house' (probably a personal bathroom for the ladies) for Miss Corry and Miss Allen (possibly Lady Louisa's personal maid).

In the summer of 1792 Buckinghamshire invited Belmore to visit Blickling with his granddaughter, Louisa. Belmore wrote:

> 'I am so deep in mortar that I cannot do myself the honor of paying my respects at Blickling this summer but hope in the succeeding summer to present your granddaughter to you, please to present my affectionate compliments to Lady Buckingham, Caroline & Emily'.

Buckinghamshire, replying on 26 June, said, 'we hear much of the magnificence of your (temp) Seat'.[11] The unfinished word 'temp', deleted in the final version, suggests that Buckinghamshire, in his usual bantering style, was about to refer to the house as a temple – thus anticipating, but humorously, de la Tocnaye's disparaging remark. Buckinghamshire's familiarity with Belmore may have warned him that he would not appreciate the joke.

Although plasterwork on Joseph Rose's designs had begun the previous summer, only one man was employed so progress was slow. Captain Cole, no doubt on Belmore's orders, wrote to Rose asking that more men be sent to speed up the work. Wyatt was sending designs with the men, designs that had been finished some 12 months previously. Rose claimed that he had to pay the new men extra wages because they were reluctant to travel to Ireland:

> 'I have (at last) sent you four more plasterers (very good ones I believe) but I have been obliged to give more wages, otherways they would not have left England'.

Rose then gives the reason the men had used to explain their reluctance to travel across the water:

> 'My men are rather afraid of being pressed, why they should be I cannot tell, as none of them are sailors. If any thing of the kind should happen I hope your Lordship will stand their friend – I hope your Lordship will excuse my leaving this letter open for if they should be taken hold of by the Press-Gang this letter will convince them they are going to work for your Lordship'.[12]

The plasterers were not completely mistaken in their fears about being pressed (that is, forcibly enlisted into the navy), although, strictly speaking, the impress was supposed to be of men who had some connection with the sea or boats – for example, on rivers or canals – or of those with skills immediately useful to the navy. Many men were pressed at sea rather than on land. Landsmen took a long time to train and were usually volunteers. However, after the outbreak of the French war in 1793 the navy needed many more men and a long journey through ports and across the Irish sea may have seemed threatening.

In June, Rose was worried because the reluctance of the plasterers to go to Castle Coole had spread to the ornamental specialists and costs were rising, which Belmore was probably already complaining about. The whole Irish project seems to have been getting on top of Rose:

'I am rather afraid I shall have some difficulty in getting the ornamental men to come – I understand that there are letters come to London from the last men I sent your Lordship saying that it is an unhealthy place, that *most of my men are ill* and that there is not lodgings for them *but in damp rooms* indeed my Lord if you should also now or hereafter *be dissatisfied with me* for it costing you more money than you expected I shall wish that I had never seen Ireland'.

Belmore approved the estimates, excusing Rose from the need to visit Castle Coole.

1793

Labourers are laid off during the course of this year (some names are scratched out). Marble is brought in from Crawford and Partners in Dublin, possibly for the chimney pieces.

26 April – Stewart writes a memorandum for the attention of Captain Cole: 'Will the windows in the saloon be plate glass – I think they shall indeed – this ought to be settled with Mr Andrews [the joiner in charge] before he goes'. Andrews takes over from Stewart in signing weekly accounts when, finally, the only work left is joinery. Presumably the window frames have been made to suit the weight of plate glass, which may be necessary because the large windows in the saloon will be used as access ways to and from the steps to the lawn outside. This is thought to be the first mention of the use of plate glass in Ireland.

The design of the hall causes Stewart a problem and he writes to Cole again:

'The niches in the hall will never finish in an agreeable manner – then make them square fireplaces and then they can be fitted up with stoves in them as well and better than if they were niches'.

Week ending 16 November – work takes place on the new canal and walled garden: 'carpenters 2 boys & 2 labourers 3 at hanging a gate on the wooden bridge on new lake' and 'a gate for Croker's bog'. In the same week a fatality – that of 'Jim Martin', is noted.

1794

By February there must have been some notion of the house being completed, for rings for picture frames are paid for.

'Enniskillen Crane, Wm Hudson, cranemaster, 1794: one hogg weighed 169 lbs' – very likely a pig for feeding the men.

Week ending 8 March – the stonecutters work on the steps for the 'great stairs'.

Week ending 31 May – the metal stoves (two in the saloon and one at the bottom of the back staircase, in the basement) are delivered from Dublin and signed for by Martin Allen (possibly the husband of Mrs Allen, who may have been Lady Belmore's maid).

Richard Westmacott supplies 'statuary drapery marble chimneys for the library, a richly carved statuary marble chimney piece for the drawing room, dining parlor, breakfast room, two for the hall and superior statuary slabs to hall chimney'.

A boat is loaded at Hungerford Wharf with six masons and four polishers.

Iron cramps, brass wire, straw and polishing materials and superior strong deal packing cases are supplied.

Six sets of black marble slips for grates and superior lapis marble are brought in, plus insurance, to Ballyshannon.

April – 'Carpenters put up surround in Venitian window. Also putting up surround to Wyaticol Window'.

Week ending 19 July – '8 Carpenters employed at fitting lodging for Mr Bartoli' (the specialist in the Scagliola surfaces put on the columns in the hall). Bartoli seems to have finished by 27 June 1795, when the last payment is made to Manuel, his subcontractor.

'Temporary Tables for Old house made week ending Aug 30th' – perhaps because a start has been made on moving furniture into the new castle, but this is not explained.

Week ending 6 September – 'Carpenters employed at Skellatons for Skylola columns'.

Sir John Caldwell's boat is still engaged in bringing Portland stone. On Monday 15 September joiners make a writing desk for Mary Anne, the new Lady Belmore.

On 24 March 1795, Rose, unwell and unhappy about the business again, had to confess to his evident embarrassment there had been a misunderstanding about the wages of the plasterers which would need more money from Belmore. Finally, in spite of increasing pain and under pressure from Belmore to get on with things, Rose explained the arrangements he had made for his prefabricated casts and moulds to be sent securely to Castle Coole via Liverpool and Dublin: 'I have sent off eight packing cases containing the casts and moulds for the capitals and frieze for your saloon – I must conclude as I am in great pain'. Belmore annotated this letter: '1795 March Rose about wages of his Plasterers – to be compared with his letters at Castle Coole under the leaden weight on my writing table in the Studdy'. This would have been the study in the Queen Anne house. A leaden weight may well have been expressive of Belmore's feelings about the cost of building at that time. The next known exchange of letters does not occur until 1796.

1795
Monday 30 March – the stonecutters make holes for the balusters in the great stairs.

Monday 6 April – the joiners fix ornaments to the pilasters in the drawing room.

9 May – the stonecutters finish the portico.

November and December – the 'engine house' (pump house down by Lough Coole to supply water to the house) is built.

Painters are at work, suggesting a great deal of the building work had been finished, and the mahogany doors for the hall are installed. Work continues in the east wing and the dormer windows in the old house are repaired.

Grates and a seat for the water closet are fixed.

By December a mason prepares the chimney pieces.

The cost of the library chimney piece described as a 'statuary, drapery, marble chimney piece' is £126 and is signed by Wyatt.

Belmore continued to be harrassed by the mounting costs of building, as well as its difficulties. In 1796 there was a problem in obtaining a particular colour; and the moist air of Fermanagh spoiled Bartoli's work on the Scagliola columns in the hall. Rose was at a loss:

'As I did not know what was best to be done when the columns mildew'd I asked Bartoli (for my own information) he told me that wiping them dry when there appeared a decay on them which would certainly be the case in warm moist weather was the best that could be done – you will in general find the same on all painted walls where there is no fire kept'.

By September of that year the problems of cost had built up. When Rose came to do his accounts in response to Belmore's understandable desire to see them as soon as possible, they filled too many sheets to be conveniently posted, and they amounted to considerably more than even Rose had expected. He pleaded that the extra costs were consequent on alterations and additions and asserted that, even at the higher price, he was the loser:

'my bills amount to considerably more than I thought they would when I was last at Castle Coole – but from Shire's letters I understood there was [sic] alterations and additions – the staircase ceiling was then intended plain, the basement story *the remaining part* done in common plastering which has now been finished in the best manner – but not to tire your Lordship, I must leave the work and the bill to speak for themselves – I shall only add that I firmly believe the ornaments has cost me more money than I have charged … If your Lordship has the least wish for my bill to be looked over by Mr Wyatt, I will give him a copy and he will give you his opinion of it. I only mention this, my Lord, as I wish you perfectly satisfied before you pay the balance. I shall only add my Lord that I wish you good health and many, many happy years to enjoy your new house'.

This last letter was not dealt with by Belmore at all, possibly because his cash-flow problems obliged him to put off payments where he could. For example, in May, he was forced to sell his hunting lodge and land in Westmeath for £1,500. When a reply was finally sent it was by Lady Belmore more than a year later.

1796

January – labourers begin levelling the ground opposite the principal front of the new building. The levelling accounts show the work of levelling going on all around the new house, employing between 70 and 80 men.

January – pilasters are made for the saloon and joiners make bedsteads for the attic rooms.

A crane for the cellar is made. (The crane is still in place in the beer cellar.) Departing stonemasons' boxes are sent away to Dublin and only two stonecutters remain: they make marble chimney pieces for the east wing.

February – carpenters work on a new carriage and at 'Cabriol'.

March – another writing desk is made for Lady Belmore and carpenters square ash for 'Stillions' for the beer cellar. The joiners also make the mahogany doors for the 'great staircase'.

Only one stonecutter is left.

Carpenters make a box for the water closets of Mr Corry and Lady Belmore.

April – the paperhanger and chimney sweep get to work. There is more whiskey for the labourers and watchmen.

May – joiners make the chimney piece for Mr Corry's room.

Locks, hinges, latches, bells and furniture arrive from Edward Hanly of Birmingham via Holyhead. The bellhanger is Thomas Wells.

Week ending 19 June – joiners fix the ironwork to the 'great stairs' and stonecutters make plinths for stoves.

Week ending 25 June – cleaning the house begins.

Tables are made for Mr Corry's servant's room, and for Mr Poole the butler's room.

In August cases are made for the billiard room and the carriage of looking glasses from Dublin is paid for.

Week ending 1 October – one labourer works with Mrs Hackett, the housekeeper, on the cupboards and fittings going into the housekeeper's room.

Doors are hung for the 'Greenhouse'.

Cleaning the house continues.

October – seats for the tables in the servants' hall arrive.

10 December – Richard Atwell is paid for surfacing the road underneath 'the subterenus passage to the new building'.

December – the circular plinth for the saloon is made and fixed and the saloon windows are put in.

Sashes for the 'Desart [dessert] room' next to the dining room and beer stands for the ale cellar are made.

A press for Mr Poole's room, a press for the Servants' Hall and a press for the barrack room (a room shared by several servants and sometimes by single gentlemen guests) are put in.

A meat screen for the kitchen and a screen for the kitchen fireplace are made.

Wardrobes for the lady's maid and for 'Mr Christofar' (Christopher Armstrong, valet) are installed.

The plinth for the drawing room is made.

Work is done in the larder, the bakehouse and the dairy. A cupboard for the china dishes is put in.

A wardrobe for Mr Poole's bedroom is put in.

Rails are fitted in the back staircase to hang hats and coats on.

A wardrobe for the housekeeper's bedroom and a wardrobe for the butler's bedroom are put in.

Old chairs are altered and stools are put into in the servants' hall.

'Magnificent' but Sadly Wanting Furniture

In the summer of 1797 someone left a pan of hot ashes on the main staircase of the Queen Anne house. The stairs caught fire and the house was destroyed. Belmore and his family, Lady Belmore, Somerset (now aged 23), Lady Louisa (now 16), his illegitimate children, Maria (13), John (10) and Armar (4), as well as his servants, had no alternative but to move into the new house, even though it was not yet ready. Furniture, books, pictures, household utensils of all kinds and family papers were rescued: the old long-case clock which stood on the stairs is still at Castle Coole (although not in the rooms to which the public have access), the scorch marks of the blaze visible on its back. Although the actual building of the new house itself had been completed, a team of joiners – Peacock, Berry, Barni, Robinson, Moor, Clark, Brian Miller, Lee, Kernel and Terry, directed by the head joiner, John Andrews – were still making furniture and finishing details such as the mahogany banister rails. The smell of paint must have been everywhere as the painters – Thomas O'Hara, Michael Byrne, John Mason, John Willis, John Rogars and Simon Stroker – were still decorating the house and furniture. The wiring for the new system of bells was installed by Richard Wells and covered by the joiners. John Stewart of Montgomery Street, Dublin, a specialist 'Carvar', was still working on the curtain poles for the breakfast parlour window. Labourers under the supervision of Mrs Hackett, the new housekeeper, did their best to clean the house from top to bottom but the removals by teams of workmen must have made for a busy and confusing time. The cleaning would continue for another four years.

1797

The joiners make: a dining table for the dining room; pier tables for the breakfast parlour, dining room and drawing room; dressing tables, writing tables and banisters. They also have to make a coffin for Henry Stewart, who dies at work.

Week ending 26 August, carpenters make a table for the housekeeper's room, the sarcophagus for the sideboard to the dining room, (the sideboard pedestals have been made the previous week) and washbasin stands for the attic rooms. They also make Lord Belmore's bedstead and curtain laths for it, Lady Belmore's bedstead and complete work in Miss Corry's bedroom.

Mr Corry's bookcases are made, as well as a table for the 'Desart' room and a fanlight for the water closet. The library bookcases have been made in April, as well as frames for flower stands for Lady Belmore, 'ladars' (ladders) for the water closets, turf boxes, 'flooting the frees [adding a coat and levelling the surface of the plaster] of the Bookcases Library'.

Spit racks are made for the kitchen; the force pump is worked on; and Lord Belmore's jaunting car and coach are repaired.

Mrs Hackett, the new housekeeper, had taken over from Rose Cowley, who had been housekeeper in the Queen Anne house for some years. It was a more responsible position because the housekeeper was now in charge of a much larger house and many more servants. In the absence of the Belmores, who usually took Poole, the butler, with them, she was head of the house's team of servants.

Castle Coole was now a house in the modern taste, replacing the old-fashioned gentleman's home, the Queen Anne house, with a new style of living for a noble family. Essentially, this meant that everyone had their own accommodation and the servants no longer lived cheek by jowl with the family. The stricter separation of servants from the family meant that those servants who lived in, were lodged in the basement or in the attic, and those who came in during the day entered through the tunnel into the kitchen in the basement. Visitors with the right credentials were ushered into the great hall from the imposing, central front entrance and then, depending on the occasion and their rank, into the library or breakfast room. The hall and saloon were used for balls and other formal ceremonies. The family lived in the east and west wings with their own entrances through the doors in the columned 'greenhouses'.

The Library at Castle Coole

An inventory made by Mrs Hackett in 1802 reveals that the new house was sparsely furnished. Some furniture had been designed by Wyatt and made by the joiners on site – for example: in the great hall, the hall chairs; in the dining room, two pier tables, the sideboard, pedestals and urns and the wine cooler; in the saloon, pier tables; in the library, the bookshelves, a knee-hole library table and two mahogany tables; in the state bedroom, a wardrobe and a chest of drawers, which were part of a total of six wardrobes and chests of drawers made by the joiners on site in 1798.[13]

Some furniture was brought over from the Queen Anne house. The inventory refers to items sent to Belmore's houses in Bath and at the seaside in Bundoran. Perhaps a man of his generation would not set so much store by a great deal of furniture but a visitor, some years later, in 1805, remarked, 'The house is certainly most magnificent, but sadly wants furniture'.[14]

In contrast, the servants' quarters in the basement were completely furnished. They all had the usual beds, bedding and quilts. While some quilts were of dark cotton there were coloured quilts, check curtains and mahogany furniture for the more privileged upper servants, including the coachman. The basement also had a sunken bath with a supply of piped water. This may have been used by gentlemen returning from hunting, shooting and fishing. There is also a small room near the servants' hall which was originally a space for powdering wigs. Wigs were, however, going out of fashion, at least for younger men and women, by the time the house was completed. They continued to be worn by servants.

The landscape of the demesne was also sparse: in his diary Thomas Russell wrote:

> 'To Eniskilling Lord Belmore's house at Castle Cool the most magnificent. The situation fine. The grounds exquisitely form'd. The trees finely scatter'd. Beautiful water. It wants, however, a apple [orchard?] and thick woods and great water to be answerable to the house'.

The apple and cherry trees had, of course been chopped down to make room for the house on their original site on top of Forth Hill. Russell visits again the next day: 'Walk through Lord Belmore's fine domain'.[15]

Belmore spent a great deal of time in his later years in Bath and at Bundoran, which may explain why he had not turned his mind to furnishing the house. He was taking the fashionable cures of the time: 'I intend going to the sea tomorrow and please God will dine here on Tuesday'. Seawater had become the recommended cure for the chest problems and rheumatism that plagued him. He rented accommodation from his friend, Sneyd, the wine merchant and member of parliament, also his neighbour in Dublin.

While it was true that Belmore was strapped for cash at this time, so too were his bankers, La Touche and Finlays. Money was scarce because of the economically and politically troubled times. In spite of the naval victory at the Battle of St Vincent on St Valentine's day, rumours of invasion by combined French and Spanish forces, fears of mutiny at Spithead and a run on provincial banks in England caused panic. The Bank of England suspended cash payments to banks. There was a run on English and Irish banks from February 1797 onwards, so it may have been that those factors as much as Belmore's own financial state that made it hard for him to raise money.[16]

The end of 1797, which had been a difficult enough year for him with his growing cash-flow problems, saw the beginning of the steady decline in Belmore's health. His doctor's bill shows many prescriptions during the period 1797–November 1801 for what were probably breathing difficulties, with congestion and chest pains: 'expectorating mixture', 'blistering ointment', 'Burgundy pitch plaster' and 'drawing plaister to dress his Lordship's back'. Ill though he was, Belmore was constrained to write personally to Sir John Caldwell to get him to pay over Mary Anne's dowry of £2,100.[17] The squeeze on credit in 1797 was biting:

> 'I flatter myself you know me so well that nothing but the utmost necessity could induce me to call on you for the payment of your sister's fortune. The fact is I am indebted to my Bank £4,000 and the terms are such that they must be paid. This is the language of their letter and without your friendly assistance it will be impossible for me to preserve my credit'.

To add to his expenses he had also just purchased the borough of Ballyshannon from Thomas Conolly for £12,000 and to Caldwell he confessed:

4th December 1799

Dear Sir John

    I flatter myself you know me
so well that nothing but the utmost
necessity could induce me to call on
you for the payment of your sisters
fortune. the fact is I am indebted
to my Bank £4000 and the terms
are such that they must be paid
this is the language of their Letter. and
without your friendly assistance
it will be impossible for me to preserve
my credit. You must know. that
my house and the Borough of Belly=
=shannon has made me as poor as
a Rat. and Bankers in these times
cannot venture to advance large sums
for any length of time. I have offered my

Bankers to assign them undeniable security for the amount of their demand which they have refused. as nothing but the bank will answer them, which must justify me for requesting you will as soon as possible pay the contents of your Bond. to

my Dear Sir John.

Your affectionate.

Belmore

Sir John Caldwell Bar

Letter from Belmore to his brother-in-law, Sir John Caldwell

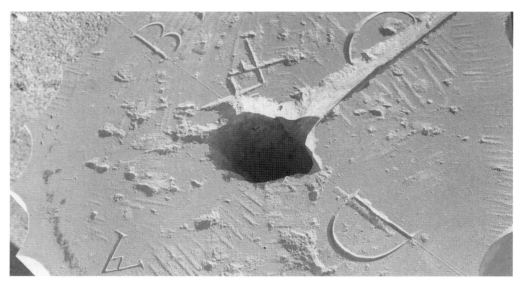

18th century mason's mark on a column at Castle Coole

'You must know that my house and the borough of Ballyshannon has made me as poor as a rat and bankers in these times cannot venture to advance large sums for any length of time. I have offered my bankers to assign them undeniable security for the amount of their demand which they have refused as nothing but the cash will answer them, which must justify me in requesting you will as soon as possible pay the contents of your bond to, my Dear Sir John, your affectionate Belmore'.

Belmore was now looking for as much time as he could get to pay bills. Using his illness as her husband's excuse for not writing sooner, the Countess herself wrote to Rose. Although there is no copy of her letter, its tone and content must have been rather high for it severely upset him: [18]

'I have just now received a letter from Lady Belmore. I am very sorry my Lord that you are so unwell as not to be able to write yourself but the letter has so alarmed me, that I cannot help answering it immediately'.

The Belmores adopted an age-old device for delaying the correspondence even further by suggesting that they send Rose a copy of his costings, thus putting off the argument for another week or two at least. But Rose was more than ready to meet that tactic:

'you need not, my Lord, give yourself the trouble of sending me a copy of my calculation I made of the plasterer's work when at Castle Coole in July 1794, *from my memorandums* I recollect the whole of the conversation that led to it and I am sure I did not mean at that time to deceive you, it was guessed at without any measurement – I have every paper I believe relating to your business, *every letter* I have received from your Lordship, *and copies* of those I wrote to you, also every letter I received from Shires, Mr Stewart and very happy indeed I am now that I have preserved them. I must own I did not expect *such a letter from your Lordship* as I have received from Lady

Belmore – and this after you had received my bill more than *twelve months ago* – and the business had been finished *nearly two years*'.

Then Rose once again raises the real reason for the increases in cost – the fact that in several respects Belmore had changed his mind about designs and quality. He suggests, as he had done in a previous letter, that Wyatt be called in to arbitrate. It seems that Rose was seriously upset, finishing his meticulously detailed letter with a rather sad, emotional appeal to the notion that Belmore and he had become friends:

> 'but my Lord you must excuse me, I am fully determined to fix it one way or another – I cannot be kept in suspense, nothing of this kind has happened to me before and think *how greatly must be my disappointment* – I thought I had added you to the number of my friends – you must excuse me if I write again if I do not receive an answer soon – *I am very uneasy*'.

Rose did not live to receive the last payment due to him. It was paid to his executors in September 1804.

1798

Peter Canan's bill is rendered for 'painting bason stands, a dressing table and an iron chest in green and white, panels of commodes in green and repairing in white the heads of balls in Billiard room, Studdy and Dining room'.

A great many lamp stands are made; bookcases are made for Lady and Lord Belmore; cleaning the house continues regularly.

In February tripods are made for the hall; in March, a screen is made for Lady Belmore. Apart from fitting the back-stairs handrail the joiners mainly make furniture, for example a pier table for Lord Corry's study, tea and sugar chests and washbasins.

Workers are engaged in repairing floors and 'hanging up picktors in Lady Belmore's work room' until the beginning of November. Cleaning continues and then, at the end of September, packing cases are made for the last of the workmen going to Dublin.

During 1801, King and Stewart were still supervising basic work in the gardens and grounds of the new house.

1801

Daniel Bready, William Murphy and Thomas Martin are at work 'Taking down trees', Richard Atwill is engaged with breaking stones, laying them on the new road leading from the house to the stone bridge, crowning, gravelling and repairing. Stones not used are left at the western end of the house, by order of Alexander Stewart.

'Thos Kerr, per A Stewart, work on new road and measuring land; painting & whitewashing grates etc and work on Turf house in company with Mr Stewart; also to laying out a road to Lisnaskea'.

Chapter Eight

Viscount Corry Comes of Age[1]

The Marquess of Abercorn, 'Don Magnifico' to many, accused Belmore of making politics his only aim in life. However, he was himself obsessed with politics, chiefly as the way to achieve his ambition of becoming lord lieutenant of Ireland. To do this he needed to demonstrate his primacy in the politics of Tyrone, but two things stood in his way: his own personality, seen by his contemporaries as absurdly vain; and Belmore, his implacable opponent – who, Abercorn complained, 'showed marked incivility to me'.[2] That was not really surprising since he himself admitted that he spoke to Belmore 'de haut en bas'.[3] Even Abercorn's old school friend, the Prime Minister William Pitt, found his manner virtually insupportable:

> 'appointing Abercorn as Lord Lieutenant was out of the question though he was so desirous of it. He would be the most unfit person in the world. His pride is carried to such an excess as to be quite ridiculous'.[4]

The contest was personal as well as political. Abercorn's political agent, John Stewart, openly admitted that it was 'certainly a very favourite object of the Marquis to exclude Lord Belmore altogether'.[5]

From 1789 onwards the struggle between Abercorn and Belmore to gain control of the machinery of political life in Tyrone involved them in manipulation of militia appointments, patronage, the registration of freeholders, canvassing, contests and polls. Although his health was beginning to fail, Belmore had a new ally – his son, Somerset, Viscount Corry, who was approaching his twenty-first birthday and would soon be able to stand for election to the parliamentary seat.

Corry's character would come to be of great significance in the political battles that faced him and his father in the 1790s. He was a man of strong opinions, expressed in strong language. When he was about 16 he had suffered a severe injury to his right leg and, as a result, was permanently lame. He never recovered the full use of his leg and had to ride a horse with a specially adapted saddle, somewhat like a lady's. He even hunted in this way. Once sufficiently recovered from his accident, he had been sent away with his tutor to Lisbon and, shortly after his seventeenth birthday, had set sail from there on a voyage round the Mediterranean from which he was not expected to return alive. That, at any rate, was the opinion of his tutor, expressed in a letter to his father, written during the voyage.[6]

Corry's diary of the voyage opens on 23 May 1791, the day he left Lisbon:

> 'Embarked this day on board the Valentine Snow of 159 tons (a two masted sailing vessel like a brig and equipped with guns) commanded by Captain John Cobb with Mr Myddleton, Dr Crawford, Mr Scott and Mr Christopher Kohn. The Prince of Luxembourg, Mr Paul George Junior, Mr Williams (our landlord) and George Ross (our valet de place) pay'd us a compliment of a visit at 5 o'clock in the morning'.

Somerset, Viscount Corry as a boy

The voyage and sea air not only improved his spirits but also restored his general health. He enjoyed himself enormously, feeling a sense of restored well-being that completely escaped his companions: 'My health, appetite and spirits are uniformly good. My friends are continually sick'. A year later, he was fully recovered in his general health, as evidenced by a remark of Buckinghamshire's. Writing to Belmore in May 1792, Buckinghamshire refers to 'the reestablishment of your Son's health'. This, Corry's first Mediterranean voyage, was an experience that gave him a lasting love of sailing. Whether his injury and his anticipated early death coloured his attitudes, or whether he was just a man who took no prisoners, is a matter of choice – but Abercorn accused him of being too ready to use 'that line of language and conduct which throws away the scabbard'.

Thomas Knox, who was nominally Belmore's political ally, was actually double-dealing. In April, he advised Abercorn to ease off Belmore, all the better to control him:

> 'In Tyrone you must for some time continue as spectator of its politics. My engagement with Lord Belmore places me in an unnatural state of opposition to you ... I would place myself in a situation that Belmore and Stewart should look up to me with that degree of anxiety that always proceeds from uncertainty. I would teach them to think that I could move the machine at pleasure and in that degree of suspense would keep them, ready always to take advantage of circumstances ... Would it not, then, be expedient that all symptoms of hostility towards Belmore should disappear and that a degree of cordiality should be assumed towards him?'

This devious suggestion was swept aside by Abercorn's pride: 'I will say in one word that I would rather give up the county forever than make the slightest advance to Lord Belmore'.

Following the Militia Act of 1793, Abercorn, as part of his political ambitions, sought to control the appointment of officers in the Tyrone Militia. He was its figurehead commander until he resigned in 1800, and Thomas Knox was its lieutenant colonel, or effective commander, until he and Abercorn quarrelled in 1794, and Nathaniel Montgomery Moore of Aughnacloy, Tyrone, succeeded him. Belmore, for his part, had since 1791 raised and paid for his own volunteer company of Omagh. His accounts show a bill:

'to Alex Tate, Looping and Cockade charged to Lord Belmore's account: to Officers hatts & Cockades, to Gold Trim, to 57 Private Men's hatts with tinsel bands loops and Cockades, to Box and Cord: £45.15.0'.[7]

The Tyrone Militia, however, was intended to be a properly trained and disciplined army reserve. It was important to Belmore, for prestige and for Corry's career, that his son should be commissioned, with a rank suitable to his social status. Abercorn could not refuse the commission but baulked at too high a rank: 'I certainly will not consent to Lord Belmore's son as being more than Captain'.[4] Belmore was insulted and Knox advised Abercorn, 'It is apparent that Lord Belmore and his friends are refusing to have anything to do with the Militia'.[8]

When Corry came of age in 1795, Belmore resettled his estates to give his son a life interest and an increased income. It was Corry's first step towards taking more responsibility. Belmore desperately needed his support because, only two years earlier, Thomas Knox told Abercorn:

'Belmore had been in so distracted a state of mind for these last three years, owing to the desperate state of his son's health and the misconduct of his wife, that he had almost entirely secluded himself from society'.

Also, Corry's place in the world as his only son and heir was increasingly important to Belmore, not just for the succession but also to secure a future for Belmore's other young children. After Belmore's death Corry would, in effect, be their guardian.

Belmore's own worsening health meant that his political activity in the 1790s was increasingly confined to a behind-the-scenes struggle. He usually voted in the House of Lords by proxy. Given the family tradition, the first business to attend to was to get Corry into parliament as member for Tyrone in the elections for the parliamentary session beginning in 1797. This meant getting in votes and taking on the opposition in the shape of Abercorn's latest political manager, John Stewart of Athenree, Tyrone.*

From 1795 to 1797 correspondence, especially between Stewart and Abercorn, throws light on the struggle and on Abercorn's feelings about it and about Belmore and Corry. They were a thorn in his side. This was shown clearly in a remark of one of Abercorn's agents, James Galbraith, after Belmore's death, saying that Belmore had died 'in the most obliging manner possible to preserve the county's quiet, which is a great blessing'.

Early in the year John Stewart was plumbing the depths of opposition by trying to establish that Corry was not old enough to contest the seat. On 10 January he wrote to Abercorn:

*John Stewart was, over time, MP for various boroughs and later represented Tyrone at Westminster. From 1798 to 1799, with Abercorn's help, he became Irish solicitor general, and he was attorney general from 1799 to 1803.

John James Hamilton, 1st Marquess of Abercorn KG PC (Ireland)

'I have been enquiring about the age of Lord Belmore's son. Some say he will be 21 years old next June, but I believe he will not be of age till the end of this year'.

The records disappointed him. He reported on 21 January that he had 'found by the parish registry in Dublin where young Mr Corry was born, that he will be of age the 4th of next July'. Stewart's hopes were raised again when, on 28 February, he was able to report rumours of differences between Belmore and Corry about raising money on the security of their estates (see page 82 *ante*) and added, in the hope of discouraging their political ambitions:

'I'll not forget to talk of the great expense and the provisions your Lordship is making for that purpose and your determination to support the contest'.

But the differences were not there and on 5 March Stewart had to admit: 'I fear the report I mentioned to your Lordship of Lord Belmore and his son is not well founded, so we must persevere vigorously in Tyrone'.

In the meantime, Belmore and Corry were making their next moves in the political game. The accounts show that Belmore spent a great deal entertaining the 'inhabitants' of his Tyrone estates.[9] This registered with Stewart, for he wrote to Abercorn on 29 January:

'It is now really necessary in Tyrone to exert all our powers, for the exertions of Lord B and his friends are really extraordinary, when we consider the value of the property from which they produce such numbers'.

This was a reference to the practice of increasing voter support by turning leasehold tenancies into apparent freeholds with an annual value entitling them to vote. Abercorn now desperately needed to find out how many voters Belmore could count on by this device. He was also only too well aware that even greater voter numbers were achieved by subdividing the holdings of the fictional 'freeholders'.

Stewart's enquiries drew a blank:

'I cannot give your Lordship an idea of the divisions and subdivisions of farms on Lord Belmore's estate for the purpose of making freeholders. Indeed, their numbers are such that they talk with much confidence, and think, from your not making any, you do not seriously intend to contest the county with them. This I know to be their constant discussion through Tyrone at this time'.

Abercorn was so intent on contesting Belmore for the county that he raised the possibility of creating freeholders on his own estates, but Stewart thought that too artificial: 'to execute new leases merely for the purpose of making freeholders is not altogether eligible'. He does add, however, that should any leases fall in, it might be different.

By July Belmore pulled off a major coup in successfully resurrecting his political partnership with Thomas Knox, whose election for Tyrone he had assisted in 1790. Knox had offended Abercorn by resigning from the Tyrone Militia to pursue his own militia and political ambitions in Dungannon. Abercorn thereafter withdrew his support from Knox. At this point, in 1795, Knox went over to Belmore. Writing to Abercorn about this on 29 July 1795, Stewart suggested:

'I think the state of the county of Tyrone now offers success to your interest on easy terms. Tom Knox was always the enemy of James Stewart's interest, and his junction with Lord Belmore is looked on in the county as a direct attack on Stewart. The people are angry at it, for neither Lord Belmore nor Knox are at all popular ... if due care is taken in registering all our friends (as every man must now register) I hope we will be able to see a majority against this Lord Belmore'.[10]

'Registering all our friends' is a reference to a manoeuvre Stewart described as 'a great stroke against Lord Belmore's interest'. It was a change in the law by the introduction – by Stewart himself – of a new and universal register of voters, which he hoped would counter Belmore's ability to create freeholders and win the county election. He had urged for some time that if Abercorn could only register some 800 or 900 votes there would not be any contest with Belmore again. Even so, Abercorn dismissed Thomas Knox's association with Belmore as a piece of bad luck. This was a serious underestimate of both men and when, in August 1795, a quarrel of some sort arose (its exact nature is unknown) between officers of the Tyrone Militia, the sensitivity of the Abercorn camp to pressure from Belmore was revealed once more. In a letter to Abercorn, George Knox wrote:

'This militia business has made a great noise in this county and is rendering Montgomery Moore [the member of parliament for Tyrone, in the Abercorn camp] unpopular. Of course, it is taken hold of by the Belmore party'.

It was also taken hold of by Charlemont*, who obviously had a hand in the matter, for by May 1796 he was able to tell Stewart that Montgomery Moore 'was wholly out of the question and you and Corry are peaceably to be elected'. After an 'explanation' between some friends of Belmore and Abercorn the matter was settled and Thomas Knox, too, was delighted by an arrangement which he was confident would return Corry and Stewart without opposition. Montgomery Moore withdrew his candidacy for Tyrone and was doubtless mollified by being returned for Strabane, one of Abercorn's boroughs.[11]

Abercorn was a reluctant party to the explanation for he was determined to keep the number of his registered voters on his estate 'always above the numbers of Lord Belmore's'. He recognised that a contest between them would inevitably come in the future.

In early 1796, Belmore set out to fix the election of a sheriff sympathetic to his interests and Stewart made every effort to counteract it. The sheriff was the chief executive official of the county in both civil and criminal matters – presiding, for example, over elections – and he was usually the nominee of one of the landed families. Abercorn reacted indignantly ('of course Lord Belmore must not be gratified with the slightest interference about Sheriffs') and later that year, even though Belmore had failed to secure the election of his nominee, Abercorn raised the stakes:

'as it is evident that Lord Belmore will be glad, whenever he can, to assume airs of victory and triumph, I think it is necessary for us never to give up on a single instance the nomination of Sheriff and everything else in the county'.

By September 1797 Abercorn had decided to sell his borough of Augher but wanted not less than 16,000 guineas for it, to make a profit of nearly £4,500 for a purchase made just seven years previously. The increase may, however, have merely reflected inflationary times. He was happy to think that Belmore could not afford it. In a letter to Stewart he scoffed, 'Lord Belmore else would like it, if he could raise the money'. Stewart agreed that Belmore's cash-flow difficulties would prevent him from buying Augher; in any case, he was having difficulty filling his seats with suitable candidates:

'I know Lord Belmore was much pushed to make out by at least seven loans the price of Ballyshannon and is, therefore, I fear not likely to purchase. I know three gentlemen who refused to accept returns from him for one seat which he still has vacant and he has returned his two attorneys, King and Babington for the other'.[12]

*Lord Charlemont, 'the Volunteer Earl' (1728–1783) had considerable social influence in Dublin and London but, aligned with Grattan, he became an advocate of Irish constitutional independence and opposed the union. He took a leading part in the formation of the Volunteer Corps and was made commander in chief of the Volunteers in 1780. He was president of the Volunteer Convention in Dublin in November of that year.

Mary Anne (Caldwell), Countess of Belmore *c.* 1830 by G F Mulvaney ARHA

Belmore then struck at Abercorn by threatening to take away Abercorn's patronage of the distributorship of stamps in Omagh, vacated on the death of the incumbent.[13] Stewart warned Abercorn:

> 'The distributor of stamps died in Omagh the other day … I dined afterwards with a friend of Lord Belmore's, and somehow the conversation turned on the death of the man whose place was vacated, and it was mentioned that Lord Belmore had applied for it, and considered the *town* of Omagh in his patronage, and that it was actually promised to *him*'.

The 'somehow' is scarcely believable, since the fight for patronage between Belmore and Abercorn would have been a hot topic at any dinner party. Stewart felt the affront to Abercorn:

> 'I went, therefore, this day and asked Mr Pelham if Lord Belmore had applied. He told me he had and showed me his letter. I replied, the town of Omagh is within 6 or 7 miles of Lord Abercorn's house. The town is the property of my father-in-law. Mr Pelham directly said that he never made the smallest promise to Lord Belmore, and did not even answer his letter, and that any person Lord Abercorn named should have it. I then begged of him not to fill up the appointment'.

To Abercorn's delight, his own nominee who got the job was Belmore's former protégé, 'which will be an additional mortification to Belmore'. However, Belmore's mortification may have been eased when, on 20 November 1797, he took a further step up in the peerage as Earl Belmore of the County of Fermanagh by patent of privy seal on 9 October, and was introduced into the House of Lords on 9 June 1798.

In fact, politics and even rebellion were not Belmore's major concern, for in 1798, at the age of 43, his wife was pregnant. The risks of pregnancy, even for women much younger than Mary Anne, were great. Early in December she went into a very protracted and painful labour. Lady Moira had once described to Henrietta Belmore her own anxieties during her daughter's confinement as 'watching for misfortune & misery to be announced in some unfavourable symptom every hour she passed with her'. Such contemporary fears may well have reflected Belmore's own feelings.[14] However, the crisis passed and Belmore was able to write to Lord Gosford at Market Hill on 19 December:

'My dear Lord, I have the pleasure of informing you my dearest Lady Belmore is now as well as can be expected, quite out of danger. She was in severe pain for *one hundred and three hours*. The child is dead, but thank God she is as well as can be expected'.[15]

The Countess must have had a strong constitution, for she recovered quite quickly. Belmore immediately wrote to her brother to announce the good news:

'Our dearest M A is recovering as fast as possible. She has slept well the last two nights – she has sat up from two to eleven in the dining room, however I am determined to remain here untill sometime next week, when I hope she will be quite rested'.

Once recovered, Mary Anne resumed her active interests, first among which was horse racing and horse breeding, which Belmore himself also enjoyed. He was among the first subscribers to the *Irish Racing Calendar* and she was the first lady owner to be recorded in it. Her mare Miss Boxer competed for the Long Stakes at the Curragh October meeting of 1800, but was unplaced. There were two especially well-known horses at Castle Coole, named Pilot and Traveller. Traveller's winnings are given as 125 and 100 guineas at the Curragh in 1799; 125, 100 and 50 guineas and a king's plate in 1800; 100 and 70 guineas and two king's plates at Hillsborough, and 60 and 50 guineas and a king's plate at Loughrea in 1801. Following his successes he was advertised in the *Erne Packet* as available for stud at a fee of eight guineas per mare, with a sovereign for the mare's groom. Pilot did not have a racing record but, like Traveller, did have a good pedigree. Traveller was regularly and successfully raced.[16]

Lady Belmore liked Bath and its social life and she persuaded Belmore to go there with her as often as possible. After his death in 1802, she lived at 17 Royal Crescent for 30 years, during which she received her widow's jointure of £1,000 a year. She is mentioned in *The Salisbury and Winchester Journal* for 22 October 1813: 'The Countess of Belmore bespeaks a Play and Farce to-morrow evening, when, without doubt, there will be an overflowing house'. For a long time she presided over balls held in the Assembly Rooms and was the model for Lady Snuphanuph in Dickens's *Pickwick Papers*. She survived the second and third Earls, dying in 1841 at the age of 86.[17]

Chapter Nine

The Dreadful Question: Lord Viscount Corry, Belmore and the Union Bill

The proposition of a union between Ireland and England had arisen more than once during the eighteenth century but was usually seen, in the language of the time, as 'visionary'. Pitt's union project was part of a grand design for the security of the newly emerging British Empire. In Ireland, there were increasing economic and security problems caused by the French wars and the 1798 rebellion.

Underlying the country's difficulties was the perceived inability of the Ascendancy parliament to provide government inclusive of Catholics. In contrast, many parliamentary gentlemen thought that the nature and quality of government was improving, based on what they perceived as the 'constitutional settlement' of 1782 and the success of the militia in dealing with the uprising of 1798. Corry was one of those. His ideas about constitutional law and economics had been much influenced by a tutor, Thomas Townshend, who in 1797 was brought in to sit as member for Belmore's borough of Belturbet. He was a barrister of Gray's Inn and, with the backing of Belmore, had been called to the Irish Bar. In the parliamentary lists for 1799 he was described as 'a scholar and pedant and better qualified for the situation of usher to a School than any other in life'.[1]

Townshend was very fond of Corry and was probably responsible for the particular interest in constitutional law and economics that Corry was to exhibit in the union debates and in later life. A specific belief expressed by Townshend about the English constitution was that it 'should be always taken as an immutable thing in principle'. Corry extended this notion of the immutability of constitutions to Irish circumstances. Townshend followed his patrons' line, and probably his own inclination, by voting against the union.

In January 1798, in his first ever session as an MP, Corry moved the address to the Crown in answer to the Lord Lieutenant's speech. This was perhaps indicative of his abilities, which were to be tested to the full in the heady atmosphere of debates and parliamentary manoeuvres against the union project.

Corry added a military career to his political one. He was captain of two Tyrone companies of yeomanry, the Lowreystown and Six Mile Cross Corps, but they were both infantry and were amalgamated in about 1810. There is an entry in Alexander Stewart's building returns for 1 January 1798, 'making Standors for the Colours Lord Corrys

Cavalry', but there is no record of him holding commissions in any cavalry units. It may simply have been that he and his fellow officers in the infantry were mounted.[2] The officers of the Fermanagh Infantry, in 1797, were Captain Somerset Lowry Corry, Lieutenant Richard Dane and Second Lieutenant James Dane.

But although Corry had started out well in his political and military careers, one of his personal relationships caused consternation when it went out of control on a social occasion at Castleblayney, Monaghan in February 1798. A witness wrote:

> 'A poor distracted girl, Miss Brooke, who at a ball at Lord Blaney's, when they went down to supper, asked Mr Corry, a son of Lord Belmore's, for his pen knife, which refused as not being sharp, she answered that it must be sharp as it was to cut leather, and seizing a dessert knife at the same instant made two attempts to stab herself both which proved ineffectual (the latter I think unfortunately), wounding the young man's hand severely who had caught hold of the knife. Handsome, genteel, a fortune of £12,000 but always melancholy and deranged at the time, whether from love or madness or both, there is one other, and perhaps but one that truly knows. Several ladies fainted but still the dancing went on, perhaps from a delicate possibility that the affair might pass unobserved'.

The witness was the renowned radical Dr William Drennan, who thought Miss Brooke a lunatic for love – a particular lunacy that, much later, would have its consequences.[3]

In 1798, Abercorn, unwilling to join his regiment in Ireland, decided to resign as colonel of the Tyrone Militia. He wanted to have Montgomery Moore appointed in his place, but Moore was turned down by the Lord Lieutenant, Camden. At Abercorn's suggestion Corry was appointed in November. Montgomery Moore was not happy about this and Major Vallancy, the adjutant, who had gone through some tough times with the regiment, could not be 'in any manner reconciled to the change'. He looked for another commission, unsuccessfully. The regiment had not always maintained the strictest discipline and Corry, the new broom, found the remaining officers ill disciplined. They failed to pay their mess bills on time and Corry, rebuked for this by his superior, General Alexander, replied bluntly:

> 'Every means that have been taken to induce the officers to be punctual in the discharge of their debts, have failed and it is now a fact becoming a regimental disgrace. I know of no other means to be taken than by your issuing an order for settling the accounts of the mess on some certain day. If there should then appear to be any debts unpaid, any officer neglecting to attend to your order to be brought immediately to a court martial'.

That cannot have made him popular. Even more irritating was a bungled change to officers' uniforms, involving the addition of feathers to their hats. The feathers could not be found, which inevitably caused a fuss. After Corry reported the loss they turned up addressed to the wrong officer. The feathers had been at camp all the while and for a long time. The duty officer blamed the laziness of his officers for not finding them sooner. An exasperated Corry suggested, 'for God's sake make them go to drill … if it be necessary for soldiers it surely is for officers who are supposed to instruct them'.[4]

His military service, mainly in Cork and Mullingar, was uneventful, except for his presidency of a series of courts martial trying rebels for murder and robbery. His penchant for discipline, however, produced its results – there is a commendation from the commanding general in November 1800 for the regiment's exemplary good conduct during seven months of duty in the Mullingar district.

Castle Coole itself was only lightly touched by rebellion. Corry's sister, Lady Louisa, a very high-spirited 19-year-old at the time, used to go out to look for rebels in the dark but 'never saw any that were worse than her'. The only rebel connected with Castle Coole was Croker (or Crocker) the gardener, who was caught training men on a hill close by. He was sent for trial but acquitted by the jury and, as was the custom then, he was taken in a cart to the border of County Fermanagh and there released.[5] Corry experienced problems in Tyrone, where acquittals of alleged rebels by sympathetic jurors were so common that it was difficult to find anyone to serve at all:

> 'in Tyrone Mr Corry, Lord Belmore's heir, who had been unable to induce his tenants to serve, had himself acted as foreman of a petit jury on which several grand jurors served'.[6]

In 1799, the government made their first attempt to achieve a union. On 22 January an address was moved in answer to the Lord Lieutenant's speech expressing the King's 'anxious hope' that parliament would find 'the most effectual means of consolidating … into one firm and lasting fabric, the strength, power and resources of the British Empire'. This was Pitt's fundamental policy. Fourteen lords, including Belmore, were having none of it and signed a formal protest against the proposal. Belmore and five other lords protested again on the third reading of the Bill to suppress the rebellion – not because they did not want the rebellion suppressed (for they expressly said that they 'abhorred' it) but because they thought it was not serious enough to 'justify the passing of an act, by which … the essence of the Constitution is universally subverted, and the freedom of our Civil Government is changed to Military Despotism'. In 1799, the Union Bill was defeated by one vote in the House of Commons.

The government tried again in 1800. On 10 February a motion was introduced into the House of Lords by the Lord Chancellor to confirm the lords' agreement to a union. It passed by a majority but, again, Belmore signed (by proxy) a protest in company with 23 other lords. On Friday 13 June a final vote in the Lords passed the Bill and, again, Belmore signed (by proxy) a protest with 19 other lords.[7]

A few days before the King's union message was introduced into the House of Lords, Castlereagh introduced it into the Commons. Corry spoke briefly and virtually dismissed it. He would not discuss its details. He looked upon the parliament of Ireland as unable to entertain the proposition. He would look on in silence and give his vote against every step that should be taken in prosecution of the measure. In March he took one of those steps when he seconded Sir John Parnell's unsuccessful motion to dissolve parliament before the Union Bill could be dealt with.

Somerset, Viscount Corry and his wife Lady Juliana (Butler) by Hugh Douglas Hamilton

Outside parliament, petitions and meetings were organised in Dublin and the counties of Ireland against a union; anti-union clubs were formed and dinners held to rally support; there was even an anti-union uniform advertised for sale by an enterprising businessman.[8] Among the toasts at an anti-union dinner held in Cork were:

> 'Sir John Parnell and the other honest Irishmen who prefer their country to the wages of corruption. Mr Grattan the father of the Constitution. Lord Corry and the friends of the Constitution in the North'.

Two weeks after its introduction into the Commons, the Bill was ready for its final form and Corry complained he considered it 'a matter of great precipitation' to ask the House to agree to it so suddenly. He would, he said, the next day propose a motion against it.[8]

Why did Corry begin his first session as an MP with implacable opposition to the proposed union; and why, after the project was defeated in 1799, but renewed in 1800, did he go on opposing it when he must have known that continued opposition would adversely affect his prospects of advancement after the union came into effect? It was said that he felt pledged to John Foster, Speaker of the House of Commons, who was emphatically against union, and whose *élève* he was. Therefore, he would not retreat from opposition.

However, ministers saw Corry as much more dangerous than as a mere follower of an elder statesman: they suspected that he was organising resistance on a county-wide basis in Tyrone, where opposition to union was strong. In September 1799, the suspicion was confirmed by no less an opposition figure than Charlemont himself, who revealed that attempts were being made in Tyrone to obtain signatures to an anti-union address, in support of which written 'hints' were sent to Corry.[9] Corry was thus seen as part of a

Somerset, Viscount Corry, opponent of the Union, by Hugh Douglas Hamilton

group, which included especially the Chancellor of the Exchequer, Sir John Parnell – who was dismissed from office because of his opposition – and William Saurin. Saurin, a lawyer and MP for Blessington, was in the Lord Lieutenant's eyes, 'a declared enemy to the measure'. He had been ready to organise armed resistance to the proposal but, threatened with the removal of his status as a King's Counsel, abandoned that idea. However, his verbal resistance was increasingly violent. He advanced arguments that union was against the competence of parliament and the sense of the people, which would entitle them to resist. These were 'dangerous doctrines' in the government's eyes and they were precisely the arguments advanced by Corry in his speeches in the Commons where he 'delivered the language of opposition'. Corry's true role as a spokesman for a larger opposition group is shown by his offer to Castlereagh, in February 1800, to give the proposal 'a fair assistance' if the government agreed to a postponement until the next session of parliament, and if the measure was then favourable to the country. Castlereagh, 'with the utmost civility', declined the offer as inadmissible.

A full-length painting of Corry by Hugh Douglas Hamilton in 1802 in the breakfast room at Castle Coole shows him standing defiantly in front of a table on which the Act of Union is shown while, under his left hand, is his address to the King opposing the union.

In the House of Lords, Belmore also aligned himself with the most vociferous opponents of union, such as the Marquis of Downshire, Lords Charlemont, Enniskillen, Bellamont, Powerscourt, Ely and others. They were each put under pressure by government to give up opposition. Downshire, for example, a particularly energetic opponent, was dismissed as colonel of militia, as governor of Down and from membership of the Privy Council. Belmore and Corry must have seen that they were taking a last stand against an attack on what they conceived, however mistakenly, as their independence in their territory of Ireland. They did not want to interfere in England and they expected England not to interfere with the 'constitutional settlement' of 1782 and subsequent commercial arrangements.

In the intensity of his opposition Corry, characteristically, resorted to very blunt language, even though he clothed his feelings with arguments of 'constitutional' principle. His speech contained over 20 expressions abusing ministers, including 'corrupt', 'rash', 'desperate', 'wanton', 'strange passion', 'dangerous', 'insulting' and 'degrading to this kingdom', 'artful delusions', 'rashness', 'arts and stratagems to procure from individuals of the lowest order, some of whom were their prisoners and felons, scandalous signatures against the constitution', 'public abuse' and 'perverted use of the Place bill'.

On Saturday 7 June 1800, when the Bill was read for the third and last time, Corry made his final speech, repeating in dramatic terms his three main arguments: that the economy of the country would be ruined; that the union was obtained by corruption and that it destroyed the constitution, which he regarded as above and beyond the power of parliament. He concluded, addressing the Speaker:

'I will not hear you put the dreadful question "that this bill do now pass". I hope I shall be permitted to avert my eyes in the last moment of the constitutional independence of my country'.[10]

When the House was finally and formally adjourned, John Foster walked out with 41 members:

> 'uncovered and, in deep silence, the mob accompanied them to the Speaker's residence. On reaching it the Speaker turned round, bowed to the crowd, entered his house and then the whole assemblage dispersed without uttering a word'.

As for Corry, he returned to his house in Rutland Square, accompanied by Lady Louisa, who had been present at the last debate – in the gallery, where she had accompanied her aunt, Lady Castlereagh.[11]

Shortly after Corry's last speech, Belmore himself signed (by proxy) a protest against the union in the House of Lords. This was signed by over 20 peers, including Lords Leinster, Meath, Granard, Moira, Charlemont, Strangford, Powerscourt and Farnham. It set out, broadly, in ten long paragraphs, the same arguments dealt with fully in Corry's speech. His opposition to the union was firmly grounded in his family and parliamentary history and his determination to see the Protestant Ascendancy preserved. For the same motives he signed a protest against the Compensation Bill, even though it was to compensate him generously for the loss of his political interest in the boroughs of Ballyshannon and Belturbet.[12]

These protests were Belmore's last parliamentary acts and they were carried out by proxy. He was probably already in Bath. On 10 December 1800 he made his last will. Corry was taking more of a hand in affairs at Castle Coole, subject only to the demands of his military duties, but he preferred to spend his time at Mount Juliet, County Kilkenny – the home of his future wife, Juliana Butler, daughter of the Earl of Carrick. This was virtually a family home for him, since it had been his mother's home as well as that of Juliana, whom he was to marry by special licence at Mount Juliet on 20 October 1800. On the eve of their marriage he ordered a specially made carriage from London for them:

> 'a chaise with a box to take on and off so that it may be either used as a street carriage or for travelling. I should wish it to be very complete and finished in the highest manner – The Butler arms must be quartered with mine on it'.

It was intended that the couple should live in the old Lowry house at Aghenis. [13]

Mount Juliet, Thomastown, Kilkenny built by Somerset, 1st Earl of Carrick after his wife Juliet

Chapter Ten

'Lord Belmore's death puts an end to all our doubts and difficulties'

In spite of his ill health and absence in Bath, Belmore continued his political manoeuvring unabated. On 30 November 1801 Abercorn was incensed at finding that Belmore had written to the Prime Minister, Addington, attempting to do a deal that would enhance Corry's chances at the next election and frustrate the ambitions of Stewart and Abercorn for Stewart to be elected:

> 'I find Lord Belmore, the violent opposer of the Union, offers you two or three votes in Parliament upon condition of your supporting Lord Corry against the Attorney General [Stewart], that is, his interest against mine in the ensuing election'.

Abercorn reminded Addington that they were old friends and that he 'has full as many [seats] in parliament as Lord Belmore, *though I do not job* them'. The last comment was pure spite, since Abercorn himself was by no means averse to 'jobbing' – that is, buying seats for votes and selling them for profit. In the event, Addington rejected Belmore's proposition. Abercorn's dig at Belmore, made by deliberately classing his opposition to union as 'violent', shows how Belmore had made himself vulnerable to being blackened in the eyes of government.[1]

On 26 January 1802 the final instalment of the compensation due in respect of the abolition of Belmore's interests in his borough constituencies was paid.[2] Election manoeuvres were once again under way between Belmore's Tyrone interests and those of Abercorn. This involved using persuasion and negotiation to secure the votes of those entitled to vote. The strength of Belmore's influence in Tyrone caused Abercorn 'doubts and difficulties'. Corry was, of course, still MP for Tyrone and would be running again. And while Abercorn still wanted to be top dog in Tyrone, Belmore and Corry were still always in his way. On 10 January 1802 Stewart remarked in a letter to Abercorn that 'Lord Corry's advertisement is violently high'. (The advertisement was the means by which a candidate addressed the electorate and the county generally.) Belmore's determination to win is reflected in the comments Abercorn makes about him.

On 17 January 1802, Stewart wrote again to Abercorn:

1800 The Acct Bt forward ——————— £8 | 9 | 0

Feb. 23 A large Expectorating Mixture as usual for Lord Belmore | 3 | 6
24 The Same Mixture repeated for his Lordship | 3 | 6
Two Ozs of Paregoric Elixir Doris the Bailiff ——— | 2 | 2
A Packet of Lime flowers for a poor woman [p] her
Ladyships order | 3 |
25 The Expectorating Mixture as usual for Lord Belmore | 3 | 6
26 The Same Mixture for his Lordship | 3 | 6
27 The Same Mixture repeated for his Lordship —— | 3 | 6
The Drawing plaister repeated for Do | 2 | 2
28 The Expectorating Mixture repeated for Do | 3 | 6
March 1 The Expectorating Mixture repeated for Do | 3 | 6
2 The Same Mixture repeated for Do —— | 3 | 6
3 The Same Mixture repeated for Do | 3 | 6
The Drawing plaister repeated for Do —— | 2 | 2
4 The Paregoric Elixir repeated for Dooris —— | 2 | 2
A box of Alterative pills for one [Kerr] [p] your
Ladyships order and Dr [Shaw]ts [feet] | 2 | 6
A Detergent Wash for the Same Man [p] Do | 2 | —
The Expectorating Mixture repeated for his Lordship | 3 | 6
5 The Same Mixture repeated for Do | 3 | 6
6 The Same Mixture repeated for Do | 3 | 6
7 The Same Mixture repeated —— for Do | 3 | 6
8 The Same Mixture repeated for Do | 3 | 6
9 Four Ozs of Paregoric Elixir for Do | 4 | 4
10 The Expectorating Mixture —— for Do | 3 | 6
The Drawing plaister repeated —— for Do | 2 | 2
19 The Expectorating Mixture repeated for Do | 3 | 6
Apr. 3 A Purgative powder for Lady Louisa | 10
4 The Same powder repeated for Do | 10
7 A Purgative powder for Dooris the Bailiff | 6
14 The purgative powder repeated for Lady Louisa —— | 10
May 5 An Oz Columba root in Powder [p] Ladyships order | 4
Nov. 17 An Expectorating Mixture as usual for Lord Belmore | 3 | 6
A Burgundy pitch plaister for Do | 1 | 4
19 The Mixture repeated for Do | 3 | 6
21 The Same mixture repeated for Do | 3 | 6
22 The plaister repeated for Do | 1 | 4
23 The Expectorating Mixture repeated for Do | 3 | 6

£13 | 14 | 8

Extract from 1st Earl Belmore's medical bill 1795–1801

'I met Lord Corry in Dungannon. He was going to see James Stewart. I have not yet heard what passed there. I know, however, he is completely alarmed … Corry's friends were making way with some of the Presbyterians, stating the folly of their taking the first law officer of his Majesty for their representative'.

Corry had been returned unopposed in 1797 with James Stewart, who still remained a favourite of the Presbyterians, and for this reason alone he may well have been returned with Stewart again in 1802 had his father lived. However, in January, John Stewart was not to know how matters would turn out. He knew that Belmore was unwell and this is reflected in comments he makes when writing to Abercorn on 30 January 1802:

'The considerations of the county must occur … to our minds … with care and attention … Lord Hamilton [Abercorn's heir] will not have opposition. Lord Belmore is far from a healthy man. I doubt if he will live till Lord Hamilton will be at age. I feel a strong inclination of the county gentlemen to keep the county quiet, and finding Lord Corry in possession some would support him who would, in the event of his father's death decidedly go with our interest … Lord Charlemont has lately declared for Lord Corry'.

By the beginning of February, Abercorn was ready to give up the struggle against Belmore and Corry and to defer to John Stewart's ambition to step up from solicitor to attorney general. Abercorn wrote to Stewart on 2 February, the very day of Belmore's death:

'I see there are so many different interests in the county to be managed and canvassed and courted, so much of the trouble which I hate most, and am most unfit for, and so much uncertainty at last, while Lord Belmore makes electioneering the sole object of his life, that if my son sees things as I do, he will think representing the county, unless with more quietness and unanimity, very little worth his while'.

Stewart did have some news of Belmore. On 4 February he wrote, 'I hear Lord Belmore is not well? He is in Bath'.

Because of his poor health, from the late 1790s onwards, Belmore spent a great deal of time in Bath with his wife Mary Anne, his daughter Lady Louisa, his illegitimate daughter Maria and his illegitimate sons Armar and John. They were all there in the winter of 1801–1802 and, probably because he intended more or less to retire there, he decided to buy one of the larger houses in the middle of Royal Crescent – number 17.

While he was negotiating the purchase they all lodged nearby in Brock Street, in a house that Belmore had rented for 12 weeks. He was suffering from chest and breathing difficulties and was often feverish. His wife and daughter attempted to dose him with Dr James's powders, a popular remedy for fevers. The writer Fanny Burney had unlimited confidence in its therapeutic value and Horace Walpole said he would take the powder if his house were on fire. Belmore, however, detested its taste and refused to take it.

On Tuesday 2 February the women slipped a dose of the powder into Belmore's food. Shortly afterwards Lady Louisa heard him fall in the front parlour. It must have been a sudden and heavy fall because some damage was done to the furniture. She rushed to him, but he was dead. She blamed herself, believing that he had choked on the powder, but it is more likely that he had actually had a massive heart attack. He was 62 years old.[3]

Abercorn's worries about Belmore were ended by the news of his death, and he wasted no time in showing his relief when he wrote to Stewart: 'Lord Belmore's death puts an end to all our doubts and difficulties, for it is surely impossible that a serious opposition to you can be attempted?' Abercorn now felt confident that he could freely exercise his patronage and secure the vacant seat of the Chief Justice, which, they anticipated, would favour Stewart's own legal ambitions:

> 'Lord Belmore's death removes all doubt from my mind as [to] the Chief Justice's seat.
> I am happy at the opportunity it offers of establishing our favourite object'.

He becomes very optimistic about the future of Tyrone politics without Belmore because 'many of my nearest friends [are] now disengaged from old promises made to Lord Belmore'.

The immediate, practical consequences of Belmore's death were dealt with by David Babington, Belmore's solicitor and man of business. First Babington emptied the dead man's pockets. In Belmore's pocket book he found 70 pounds and 16 or 17 guineas in gold. Then he paid various household bills and arranged for an inquest, 'opening of the body and ascertaining and reporting on the cause of his Lordship's death'. There was some difficulty in getting the body back to Ireland for the wake:

A view of The Royal Crescent Bath by Thomas Malton

'Paid expenses twice to Bristol to charter a vessel [to take the body back to Ireland] first with Mr Healy and afterwards to Mr Span, the Captain first agreed with having retracted and refused to receive the corpse on board'.

Even when Belmore's body was eventually taken back on the ship *Britannia*, accompanied by his servant McConnell, the cook, there was trouble. On 1 March John Poole was paid in Dublin for his journey to Rostrevor to await the arrival there of the *Britannia* and the corpse of the late Earl, but the weather was so bad that they had to divert to Dublin:

'Paid the different Custom's House Officers on landing the corpse of the late Earl at Georges Quay, the Capt of the [Parkgate packet] ship having put into Dublin contrary to his agreement'.

Finally, there was the funeral and the customary gathering of his tenantry for the wake:

'Paid going with the present Earl Belmore to Armagh the expenses of the different people at there, who came to attend the funeral, thence to Caledon, and the expense there for the lower orders of the people, Captain Pringle [Lord Caledon's agent] having entertained the better orders'.

Belmore was buried in the original Lowry family vault at Caledon. Babington's final act on Belmore's behalf was to prove the will at Doctor's Commons in London, where probate matters were dealt with.

In February 1802, John Poole, Belmore's butler, was paid:

'the balance of his travelling accounts in England in 1801 being the difference between £224.1.1 which he had expended and £192.7.3d which he had received, in which receiving was included three guineas found by him in the late Lord's pockets at his Lordship's death'.

Poole, charged with the financial arrangements for the funeral and wake, had been provided with a new saddle case into which he put 60 guineas given him by Babington. Babington worked out what had been spent simply by counting what was left of the 60 guineas after Poole's return to Babington's Dublin office.[4]

The Financial Background of Armar Lowry Corry

Babington's arrangement with Poole reflects the unsophisticated accounting methods of the time and it is no surprise that an accurate calculation of Belmore's true financial position at any one time was not really available to him or his men of business in Counties Fermanagh and Tyrone, who went about things each in his own way.[5]

A summary of Belmore's income and debts made during 1779–1780 for the treaty in anticipation of his marriage was, no doubt, intended to impress, but it does provide a starting point for looking at his financial life.[6]

His income in 1779 was contrasted with the increases he expected over the next few years as leases were renewed. Rounded up slightly, the settled land at the Castle Coole

The Lowry family vault at Caledon, Tyrone

estate and in Counties Tyrone and Armagh brought in £5,000; the unsettled land at Six Mile Cross, Tyrone, Longford and three small estates in Fermanagh, Tyrone and Monaghan brought in nearly £3,500; the Churchlands of Castle Coole with some leases in Tyrone and Dublin brought in £2,500 – a grand total of £11,000, which was expected to rise to about £17,000.

One of the misleading aspects of the summary was that the figures were taken from rent rolls, which made no allowance for arrears, and recorded what was due, not what was collected. Arrears were always a problem and amounted at one time to just over 15 per cent of the total rents due.

Belmore's debts were reckoned at £22,400, and credit was given for debts of £7,000 owed to him – a net indebtedness of £15,400. Showing debts as assets was not unusual, even though it was possible that they might not be repaid on time or at all. They usually carried interest of four to six per cent. Some debts, mainly small amounts due to relations, on which he paid about £1,400 a year in interest, were not shown.

The forecast rise in his rental income was not achieved as quickly as expected. In fact, until the 1790s, there was no appreciable increase at all. Belmore took some land in hand at Castle Coole to make his new landscape park – which probably explains the more or less similar levels in rents from that estate, in spite of some slight increases in the tenancies that remained.

By August 1789, Belmore's debts stood at just over £25,000 and, although he had taken steps to reduce them by January 1791 to almost £21,000, he was paying out nearly £4,000 a year in rent, interest, pensions and annuities from a gross income of little more than £13,000 a year, leaving him just over £9,000 a year for his own use. By 1800 his debts had risen to some £70,000 plus the £20,000 due to his daughter Lady Louisa under his marriage settlement of 1780. As a consequence, his interest and other outgoings, including an annual allowance to his son, had risen to nearly £9,000 a year, leaving him with a net income of about £8,000 from an increased rental income of over £16,600. Rents from the demesne only just met the expenses of the demesne itself; the farm showed no profit and rent received from his Dublin property was offset by the expense of the house in Sackville Street.

Belmore had been forced to borrow more and more to finance the cost of building his new house and to maintain his influence in the House of Commons.[7]

Although Belmore had expected the house to be completed by 1793 at the latest, the final reckoning did not arrive until shortly before his death. He had made a fundamental miscalculation in thinking that the project could be paid for out of his income. On the original estimate of £33,000 that might just have been possible. But the final bill, estimated at some £54,000, rose in the end to £70,000 or more. Between 1793 and 1800 the cost of politicking added at least another £20,000.[8]

He paid Thomas Conolly £12,000 for the borough of Ballyshannon. As it turned out, the government would pay him £15,000 in 1801, in compensation for the borough's loss as a result of the Act of Union. At the beginning of the 1780s he had purchased Belturbet from the Earl of Lanesborough for 8,000 guineas. He would also receive £15,000 in compensation for this. Because of the union, then, his purchases of borough patronage made a profit – but this was, at the time, an unforeseeable outcome. In the meantime, Belmore had to increase his borrowing to finance the purchases and they must have contributed significantly to a tightening of his cash flow. Belmore revealed how nervous he was about his creditworthiness in notes to his agent, for example:

> 'Could you borrow five hundred, if the notes cannot be had, as my credit is at stake for this payment and rather than be disappointed I would send John Poole over with the cash – I want two hundred for our man in London and 300 for a man in Birmingham – pray let me hear from you soon. I received your letter in which said you had sent thereby £750. I never will be at ease until I pay that Bond off'.[9]

In 1813, the second Earl's accounts showed encumbrances created by his father in his lifetime as a total of £90,000 – a sum which can only have included the cost of building the new house and £20,000, Lady Louisa's fortune, stipulated for in her mother's marriage settlement. His death added a further £11,000. He left legacies of less than £4,000, including £3,000 to his illegitimate daughter Maria, £300 to his widow and some smaller legacies – less than £500 in total – to family and servants. The purchase of 17 Royal Crescent was completed for £7,000. It was now to be a residence for the dowager Countess. There are two allowances in the 1813 account (£1,000 for Corry and £5,000 for Lowry), which it is not clear actually arose from the first Earl's death. His total indebtedness after his death, therefore, was about £101,000 or perhaps £107,000 – interest on which, at average rates, would have been about £4,000–£5,000 a year. In addition, annuities were just over £3,000 a year, although they dropped to just over £1,000 a year on the death of Henrietta Belmore, less than three years after that of Belmore.[10]

It is quite possible that Belmore would have made efforts to control or reduce his indebtedness as he had done between 1789 and 1791, but by the end of the century Belmore was certainly strapped for cash and was struggling to keep up his reputation for creditworthiness. In April 1799, he began to take hard decisions. He sold his house in Dublin, which the family had owned for many years. He wrote to Samuel Galbraith:

'I need not tell you you are heartily welcome to sleep in this house if it is not sold and, if it is, you may sleep at my son's house, No 46 Rutland Square next door to Babingtons – this house cannot hold my servants besides I want the money and if the taxes become better I can easily get pick and choice of houses to buy and, for a year or two, I can hire one by the year'.[11]

Belmore's outgoings were not unmanageable at the time of his death. About 60 per cent of his 'debts' were made up of family obligations from wills and settlements, pensions to retired servants and poor people and rents due by him, for example, to the Crown or the Church. In 1791 his interest payments were only about 11 per cent of his gross income, rising to a probable maximum of some 30 per cent in 1800 – surely acceptable proportions under the strictest notions of debt control.

A factor in the tightening of Belmore's access to capital was his resettlement of his estates when, in 1795, Corry came of age. When a son came of age the father's absolute interest was turned into a life interest, and the estates resettled on his own eldest son for his life. Father and son could profit from the arrangement. The son was given an increase in his income in return for the resettlement of the estate; the father gained by ensuring the estate was kept in the family and continued to take the estate's income, subject to the increased payment to the son.

The father could also take the opportunity to raise capital by charging the estate, or exclude some of the land from the settlement if he so wished. The latter is exactly what Belmore arranged with Somerset, 'on the morrow of All Soul's 1795'.[12]

Belmore agreed to limit himself to a life interest, entitled to income only, with no right to sell land to raise capital, in return for Corry, in his turn, taking a life interest plus £1,000 a year. Belmore also retained for himself the 45 acres of land at Drummin, Armagh (in the middle of the Richhill estate), which had come down from the Lowry family. It was left at his absolute disposal, most likely with a view to its sale. However, it was not sold until 1814, when it realised slightly over £2,000.

The effect of this arrangement was that Belmore could not sell land to raise capital without the consent of Somerset – who, naturally, would want to sell little or nothing, since that would reduce the value of his own inheritance. Belmore could raise money by mortgage but this was limited by the availability of people or banks willing to lend on the security of land subject to life interests. In any case, the amount that Belmore, as a life tenant only, could borrow would be significantly lower than if he were the unrestricted owner. Even his formal power to mortgage was effectively limited by his need to have Somerset's cooperation in the management of the estate for the benefit of the family – the practical importance of which, as Stewart's letters to Abercorn have already shown, was certainly appreciated by their political opponents.[13]

Part Two

The Lame Earl: Somerset, Second Earl Belmore, 1774–1841

Chapter Eleven

Situation, character and fortune

While Mrs Hackett made her inventory of the furniture and furnishings at Castle Coole in 1802, soon after the death of the first Earl, Somerset Lowry Corry, 26 years old and now Earl of Belmore, had to take stock of what he had inherited and what he proposed to make of his life. He had his own house in Rutland Square, Dublin but, after his marriage in 1800, the old Lowry house at Aghenis became his country home. On 24 December 1801, Juliana had given birth to a son, who was named for his grandfather, Armar.

The new Earl Belmore had his commission in the Tyrone Militia and had been elected member for Tyrone in 1797. Therefore, while he remained Viscount Corry the heir, no matter what difficulties there were after his opposition to the union, he could simply have enjoyed life. The Castle Coole he had grown up in was the comfortable old Queen Anne house, family home of the Corrys, set in a renowned, wooded demesne. He had also spent a lot of time with his late mother's family at their home, Mount Juliet in Kilkenny – an elegant mansion set in an extensive demesne of ash, elm and beech trees overlooking the river Nore. It had been built during his young life and was completed when he was 11, in 1785.

An Extravagant Young Man

His father's death catapulted him into an entirely unsettling situation, requiring him to formulate plans that would rescue his family's fortunes after their political expectations had miscarried. He had two main fronts to fight on: firstly, finding employment for himself and getting himself back into mainstream political life; and secondly, completing the new Castle Coole.

An overriding consideration should have been to make a plan to reduce the debts left as a result of his father's death, but a determined (not to say pugnacious) person like Belmore was not about to allow money to put the brakes on his ideas. Cost what it might, his project was essentially to put himself and his family back on the map.

In reality, there was little alternative for him unless he was to languish, unnoticed, in the north-west of Ireland. That was not in the nature of the man. Although he was to become known locally as the lame Earl, there was nothing in the slightest bit lame about his character. He needed to establish his family in a society whose centre of gravity had shifted to England. While an Irish aristocrat could present himself, as he himself had done, as English when travelling abroad, in English society he was never considered English. He was Irish, his peerage was Irish and he started in English life as an outsider. This meant that he, and others like him, had to make extraordinary efforts to impress themselves on the power centre in England. His character would not allow him to submit to being an outsider, and the inevitable result was his programme of assertive expenditure calculated to keep his ambitions and his family in the news and in the centre that mattered – London.

Actually, although his finances needed care and attention, they were not beyond control, and he could still expect to obtain plenty of credit. Rental income from all the estates rose, in the 20 years from 1790 to 1811, to over £22,000 a year, although some of the increase was, no doubt, the result of inflation. Rents from the Tyrone and some of the Longford estates came in at nearly £16,000 a year and rents from the Castle Coole estate and the rest of the Longford and Monaghan estates totalled some £6,500 a year.

However, during the same period, the family's average expenses almost exactly equalled their income. This meant there was no money immediately available for dealing with his liabilities of somewhat more than £100,000. Interest payments of about £5,000 a year and annuities of £3,000 cut deeply into his gross income. Henrietta Ancram's annual £1,000 would cease with her death in 1805. He had, therefore, a net income rising to about £17,000 a year – within which, in the early years, he lived. But, as time went by, the momentum of his activities increased, so that far from developing any scheme for reducing his indebtedness, he allowed it to run away with him.

He began badly by selling his house and its contents in Rutland Square, Dublin in February 1806 – at a bargain price, if a contemporary account is to be believed. Altogether, he received over £3,400 from the sale of the house and just over a further £1,650 from the auction of its contents by Preston and Sons, a firm of furnishers and auctioneers. On 27 January 1806 Andrew Caldwell of New Grange, writing to George Cockburn, commented:

> 'I must tell you Lord Belmont [*sic*] has sold his house to Mr Cash, the Lottery Office Keeper, & all the furniture perfectly new to be sold by auction, the Drawing room furniture was never uncover'd, it came all from London & is the most elegant best workmanship I ever saw, the whole room is done in one stile, there is a uniformity and correspondence throughout, and if it be pull'd to pieces the merit of each article will be greatly diminish'd, there are no pictures, but in every other respect I have seen no Apartment in England of equal taste. Ld. Belmont is an extravagant young man, he won't deign to keep a house in Dublin, but has a magnificent one in the country, that he is going to furnish with boundless expence'.[1]

Belmore would later become more closely involved with Preston in furnishing Castle Coole – and just as expensively as Caldwell predicted. The new house, set in a demesne now rendered bare by his father's building works, with an atmosphere as frosty as its name, was hardly lived in and certainly not furnished for family life. It cannot have matched his own experience of a family home. Mrs Anna Walker, after a visit in June

The Broadwood piano in the saloon

1804, remarked that 'the House is badly placed – the grounds are unfinished'; it was she who made another visit a year later in and, after noticing that it was magnificent, nonetheless damned it by saying that 'it sadly wants furniture'.[2]

Apart from doing something about the house, Belmore now immediately had to assume personal and financial responsibilities for an extended family – his half-sister Louisa and his half-brothers and sisters Armar, John and Maria. Each of them had grown up and had reached the time when their lives were to take their own paths. They needed his support – as, indeed, did his stepmothers Henrietta Ancram and the dowager Countess Mary Anne, who each had settlements securing annual payments to them for the rest of their lives.

It was essential that Belmore should give Castle Coole and its demesne the significance his father had meant for it, rather than allowing it to become (as it would if left unfinished) a social and political embarrassment. One of the earliest decisions he made, therefore, was to bring life and comfortable elegance into Castle Coole. In September 1810 Belmore bought a good many pieces of furniture and mirrors at a sale of the Earl of Clonmell's effects in Dublin, at which he was accompanied by Preston, the man who had furnished his house in Rutland Square. Through Preston he furnished Castle Coole in the same striking style, but on a much larger and therefore more expensive scale.[3]

His taste for spectacularly expensive objects is shown by a piano he had made for Juliana in 1802, which was kept out of the Dublin house sale. It was a romantic gesture by Belmore in the year when Juliana had their first son, Armar. The gesture was, literally, a grand one. It was no ordinary piano, but one of a very few grand pianos made by Broadwood. The case was designed by Thomas Sheraton with cameos and medallions by Wedgwood.

It was similar to one that had been made in 1796 to be presented to Isabella, the Queen of Spain by her favourite, the minister Manuel de Godoy. Broadwood's shop in London produced the finest instruments in Europe. Juliana was a keen amateur musician as the range of her music, which is still at Castle Coole, shows. She played the harp as well as the piano, as did Lady Louisa and Maria Corry. Music, of course, was an integral part of a young lady's education.

Belmore himself took an interest in things musical. He was, for example, a patron of the Belfast Harp School in Cromac Street, which was founded in 1807. One of his tenants in Crevenagh, Tyrone was James McBride, an amateur harpist and wheelwright. He was the father of Edward MacBride, who became a well-known harpist and principal of the Belfast school. He frequently played at Castle Coole.

Neither 'object nor prospect of success'

The fact that Belmore sold the house in Rutland Square at a knock-down price simply reflected the truth that Dublin was no longer the centre of political power in Ireland. Many people also sold out at the same time, which itself lowered prices. Power had obviously shifted to London and Belmore was in a hurry to find a niche there, in order to be closer to the sources of influence and income.

Restoration to political employment and influence was the other front on which he prepared to fight. However, he had to face an unpalatable truth: he had become unemployable in any capacity that he might have felt suitable to his rank and talents. Although the militia regiments were embodied again in 1803 after the Peace of Amiens broke down, Belmore could not continue with his military career in his new role. In 1805 the army reserve tax was paid for him, but he had either resigned or lost his commission as colonel of the Tyrone Militia by August of that year.

To find suitable employment he, not unnaturally, looked for a political solution. His resistance to the Act of Union, had it been measured, would certainly not have endeared him to the government in London, but it would not necessarily have been fatal to his prospects. Others successfully negotiated the transition from opposition to acceptance of the new situation. The difference was that they had not shown such marked hostility by their associations and language. Belmore had been seen not only as an *élève* of John Foster but as the supporter of an altogether more dangerous faction, organising resistance on a county-wide basis in Tyrone, where opposition to union was strong.

Even Foster, who eventually joined up by accepting the chancellorship of Ireland, was not forgiven for the depth of his opposition. As late as 1807, Lord Hawkesbury (the future Lord Liverpool) rejected an applicant for a treasury post on the basis that he:

> 'is a decided friend of Foster's and was a warm anti-unionist. I wish well to Foster and his connections ... but we must recollect his faults and his invariable endeavours at all times to create an independent party for himself'.[4]

Belmore was too intelligent not to be aware of the difficulties his opposition would cause him in the completely changed circumstances of political life after the union. Whatever his difficulties, however, he was not easily frightened. Castlereagh had, before the union debate, offered him one of the 28 Irish representative peerages in the Westminster parliament in return for his vote in support of the government, but he had rejected that. What he decided was to go one further and demand an English peerage. One had been offered to his father at one time and now he felt it was due to him.[5]

So it was to politics that he turned first to find a fresh start, not only for himself but also for the political future of his infant son. He had little military and less political experience to offer to any government and a temperament that easily made enemies. But then a timely prospect was opened up for him from an unexpected quarter.

In the first flush of enthusiasm at the new opportunities created by the first Earl's death, Abercorn decided, through Castlereagh, to offer Belmore friendship and a political alliance so that they could control the elections for Tyrone between them. He remarked, 'though aware of the enmity of the father, I have always spoken handsomely of the son'. It was not exactly a warm-hearted offer, being made:

> 'upon the principle that, as we do not seem to have anything to quarrel about now, we might as well be on friendly terms … Certain it is that, at present, he can neither have object nor prospect of success'.

Belmore might have thought that a united front with Abercorn was one possible way to influence the government to grant him an English peerage, but Abercorn believed otherwise. While a Dublin government might have feared the political opposition of Tyrone, to the government in Westminster it would be 'scarcely an object of consideration, assuredly not of dread or even negotiation'. This was, of course, precisely why Belmore so desperately wanted an English peerage. It would give him the right of direct access to English ministers – in the same way that, as an Irish peer, he had had to Irish ministers. Abercorn well knew that Belmore was now out in the cold and would have to modify his conduct and his language to find favour:

> 'Lord Belmore's situation, character and fortune, added to a dignified line of conduct, now the measure which he had a fair right to oppose is irrevocably settled and at rest, will hold out a fair pretension to any ministers, but let me repeat again and again, that ministers here cannot be talked to and dealt with like Lord Lieutenants and their Secretaries before the union'.

He was referring to the well-known fact that, in pursuing his aims, Belmore was only too likely to use language and behaviour that, in Abercorn's phrase, 'throws away the scabbard'.

The added advantage to Belmore of making common cause with Abercorn was that it would include an understanding that Armar, his son, would be brought in to take the seat for Tyrone in 20 years time. But Belmore had a problem. He was being pressed by his former anti-union associates to side with them against Abercorn, in order to threaten the political domination that Abercorn could expect as a result of the first Earl's death.

Babington, Belmore's agent, 'very candidly' told Stewart that Belmore and he would show government that it was Belmore and not Abercorn who was 'entitled to the patronage of the county, by showing that he has the stronger interest in it'. If that were the case, Belmore might then put pressure on the government by opposing it until it was forced to recognise his power in Tyrone and agree to grant him his peerage. The question was, which way would Belmore choose – friendship and the influence of Abercorn in England, or troublesome opposition in Tyrone in the hope of making the government recognise his claim?

Since he could not be sure which course would be successful, he chose neither, but decided to wait and see what Abercorn would do. The matter dragged on into April and Belmore, frustrated by what he saw as unnecessary delay, pressed for news. He received cold comfort from Abercorn, who wrote:

> 'I cannot but be very sorry that your Lordship ever thought your present object [the peerage] 'easy' of attainment because I am too sure of the contrary; and, unfortunately, its having been so strangely prostituted, makes it every day more difficult to those more worthy of it'.

Abercorn, much more interested in getting Belmore to join him to control Tyrone politics, added that he thought Belmore would at least find comfort in their connection, thwarting:

> 'all malicious county combinations, all artful and insidious offers, all petty resentments … and freeing ourselves from the plague of even listening to the eternal suggestions of schemes and jobs and canvassings'.

Abercorn gave in sufficiently to Belmore's pressure to put forward his claim to the Prime Minister by the end of the month. Addington's reply effectively shelved the claim indefinitely. While he admitted the fairness of Belmore's pretensions, he was determined to make no promise, and while he had the greatest wish to gratify Abercorn, it was clear he thought that the object was impossible. It is quite possible that Abercorn, more interested in Belmore's cooperation in Ireland, did not press the English claim too hard, for Addington's language sounded very much like Abercorn's own earlier judgement that Belmore could 'neither have object nor prospect of success'. Belmore had no option but to accept the rejection in good part, but he must have been very hurt when, in late July, it was known that two Irish peers had been given English peerages.

Within six months of his father's death Belmore faced the reality of his exclusion from political influence. There might be nothing for him in that line until his son was eligible for election, 20 years hence. What was he to do? It was not in his character to give up. He spent the next five years on the one hand pressing Abercorn, his newfound political 'friend,' to get him a representative peerage, and on the other hand striving to demonstrate his domination of politics in Tyrone by thwarting Abercorn's nominees and getting his own elected. It was Thomas Knox for Belmore against John Stewart for Abercorn.

But if Belmore seriously thought he could press Abercorn for help and at the same time attack him in Tyrone, he was mistaken. Abercorn decided to pull out of the business for the time being:

'My sons are out of the question and, as to Lord Belmore, after what has passed, no earthly consideration should induce me either to court or engage or consent to an *engagement* with him'.

Perfectly Happy: 'Dear abode of happiness! My home!'

During the time when he was sounding out Abercorn and the English government, Belmore put in hand improvements to the Castle Coole demesne by a scheme of tree and shrub planting, taking advantage of the grants which were then being paid for such work by the government. He planted no less than 7,500 Scotch firs, 6,750 larch firs, 5,150 spruce firs, 1,400 silver firs, 4,375 alders, 6,450 oaks, 850 birches and 750 ashes – in all 33,225 trees. Much of his planting made a picturesque landscape around Lough Yoan in Drumcrin and Derryvore, which brought it and the smaller Lough Breandrum into the demesne. He further extended and improved this part of the demesne when the new Dublin Road was made in 1813 by bringing parts of Slee, Killyhevlin and Gortgonnell, between the new and old roads, into it. The whole of this scene could be seen clearly from the house until it was hidden by further planting in the early twentieth century.[6]

The area around the walled garden was also landscaped and sheltered by a belt of trees. Belmore would continue to make improvements to the landscape in later years.

Family affairs constantly demanded his attention. On 9 March 1803 Juliana gave birth to another son, Henry Thomas, a brother for Armar. Their half-brothers Armar and John, who had been at the school of a Mr Williams in Bangor until the summer of 1804, were equipped and sent away to begin the careers that had been chosen for them.

John, then 17 years old, had been recommended by Castlereagh to join the East India Company as a cadet in 1803. He was now due to go to India, having been commissioned as lieutenant in the Sixteenth North Indian Regiment. He set off with David Babington from Dublin to Beaumaris in Wales by boat and then to Osborne's Hotel in St James's Street, London. He was taken to lodge with a Mr Andrews of Woolwich for board and tuition and accompanied by Andrews on evenings out in London, for which Babington had given him pocket money. He was fitted out by Walsh and Stalker in London with his uniform and other articles at a cost of over £318. Babington also paid for a watch at Mr McCabe's of King Street, Cheapside. Belmore bought him a chain and seals for it from Mr Smyth of the Poultry, London. When he finally set sail for India he was given another £20.

Armar, aged 11, also went via Beaumaris with Babington to London where, on 1 August, he boarded HMS *Diadem* (64 guns, under the command of Sir Hume Popham) to enter the navy as a first-class or 'gentleman volunteer', the usual title given to a boy from a family of rank for his first posting. Babington bought him a silver watch and provided him with £50 for his use 'under the direction of Sir Hume Popham'.

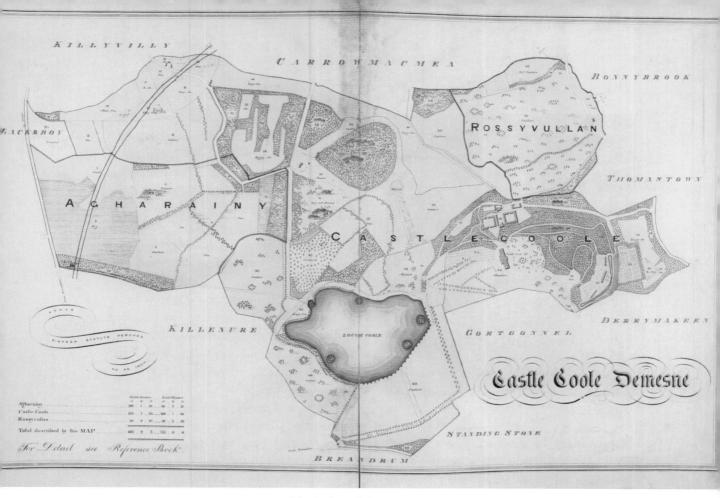

The Castle Coole demesne in 1853

Armar saw action quite soon. Popham, with Major General Baird, commanded an expedition sent to recapture the Cape of Good Hope in January 1806. In 1807, by then a midshipman, he returned to England and joined HMS *Leda*, and was at the bombardment of Copenhagen. He was badly hurt when the *Leda* was wrecked off Milford Haven in January 1808 and, very ill, was taken to London, where a Mrs O'Brien of Bury Street looked after him and Dr Babington attended him. Both, perhaps in a spirit of patriotic concern for the boy, refused any fees or compensation for their care but Belmore had a present of table linen sent to Mrs O'Brien and reimbursed Babington for Armar Corry's expenses of £150.[7]

Louisa had spent a good deal of time in London with her aunt Emily, Lady Castlereagh as part of her upbringing, and had been brought out into London society. In 1803, the *Ladies' Magazine* noticed her especially at Queen Charlotte's birthday ball, an annual society event for debutantes. Her dress was a rich pink satin with silver draperies, black lace and a train of black velvet with slashed sleeves, richly spangled in silver, all topped by a headdress of a handsome plume of pink feathers and a profusion of diamonds – 'both the wearer and the dress were particularly beautiful'.

Portrait of Lady Louisa Corry, Countess of Sandwich
by Hugh Douglas Hamilton

Louisa's vivacity and good looks attracted many people to her, especially George John, Viscount Hinchingbrooke, the 31-year-old heir of the Earl of Sandwich. The attraction was mutual and in April the following year Lady Castlereagh announced that they were to marry. The delight and rejoicing of her family and friends went far beyond their pleasure at the prospect of an excellent match. Lady Florence Balfour, formerly Cole, who had attempted unsuccessfully to reunite Louisa with Henrietta Ancram, her mother, ardently hoped her happiness would last and was delighted that she was so much in love. Enniskillen himself, in wishing her every happiness, bluntly opened his letter, 'I rejoice with you that you will so soon change the nasty name of Corry'. His family had closely supported her mother during the separation from the first Earl, with whom they had quarrelled when he would not let the mother and daughter see each other.

Belmore wrote a short but affectionate letter to Louisa about arranging her marriage settlement. Juliana's letter was longer and revealed more of the nature and style of family life at Castle Coole, a life which was affectionate, lively and full of good humour. Belmore, unable keep up the serious tone of a paterfamilias, added a cartoon to it, showing the future Lord and Lady Hinchingbrooke trailing between them a collection of children in descending order, ending with a baby in the nursemaid's arms. Belmore whimsy resulted in nicknames: 'Pigmy assures Weiza it was Cudsey did this'. Pigmy was Juliana, Weiza was Louisa and Belmore, Cudsey.

Juliana revealed her own happiness, writing:

> 'may you, my dearest Louisa be as perfectly happy as I am after being married *three years and a half*, and I cannot wish you more happiness than is expressed *in this wish*'.

She was delighted at 'getting poor Cudsey back' in Dublin after what she felt to be a long separation during his absence in Limerick, probably on militia duties. But now she and the children would be returning there with him since there was 'no fear of Bonaparte's paying us a visit'. In the meantime she had been enjoying life in Dublin, which 'has been very gay since Easter, no end to the Balls, parties and everybody agree [*sic*] that since the union it never was so pleasant'. She thought Louisa would be very proud of 'little Cudsey' (Armar) and Henry. Armar was obviously a favourite with Louisa and was 'very entertaining, and prattles away at a great rate'. Henry was beginning to walk by himself. Finally, she burst out with the following:

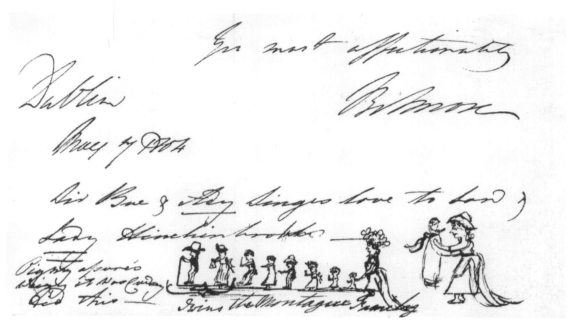

Cartoon drawn by the 2nd Earl in a letter to the Countess of Sandwich

'*Dear, dear Weiza* I am in such delight, Cudsey has just told me we are to go to London to see you … I feel so happy at the thoughts of seeing my dearest sister after so long an absence'.[8]

On 9 July of the following year, 1804, Louisa was married from Castlereagh's house in Upper Brook Street, London. The *Ladies' Magazine* reported that her bridesmaids were Lady Maria Hamilton and Lady Selina Stewart and that Belmore gave her away. Her dress was plain white muslin, with rich point lace, an elegant white satin cap, a white Brussels veil with wreaths of artificial flowers and a costly diamond necklace and arrow. 'The happy pair set off in a chariot and four for his father's seat at Swinly, Berkshire'.

Louisa's attractions concealed a strong will and a biting edge to her character. The happiness was short-lived. Louisa spent much of her married life abroad because her husband, by then the sixth Earl of Sandwich, suffered from consumption. An acquaintance in Lausanne commented in August 1817:

'Poor Lord S is dying of consumption and Lady S who is one of those unhappy people who are tormented and torment others by an unbridled temper makes the short remainder of his life sad. He is pettish with illness and provocation and although they love one another they cannot live happily together. Mamma cannot bear being with them but is obliged'.[9]

Sandwich died in the villa of Cardinal Consalvi, near Rome, in 1818, leaving Louisa a large jointure. She continued in charge at Hinchingbrooke until her son succeeded to the title in 1832. After that, she went to live for the most part in Paris in the Rue St Florentin,

Lady Belmore's Poor list

where she became well known for her salons. She returned later to live in Grosvenor Square, London. She was very friendly with the Duke of Wellington in his later years and often visited him at Walmer Castle but was noticed, unsympathetically, as 'appallingly and oppressively vivacious' at the Christmas celebrations for 1823 given in the Brighton Pavilion by the King.

Louisa had two daughters. The first was Lady Harriet Mary, who married William Bingham Baring, later second Lord Ashburton, and became a leading spirit of political, intellectual and literary society in her salons at Bath House, Piccadilly. The other daughter, Lady Caroline Katherine, married the illegitimate son of Napoleon, Count Walewski, and had a son and a daughter. Sadly, both daughters died young, before their mother.

The magazine had another family wedding to report in July of the following year, 1805. This time at Castle Coole, Belmore gave away his half-sister Maria, who married Major Charles Luther Watson of the Third Regiment of Dragoons, eldest son of the Bishop of Llandaff.[10]

The following year, 1806, was an unhappy one for the Belmores. Juliana gave birth to a daughter, Sarah, but she died soon afterwards. To add to their sadness they learned of the death of John Corry in Cawnpore, where he was stationed. He had made his will on 13 May 1806; eight days later he was killed in a duel with a Lieutenant Charles Ryan, his senior by a year. Ryan was tried for murder in the Supreme Court of Calcutta but found guilty of manslaughter, for which he was imprisoned for six months and fined 100 rupees.

The immediate consequence of the girls' marriages was to bring their settlements into effect. Belmore paid Louisa's fortune of £20,000 in full by August 1809, and in November he paid £500 to Watson, now a lieutenant colonel, towards Maria's fortune of £3,000. November was the month when the second annual instalments of rent were collected and so he then also discharged a family obligation by paying £325 to purchase a commission for Mr Eccles as an ensign for in the Thirty-fourth Regiment. The Eccles family of Fintona were connected by marriage to the Lowry family of Aghenis.

Generally though, life at Castle Coole was happy and active. It was also strictly religious, according to the Anglican faith. There were prayers in the morning, either in the chapel in the attic or in the saloon. Every room was provided with a Bible: even the housemaids had their own Cambridge edition, which they used for recording their names and making comments. Charitable work included the distribution of blankets and flannel to the poor.

The boys, when young, had tutors for lessons in the schoolroom. They exchanged witty verses with their tutor Mr Burgess, using their own name for the house, 'Castle Warm'. Warm it most certainly was in atmosphere – and in fact in the kitchens, the housekeeper's room and basement, where fires, stoves, ovens and boilers were constantly on the go. Armar, at school in Beaconsfield and a little homesick, wrote a poem for his mother, which shows a boy's feelings for home:

'Soon to my native house I will repair
And to those things which give me pleasure there,
My little island, ever neat and gay;
The parrot's talk or puppies lively play …
Dear abode of happiness! My home!
O Castle Coole to thee I long to come'.

Armar never lost his love for Castle Coole and its demesne. Mrs Walker was all too ready to succumb to the hospitable surroundings when the Belmores 'begged very hard that we shou'd stay with them':

'Both Lord and Lady Belmore improve excessively on acquaintance, are extremely good humoured, and are good enough to express great regret at our leaving Enniskillen. We worked in the evening very sociably & staid very late'.

The last sentence refers to the usual practice of the ladies withdrawing to 'Lady Belmore's workroom' overlooking the lawn and Lough Coole, in modern times called the Bow room. Dinner was usually at five o'clock in those days and was 'very handsome and served on plate'. The house accounts show what a variety of dishes could be served – soups,

The Bow room or 'Lady Belmore's workroom'

salmon, duck, trout, chickens, oysters, lobsters, oranges and lemons. There was ice from the ice house to cool food and drink and to make ice cream.

The house had a billiard room, an extensive library, lakes for sailing, swimming and fishing and an estate for riding, hunting and shooting. A visitor noted that the:

> 'lakes are stocked with wildfowl, on one, in particular, they are preserved with great care, the water seems almost covered with bold coots, wild ducks, widgeons, divers, teals, bitterns, wild geese and swans'.[11]

The oak, beech and Spanish chestnut trees planted over 50 years before, in the time of Margetson Armar, were known for their beauty and sheer size.

The fishing (especially pike) and shooting (pheasant, woodcock, snipe and rabbits) were especially good. Reflecting the long tradition at Castle Coole, Juliana showed a fondness for gardening, following the fashionable Humphrey Repton, with the result that the walled and kitchen gardens remained famous for the variety of shrubs, plants, vegetables and fruit they provided. The heated greenhouses sheltered vines, figs, peaches, pineapples and melons:

> 'The garden, where the glass is, is uncommonly well laid out. A very nice piece of water winds thro' it, and it is bordered by an extremely well planted shrubbery, where the shrubs grow very luxuriantly, and are variegated by the mixing of some fine trees – we strolled about here a long time – the day uncommonly fine – but very hot. We were all fagged with rambling about'.

Belmore loved hunting, in spite of his lameness (as mentioned previously, he had to have his saddles specially made to support his right leg in order to ride at all). In July 1809, to get more hunting near the Butlers' estate in Kilkenny, he acquired over 76 acres of land at Thomastown, Jerpoint for annual payments, on which he planned to build a hunting lodge. He also kept a pack of hounds at Castle Coole in the old farm buildings, next to the remains of the Queen Anne house, and in December 1806 he bought a new hunter.

He spent more time and money breeding and racing horses at the Curragh. For 21 December 1803 there is a record of a payment 'To John Murphy taking Grey Colt to the Curragh £3.8.3'. One of Belmore's racing grooms was James Hair, whom he regularly paid sums from £100 to over £300 to cover charges for the purchase of horses, mares and foals; for stakes placed for Belmore; for looking after Belmore's horses – including Sharpresa, who was served by a horse called Champion belonging to a Colonel Luman. Belmore's small bay horse, Buffer, won several plates and was used to serve mares, including one called Plenty, belonging to a Mr McHalley.

Belmore may have entered horses elsewhere, but in August 1810 he had to pay a Mr Hunter a 'forfeit for the Ulster Stakes run for at Derry'. Belmore kept many horses at Castle Coole, among them Chiswick Muse, whom he sold in 1810. Traveller, who had belonged to his father, was still alive, as was Pilot, who was often advertised in the local newspaper, *The Chronicle*, as available for breeding. He bought Suffolk mares from a Nat Caldwell in England and Thomas Bowen, still the coachman, brought the horses over from Ipswich to Parkgate and on to Castle Coole.[12] By 1812, however, he had decided to give up hunting in favour of other plans.

Chapter Twelve

Donegal, London and Portsmouth: The Travels Begin

On his many journeys in Ireland, to Dublin, Waterford, Bray, Mount Juliet in Kilkenny and Fortland in Sligo for the fishing, Belmore often used a cutter, which he kept near Seaview – a house he leased from the Montgomerys, relations of the Conynghams of Slane Castle, at Mount Charles in Donegal.

The cutter was the *Flying Fish*, a small vessel fore- and aft-rigged on a single mast. Its captain was Stephen Bonner.

Seaview was a good-sized house, as can be gauged from the fact that it was stated for tax purposes as having seven hearths and 24 windows. John Griffiths was the gardener. In the summer of 1813 the family must have been there, for there is an account for the hire of horses for Mr Thompson, 'when the young gentlemen were going to fish and to the Woman that took care of the house'.

There are also the accounts of Captain Bonner for work on the *Flying Fish*, including painting it and its boat in colours he listed: Prussian blue, vermilion, white, burnt umber, lampblack, Dutch pink and rose pink.

Salthill House, formerly the 2nd Earl's Seaview, Mount Charles, Donegal

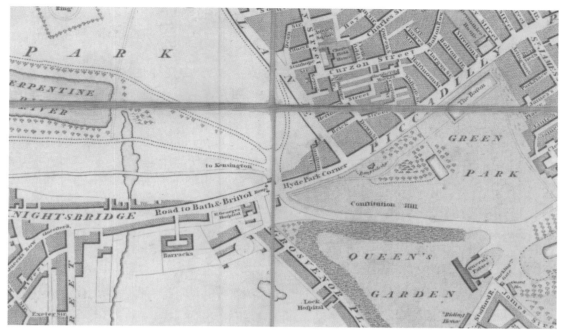

Moggs map of London 1810 showing Hamilton Place at the bottom of Park Lane
At that time, the gardens of the houses had access into Hyde Park

Ever since his life-enhancing voyage around the Mediterranean as a young but sickly man, Belmore had enjoyed sailing. As he became increasingly aware of just how politically marginalised he was, what had so far been a convenience and a pastime opened his mind to the possibility of a greater project. He set about a plan to emerge from the political wilderness by developing what was, in effect, a three-point business plan to lift himself and his family back into the centre of things. The first point was to make a move to get closer to the centre of political action; the second was to plan a voyage which would be pioneering and therefore a brilliant public relations exercise; and the third was to complete the furnishing of Castle Coole in the most fashionable style, a style he had already tried out in his Dublin house. It would take time and be expensive but Belmore hoped it would work.

First, because he wanted to be in the centre of things and because he was a man who never took half measures, he decided to buy a house in London in what is now Hamilton Place, Park Lane, whose garden edged into the south-east corner of Hyde Park. He was to be a close neighbour of the Duke of Wellington at Apsley House, which at that time belonged to the Duke's older brother, but which the Duke himself bought in 1817.[1]

On 18 February 1812 Belmore agreed to purchase 6 Hamilton Place from Mr John Sullivan for £14,000, plus £2,000 for the furniture and contents – wine in the cellar, books, glass, pictures and prints and beds (including two children's beds). Eventually, much of the finer furniture found its way back to Castle Coole, including two globes, now in the library. It amounted to a turnkey operation in that he employed William Newton of Bond Street, an upholsterer, to complete the arrangements from beginning to end. Newton's first bill of 9 December 1811 specifies 'sundry attendances and arranging the purchase of Mr Sullivan's House and Furniture in Hamilton Place', making an inventory and then undertaking substantial work, making new beds, chairs and mirrors, hanging curtains and hanging pictures. During 1812 and 1813 Newton arranged all trades to substantially alter and improve the house and stables.

In the garden, the head gardener Mr Chick supervised seven men, planting 200 sweet briars and 27 yards of box and improving the soil with dung and loam. He charged 10s 6d for 'keeping the walk through the park clean'. Belmore raised almost £17,000 to pay for the purchase through a firm called Benjamin Frayle & Co during 1811 and on 1 February Mr Ross Thompson's draft for £16,000 was delivered express to Castle Coole for Belmore to endorse as payment for the house.

He paid a Miss Jouille, an artist and perfumer in Dublin, to copy a painting of Louisa (now Lady Hinchingbrooke) and also to copy a painting of Lord Edward Fitzgerald. From her he bought a view of a mill and a Venus reclining, all of which are at Castle Coole. He also paid for an Indian cabinet.

'She's the nicest of vessels that ever was seen'.[2]

The second limb of his plan was original and dramatic. Between May and November 1813 James Kilpatrick and John Kiles, sailors, took the *Flying Fish* to Portsmouth. They were paid one year's salary of 50 guineas plus expenses and over £300 for subsistence to carry out a thorough inspection of a particular vessel. This was the *Madison*, an American schooner captured by HMS *Barbados*, whose commander was Edward Rushworth, shortly before the outbreak of general hostilities between England and America in 1812. Belmore proposed to buy her and fit her out for a remarkable voyage.

The *Madison* was also inspected by Lieutenant Armar Corry who was on leave for a month, and who was so impressed by her that he broke out into enthusiastic verse:

'The Schooner *Madison* in 1812

'Safe moored in the harbour of Portsmouth there lies
An American Schooner sent in as a prize.
She sails like the wind, as the Captain told me
And's as good a sea boat as you'll find on the sea;
But what of her sailing when the air was still, lulled,
And the boats from a Frigate exultingly pulled
Impelled by their oars they foam thro' the tide
While her empty sails flapping their impulse denied.
She was taken, sent home, and she weathered a gale
That sank of the Convoy some twenty odd sail –
She's eighty four feet to the breadth of a nail
From her stern head to her Tafferel rail
And Twenty three feet is the breadth of her beam
Her frame is fine oak with some cedar between;
Her hold is not deep, for to fly as she sails,
Her beams are laid even along on the wales.
She's planked with good oak, and her copper is stout
And the bolts through her timbers are copper throughout
The ports through her bulwark are pierced to sixteen
She's the nicest of vessels that ever was seen'.

The *Osprey* 28th August, 1819

His excitement may have been helped by the fact that, for the past four years, he had been engaged in the dull duty of blockading the French in the Mediterranean. Promoted to lieutenant, he had joined the frigate *Nereus* for duty in the river Plate and Brazil. By October 1812 he was bored again, 'brought up' for 18 months at Buenos Aires after the local revolution against Spanish domination.

He described his situation to Lady Louisa, who had become a sympathetic correspondent since she had first written to him while he was sick in Haslar Hospital, Gosport. He told her that the people of the town had:

> 'thrown off their dependence on old Spain, and to effect a complete revolution they shoot or hang every man supposed to be attached to the mother country, and, what astonished me was, the ladies go to see these spectacles and cry "viva la Patria"'.

He promised Lady Louisa that he would try to preserve for her some of the colourful local birds, which she liked to collect. By January 1813 he was fed up with lying 150 miles up the river Plate, so had gone ashore to learn Spanish. He added, after the news of the capture of the British *Guerriere* by the American *Constitution*, 'I will not be easy until we give these Americans a drubbing ourselves'. He learned Spanish well enough so that, by March, he could report he was being sent on different duties on shore, which helped to pass the time. Armar would use his Spanish again later in his career.

The defeats suffered by the British navy at the hands of the Americans gave him 'more real pain than I ever suffered before'. He describes the ladies of the country as 'beautiful between the ages of fifteen and twenty' but added that 'innocence and folly are synonymous terms throughout this country'. His relationships with women would cause him great difficulties later in life.

The inspections must have satisfied Belmore, who bought the *Madison* and renamed it the *Osprey*. The contract, which he signed on 16 June 1813, recorded that the *Madison* had one deck and two masts, length 86 feet and three inches and breadth 22 feet and ten inches, being a square-sterned schooner with no gallery and no head.

Belmore spent a great deal to turn the *Madison* from a relatively plain schooner into the *Osprey*, a completely furnished, handsome 14-gun brig, putting in new masts and sails and the most modern cabin furniture, including the very latest in water closets.

A list of the expenses incurred on board the *Osprey* from August 1816 to August 1818 shows that Belmore spent over £9,600 on fitting her out and, in addition, advanced money to dependents who were to travel with him, lifting the grand total to almost £10,500. While the conversion was being carried out and a crew being selected, Belmore took a house in Cowes (still called Belmore House). In 1815 he had become a founder member of the Yacht Club, which later became the Royal Yacht Squadron. He was travelling regularly between London and Southampton and continued to spend handsomely there. He bought himself fashionable clothes from Davidson, Dunnett & Co of 12 Cork Street, London: a silk-lined corbeau (dark green verging on black) cloth dress coat; a waistcoat with black cashmere breeches, rich steel buttons and a dress bag; a blue cloth 'Cappell'd' coat, with gilt buttons and a velvet collar; and a white waistcoat with black 'cassimere' (cashmere) and blue 'mill'd' trousers. He also bought a bloodstone ring in old gold for £200. He and Juliana often went to the opera and, in anticipation of their voyage, bought travel books such as *Syntax's Tour*, *Hobhouse's Travels* and *Clarke's Travels*.

In January 1814 Captain Bonner handed over to Captain William Ostler, who was to oversee the conversion of the schooner. Ostler signed for many items of practical use – bed linen, kitchen utensils and other domestic utensils, such as crockery and candles, which were transferred from Hamilton Place to the *Osprey*. By October he had her ready for sea trials. Accompanied by Belmore, they sailed to St Peter Port, Guernsey where they arrived on the first of November. They were back in West Cowes by January 1815.

The third important part of Belmore's overall plan was to have Castle Coole furnished and the demesne planted out so that the family would return to a perfected setting. He also intended to be back when his sons would be old enough to follow the family tradition and begin a political career. This accounts for his arrangements with Preston to furnish the house; but he also proposed to build a completely new stable and service block, placed conveniently closer to the house than the old stables and farm buildings next to the remains of the Queen Anne house. As early as 1810 work had begun on what would eventually become known as the grand yard, and by 1815 Belmore was in discussions with Richard Morrison and a builder called John Ferrall of Wexford for further work to build a steward's house, stables, coach houses and a house steward's lodge.

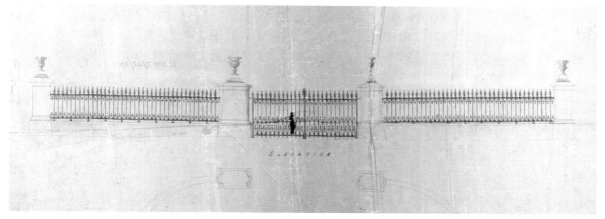

Gates and railings proposed for the Dublin road entrance

Elevation of one of three Bridges Intended for the Rigt Honble The Earle of Belmore augt 1800

Design for one of 3 bridges to cross the canal near Gortgonnell Hill

It was at this point that the sheer cost of all his activities began to impress itself on Belmore. His architectural improvements also included a magnificent set of gates for the main entrance and a bridge over the canal which ran through the walled garden, which was one of three bridges designed for his father in 1800. The grand yard had cost so much that some of the work he wanted Ferrall to do was omitted from their draft agreement so that Belmore would have more time to think about it; but time was a luxury he would not have the chance to enjoy.

An 'arduous and unexpected ... state of inconvenience'
The steward's house and some ancillary buildings were to be the only survivors of a complete review of Belmore's finances which he was compelled to carry out as a result of receiving, in March 1815, a demand from his bankers, Benjamin Frayle and Co, in England for a payment of over £10,000. This was the total of bills of exchange drawn

upon English banks by Belmore's agent in Dublin, John King Irwin, partner of the long-time family solicitor and man of business, David Babington.

Belmore was shocked, appealing to his honour and his friendship with Frayle himself to urge that he ought not to be made to pay. The debt was not his, he declared, but arose through the deceit of Irwin, who he claimed had drawn the bills as an expedient 'for his own personal ends … involving my name in an unauthorised and inexcusable form'. He had 'placed me in so arduous and unexpected a state of inconvenience that I cannot venture at once to commit myself to any responsibility for his actions'. He further claimed, 'I stand a creditor for a very large amount' to the firm of Babington and Irwin, which was in financial difficulties. He urged that since Babington and Irwin had arranged the credit with Frayle in return for receiving all Belmore's rents from his country agents, they were responsible, not Belmore himself. There are no other letters between Belmore and Frayle to clarify what happened next, but Belmore accused Irwin of cheating him of £10,000 by milking commissions. Perhaps, therefore, Belmore was obliged to pay Frayle.

What was the true position? Had Belmore been cheated or had he been blissfully unaware of the consequences of his lifestyle? The dispute continued for five years, until Irwin wrote a long letter in 1820, setting out his version of the matter and revealing the truth about Belmore's money problems. Irwin was originally appointed to control the payment of Belmore's debts and interest because Finlay's bank refused to continue to handle Belmore's business. Irwin was a frontman, whose job was to manage Belmore's affairs so as to avoid any creditors taking action for recovery. Although Irwin opened an account for Belmore at Beresford's bank, 'it was considered imprudent to allow a list of the permanent debts to appear' because:

> 'his Lordship emphatically said he would not leave himself to the caprice of any banker, who, by refusing to pay a very few interests, might bring all his creditors upon him'.

Irwin was, therefore, as Belmore had said himself, supposed to collect all income from Belmore's agents (including Babington, who did not retire until 1811) and handle negotiations throughout the United Kingdom, including the purchase of Hamilton Place. He explained that Belmore's normal income had been 'exceeded by upwards of £100,000' for one-off payments and for the extra interest charged for extending the time for repaying amounts due under bills of exchange. The fact that extra time was needed to pay outstanding debts itself suggests that Belmore's situation was stretched. Irwin's explanation is supported not only by his books of account but by an item-by-item analysis or double-check carried out for Belmore by his new agent, John Spiller of Omagh and Dublin.

Irwin's account shows that Belmore's total annual expenses rose markedly from just over £38,000 in 1810 to nearly £65,500 in 1813, falling back to just over £54,000 in 1814–1815. Belmore's total expenditure from 1804 to 1815 was nearly £314,500. Spiller's analysis showed Belmore's total expenditure at just over £315,000 so, over 11 years, the discrepancies in Irwin's figures, a few hundred pounds, were not the problem. On the other hand, Spiller's analysis revealed that Belmore's average annual expenditure was almost £29,000 a year, at least £2,000–£3,000 a year above his income. If £10,000 were indeed missing it was not in Irwin's hands.

The average hides the fact that in the first five years Belmore's expenditure was at the rate of just over £10,000 a year, but increased dramatically in the five-year period from 1810 to 1815 to an average of nearly £51,000 a year. These were the very years in which he had undertaken his three-point plan. Spiller's analysis itself also shows the deteriorating position. Interest paid on loans managed by Irwin from 1810 to 1815 was just over £28,000. This confirms that those loans were about £90,000, a figure Belmore himself acknowledged. But these were in addition to loans raised by his country agents, Perry in Tyrone (£35,000) and Dane in Fermanagh (£14,000).

Belmore managed to repay his principal debt of almost £28,500 by means of further loans, sales of land, bank stock and debentures, but his own expenditure and his family obligations, added to the first Earl's building costs of £70,000, left his debts at about £139,000 by 1815. In fact, in future, they would double.[3]

He had advertised Jerpoint for sale in 1812, hoping to get rid of the liability, but the place did not sell until 1853, 11 years after his death. As a result, it cost over £16,000.

Belmore does not seem to have taken the matter further after Irwin's letter, but not even the shock of Frayle's demand was enough to set him back. Making room for borrowing a bit more than the £139,000 he already owed, he simply calculated his annual interest on £150,000 as £9,000, added that to some other obligations, allowed himself £12,000 a year and reckoned that left him a balance for contingencies of £2,400 out of what he thought was his annual rental income of £26,000. The only part of his plan he was prepared to curtail was the work on the grand yard and the improvement to the front gates at Castle Coole. He drew a line under those projects, put the whole unpleasant experience behind him and turned his attention to the much more appealing prospect of his voyage in the *Osprey*.

'Repose from the harsher anxieties of existence in this country … a land of theology, warfare and fog'

One of his reasons for the voyage was, as he later said himself in a letter to Lady Hester Stanhope, the lack of interest politics held for him at that time. During the course of 1816, Sir John Stewart, who had by now been MP for Tyrone for some years, actively canvassed government ministers to secure Belmore's election as a representative peer in the next election. Three peers had been elected at the beginning of March and others had been elected in previous years, so Belmore was still being overlooked. Lord Enniskillen also urged Belmore's claims. Stewart attempted to press the Lord Lieutenant by asserting that Belmore's 'weight in some counties, and particularly Tyrone, is very powerful' and he could as easily oppose government as support it, were his claims to be ignored:

> '[If] parliamentary influence is of any consideration in the choice of a representative peer, in this instance it is great. If property is to be considered, are there six peers residing in Ireland that have such an estate and so splendid a residence, with every suitable appointment'.

Adding insult to injury, the Lord Lieutenant told Stewart that Belmore's friend and brother-in-law, Carrick, was probably next in line and recommended Stewart to see what Castlereagh could do. Although Castlereagh was 'decidedly interested' in favour of Belmore's election he passed the buck to Peel and the matter lapsed. Stewart, obviously discouraged, regretted that Belmore himself had not been present to support his claim. Belmore must have realised then that he would have to wait yet again, and it was not until 1819, three years later, that he and Carrick were elected.

Although his failure to achieve an English, or even an Irish, representative peerage, was perhaps good reason for travelling abroad and one he was willing to admit to, his increasing indebtedness must have made the prospect of getting away from his creditors very attractive. He could then hope for what his old tutor Townshend, in a letter of May 1817, described as 'repose from the harsher anxieties of existence in this country … a land of theology, warfare and fog' – and, he might have added, creditors. Townshend, ever the pedagogue, could not resist advising Belmore at length to adopt 'a liberal frugality', so that his fortunes could soon take a favourable turn. But, warming to his subject, he warned:

> '*Punctuality* in your engagements here is I take it, a grand necessity never to be lost sight of – & that maintained I do not see anything to cause any severe shock in the rotation of business. It has often struck me that if I were placed as you are, I would send No 6 Hamilton Place to the Market under Newton's auspices & the produce I would reserve untouched for any emergency that might occur. It is morally impossible to raise £10,000 in Ireland – & during this necessity, a capricious creditor, or the Executor of a Creditor out of the exigencies of the case, may call in the principal of a debt – any delay in complying with it – & delay there must be in such a case, may raise false alarm, excite others to make demands also upon various pretences to cover apprehension – & then tho' all were surmounted at length, the expence would be great, & the vexation severe. If the House in Hamilton Place should become untenanted, you may dispose of it as quietly as you purchased it – your being abroad is a fair excuse for so doing … The main piece of prudence is to have ten or twelve thousand pounds for emergencies – if it were only to take you out of Agents' hands even it would be wise'.[4]

Townshend's advice may have been sound but 6 Hamilton Place was too significant a part of Belmore's strategy for it to be given up. He would hold on and use it for another ten years. In the meantime, he was ready to embark on his most original project.

Chapter Thirteen

'Something so novel, so interesting (in this degenerated age)'

Belmore proposed to take his whole family on board the *Osprey* for a journey around the Mediterranean, disembarking for travels through Egypt and into the Holy Land. It was to be the first voyage of its kind by a European family. During 1814 kitchen utensils and other items of practical use were transferred from the house in Hamilton Place onto the *Osprey* and the family spent a large amount of their time in West Cowes and Southampton between January 1815 and August 1816, when they were ready to set sail.

Belmore would be taking his wife and children, Dr Richardson (a medical man, who was to chronicle the whole journey), the Reverend Robert Fowler Holt (the children's tutor) and the family's pet dog, Rosa. Holt was an Eton scholar and graduate of Brasenose College, Oxford. There were two maidservants, one of whom was Sarah Dane, a young member of the Dane family of Killyhevlin, Enniskillen. Last, but by no means least, there was a babe in arms, Juliana Brooke. She was the daughter of Lady Marianne Brooke, wife of Lieutenant General Sir Arthur Brooke of Colebrooke. Belmore was said to be her father. There is a pencil drawing at Castle Coole, initialled by the artist in 1821, of a very pretty girl aged about seven, who is almost certainly Juliana Brooke.[1]

Belmore and his half-brother Lieutenant Corry carefully planned the Mediterranean odyssey. They needed to, for they were to lead a party which included women, two young boys and a baby on what was virtually a regal progress through almost uncharted territories (and was later seen as just that by other travellers).[2]

Lieutenant Corry, until the end of Napoleon in June 1815, had been on duty in the English Channel on the *Tay* but had recently returned from Brazil on the *Montagu*. With Belmore he prepared a full set of sailing and disciplinary instructions for the crew of 32. Stores were loaded at Southampton and articles between Belmore as master and commander and the crew of over 30 were signed at Southampton in July 1816. Among the crew, apart from seamen, were: a mate, James Manley; a boatswain, Maurice Kean; a carpenter, William Loader; a sailmaker, Robert Thomas; a steward, John Vogwell; a ship's cook, Benjamin Clarke; a cabin cook, Richard Darling; and a gunner, Samuel Bates. During the course of the voyage, seamen came and went; local cooks and pilots were taken on, as was a surgeon. Six wives accompanied crew members, whose numbers never

Pencil drawing of young girl, possibly Juliana
Brooke by unknown artist 'LJW'

fell below 30. Their wages until the end of the voyage in 1818 amounted to almost £2,700. Belmore and Corry took a hand in sailing the brig with Captain Ostler and made regular notes of latitude and longitude as the *Osprey* voyaged on.

The long and careful preparation and the size and range of crew and equipment all show that Belmore's real plan was not simply to escape from boredom and creditors – it was to discover Egypt and the Holy Land for himself. The two regions were linked not just by geography but also by the cultural concerns then flowering in Europe, under the influence of French descriptions of ancient Egypt and its monuments. It was a culture described by Richardson as 'the modern passion for exploring the ruins of ancient towns'. In addition, a visit to the Holy Land was undoubtedly a project dear to the heart of Juliana, a devout Christian.

In Belmore's mind, antiquities were important business, calculated to draw attention to his personal enterprise as a collector and connoisseur. He had carefully studied the works of many earlier travellers in the region – Sonnini, Savary, Chateaubriand and Volney among others. Henry Salt, whose book on his travels in Abyssinia had made him famous, was invited to Ireland by his patron, Viscount Valentia. Salt was fêted in Dublin in 1814 and accepted an invitation to stay with Lord Caledon in Tyrone. He was there for six weeks. In May 1815 he was appointed British consul by none other than Castlereagh, Belmore's close family and political connection. It seems probable that Belmore knew of Salt and his prospective employment in Egypt, where Salt was encouraged by the terms of his appointment to make 'temporary excursions' to any places which might further the government's knowledge of the province. Furthermore, Salt had been asked by Sir Joseph Banks to collect for the British Museum, and by the Society of Antiquaries to collect fragments of inscriptions.

The *Osprey* set sail on 21 August 1816 from Southampton. It was bound for Gibraltar, where it arrived a month later, not long after the successful attack on Algiers by the British and Dutch. These were heady times and, to cap it all, the Inniskillings were stationed there. Celebration was called for and Belmore responded by giving a ball on board for local gentry and the Inniskillings themselves, their band providing the music. Sergeant and Mrs James, who later worked at Castle Coole and lived in the Heather Lodge, enjoyed the party, as did many of the sailors.

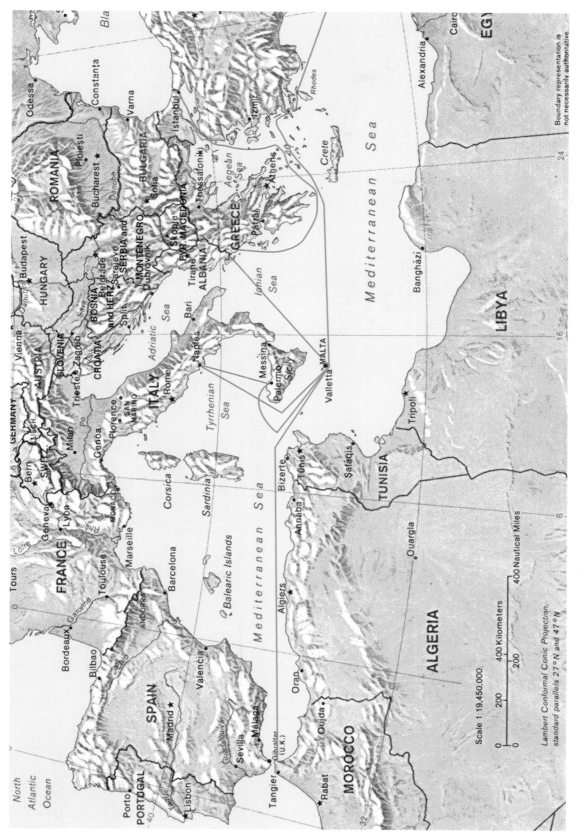

The *Osprey's* route in the Mediterranean towards Greece and the Middle East

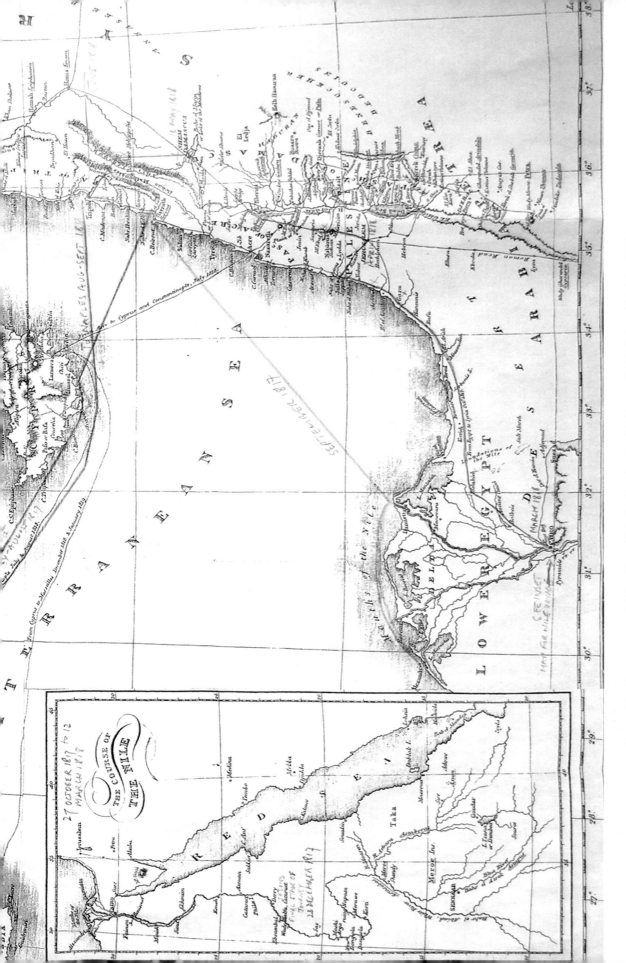

Voyage of the *Osprey* on map copied from Irby and Mangles, Captains, *Travels in Egypt and Nubia, Syria and Asia Minor* 1823

After ten days there they went on to Malta ('excellent harbours, white houses and good linen'), anchored in 'the beautiful bay of Syracuse' and then sailed for Messina, which they left on 3 November to winter in Naples from 6 November until the end of March 1817. In Naples, Richardson's impressions ranged over the beggars assembled in the early morning round boiling cauldrons 'to scald their lips on the boiled chestnuts' through 'the sprightly gaiety of noon in the passing throng that crowd the Toledo' to 'the seductive brilliancy of the evening assemblies in the ball-rooms and theatres' but he also recorded his disgust at the gulf between rich and poor, at the hypocrisy of priests indulging themselves in every café, at the miracle-mongers working in the cathedral and pimps on every corner. They did the usual tour of Pompeii, Paestum and the Roman remains in the region.

Heroical Incidents

Belmore's instinct for public relations revealed itself clearly in March and April 1817; although his was a private venture he did not intend to hide his light under a bushel. He had already secured a letter of marque for the *Osprey* as a privateer which authorised it take enemy ships as 'prizes', but this was directed against the Americans, who were not likely to show up in force in the Mediterranean. Nevertheless, there was, he thought, trouble in Malta, so he offered his services to the government, proposing to sail there and sort it out. His offer was, with the utmost politeness, rejected in terms which suggested he had jumped the gun. William à Court, the government's envoy at Naples, replied to Belmore's proposal on 24 March 1817:

> 'I have a thousand thanks to offer you, both on my own part, as well as that of the Govt, for your obliging proposals of proceeding direct to Malta, should the public service require it – I am happy to say that the negociations in which I am engaged are in no way connected with our own immediate interests, nor by any means of a warlike nature – we are now merely giving effect to some of the provisions of the Treaty of Vienna, that have, from unforeseen circumstances, remained unsettled till the present moment'.

His second effort was also calculated to draw the attention of those in places of influence to his enterprise. He wrote to Castlereagh, asking him to get the formal permission of the Prince of Wales for him to wear the Prince's uniform. This time he was successful. General Bloomfield wrote to Castlereagh on 10 April 1817:

> 'I did not fail to submit your Lordship's letter of this morning to the Prince Regent, conveying the request of Lord Belmore to be permitted the distinction of wearing his Royal Highness's uniform, and which his Royal Highness, in the most gracious manner, was pleased to sanction. I rejoice to continue the best possible account of HRH's health'.

Castlereagh sent on the good news immediately. Which of the many uniforms, naval or military, Belmore adopted is not known but, in any case, Belmore's public-relations efforts produced results. In early May, he had a letter from Townshend from Dublin telling him:

'the London newspapers of a very late date, had sent you [to] Rome, involved you & all your escort – numerous & well armed as they were – in a most grievous battle, with a body of Italian Banditti, whom a long argument carried on with guns and pistols could not easily dissuade – out of a very obstinate predilection for your moveables. About this heroical & sanguinary incident you are silent, and therefore I presume the London newspapers are somewhat in error'.

There certainly was a uniform because 'an *Osprey* waistcoat and pantaloons' are listed among Juliana Belmore's clothing.

The Tiger of Epirus and the Nun of Syria

The *Osprey* returned to Malta in April 1817 and stayed until early May, without incident other than the loss of the boatswain, Kean, on 25 April. Drunk, he fell overboard and was drowned. In May the *Osprey* set off for the Ionian Islands and, at Corfu on 4 June, fired off a salute in honour of the King's birthday. Next, they called in at Santa Maura (Lefkas), where Belmore, provided with extracts from the journal of a Danish traveller in the Peloponnese, Dr Bronstead, lost no time in putting them to good use. Three hours later they anchored at Seyada on the coast of Epirus, disembarked and travelled across country to Joannina, the capital, to meet Ali Pasha 'the tiger of Epirus' who had set up an independent state there.

Richardson, having experienced the rough local bedding, advised every traveller on land 'to carry with him a mattress, blanket and sheets, if he has not previously reconciled his skin to the harrowing affair of a hair cloth', and added, obviously in one of his frequent surly moods, 'In which case he may do as he pleases'. Their skin suffered more when they decided to bathe in what Richardson's classically inspired imagination called the river Styx, and found themselves in the swim with 'water snakes, efts, leeches and toads'. From the islands they went to Constantinople and visited the classical Greek sites – including Troy, where Richardson cleaned and dressed the wound of a young Greek man, in return for which the young man's friends gave them a lamb. The sailors adopted it, fed it biscuit and grog and called it John of Troy. At Delos, Belmore suffered a seriously painful attack of gout, which continued to plague him for almost three months.

They called in at Rhodes in the first week of August and by the last week had arrived, via Cyprus, in Beirut, where Belmore wrote immediately to Lady Hester Stanhope, who was known locally as 'the Christian Woman', but in England as the 'Nun of Syria'. She was not at home, but in a reply typical of her style, wrote:

'I am not at present at my Convent but encamped in the neighbourhood as I feel it much pleasanter in hot weather to lead the life of a wandering Arab, than to be confined by stone walls'.

She was more than ready to give advice, although she showed her prickly sensitivity to criticism in the ending of her letter:

'it is my wish to be useful to my countrymen in every way in [my] power, and if I have ever held back, it has been from some of them (who Burke and Wyndham would dignify with the title of blackguards) having accused me of giving myself airs, and taking upon [myself] to protect those I only wished to serve'.

She offered them the use of her convent, a very strong ass and her maid for Lady Belmore.

At that time Belmore had intended to go to Acre and Jerusalem but his gout, and Hester Stanhope's advice, changed his mind and he decided to go to Cairo. Jerusalem would come later. Her advice, which was lengthy but accurate, began with a handsome compliment:

> 'There is something so novel, so interesting (in this degenerated age) in a father travelling for the instruction of his children, and in a woman accompanying her husband upon hazardous journeys, instead of devoting her time to folly and dissipation, that for *once*, I feel no sort of apprehension of my motives being misconstructed, if I take the liberty of giving you my candid opinion upon your plans, which you can act upon or not, as you like'.

Now was the time for visiting Cairo, she said, and the spring for going to Jerusalem 'when Pilgrims of all nations visit that place and all the ridiculous ceremonies are performed'. The coast was dangerous in the winter, a fact subsequently confirmed by one of Belmore's officers who had been sent to find a safe port. She added:

> 'Go immediately to Egypt and return here before winter, to establish yourself in a house from whence you could make vastly interesting excursions'.

She had asked him for any political news, 'for I was born a politician, with all my grandfather's patriotic sentiments, but with his same principles of independence'. Her grandfather was William Pitt the Elder, Lord Chatham; the younger Pitt was her uncle.

Alas, Belmore could offer no political news, writing that as far as he was concerned 'the political state of Europe at present affords no variety'. But, attracted by Hester Stanhope's independence, he overcame the pain of his gout and rode with Juliana and the boys to the convent on a day trip. A piece of advice – a piece of her mind, even – might suggest that he took the boys as well. It seems that one of them, who could not keep still, attracted her attention and a warning:

> 'Your son also ought not to be allowed to jump about when out of doors like an English boy, for it is not only unlike the conduct of children of distinction, but it is that of *dancing boys* in this country and he might be insulted'.

At the beginning of September, following Hester Stanhope's advice, Belmore decided to set off for their first major destination, Alexandria, where they arrived on 7 September. Richardson writes that it was at Alexandria that he began the 'particular narrative' of the travels, later published as *Travels Along the Mediterranean in Company with the Earl of Belmore*. Richardson's is the only narrative of the travels and, for that reason, has inevitably been used to describe the party and the sights and events they experience. It has to be said, though, that Salt disliked Richardson because 'the rudeness of his character was

From my tent
Saturday 12 oclock

My Lord

I have this moment rec'd yr letter of the 22 ins.
& was about to return to my residence upon
the heights of Lebanon, but in the hope of
being useful to you & Lady Belmore, I shall
defer my departure untill I have given
the necessary orders for yr reception at
Saide, as the Governor is at this moment
absent, & also informed Soliman Pacha
of yr intended arrival at done.
I am not at present at my convent but

Extract from a letter written by Lady Hester Stanhope to Belmore

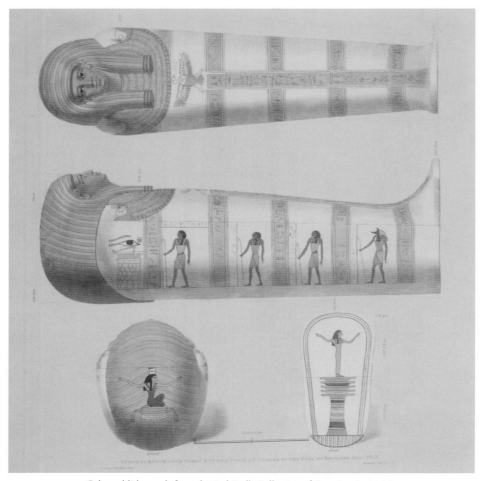

Coloured lithograph from the 2nd Earl's Collection of Egyptian Antiquities
published by the Royal Society of Literature 1818

too evident' and at times 'unbearable'. In fact, rudeness led to Belmore parting with the doctor on bad terms in July 1818, a year before the voyage finished and they began the overland journey home.

Salt thought Belmore showed great patience in putting up with Richardson, but understood that this was necessary for the retention of the doctor's medical skills. In actuality, though, the doctor's skills were not called upon for the Belmore party at all throughout the voyage. The only complaint was Belmore's gout, which medical skill of the time was quite unable to treat. Richardson treated conditions such as blocked ears, opthalmia or conjunctivitis (a common problem) and wounds of various kinds, which he was able to clean and cover. A reading of his version of the travels suggest that his rudeness included a singular interest in all things female, whom he treated as their husbands' request.

Nonetheless, his recommendations that a pasha should have a warm bath and other successful consultations produced gifts for him and a welcome in many places for the party. Eye and skin infections were a common risk in the sand and wind of the desert, as were stomach upsets and chills caught from contrasts of daytime heat and night-time cold. In the absence of pharmaceutical remedies many conditions were treated by whatever diet, foodstuff or liquid was thought to be beneficial. Hester Stanhope, for example, recommended quince jelly as an astringent and Sarah Belzoni used tea for opthalmia and many other problems.

As for Richardson's book, Salt commented that while it would be full of interest 'as far as respects the state of Christianity in the East, he was neither a profound observer – nor by his shortness of sight capable of forming any judgement of the important monuments of antiquity which he [had] so good an opportunity of visiting'. Later, Salt classed Richardson's work among the ephemeral productions of travelling authors 'who, as the Indian expresses it, take walk – make book'. Hester Stanhope herself warned Belmore against being in too much of a hurry 'and not to risk being misinformed upon many subjects, for the journal of most travellers I have seen is only fit to be put in the fire'.

Richardson's account is nonetheless useful as a record of the places visited with some comments on the activities of the Belmore party, and he needed no particular expertise to write it. The one person who, rather surprisingly, did not write an account of the travels was Holt, the boys' tutor and Eton scholar. Perhaps he and the rest of the party had more input into Richardson's work than Richardson ever acknowledged.

They stayed in Alexandria for a month, eating and sleeping on the *Osprey*. When they set out on asses to explore it they:

> 'entered immediately on the field of ruins ... with here and there the end of a beautiful column, or the angle of an enormous stone cropping out, to break the continuity of the drifted sand unconsolidated by aught of vegetable growth'.

They came across two beautiful obelisks, covered with hieroglyphs, one still erect but the other on its side on props 'as if prepared for a journey: I believe accident alone has prevented its being in England'.

They then went into the catacombs, firing off a musket and blowing a bugle to frighten off jackals and bats, and crawled on hands and feet, each with a lighted candle, through musty, damp chambers filled with bones until, finally, the choking sand prevented them going any further. Richardson saw Alexandria as the connecting link between Egypt and Greece, holding the key to unlock the hidden mysteries of the hieroglyphs – which at that time had not yet been deciphered. But they were anxious to get on and 'Alexandria is not Egypt; which, he that hath not seen, hath not seen the greatest rarity in the world'. At five in the morning of 22 September 1817 they transferred their luggage and themselves from the comfort of the *Osprey*, which was to go on to Cairo, to a 'djerm', a local shallow-draught riverboat with a lateen sail and an awning for shelter from the sun, and set sail through the bay of Aboukir.

Four Remarkable Men
As soon as the *Osprey* tied up in Bulac, the port of Cairo, on 28 September 1817, Belmore sent a messenger to Salt 'to acquaint him of our arrival'. Salt immediately came to welcome them personally, bringing with him the Pasha's carriage (the only one in Egypt)

for Juliana and a horse for Belmore. Once the rest of the party had taken donkeys from stands, 'nearly as common as stands of hackney coaches in London', they set off to Salt's house to stay as his guests. Soon after his arrival, whatever ideas Belmore had previously entertained about the nature of his travels were to be opened up to the influence of four remarkable men who turned up at Salt's house. They were the naval officers Captains Irby and Mangles, a Swiss explorer named John Lewis Burkhardt and the amazing Giuseppe Belzoni.

Irby and Mangles, both in their twenties and both retired from the navy, had set out together to travel through Europe but their admiration for antiquities and sheer curiosity had drawn them to Egypt. Burkhardt, who had so immersed himself in the Arab way of life and language that he was now usually known as Sheikh Ibraham Ibn Abdullah, had since 1812 travelled extensively in what is now Jordan; he was the first European for 600 years to see Petra; he had gone into Nubia a good distance up the Nile and, on his way, explored Thebes. He had a Scottish servant and friend, formerly a soldier, who had been captured by the Turks, enslaved and forced to become a Muslim, called Osman. Salt had successfully persuaded Mehemet Ali to give Osman his freedom.

Belzoni was an Italian from Padua, at six feet eight inches tall a giant of a man, immensely strong, whose chequered past included appearances in pantomime on the London stage as the giant in *Jack and the Beanstalk* and many appearances as the 'Patagonian Strongman' at fairs and theatres around the country and later around the Mediterranean. He claimed that hydraulics was 'a science I had learned at Rome' and in Malta in 1815 he was hand-picked by an agent of the Pasha of Egypt to build waterwheels to his own design. He and his wife Sarah, a Bristol woman, and his young Irish servant James Curtin were at the trial of his first waterwheel run before the Pasha in June 1816. It was technically a success but the Pasha's enthusiasm resulted in his ordering men, including Curtin, to be substituted for oxen 'by way of frolic'. An accident occurred, in which Curtin's thigh was broken. The Pasha's advisers considered this an ill omen, so the project was abandoned and Belzoni was sacked.

Subsequently, Burkhardt excited Belzoni's enterprising spirit by his tales about upper Egypt – in particular by his account of the gigantic head of young Memnon, which lay, separated from its body, in a temple at Thebes. It was considered the most beautiful piece of Egyptian sculpture then known but all attempts to remove it had failed. Belzoni could not resist the challenge but lacked the funds to do anything about it – until Salt, the new British Consul, turned up. Salt, to whom Burkhardt introduced Belzoni, saw immediately the opportunity Belzoni's skills, allied to his own interests, presented and thought Belzoni's planned journey to recover the head for the British Museum 'a godsend indeed'. Although they fell out later over the meaning of the agreement each thought he had made, it was this initial enthusiasm that set Belzoni off on his famous series of excavations – including the recovery of the head, which was later immortalised by Percy Shelley as 'Ozymandias, King of Kings'.

These, then, were the men whom Belmore had the good fortune to meet at Salt's house and who, undoubtedly, caused him to take his Egyptian travels even more seriously. He

Coloured lithograph from the 2nd Earl's Collection of Egyptian Antiquities
published by the Royal Society of Literature 1818

could rely on his party's collective sense of adventure and spirit, for which they had each
been praised – Belmore and Juliana by Hester Stanhope, Captain Corry and Robert Holt
by Salt ('in Mr Holt I conceive you have been most fortunate – and the Captain with his
fine natural spirit and agreeable manner is absolutely formed for travelling'). Agreeable
manners were essential for people locked together for months in ships and travelling groups.

While Belmore thought out his next move they did the usual things, discovering Cairo
and making a trip to the Pyramids. Richardson's descriptions of his journeys around Cairo
are rather tedious, as he himself by now must have been to the Belmores, who seem to
have left him very much to his own devices. Belmore was still suffering from gout so a
pause would have been welcome. Juliana Belmore and her maid probably stayed close to
Salt's house until Turkish dress was acquired for her. Although Hester Stanhope thought
attitudes to European dress in Cairo more liberal than they were in Syria, the Belmores
took no chances since she had strongly advised:

'the more Lady B covers her face … the more she will be admired and considered the wife of a great Pasha for it is quite impossible to say how the Turks in Syria are horrified with the European customs'.

In Cairo she covered her head and face, but away from Cairo she certainly took no chances and wore Turkish dress, as did Belmore. Their wardrobe included: a blue robe, two jackets and breeches; a red robe, jacket and breeches; two coloured robes and waistcoats; two turbans and sashes; three Bedouin outside robes and a white Bedouin robe; a white cloak and large blue robe; two silk shirts; a pair of boots trimmed with gold; a saddle cloth; red breeches; a very fine white robe; a large red cap; three small red caps; five pairs of yellow slippers; two embroidered caps; and two Tripoli shirts. Some of these were Belmore's. Later, in Damascus, Juliana Belmore's disguise allowed her a freedom of movement, remarkable for its time, to explore the city.

Belmore's gout finally eased off and Salt was able to take the men and Belmore's boys to meet the Pasha, Mehemet Ali, 'worthy successor of the Pharoahs', at his pretty summer

Dendara,	RDK 93	James Livingston	Iˣ LIVINGSTON N12 1817+ OSPRAY

Dendur,	RDK 1164	John Patterson	J. PATTERSON
	RDK 1163	James Livingston	J. LIVINGSTON JANUARY·1·1818

Philae	RDK 597	James Livingston	J LIVINGSTON
	RDK 1167	John Patterson	Jⁿ PATTERSON 1818

James Livingston	Age 28
John Patterson	Age 30

Names of the 2 seamen, principal carvers of the Belmore/Corry graffiti

palace in Shubra, just outside Cairo. He was actually a Romanian soldier of fortune in the service of Turkey. He welcomed them, expanding warmly on the prospect before them: the Nile, the grain-covered fields, the Pyramids of Giza, the bright sun and the cloudless sky and remarked that England could offer nothing to equal the greenery, since it was 'steeped in fog and rain for three quarters of the year'. To emphasise the point he shivered and then gave a hearty laugh. He offered to give Belmore every possible facility for his journey up the Nile, but warned him against the certainty of Arabs stealing from him if they got the chance.

Leaving their names behind them at the 'transcendent Pyramids'

On 10 October 1817 they all set out with Salt on a trip to see the Pyramids of Giza. Juliana wore her Turkish dress for the first time. As the Nile floods were at their height they had to approach the Pyramids by a circuitous route on a canal boat, instead of riding there in an hour. They lost their way several times in the maze of branch canals, so the journey took all morning. They had several glimpses of the Pyramids as they approached their landing place, about three quarters of a mile away, and were seriously disappointed that they did not seem as large and grand as they had been led to expect. However, when, unsteadily and on 'miserable asses' they arrived at the base of the two largest, they realised how gigantic they really were. They lodged their equipment in the 'Sheik's cave' – the shell of an ancient mansion – had a quick meal and began measuring and exploring the 'transcendent' Pyramids. They went through the passage into the Great Pyramid, candles at the ready, descending further and further through the various chambers to a depth of just over 200 feet. Looking directly upwards they could see open air, a view that at night pointed directly at the Pole Star. A little further on they came to a large chamber, 66 feet long, said to be in the exact centre of the Pyramid, cut out of the rock below the Pyramid itself. They retraced their steps and reached the open air, exhausted by their efforts in the dusty, hot atmosphere of the passages and chambers.

Led by Salt, they had in fact gone further and deeper into the Pyramid than modern tourists do. Next, they climbed to the summit, helped by the step-like construction of the sides, Richardson commenting that 'Lady Belmore ascended it with the most perfect ease, and none of the party experienced the smallest difficulty or vertigo'. He was surprised by the freshness of the stone at the top, injured only by 'the knives and chisels of visitors, who, anxious to perpetuate their arrival on this lofty station, had left their names behind them'. Belmore and Juliana added to the scars by having their names carved there, as did Captain Corry, who became the most enthusiastic perpetuator of his name throughout the travels. The carvers were two of the *Osprey*'s seamen, John Patterson and James Livingston.

In the evening, still tired, they paid an Arab to run up to the top of the second Pyramid. They slept in the 'Sheik's cave' that night and the next morning went to examine the Sphinx. Much of the Sphinx had been excavated a few months before but was now covered again by sand, which had been replaced partly by Arabs and partly by the wind. Richardson commented that the whole spot was covered with excavations, structures and mausoleums – 'a dreary waste of up and down, as the drifting winds permit the sand to settle'. They then packed up and returned to Cairo by the canal boat, 'the oars keeping time to the song of the boatmen', and 'the merriest of our songsters concluded his warblings by showing us how well he could imitate the braying of an ass'.

Bad news awaited them on their return to Salt's house. Burkhardt, in Salt's own words 'the only conversable friend I had in Cairo', had contracted dysentery and, in spite of Richardson's attempts to help him, died. Salt's devastation must have cast a shadow over the whole party and was a reminder of the dangers facing travellers at that time.

A 'great undertaking for Lady Belmore and the little girl'

Belmore, fired up by what they had seen and done so far and by the accounts of Belzoni about his work in upper Egypt, made up his mind to see more. This was his chance to take advantage of what he had learned and perhaps even share in the reputations for enterprise and knowledge being acquired by his new friends. He decided to go to upper Egypt with Salt, but it was risky: 'your plan embraces a wide field indeed and seems to me a great undertaking for Lady Belmore and the little girl'.[3]

Belmore was not to be put off:

'The noble Traveller having now resolved to extend his researches into Upper Egypt, many articles necessary for our accommodation were brought from the *Osprey*'.

The brig was then sent to winter at Malta while, in the evening of 27 October, at Bulac, the party boarded the large two-masted boats commonly used on the Nile, called maashes. Five maashes were provided: one for Belmore and Juliana with Juliana Brooke, Sarah Dane and Belmore's valet; one for Armar, Viscount Corry and his brother Henry with the Reverend Mr Holt and another servant; one for Captain Corry, with a sailor as servant and Dr Richardson with a Nubian interpreter; a mess boat with cook and superintendent; and one for Salt with a servant.

For Salt, this journey held out the prospect of further studies of Egyptian antiquities, an important part of his official duties, and also afforded an active antidote to the pain of the loss of his friend. The Belmores were now also his friends and there could not have been better company for him in the circumstances. He joined them at five o'clock the following evening and the small fleet set off up the Nile, which was still high. The wind rose, the maashes were tossed about in the rough water and the jolly boat attached to Captain Corry's maash broke loose, setting off a shouting match between the sailors and their chief. In the confusion, their vessel ran aground, crushing the prow. Repairs were carried out during the night while they moored by a small village and the following morning they set off again, catching up with the others at ten o'clock.

On 31 October they moored by the ruined village of Antinopolis, built by the Emperor Hadrian in memory of his son who drowned in the Nile, and had a quick tour of the ruins, columns, arches and houses before setting off again to Alrairamoun, a large village on the west bank, where there was a new sugar factory managed by an Englishman, Mr Brine. Richardson was most interested in the factory's rum production, which he

Temple of Dendur, details showing graffiti of Captain A. L. Corry and the 2 seamen carvers

criticised for not having the 'exquisite flavour' of West Indian rum. Brine, with his own interpreter, accompanied them when they left on their way to meet Mahomet Bey, Mehemet Ali's son-in-law.

At ten the next morning they were all received in a low, cool room, laid with mats and cushions. They drank coffee and smoked the usual pipe, discussing, amongst other things, the Bey's fear of Russian interference in the region. Belmore presented him with a brace of handsome English pistols and, when they returned to their maashes, they found presents of sheep and salt butter in return. There was also an invitation to a review of the Bey's cavalry, together with target practice. There was a sham fight in which two sides, commanded respectively by Mahomet Bey himself and his lieutenant, charged at each other, wheeled, rallied and fired. Inevitably, the Bey won. He chased his lieutenant from the battlefield at full speed, close up to where the Belmores sat, then engaged him in a spear fight – wheeling around, parrying and thrusting skilfully for about ten minutes.

Coffee and pipes followed, during which Captain Corry set up his sextant to take some meridian observations. He explained the calculations and then presented the Bey with a note of the exact latitude of the 'battle' ground, much to the latter's amusement and satisfaction. There followed the next act, which was target practice – firing at a gallop at small earthen pitchers placed on a rock above the riders. Each rider started from 300 to 400 yards away with his musket slung over his shoulders. One after the other, in quick succession, each rider drew the musket over his head with both hands as he galloped up to the target, fired, rode round to the rear and began again in his turn. When this sport eventually ended they all returned to the town, took leave of the Bey and returned on board the maashes.

'Everything seems to speak and move around you'

Richardson thought that such cordial receptions were due to the rank of 'the Noble Traveller', but another influence was at work. In a letter to Hester Stanhope, written after the Egyptian journey was over, Belmore acknowledged the debt he owed to her influential connections, which eased their way as far as Thebes.

Thebes would be their next major stopping place, with a pause to examine the temple at Dendara – a pause that was to stimulate Belmore's ambition to become a serious collector. At a previous short stop Salt and Belmore had taken the opportunity to ride away for about an hour to some catacombs. Salt opened one and they found two well-preserved mummies whose nails and skin were quite fresh.

They reached the temple of Dendara late in the afternoon and their first impression was that it stood in 'a black field of ruins'. When they approached the temple itself, however, any disappointment melted away. Advancing among the ruins for a few hundred yards they came across an elegant sandstone gateway covered with sculpture and hieroglyphics. Over the centre of the doorway was a beautiful sun symbol, a globe embellished with a serpent and wings. On the walls of the passage through the gate, wrote Richardson, 'some of the female figures are so extremely well executed that they do all but speak'. The temple's strikingly beautiful symbols, painted figures, sculptures, sacred boats in procession and hieroglyphics left them all (including the normally loquacious Richardson) speechless:

'No part is without its decorations, everything seems to speak and move around you … the mind is astonished, and feels as if absolutely introduced to beings of olden time, to converse with them, and witness the ceremonies by which they delighted to honor their God'.

The impact of the temple was overwhelming. Salt had with him the illustrations of Dendara done by the French in 1798 in the *Description de L'Egypte*, to compare them with the originals. In the excited discussions which followed they praised the French for acquainting the world with Egypt's antiquities and criticised the English for failing to play their part. England, so far, had only fragments to exhibit, which could never be satisfactory. Now was the time to do the work while the building was in perfect condition and all that was necessary was to remove rubbish which had accumulated around it:

'But a few years hence the object may be impracticable, and Dendara, like Karnak, may be trodden under foot, and looked at in scattered fragments'.

It was nothing short of disgraceful, they agreed, that the many in England who had the means did not have the will to do it 'so that it could be seen in England exactly as it is in Egypt'. Discussions of this kind encouraged Belmore to believe that collecting and transporting antiquities to England was entirely justifiable. The Egyptians and Turks were interested only in treasure hunting. Corry, perhaps not quite such a romantic as the rest,

View of Grand Cairo by Henry Salt 1809

seeing that Irby and Mangles had previously carved their names on the parapet of the temple roof, had Livingston add theirs.

When they reached Thebes at half past seven in the evening of 16 November, all that was to be seen of its glory 'was a field of ruins'. At this point, as if it were one of his stage appearances, Belzoni turned up with Salt's secretary, Henry Beechey, to welcome them to Thebes and to take them off to see to admire and be astounded by his discoveries of the 'celebrated tomb of Psammethis'. Belmore and the others were to be the first 'English' travellers to enter it. Salt described the tomb as 'exquisitely painted, and with the colours as fresh as on the day it was completed'. Salt and Beechey copied the paintings in brilliant watercolours.

Belzoni's own narrative confirms that Belmore's ambition to collect was excited by the discovery:

> 'They were delighted when they saw it; and as his Lordship was anxious to find a tomb, I pointed out two likely spots of ground in the valley of Beban el Malook, but they turned out to be two small mummy pits … During his stay his Lordship made many researches, and was pleased to send down the Nile two of the lion-headed statues I discovered in Carnak. Thus, with what was found and brought by the Arabs, he accumulated a vast quantity of fragments, which, when in Europe, will form a pretty extensive cabinet of antiquities'.

Henry Salt was also enthused and stayed for four months making excavations. Belmore left for Nubia after, in Belzoni's words:

> 'His Lordship and family had been at Thebes for some time, and had accumulated no small collection of antiquities; indeed, I esteem it the largest ever made by any occasional traveller'.

Belmore and his party were so immersed in the excavation work that they seriously considered abandoning a trip further up the Nile. However, the Nile waters were about to recede, making a longer trip impossible – so, after further thought, they decided to go on and return later to the Valley of the Kings to resume excavation work 'with greater vigor'.

Before they left, they had a visitor – the former French Consul, Bernadino Drovetti, who was soon to be consul again. A successful collector of antiquities himself, he was, according to Richardson:

> 'the only Frenchman I ever saw in all my life completely run out of the small change of compliment and admiration. He was so lavish of his civilities on entering the tomb, and everything was so superb, magnifique, superlative and astounding, that when he came to something which really called for epithets of applause and admiration, his magazine of stuff was expended, and he stood in speechless astonishment, to the great entertainment of the beholders'.

To the Second Cataract on the Nile

They left on 22 November to make their way to Aswan in Nubia, stopping at villages on the way for eggs, milk and butter and calling, through their interpreter, to be shown any

Temple of Dendur, details showing graffiti of the 2nd Earl Belmore

antiquities which might not have been snapped up by previous travellers. The villagers in this part of the region – elegant, slender and black complexioned, forerunners of the tourist trade – would offer them a gallimaufry of objects, from Roman coins to beetles, beads, vitrified rings and statues, most of no interest at all. They had been warned never to go ashore without arms, the Nubian men themselves always carrying a long-shafted spear, with a knife tied onto their left upper arm – which they could use with great dexterity in either hand.

Belmore's objective was to reach the second cataract on the Nile, and to do this they all had to be transferred into a flotilla of small boats, with coverings of straw and palm mats to shelter them from the sun by day and the damp by night.

At Aswan they had laid in plentiful stores – sheep, poultry, two milch goats and bread, the like of which for quality and taste Richardson had never eaten in the whole of his life. Belmore, to Richardson's relief, 'had taken care to be well provided with a due assortment of the juice of the grape, before we left Cairo'. Butter, lentils and vegetables could be bought at villages on the way.

Belmore and Juliana, with little Miss Brooke and two servants, led the way, followed by Holt, Armar and Henry with a servant in the second boat, Captain Corry and Richardson in the third boat with a sailor as servant and, bringing up the rear, the cook and a servant with the supply boat. They were about to sail on 7 December when it was discovered they had forgotten to bring their colours (the British ensign). Belmore refused to sail without them so a sailor was sent back for them and, by 11 a.m., colours aloft, they were able to set off.

Every day, each party breakfasted on their own boat and, at sunset, they moored and spread a mat on the bank to dine together, a happy company. After dinner, on the evening of the eighth they made their way by starlight to wander round the ruined temple of Gartaas and on the ninth reached Kalabshi to visit the temple there. Belmore was the first to arrive and was immediately confronted by a young spear carrier, who demanded 'baksheesh'. 'I am going to take a view of the temple,' insisted Belmore, 'and will give you baksheesh when I return'. One look at Belmore in his Turkish dress, armed with his sword and pistols, was enough to persuade him to give way, saying repeatedly, 'A Turk is a good man'.

Belmore returned to the boat for Juliana, by which time the others had arrived. After they had inspected the temple and paid for some antiquities the interpreter was ordered to pay the promised baksheesh. Captain Corry took one of his many observations here. Subversion appeared shortly afterwards when the interpreter admitted he had not paid the baksheesh because the locals had stolen his coat. He was severely admonished for demeaning his master's reputation, although there was some relief that the locals had obviously been so content with their sales of antiquities that the interpreter's duplicity had not bothered them.

Belmore, Captain Corry and others would hop off their boats to walk along the bank and shoot pigeons and 'partridges of the desert'. After the trouble with the interpreter, they were threatened by an Arab commanding a boat sailing alongside them. He aimed a musket at Captain Corry who was walking on the bank, armed only with a sword, but Corry was quickly passed a pistol from the boat and, backed up by a musket aimed by one of the sailors, persuaded the Arab to steer quickly away.

As they went further up the Nile the winds fell and the sailors had to 'track' or pull the boats from the bank, which slowed them down a great deal. When sailing was possible, Belmore went ahead faster than the others. At the temple of Dekaa he was up early in the morning and spent several hours studying it before everyone else arrived.

The presents the Nubians liked most included gunpowder, which Richardson thought would be used to fire at them unless it were given just before they left. The usual presents were soap, tobacco, coffee, musket flints and – to guarantee temporary friendship – a sword or double-barrelled gun. To women, Juliana Belmore normally gave beads and mirrors, which were popular.

On 20 December they arrived at the temple of Abu Simbel, which had been excavated by Belzoni.

Although it had recently been entered by an English party under Colonel Stratton of the Inniskilling Dragoons, the entrances had been covered by drifting sand. After some difficulties and setting to it themselves, they persuaded the sailors and their chief to help them clear away the sand. Suddenly, large stones began to roll down from the top of the pyramid and drove them from the work. The Arab attacking them made no attempt to conceal himself or to be persuaded to stop so Belmore had the sailors fire at him. He ran off, chased by Yanni, the Greek servant, but managed to get clean away. The man's anger had been on account of the interpreter yet again failing to pay him the baksheesh agreed for allowing the party's two milch goats to be pastured in his cornfield.

The next day they stopped at Ishkid, a village where two chiefs lived in such a rare, magnificent state that Belmore decided, being now only five hours from the second cataract, to stay overnight. After he had visited them, the chiefs sent him seven sheep; in return, he sent one a set of coffee cups and the other a travelling carpet. During their usual dinner on the bank a messenger arrived from one of the chiefs, leading a little black boy who was to be given to Belmore as a slave. Despite the astonishment of the interpreter and the messenger that there should be any scruples about accepting such a handsome present – which, they insisted, could not properly be refused – it was eventually rejected 'on the principle that neither an Englishman nor a Christian can consistently accept of a slave'. The unfortunate boy was returned to slavery.

On the morning of 23 December they were overjoyed to have reached the cataract, the end of their journey, Belmore being anxious to get back to the Valley of the Kings. They climbed to the summit of a tumulus to survey the cataract as it fell and split, divided by rocks and islets, into several streams.

Afterwards, on the bank of the river, though the surroundings were barren, they celebrated – with plenty of French wines, porter, and a bumper of the best Irish whiskey – the birthday of an infinitely more fortunate boy, Viscount Corry, who was 16.

On Christmas Eve they were provided with an ass on which Juliana and Miss Brooke rode alternately, the rest of the party scrambling through the sand as best as they could, and did a round trip around the area of the cataract. Belmore took observations and the whole party engraved their names on suitable rocks, some of which already bore the names of English travellers. Captain Corry had left in the morning to travel the ten-day journey to Saie and to join them again in Cairo. However, when they returned to their boats for the journey back down the river to Aswan, to their delight, he had returned. The accommodation he had been promised had not materialised.

'Work hotly plied': Back to the Valley of the Kings

They arrived back at Aswan in the New Year of 1818 and transferred into to their maashes, finding it strange to be dining again on board and not out in the open. But Belmore was not about to relax. Before leaving he wanted to excavate inside a local temple in the hope of finding a well that was thought to be there. He got permission to do so and with a dozen labourers from the *Aga* armed with spades and buckets, they began.

'No attention was paid to opening the door, or clearing the rubbish from the exterior of the building, though that would have been the most regular plan of conducting the examination, but we had not time for that'.

The space inside was too small to allow all the labourers to dig at the same time, so they took turns to dig, 'the work hotly plied', to a depth of about 14 feet, but they found nothing. Richardson lost interest and wandered off to see the ruins of a convent, so there is no evidence that they filled the hole in before they left on the morning of 7 January. They were rowed down the Nile, stopping to look at ruined temples and villages on the way but were delighted when they finally reached Luxor and moored at the western bank by the sycamore tree.

Here, they were greeted by Salt and Beechey with dramatic news. Princess Charlotte was dead. She had died of post-partum haemorrhage and shock at two o'clock in the morning of 6 November. They had seen her only 18 months previously, a 'lovely Princess in the hey-day of her spirits, as she drove rapidly along with the husband of her choice' amid the applause of the onlookers. 'The gay spirits of the party were stilled'.

Coloured lithographs from the 2nd Earl's Collection of Egyptian Antiquities
published by the Royal Society of Literature 1818

They spent the next week in preparing for a journey back into the Valley of the Kings and giving Salt an account of their journey into Nubia. Salt wrote to his friend and patron, Lord Mountnorris, in January about their experience:

> 'they never enjoyed anything more than this voyage, the climate being most delicious. Fortunately, Lord Belmore had with him a very fine sextant, and his brother, Captain Corry, is a very accurate and attentive observer: they have taken many observations, indeed, at every place they have touched at'.

Belmore went with Salt to have a look at the antiquities that had been collected for him by 'the diligent and faithful Greek', the 20-year-old Giovanni d'Athanasi, known as 'Yanni', who had recently chased off their attacker from the Pyramid. Among the usual collection of stone jars, scarabs, small statues and stones covered with figures and hieroglyphics, was an ancient deal door, with hieroglyphics and the figure of Osiris carved in it. Belmore gave it to Salt, who later sold it to the British Museum. They then went on into the Valley of the Kings and, after admiring the watercolours of Salt and Beechey, which are now also in the British Museum, Belmore made a general survey of the ground and got to work. He was the first nobleman to get there and the first to take his family with him.

He 'kept a number of Arabs constantly at work, set an example of the most commendable industry and perseverance' in directing and superintending the excavations. His efforts were crowned by a magnificent collection, which is also in the British Museum. In the many mummies which they discovered they found beautifully coloured papyri, the most perfect of which 'and the best unrolled I have ever seen, belongs to the Earl of Belmore, and was unrolled by himself'.

Belmore spent some time and considerable trouble lifting a granite sarcophagus from the bottom of a deep tomb halfway up the mountain above the village of Gornou. The Herculean effort was wasted because when Belmore saw it in the light he was forced to admit that it was not worth transporting to England.

'All the pomp, parade and grandeur, of luxurious speculation'

A notion of the sheer size and impact of Belmore's family party and, indeed, Salt's entourage, is evidenced by the impression of two Frenchmen who saw them in action. Frederic Cailliaud, a mineralogist, who met them in the Valley of the Kings in January, noted that the rivalry between the foreigners was so great that the Arabs were able to take advantage of it in their dealings. At Karnak, there were even lines of demarcation drawn between the French, English, Irish, Italians and others. Comte Louis de Forbin, the other observer, was not happy about what he saw of the Belmore party but his mocking description may do them more justice than he wished:

> 'Lord and Lady Belmour had been visiting a part of Nubia, indulging themselves in all the pomp, parade and grandeur, of luxurious speculation. Four large bateaux were in the train of the one that contained them, husbands, wives, young children, chaplains, surgeons, nurses, cooks'.

Among the ruins at Luxor Forbin encountered, at almost every turn, 'an English waiting woman, in a rose coloured Spencer [a short, close fitting jacket], a parasol in her hand'. Perhaps this was Sarah Dane. Cailliaud, who was also received by them with great kindness, formed quite a different impression: of Salt, 'with a numerous suite, some in tents and some lodged in tombs'; and of Belmore's 'very long suite'. Juliana Belmore he found particularly impressive because she 'displayed courage far superior to her sex … every day exploring catacombs with great perseverance'. Cailliard's friend 'Riffo' (Jean Jacques Rifaud – artist, sculptor, traveller and adventurer) was also enchanted by Juliana, whom he encountered at Karnak.

He was so enchanted, in fact, that in an excess of gallantry he invited her to dig in a spot until then jealously reserved for the French. Much to his annoyance, his gallantry cost the French dear. Almost at once she was rewarded with the discovery of the funerary boat of Mutemwia, the principal wife of Thutmose IV and the mother of Amenhotep III. Although Mutemwia's head and the stern of the black granite boat are missing, a small female head inscribed with her name, delicately carved, with the narrow almond-shaped eyes typical of the time, was found close by. After they returned to England, the Belmores gave the boat to the British Museum where it can be seen to this day. It remains a unique object.

After nearly a month of excavating the Belmore entourage felt some pressure to leave for Cairo before the plague season struck, which was usually by the beginning of April. On 10 February they cut loose and floated down the Nile past Karnak, light from the rising sun flooding the mountains opposite Gornou. They dropped down to stop and look at the temple of Dendara one last time, shot crocodiles on the banks of the river, were entertained to see groups of dervishes with their flags and colours and admired the white dovecotes on the roofs of village houses. The weather turned cloudy and wet as they glided down to Osyout where Richardson treated Ahmed Bey – 'a battered sot'. While there they examined rock excavations and then rowed away, the weather now turning mild.

Encountering dervishes again, Belmore and Richardson received the attentions of one who, calling upon the name of God in long, hollow tones, breathed upon their faces as a blessing. They then called on Mr Brine, the sugar manufacturer, and rode to inspect the temple at Oschmounein, which they had missed on their way up the river. They rode to make a courtesy visit to Mehemet Ali's uncle. Embarking once more, they revisited the ruins of Antinopolis, but on the first of March ran aground. They had been on the move again for only a few hours when then ran aground again and had to spend the night in the middle of the river. Freed again, they went on but got stuck two or three times. They reached a mooring from which they could walk through the fields of corn and grass to see the statue of Memnon. They had not realised that there would be a heavy dew, which soaked their shoes and stockings.

Their next visit was to the pyramids of Daschour and eventually they sent the boats on to Giza, while they themselves rode asses along the edge of the desert to the Pyramids. They were informed by the local Arabs of Belzoni's success in opening the second Pyramid some ten days earlier, and immediately went to see it, even though it was late.

length. 7 feet of Black Granite —

Sketch by Belzoni of the funerary boat of Mutemwia

They were, once more, the first Europeans to see the result of Belzoni's work. After that, it was a short distance to the port of Bulac in which they arrived on 12 March 1818 after a journey of some 700 miles, 'as happy to step on shore as they had been impatient to step on board'. Their luggage accompanied them back to Salt's house and their collection of antiquities was carefully packed and sent by boat to Alexandria, on its way to England.

'Like a London Lord Mayor's show'

In the meantime, the family had to prepare for the next leg of their journey, over land to Syria and Palestine. Belmore was armed with an excellent itinerary written out for him by Irby and Mangles with details of routes, stopping places and historic sites. He also had travel advice from William John Bankes (1786–1855) – explorer, Egyptologist and adventurer – who during his travels put together a large and immensely important private collection of Egyptian artefacts.

The whole party were now bronzed by the sun and wind and the men had grown luxuriant beards and moustaches, so that when they exchanged their tattered European clothes and shoes for Turkish dress they must have looked quite authentic. The women had already become accustomed to wearing their Turkish outfits. While preparations were being made they rode out to visit local excavations and villages. Finally, on 25 March 1818, all was ready – horses, asses, camels and dromedaries. 'Like a London Lord Mayor's show', they set off – Belmore on the Sheikh's own dappled horse, one of the English sailors on the only other horse, holding the four-year-old Miss Brooke in front of him, Juliana Belmore and the rest bringing up the rear on the asses, which brayed and flapped their long ears.

Coloured lithograph from the 2nd Earl's Collection of Egyptian Antiquities
published by the Royal Society of Literature 1818

The male servants were on camels with the luggage. One sheikh led the whole procession on a dromedary and the other sheikh brought up the rear with the baggage. The travellers carried a tin flask, holding three pints of water, tied to their saddle bags. The flask was covered with a wad of cotton under a leather covering and, when filled and wet in the morning, was kept cool all day by being hung on the shady side of the saddle. The men had a brace of pistols in the left side of their belts and a dagger on the right, a sword slung around the shoulders, a flint and steel with a piece of amadou (a fungus used to catch the sparks) and a bag of tobacco tucked into their kaftans:

'Thus accoutred, with a haversack slung across the saddle, stuffed with bread, onions and cheese, a small tin pot, a cup and some coffee, with a persian or travelling carpet, which is about the size of a hearth rug, folded beneath him, to spread upon the ground when he lights to repose, the traveller shoulders his pipe, smokes and muses along at the rate of three miles an hour'.

Belzoni went with them until, on the second day, they parted company when he went off to investigate the ruins of Heliopolis. Belzoni's wife Sarah also made her own way to Jerusalem, where, after several adventures, she joined the Belmore party, happy to be welcomed into a comfortable and safe environment for a time.[4]

The journey to Jerusalem was through Gaza to Ashkelon, Ashdod, Jaffa and Ramala. The only incident on the way was an attempted ambush by an Arab, who caught hold of Captain Corry's bridle and held back his horse. Belmore drew his sword and Captain Corry took aim with his musket but when one of the muleteers told the Arab they were under the protection of the Governor of Jaffa the 'ragged, red-haired knave slunk across the field to his thievish den'.

Drawing by J J Chalon showing Lady Belmore in Palestine,
followed by a sailor holding the infant, Juliana Brooke

On 13 April at half past three in the afternoon they arrived at the house of Ibrahim Abougosh, 'the chief of his tribe, the prince of the Arabs, and a plunderer of pilgrims'. With a letter from Lady Hester Stanhope and his brother as their guide they had nothing to fear and were welcomed into the chief's own house, where dinner was served by the light of a single candle in a large room with a low sofa around the walls. The dishes of rice, chicken, boiled and minced meats, stuffed cucumber-like vegetables and other spiced dishes were set at their feet. They were supposed to begin before their host, but there was nothing to eat with, the only spoon being used to put yoghurt on the rice. Belmore rescued them from embarrassment by asking the chief 'in the name of Allah' to set them an example, whereupon 'he tucked up the long dangling sleeves of his shirt as far as his elbow, and thrust his washed hand into the mountain of rice that smoked before him'. They watched the chief and copied his way of eating, 'talking, laughing and enjoying ourselves', until they could eat no more.

Afterwards they persuaded the chief to drink tea with them, unpacking their own tea-making equipment from their baggage. Belmore handed Hester Stanhope's letter to the chief who read it and then passed it round to his brother and companions to read. He had had the honour of entertaining her ladyship in the same house, but his brother had a question about her: how could she think of travelling with so many maidservants and no husband?

About eight o'clock dinner was over and Belmore, Juliana and family stayed in the same room, fitting up their own cots and hammocks. Captain Corry, Holt and Richardson slept on beds on the floor of a small, adjoining room. They set off early the next morning, having watched the chief despatch a body of his men on horseback to attack caravans or pilgrims passing through his territory. Jerusalem was only two and a half hours away and so, the same day, they arrived at the Latin convent of San Salvador, where they were to stay. On entering the guesthouse opposite the convent, whom should they see again but their old acquaintances Irby, Mangles, John Bankes and Sarah Belzoni, accompanied by Thomas Legh. It turned out that all of them had been in Jerusalem for some time.

Their conversations must have been intense and interesting. Legh, a British MP, had published an account of his journey up the Nile in the autumn of 1812. He was one of the first Europeans to visit the archaeological sites above the first cataract.

Richardson's account of Jerusalem is, just as Salt might have expected, an extended guide for the Christian traveller and contributes little to the story of the Belmores. His medical services were much in demand and he was more or less left to get on with providing them. Still, the Belmores were there themselves as Christian travellers and made the usual tourist itinerary round the holy city. Belmore's gout was troubling him again so it is not surprising that a glimpse of Captain Corry shows him as the only one of the party to join the annual procession of pilgrims to the river Jordan.

That, however, was not Captain Corry's only adventure. Bankes was itching to excavate a blocked entrance to the Tomb of the Kings but had not been able to get formal permission from the Governor of Jerusalem to do so. They decided to do it anyway, illegally and by night, armed with pickaxes and farming tools.

'Late in the evening we quitted the town secretly, from different gates, to avoid suspicion, and assembling at the rendezvous after dark, found we mustered a working party of ten persons, viz. Messrs Bankes and Legh, Captain Corry and ourselves, together with five servants, including two of Lord Belmore's sailors, whom his Lordship had allowed to assist us'.

The two sailors were almost certainly Patterson and Livingston again. They worked all night, seaman-like, in two watches, digging and clearing away the rubbish, a servant keeping guard against discovery. They had forgotten to take spades and so had to clear the rubbish with their hands but, at a depth of ten feet, encountered an immense block of stone, which they could not even move. Exhausted, they crept back to bed. The next morning Captain Corry, Bankes and Mahomet (a janissary) followed Belmore's advice by heating the stone and pouring cold vinegar on it, and managed to break it. Perhaps Belmore had learned this technique from masons working at Castle Coole.[5] No sooner had they managed this than they were discovered by the Turks and reported to the Governor. The whole portico was walled in to stop any further attempts.

On 8 May they left Jerusalem and went to Tiberias by way of Nablous. One evening in Tiberias they were visited by an elegant person dressed as a Turkish nobleman. It was Lady Hester Stanhope – who 'looked remarkably pale, but I believe was in tolerably good health, and conversed in a cheerful and sprightly manner'. Their next stop was at Nazareth, where they left Sarah Belzoni. At a nearby village Juliana Belmore experienced the close personal attentions of the wife and family of the sheikh who led their caravan. They inspected Juliana and her dress in her tent and were reluctant to leave until driven away by an Albanian soldier who travelled in the caravan.

At seven o'clock the next morning, in the bracing, fresh air they left, winding their way through high mountain scenery, dominated by the snow-capped Gibl Sheikh, and eventually descended into the plain of Hauran on the way to Damascus. After travelling for three hours in the intense afternoon heat, they pitched their tents by a small stream and bought bread, milk and vegetables from the nearby village.

The next morning they left, as usual, at seven o'clock for Damascus, and travelled for seven hours. Passing through a plantation of large, heavily laden walnut trees, they arrived at the walls of Damascus by the west gate. They went along the street called 'Straight' until they reached the Franciscan convent where most of the party were to stay. Belmore and Juliana, however, stayed in the house of an eminent French surgeon, M. Chaboiçeau. They visited the Pasha, Ahmed Bey and were given the usual pipes, coffee and lemon sherbet. Ahmed Bey asked Belmore for an account of their journey so far and then, waxing philosophical, asked him whether the earth moved round the sun or was stationary. When Belmore explained the earth's rotation, the Pasha asked how it was that, as the water must sometimes be undermost, it did not fall off. They all laughed, but as they could see that the Pasha really thought the question unanswerable they discreetly said no more. When the Pasha complained that he could not enjoy conversation as he used to because of deafness, Richardson arranged to see him the next day and cleaned out his ears. After that he seemed to hear acutely and news of the operation's success spread rapidly

النعم مصطفى اغا حاكم شرفيه زيد

صدلا الرقيم الديواني من ديوان مصر المحروسه خطابا الى ذوي الاماجد والاعيان

وفي بقايا البلاد ومشايخ القرى والنواحي بقلم شرفيه وقوه الامائل والاقران الحاج يعقوب اغانا

العريش زيد توقيره تحيطون علما ان القادم على طرفكم رافعه الخواجه مليورت الانكليز متوجها الى

بقصد السياحه هو وحريمه واتباعه فعند مروده عليكم كلما يلزم له الحال من الماكل والمشرب بأخذ

بالثمن حتى يمضى الى المحل مقصوده وتكونوا معينين ومساعدين له في خصوص ذلك ولم احدا يعارضه

في مرود وعبوره ويكون له ومن بمعينه الحمايه والصيانه ولم تدعوا احدا يتعرض له بوجه من الوجوه

فبنا على ذلك اصدرنا هذا الرقيم الديواني من ديوان مصر المحروسه جنه تعالى لدى وصوله اليكم ويصير معلوما

بمضمونه ومقتضاه وتخالفوه اعلموا واعتمدوا غايته تعرفوا الاعمال

(١٤)

Example of laisser passer through a sheikh's territory

158

through Damascus. Richardson spent a great deal of his time afterwards in treating a succession of patients.

The fame of the party spread as they moved around the town and its bazaars. Juliana Belmore had been advised to 'muffle herself up and walk about as the ladies in the country' did, but she refused to do so. Wearing her Turkish or Mameluke outfit, she walked as bold as brass into the large open-air cafés on the riverside:

> 'sat down and took her hookah and her cup of coffee the same as other members of the party, unnoticed and unannoyed: a proof of her ladyship's resolution, and of the eager desire of knowledge that led her to examine everything of consequence'.

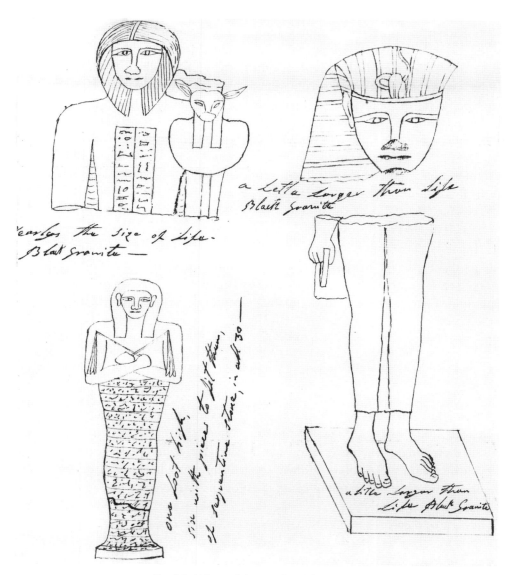

Sketch by Belzoni of objects collected for Belmore

She had, of course, the example of both Hester Stanhope and Sarah Belzoni to encourage her. The men also wore Mameluke costume, which was not customary in Damascus, and meant that they appeared at first to be from Cairo. But when it was discovered they were actually Europeans and Belmore was 'an English Consul', greater interest was shown in Juliana, who had to be passed off as a clerk. 'Why then has he no beard[?] He seems old enough', was countered with, 'It had not happened to grow, there were sometimes odd cases like that'. The oddity was shrugged off as the will of God. In their tours of the city they were shown the houses of Judas, which had been the lodging of St Paul, and of Ananias, who restored the saint's sight, and also a section of the city wall down which Paul was lowered in a basket.

They had wanted to visit Palmyra, but there was conflict between the Arabs and Turks which made it too dangerous. So, on 4 June, the cavalcade set off through the city gate, up the hill for a last look back at Damascus, and then pressed on to visit the ruins of Balbec. Here they measured, inspected and studied what remained of the old buildings for the rest of the day and then set off again to reach the base of Mount Lebanon, where they camped for the night by a stream and under the shade of a walnut tree.

The following morning they began the climb up the mountain, zig-zagging up the steep incline until, after just over an hour, they reached the patchy, melting snow at the top. They could see the sea in the distance, the mountainous foreground which hid the plain of Tripoli, and the hillside villages. And they could not help but look behind them in the direction of Nineveh, Baghdad and Babylon, which conflict had prevented them from visiting.

On their descent they came to the famous cedars of Lebanon, 'large and massy, rearing their heads to an enormous height', and then passed on to the village of Eden where they were regaled by the local Sheikh with the usual pipes, coffee and lemonade.

Two days later, on 13 June, they set out for Tripoli where, passing through the town, they camped by the beach, near the marina where they could see the *Osprey* riding out in the bay:

> 'The sheikh of the caravan, the soldier, the interpreter, the servants, the tent pitchers, are all paid off … On the morning of the 17th our tents were all struck, and by twelve o'clock we all got on board, and immediately set sail for the island of Paros'.

The first thing they did on board, on seeing their weather-beaten faces in a mirror, unrecognisable with beards and moustaches, was to shave and then to take off their Turkish dress and put on 'the light and comfortable garb of Europeans'. Sailing was made difficult by contrary winds forcing them to tack constantly but they made their way by Rhodes, Patmos and Naxos to the island of Paros and anchored in the same station they had used the year before.

From Paros they went by Delos, Milos and on, at a rate of four knots in a favourable wind, to Malta, where the *Osprey* was quarantined for 15 days. At Malta, afterwards, Richardson parted company with the Belmore party. They were delayed there until 16

August 1818, when they left for Naples. From Naples during August, September and October they went to Rome, Messina, Palermo, Catania and Augusta and Belmore put together a collection of the usual artefacts purchased by travellers on the grand tour, such as bronzes, Roman armour, statues, decorated tables and Etruscan vases. In Rome Pietro Maria Vitali made various decorative items in marble for Belmore. In all, by August 1818, there were no fewer than 37 cases of antiquities in a Naples warehouse.

At the beginning of December 1818, the old stalwarts Patterson and Livingston were left behind in Malta to supervise the arrival and transfer of Belmore's Greek and Roman antiquities into a vessel bound for England. His Egyptian collection did not fare as well, for Pearce, who had charge of them, died before they were properly listed and packed. Plague broke out in Cairo and they were hurriedly put into a large packing case and sent off to Alexandria – where, in December 1820, they still awaited onward transmission to England.

Salt explained this in a letter to Belmore at the end of November. The most important items were a fragment of a statue, a small statue and the fragment of the processional boat of Mutemwia previously mentioned. He enclosed sketches of the former, with a drawing of what he thought the broken section of the boat might look like.

Many smaller figures Salt thought of little value and one poor statue and a mummy case were hardly worth the carriage. He offered to send Belmore a fine mummy and its case in their place. In fact, worse was to follow when Belmore found his antiques had been carelessly turned out for examination by customs officers in the quarantine building at Malta:

> 'I have had the mortification to find a terrible wreck among my antiques … many of the best of my small figures broken to pieces – most of the papyrus ground to dust and everything laying jumbled together in the Lazaret as so much rubbish'.[6]

Even after Belmore had arrived back in England he was receiving confirmation of further shipments from Naples:

> 'I have, according to your Lordship's directions, shipped on board the *Ann* bound for London two cases containing 33 Etruscan vases, large and small, a helmet and part of the breast plate inlaid with gold, a hand of bronze on an alabaster stand. The hand is of the most expensive Greek antique workmanship, and two small boxes in the shape of those in the tea caddies of amber, they are of the 15th century and belonged to the Cardinal Mattei. I hope you will approve of the above trifling articles; I paid for the above 323 Ducats, about 54 pounds'.[7]

The bill for warehousing the whole of his collection – Egyptian, Greek, Roman and modern Italian – for a year (August 1818 to August 1819) amounted to almost £3,000.[8]

Finally, after discharging the crew of the *Osprey* and selling the brig (it is believed, to the King of Naples), Belmore took his family and servants over land via Florence to Geneva, Paris, London and home to Castle Coole, where they arrived in the spring of

1820. They were met at Castle Coole by local dignitaries and crowds of people from Enniskillen. A local English teacher, John Murphy, wrote verses for the occasion, which he had printed and circulated in the hope they would get him Belmore's attention and a job:

'Written after his Lordship's Arrival at Castle Coole

'Welcome! Welcome! Lord Belmore
From your long and tedious tour
Furnished well with foreign lore
And foreign rule;
Back to the hospitable door
Of Castle Coole'.

The verses ran to 22 pages, written under a pen name 'A Fermanagh Peasant'. Someone wrote 'not worth much' on the front page, so Murphy fared no better than Wordsworth before him.[9]

Shortly after Belmore's return, reminders of his adventures came in letters containing two separate accusations against him – one of looting and the other of murder. The first was a claim for compensation from Belmore for stealing one statue and mutilating another at Marathon. He denied this and it was not pursued. The second accusation was aimed at both Belmore and Belzoni. It was alleged to the Academy of Science in Paris that they had murdered a Piedmontese in the service of the French Consul, Drovetti, by throwing him overboard into the Nile. Belmore described the allegation as 'a malicious calumny' due to 'the jealousy's which unfortunately exist in Egypt among the different persons who are engaged in Antiquarian researches'. The facts were that the Piedmontese had begged a passage in the boat carrying Belmore's collection from Thebes to Cairo. An inquiry by the captain and the local chieftain established that the Piedmontese was drunk and while sitting on the side of the boat 'accroupi as is common in that country to wash himself, he fell in and was drowned'. No more was heard of the affair.

Chapter Fourteen

A Stern Father and the Advantages of a Fortune

Anyone who has been away for a considerable time from home or work will have experienced the pleasure and the pain of settling back into routine. The Castle Coole Belmore now entered had been improved by the new furniture he had ordered from Preston and by the addition of the new stableyard below the house, designed by Richard Morrison and subsequently known as the 'grand yard'. The planting near the new Dublin Road entrance and the laying out of a new approach to the house were finished, except for the installation of the magnificent gates and railings Belmore had had designed. These proved too expensive to build.[1]

While Belmore was on his way home in 1819, a vacancy arose in the Irish representative peerage and in February Lord Liverpool had confirmed to the Duke of Wellington, canvassing for Lord Westmeath, that he was 'under an engagement to Lord Belmore'.[2] With government support Belmore was duly elected.

Important though a representative peerage was for access to ministers in London, in Tyrone and Fermanagh nothing had happened so far in the years since the union to change the circumstances of Belmore's political influence or social standing. On his return, Ireland was still not the scene in which he would find anything particularly interesting for himself. In any case, his worsening financial situation was enough to occupy him and it was about to be made three times as bad by his obligations as a peer. Firstly, all peers (representative or not) were strictly required to attend the divorce proceedings against Queen Caroline, which began in the particularly hot August of 1820 and ended in failure in November. Secondly, peers had to attend the coronation of George IV in July 1821. And thirdly, Belmore had to make expensive preparations for the new King's proposed visit to Ireland shortly afterwards. Mementoes of all three, all at Castle Coole to this day, would remind him of the cost of the year 1821: a gold coronation medal, a large specially made volume of cartoons and transcription of the trial of the Queen, and the refurbished state bedroom with its elegantly beautiful state bed.

He had not, as yet, paid for most of the furniture and furnishings – many of which, as a result, had been left for nine years in a Dublin warehouse. Preston was in despair. Not only had he not been paid, but he had also had to pay out of his own pocket for cleaning up, burnishing and replacing spoiled articles. Silk to the value of £200 had been ruined. Preston had sent a bill by special messenger to Paris as Belmore was on his way back from

Gold medal commemorating the coronation of George IV

his travels but, getting no result other than complaints, he called personally at Hamilton Place to see Belmore. Spiller had been alarmed by Preston's demands for 'thousands' and refused to do anything until Belmore reviewed the whole situation. Belmore then consulted solicitors. The matter was not settled until 1830, when he and Corry had to join together to execute a formal deed for paying Preston £11,000 in three annual instalments in May 1832, 1833 and 1834.[3]

In the meantime, George IV dallied at Slane Castle with his mistress and ended his tour so Belmore was, at least, spared the actual arrival of the King at Castle Coole, an honour his finances were well able to do without.

Belmore had been shocked by misunderstanding Spiller's accounts for the 12 months to May 1821, thinking that he had spent £10,000 in London alone. Nonetheless, he had spent overall almost £10,000 in Irish currency, or £9,000 English, on what Spiller called 'the positive expences of your establishment'. This meant that interest payments, family annuities and many other costs were not included and the expense of the King's affairs meant the general expenses were considerably underestimated. For the following two years, 1822 and 1823, London expenditure reached just over £3,000 English from his personal accounts and just over £6,000 English through his accounts with the bankers Puget and Bainbridge.[4]

The *Osprey* voyage, contrary to the usually accepted wisdom about such enterprises, saved no money. During the five years from 1817 to 1821, a total was spent through Puget and Bainbridge of more than £21,000 – over £4,000 a year. The two-year voyage itself cost about £10,500 up to August 1818. Belmore had, as already seen, spent about £10,000 on converting and fitting out the *Osprey* and preparing for the voyage. His annual income from Tyrone (now nearly £15,500 Irish), from Fermanagh (nearly £8,000 Irish) and from Longford (about £2,000 Irish), a total of £25,500 Irish or almost £23,000 English was absorbed by debt servicing and other expenses, but he was spending another £10,000 a year or so above that.

Belmore's own estimate of his debts, which had stood at £139,000 in 1815, assumed that they had risen to £150,000 by 1823. However, they were almost certainly more, taking into account the *Osprey* costs, election expenses, the furnishing of Castle Coole, of his house at Cowes on the Isle of Wight and of Seaview and the *Flying Fish*. Even at £150,000, interest payments alone were running at no less than £9,000 a year.

The fact is that nobody had a real grip on Belmore's financial situation, since his accounts were split between his local agents and Spiller and whichever bankers he managed to keep with him for the time being. There were several of these over the years. The lack of a complete overview no doubt suited him for the time being. That way he could play one agent or creditor off against another – but it would eventually end in tears. It was the Artemus Ward school of finance, but carried to extremes: 'Let us all be happy, and live within our means, even if we have to borrer the money to do it with'.[5]

Belmore's Fermanagh accounts for the three and a half years to January 1822 confirm that his total expenditure was almost £31,000, a rate of almost £9,000 a year. Income of £2,000 from the sale of cattle added to his Fermanagh rental income of £29,000 was just enough to cover it. In addition, his agent Richard Dane's fees were about £4,500 for the period, so Spiller could not be paid as he should have been: 'I have had no further amounts from Fermanagh since my last letter to your Lordship'.

In 1822, Armar and Henry went up to Christchurch, Oxford to complete their education. Then two unexpected events changed Belmore's political perspectives. In August, his most important political ally and connection to government, Castlereagh, committed suicide – a serious setback to Belmore's hopes of employment. These would eventually come to depend on the political fortunes of Castlereagh's illustrious friend, the Duke of Wellington.

Nearer home, General Sir Galbraith Lowry Cole, Somerset's cousin, resigned his seat as member for Fermanagh on being appointed governor of Mauritius. The county was usually represented (and had been since the seventeenth century) by a member or a relative of the Enniskillen family, but the Earl of Enniskillen's son, William Cole, was not yet old enough to contest the seat. Belmore immediately saw that this was the ideal opportunity to get his eldest son into the Westminster parliament as member for Fermanagh, even though the family's political heartland had been in Tyrone.[6]

'I have not lost a moment,' he wrote to Enniskillen. 'I have decided in bringing Corry forward, and your immediate interference with your friends will most essentially contribute towards his success'. As a result, Armar had to leave the university and return to Castle Coole to fight his first election. The manoeuvres which followed were typical of the style of politics of the time. Candidates, chosen by the landed families of the county whose interests they would represent, would either have to fight each other in an election or negotiate to be returned unopposed.

It was to be a bitter and expensive contest, for Corry's opponent was Sir Henry Brooke. The Brookes of Colebrooke had represented the county during the previous century but had been left behind in the race for a peerage by, amongst others, Belmore's father. Sir Henry now sought to get back into the game. The political bitterness was perhaps coloured by the relationship between Belmore and Lady Brooke mentioned earlier.

Corry spent a great deal of time and money travelling around Fermanagh, canvassing the freeholders, who were the only voters. 'Nothing has been left undone that activity can

The State bedroom, Castle Coole

accomplish … and Corry, etc have been very successful in the canvass,' wrote Belmore to Enniskillen in August. They then joined forces, arranging meetings at Castle Coole and Florence Court or writing to bring as many of the local gentry as possible to their side. The use of their powers of patronage enabled them to secure support by promising to appoint voters to positions they wanted, such as burgess of a borough or sheriff of the county. Towards the end of January 1822 the tension was building and Belmore, wanting to increase the pressure, wrote from Castle Coole to Enniskillen:

> 'I wish you and Hamilton would come over here. He can occupy Henry's room on the *ground floor*, close to the *water closet*, and handy for any *friend* he might wish to visit him'.

Their efforts were successful. Oddly, Armar, like Cole, was not himself of age when the election itself began, but the process took so long that he had come of age by the time he was elected in March 1823. Henry Brooke had retired from the contest as hopeless, but it was a Pyrrhic victory for Belmore and his son. The cost of electioneering amounted to no less than £8,000 and, as has been seen, this was money that Belmore did not have.

Nonetheless, an election success and a twenty-first birthday called for celebration and nowhere could have been better to celebrate in than the elegantly Grecian Castle Coole, now richly furnished in glittering Regency style. Everything that went into its design responded to the occasion. There were floral decorations everywhere. Fires were gleaming in the Doric fireplaces on on either side of the entrance hall; the Grecian torchères threw a warm glow onto the scarlet curtains and large Portuguese mat, with its red leather border. Beyond the four porphyry scagliola columns at the rear of the hall, through the open mahogany doors of the saloon, light blazed from a large chandelier, giving a tantalising glimpse of the extravagant scene beyond. The saloon's curved space, its mahogany doors decorated with painted panels, had four gilt sofas with crimson silk, four richly embossed gilt sofa tables, four large pier glasses and rich crimson window curtains lined with blue silk and trimmed with yellow silk lace. It was the heart of an elegant space, extending to left and right through the drawing room with its wealth of gilt chairs, sofas covered with striped yellow silk and sumptuous Turkey carpet; and the dining room, the windows hung with scarlet-and-black curtains, its long mahogany table set for a buffet, behind which stood the mahogany sideboard, pedestals and an oval wine cooler, all with panels painted by Biagio Rebecca, and, set out on the sideboard, a final glowing reflection of light from the Belmore silver gilt plate. The elegance of the rooms was highlighted by the delicate plasterwork designs on the ceilings. The whole parade sparkled with light from chandeliers and candles, enhanced by reflection from the pier glasses between the windows.

After the ball was over it was back to the cold light of day. Belmore's Fermanagh accounts for the period of his absence in the *Osprey* show an increasing tendency for delaying payment of bills for as much as three years.

Hulmandel, the printer and lithographer who created Belmore's collection of *Lithographs of Egyptian Papyri* had to take proceedings to secure payment in 1825. From the middle 1820s disputes over the bills due to Preston were in the hands of solicitors. It was dangerous to fail to pay creditors, as Belmore well knew. In December 1820 he had written to Dane from Hamilton Place:

> 'Last spring Harry Maxwell was arrested in this town and Lord Carrick and I were obliged to enter into an engagement that a certain sum should be paid'.

Belmore had drawn a bill on Puget and Bainbridge, bankers, for £250, which he asked Dane to pay. The tone of the letter is unusually humble, suggesting perhaps that not all the money was for Maxwell.[7]

During the 1820s Belmore borrowed large sums amounting to more than £35,000, some unsecured but the largest secured by mortgaging the Churchlands.

For his younger son, Henry, on the occasion of his 21st birthday, Belmore provided an allowance of £600 a year secured on lands in Tyrone, reserving for himself any income above that. Maria Watson had not fared so well for she had had to press for her quarterly allowance of £100 which had fallen seriously behind on several occasions. In 1811 Maria had given birth to twins, Richard Luther and Mary Anne Juliana. Mary Anne, named, perhaps, after Mary Anne and Juliana Belmore, died young. Maria's husband Charles had sold his commission as lieutenant colonel on retiring from his regiment in 1811. He had suffered serious ill health ever since his horse had been shot by a French sharpshooter and he had been thrown from it. In spite of a strict diet and medical care he died in 1814. Subsequently, Maria seems to have lodged in Bath and Paris until she married again – to

The Enniskillen Chronicle, and
ERNE PACKET.

,010.   **THURSDAY, MARCH 13, 1823.**   Price Five Pence.

TO THE INDEPENDENT ELECTORS
OF THE
COUNTY OF FERMANAGH.

GENTLEMEN,

WITH sentiments of unbounded obligation, of gratitude and pride, I offer my most sincere and heartfelt thanks for the distinguished honour you have conferred on me. by electing me your Representative in Parliament. Deeply as I feel this exalted favor, and highly as I appreciate the proud distinction you have been pleased to confer upon me, I have yet desired to repress the voice of triumph, to refrain from expressions of exultation, and upon this occasion, to confine my address to you, within the limits of a grateful acknowledgment of your disinterested kindness, and of those indefatigable exertions which have crowned your efforts with success. But when an address has been published under the sanction of Sir Henry Brooke's name, in which, on retiring from the contest, he ascribes his defeat to *a formidable Coalition*, and *defective Registry*, I feel myself bound in justice to that independent and generous support which I have received, to deny, in the most distinct terms, that any such cause has been the occasion of his failure.

If the almost unanimous support of the resident Gentry in the County, forms the *formidable Coalition* he alludes to, such support I have received, and for which I feel grateful: and if the failure of 400 votes, which he terms *his own Registry*, form a portion of what he considers the *Independent Interest* of the County, such, when amended, must, no doubt, contribute their influence to his support. But on this point, Gentlemen, I do not hesitate from authentic documents to state, that if no error had occurred in the Registry, the result of the contest must have placed me at the head of the poll, with a majority of votes to the amount of several hundreds; and at the time when Sir Henry deemed it prudent to retire, the decision of the Sheriff on the point of defective Registry, operated at least as much to the prejudice of my friends, as to those of my opponent.

It is *not*, Gentlemen, to a defective state in the registry, to which I owe my success. It is to the energetic and decided support which the independent interest of this county have been pleased to honour me with, and which now has been termed a *formidable Coalition*.

On this support, however, I rest my hopes of future favor. My strenuous efforts shall now be devoted to a faithful discharge of those duties you have confided to me; and, while I thus hope to maintain the good opinion of my friends, my next desire is to gain the approbation of those who opposed me.

I have the honour to be,
Gentlemen,
Your most obliged,
And most humble Servant,
CORRY.

Castlecoole, 10th March, 1823.

FERMANAGH ELECTION.

In our publication of last week we brought down our narrative of the Election proceedings to Wednesday inclusive. The polling was continued with great spirit on Thursday and Friday, with an increasing majority in favour of Lord Corry. At the close of the poll on Friday the numbers stood thus—

For Lord Corry	...	1056
For Sir Henry Brooke	...	932
Gross Majority for Lord Corry		124

On Saturday morning it was signified to the High Sheriff on the part of Sir Henry Brooke, that he intended to relinquish the contest. Sir Henry did not appear on the hustings, but in a printed address, he explained his failure as arising solely from the defective state of his own Registry, by which upwards of 400 votes were lost to him; and urged his friends to lose no time in registering their freeholds as he might soon again require their assistance, in finally achieving the independence of Fermanagh.

After Lord Corry had been declared duly elected, he addressed the electors in a speech of considerable length and animation. Circumstances, he said, had occurred since he last had the pleasure of meeting them, which were decisive as to the present contest. He had now to express his sincerest gratitude for the powerful and energetic support of his friends, which gave him so large and decided a majority. It had been said, and believed by some, that this majority was owing to the defective state of Sir Henry Brooke's Registry, but that defect operated equally against himself; and if the contest had been persevered in, he had no doubt there would be a majority of several hundreds more in his favour: "Gentlemen" said Lord Corry in conclusion, "the important trust you have reposed in me shall be faithfully and constitutionally discharged. Impressed with a deep sense of the high obligations and responsibility attached to the possession of that trust, it shall be my anxious study to use it, to the best of my judgment aided by your instructions, in promoting the general welfare of my country, and the particular interests of this county. It is unnecessary, I hope, to add any thing further in the way of profession. For the rest, I confess myself wholly unable to give adequate expression to the gratitude which I this day feel—this day, which I shall ever consider the proudest of my life, and the events of which will never be obliterated from my recollection." He then returned thanks to the High Sheriff, and his Assessor, and to his Agents, after which the Court was dissolved.

The preparations for the final ceremony of chairing were, by this time, completed, and his Lordship being placed in a handsome chair, fancifully decorated with orange and purple drapery and ribbons, was borne up and down the principal street, attended by several gentlemen, and an incredible concourse of country people, whose acclamations rent the air. His Lordship bowed repeatedly and gracefully in returning the salutations and greetings addressed to him as he passed, from the windows of the inhabitants, in which were assembled all the rank and beauty of the town and vicinity. We were particularly delighted to see the Countess of Belmore herself attending to witness the gay spectacle, and indulging those feelings of amiable sympathy and affectionate joy, so natural and honorable to the maternal character in such circumstances. A band of music played before the procession, and the ceremony ended without the slightest accident or disorder.

In the evening, Lord Corry dined at the White Hart with his Committee, and Agents, the High Sheriff, his Assessor and Deputies, besides a numerous party of his Lordship's friends. Nearly one hundred gentlemen sat down to a sumptuous dinner. The choice old claret of Castlecoole cellars was laid under welcome contribution, and circulated with no sparing hand. In the course of the night several gentlemen addressed the company in speeches appropriate to the occasion, which we are precluded from reporting this day for want of room. Among a number of loyal and patriotic toasts, Lord Corry gave "the Glorious and Immortal Memory," which was drunk with loud applause. The

hour, after spending a night replete with conviviality, harmony, and good humour.

Upon a general review of the whole proceedings we cannot help dwelling with particular satisfaction on the circumstance, that, whatever spirit of angry opposition might have been momentarily excited among their respective adherents, the most creditable sentiments of personal regard, and good feeling, subsisted throughout between the candidates themselves, and that their private friendship suffered no interruption or diminution by being thus accidentally placed in political competition. Another circumstance worthy of congratulation was, the absence from the contest of all those party feelings and prejudices which give so malignant a character to popular contentions. The few disputes that did unfortunately occur arose merely from the imprudent personal zeal of some individuals on behalf of their favourite candidate.

It is a painful part of our remaining duty to state, that the disposition to riot which we noticed last week, was renewed on Friday, by a savage mob, whose only freeholds appeared to be their cudgels, and who paraded the streets in a menacing manner as if for the purpose of intimidating the opposite party. We were still more shocked to see such a mob headed by two persons holding, or who ought to hold, a respectable rank in society, but whose names we suppress for the present out of delicacy. This band of ruffians, so encouraged, finding no opposition in the streets, and being determined, as it would seem, to signalize themselves in some way, attacked the house of a publican named Noble, near the East Bridge, frequented by the friends of Sir Henry Brooke. They had made considerable progress in demolishing the windows, when the proprietor, under the impulse of the moment, and alarmed for his property, fired out among them a gun loaded, we believe, with shot, by which four of the assailants were wounded, one of them it was first thought mortally, but we since learn his life is pronounced out of danger. The other three are but slightly injured. A military party having arrived by this time, the rioters dispersed in all directions, and tranquillity was restored. We abstain, from indulging any severity of comment on this outrage, as the affair, we learn, is in progress of investigation, but the nearly fatal consequences afford strong proof of the danger there always is in exciting popular feelings, which when once set in motion, no stop short of excess.

The subjoined statement, shewing the comparative numbers polled by each Member out of the different Baronies, will be interesting to our readers as matter of reference.

	For Lord Corry.	For Sir H. Brooke.
Magheraboy,	160	60
1st Magherastephena,	23	176
2d Do.	40	180
Knockninny,	89	86
1st Lurg,	210	122
2d Do.	135	104
Tyrkennedy,	123	107
Glenawly,	216	14
Clonkelly,	47	33
Coole,	8	34
	1056	982

Majority for Lord Corry, 124.

a Christopher Salter, by whom she had two children, Elliott and Elizabeth. Elizabeth eventually married Sir Charles Henry Darling.

Belmore knew that one way out of his money problems was a marriage between Corry and an heiress but, as Shakespeare warned, 'It is a wise father that knows his own child' and Belmore was about to find out how true that was. Shortly after his election success, and perhaps encouraged by it, Armar wrote to Belmore to announce that he had fallen deeply in love, had proposed to the lady and she had consented to marry him. Belmore exploded into such a fury that Armar was afraid to see him too soon, feeling 'like a bottle of old port that has been well shaken & it is as well to let the dregs subside a little before we meet'. Instead, he wrote to Lady Louisa, 'you are the only person to whom I can speak my mind on this subject'. In this, as in many other family matters, she was the trusted confidante. Belmore himself rushed off to see her, asking her to use her influence to make Armar change his mind. The girl was Sarah Juliana Maxwell, daughter of the Reverend Henry Maxwell (subsequently sixth Baron Farnham) and his wife Anne (*née* Butler).[8]

This episode illustrates perfectly the strain Belmore was under as a result of his heavy borrowing and the intractability of his character. The unfortunate Armar admitted that he had tried his best to overcome his feelings for Sarah. He had avoided seeing her since they had last parted company at Castle Coole 18 months previously at Christmas 1821:

> 'I did every thing in my power to get over an attachment which as far as worldly interest goes I know to be so injurious to myself, &, what I assure you had more weight, so annoying to my father & mother'.

After that lapse of time, he went back to see her again at her home at Mount Juliet, Kilkenny:

> 'I spoke to Sarah for the first time about marriage, when after making pretty much the same answer, I suppose, as young ladies in a similar situation generally do, she said: "But, my dear Corry, you must allow me to say that I love you a great deal too much to listen to such a thing for a moment if you cannot get your fathers consent, & thereby be the cause of disunion between you, & all its necessary evils, & do you imagine that he will ever allow you to marry me?" To which I answered that it would be affectation in me to say that he would not be annoyed at it, but that she might make her mind perfectly easy as to his giving his consent, for it was not six months since he told me that I might marry whoever I pleased, & that the worst we had to expect was to be obliged to wait'.

Armar's confident assurance was misplaced, even though it was based on a conversation with Belmore that had indeed taken place. But now he was being forced to accept that he should at his father's insistence, think of her only as a cousin:

> 'I may & will bow to parental authority, or rather as it appears to necessity, but more than that I cannot do. If I could not get over this attachment during the two years before I spoke to her about marriage, from what passed then & since there is but very little chance of my being more successful [in] those that are to come'.

An early photograph of the saloon, Castle Coole

Although his father expressed his satisfaction at Armar's apparently compliant answer, he completely underestimated the strength of Armar's feeling that he was being sacrificed to necessity. But Armar realised they could not 'live off love, as snipes do off suction'. Had it not been for her lack of money – 'that one fatal objection' – he could have waited for any length of time Belmore proposed. Neither she nor her family would have objected to that: 'I need hardly tell you that my feelings at this moment are not the most enviable'.

Lady Louisa's reply did not help. She made fun of his predicament and told him the girl would probably end up using him badly anyway. Girls, she said, never married their first loves and she would eventually settle down perfectly well with someone else. She found his notion that he was in some way committed to Sarah just because they had spoken about marriage, extremely amusing, but, in a letter to Lady Londonderry, she feared that if he persisted it would be 'utter destruction to the silly boy'. But the boy was not ready to give in.

> 'I am at present I fear in a different state of mind than when I wrote to you. I was then in one of those calms that generally follow a great storm, for when I received my fathers letter stating the circumstances (those eternal circumstances) that precluded the possibility of his giving his consent, I must confess I was in a most thundering rage'.

He denied he was as tractable as her wit had made him out to be. He would not quietly look on if they were going to marry her to another. He said he had told his father that as he could not afford it:

> 'I supposed I must let it drop. However I could only preserve this calm for a very few days & I will venture to say that I am as ill tempered a young man as any in the kingdom – I shall now proceed to repeat to you a conversation that passed between my

father & myself last March, when I suppose I was at least as young & inexperienced, & his affairs in pretty much the same state as they are at present – After expressing the great satisfaction he derived from the result of the election he began to talk of his affairs generally & their embarrassment & observed that I might remove a great part of it by marriage, when in the fullness of his heart he made the following speech. I can swear almost to the very words – "But, my dear Corry, don't for a moment suppose that I wish to force you in your choice; you must not look upon me as one of those stern fathers, who would put himself between you and the object of your choice; on the contrary if you *this moment* told me that your happiness depended on *any woman, I don't care who she was, so that she was a gentlewoman I would give my consent, & the most I should do would be to tell you to wait a little;* & I think it my duty to tell you this now, that you may be on your guard against too easily giving way to an imprudent attachment, *knowing that whoever the object of it may be of course if she is a gentlewoman you will meet with no opposition from me!!!'* You may possibly say, you must have misunderstood him – I say, I did not. When I wrote to ask his consent or rather claim his promise what answer do I receive? Just refer to his speech before you go on. "*Your youth & inexperience* alone would deter me from giving my consent to this match even if it had the advantages of *fortune*; besides as you are not ignorant of the state of my affairs *you must reproach yourself* for not considering that I could not afford it" – Is this fair? Is it even just? Is it not wantonly trifling with my feelings, in order I suppose the more easily to gull me with my eyes shut, into selling myself to some heiress, or for some other equally worthy passion? Reproach *myself!* Who may I ask has most reason to reproach themselves, he for having made a promise which he had neither the power nor the intention to perform, or I, for having been fool enough to believe him?'

He finished his letter with a declaration of his determination never to give her up:

> 'to marry her shall always be my first & last object if I have to go the devil in the attempt & my father has nobody to thank for it but himself. If I cannot sigh & whine & look as miserable as some of my woebegone brethren I can feel as strongly & may do more'.

But give her up he did, and it would be many years before he once again showed any interest in the idea of marriage.

Henry graduated from Oxford, and, in spite of his increasing financial difficulties, Belmore backed his campaign in June 1825 for election as member of parliament for Tyrone. This was something, at least, to satisfy Belmore's political ambitions and, although he could not have known it at the time, Henry was to enjoy a long and distinguished career in parliament. Nevertheless, it was yet another expense.

Captain Corry became a member of the Royal Yacht Club in 1830; he owned two yachts, one of 58 tons called the *Dolphin*, built in 1830, and *Phoeby*, a cutter of 33 tons. But, before that, like Armar, he had run up against Belmore's bad temper when money was mentioned and it was to Lady Louisa that he unburdened himself. After his return from the voyage of the *Osprey* he had commanded HMS *Satellite* in the East Indies where he was promoted to captain in command of HMS *Topaze* and then flag captain to Admiral Sir Henry Blackwood on HMS *Leander*. In February 1822 he was invalided home. In September 1826 he announced that he intended to marry Lady Paulett, rich but elderly. It was altogether too much for his siblings. When Lady Louisa wrote to tell him, Belmore was scathing:

> 'to think of marrying Lady Paulett!!! Rich certainly, but having said so, that one monosyllable comprehends all her attractions! Good heavens, what a stomach the dog must have – Lady Paulett!! The very "pis aller" for all fortune hunters! Well, well, well! – Confound me but I would take two to one she bury's [*sic*] him'.

There was more of the same but, unfortunately for him, Captain Corry's self-confessed reputation for womanising caught up with him. The lady received anonymous letters about his amours and when she made enquiries of his friends, including Belmore, they refused to vouch for him. His reputation 'made her take lofty ground to stand upon' and she broke off the relationship while continuing to express the warmest interest in his welfare. Behind the badinage and the caricaturing of a young man marrying an old woman, however, lay a deeper hurt for Corry:

> 'My feelings have been extremely lacerated, particularly by the letter from Lord B who mentioned that I am indebted to the Dowager Lady B for raising my prospects to the rank of a gentleman, saying my father only left £500 for my education which would hardly have apprenticed me to *a mechanic*'.

Captain Corry went straightaway to the source of this canard, Mary Anne Belmore in Bath. She told him he was always intended for the law and she had always heard the first Earl say that his 'natural' children were to have a small independence and a choice of profession should they wish. He pointed out that Maria was expressly provided for and he could not credit his father would leave him to starve. Belmore had consulted Babington about some provision for Captain Corry but Babington 'suggested my considering that *enough* had been done for me *already* by his Lordship'. Belmore's opinion was that Captain Corry had 'arrived as high as Interest could push him in his profession and just in the expectation of immediate employment' he had chosen instead to marry Lady Paulett. Obviously there was classic sibling rivalry between them and Belmore was not entirely wrong, for Captain Corry admitted to hoping she would still leave him something in her will. For his part, Captain Corry felt Belmore had arranged that he should be pushed off to sea in 1805, instead of being provided with an education and a legal career.

The differences were really about money, which neither of them had. Corry needed an allowance as he had had no employment since his return from the East Indies. A naval officer in peacetime had little money and little prospect of a command, even if he had influence. Two years later, in 1828, still hoping that Belmore would use his influence to get him employment, Captain Corry found to his chagrin that Belmore was using it instead to favour one of his captains from *Osprey* days, Captain Fair, by getting Lady Louisa to write to Lord Melville on Fair's behalf. But, as for money, which he still needed, 'the repugnance I feel to discuss money matters with him is so great that I fear to trust my own judgment'.

Chapter Fifteen

Governor, Vice Admiral and Lord Chancellor of Jamaica

Since his election as a representative peer in 1819, Belmore had been able to regain access to government ministers and establish a network of connections that might find him employment, but he was too much of a Tory to attract the favours of ministers of a different political persuasion. In 1828, however, the political scene changed dramatically with the emergence of Wellington as prime minister. Belmore, always a devoted follower of the Duke, was at last able to look for employment by government. The fact that he was an Irish peer and that one of the great issues of the day was Catholic emancipation may have encouraged his hopes. Pressure for emancipation had built up since the formation of the Catholic Association by Daniel O'Connell in 1823. The Duke of Wellington himself had privately drafted proposals for emancipation, subject to conditions, as part of his thinking about the problems of Ireland. In 1825, a bill for the relief of Catholics was debated in the House of Commons, but rejected by the Lords, following an outspoken objection to it by the Duke of York, successor to the throne.

Belmore was 'favourable to the principle of concession' but was one of those whose support was conditional on certain 'securities' being given by Catholics – principally a right of the Crown, within limits, to veto a proposed bishop or archbishop of the Irish Catholic Church. Belmore saw two major difficulties in the way of emancipation on these terms. First, those who opposed securities because they thought them invalid had not shown that they would negotiate with the Catholic Church to find a way to ensure their validity. Secondly, he thought that Catholics themselves needed to recognise that some concessions would be necessary in a Protestant state – and if they did not, he would oppose their claims. He refused to sign the Buckingham House resolutions in favour of civil equality for Catholics because they referred to a time when parliament might be *forced* to concede them. Completely in character, he said, 'I entertain no apprehension that that time can ever arrive'. As it turned out he was wrong. Wellington had seen that emancipation subject to securities was not really emancipation at all and preferred a negotiated relationship with Rome. The road to emancipation was opening up.

Meanwhile, Belmore fully supported Wellington's retreat from opposition to the repeal of the Test and Corporation Acts, which had required officers of corporations to take communion in the Established Church, thus excluding Dissenters from office. Lord Holland, sponsor of the repeal, wrote to Belmore after it had been passed by a 'triumphant' majority: 'I am proud of reckoning the marks of confidence and approbation I have received from your Lordship'.

By the end of 1828, although Belmore's attitude to emancipation remained the same, his own situation had completely changed. He had met Wellington at the beginning of the year to discuss the possibility of getting a colonial governorship when vacancies occurred. On 1 August the Duke wrote to the King with proposals for filling the vacant governments in North America and the West Indies, naming Belmore for Jamaica but grudgingly describing his proposals as 'the best that can be made under existing circumstances'. More optimistically, George IV wrote at the top of the letter, 'Highly approved'.[1] After an anxious six months, Sir George Murray, the Colonial Secretary, confirmed Belmore's appointment as governor, vice admiral and lord chancellor of Jamaica, with an annual income of between £5,500 and £6,500, including salary and fees.

In December, shortly before he was to leave England, Belmore increased his personal commitment to Wellington's policies by leaving him with two blank proxy forms for the nomination of a suitable person to vote on Belmore's behalf in support of his government, come what may. As for emancipation, if the government took it up, as he expected it would, he would not offer any opposition to it. If on the other hand it were not a government measure, he would continue to hold his previous position – while he supported the principle, he had never seen a bill the details of which he could support.

> 'Still, however, I consider the expediency so pressing for endeavouring to arrive at some means of arranging it, that I should feel inclined to make considerable sacrifices to accomplish so great an end'.

In practice, Belmore would support any measure recommended by the government. His sons did not. Although Corry would have accepted an investigation to see whether, in principle, 'something could not be done', he was temporising, for when the detailed proposal for emancipation was brought to the House of Commons, Corry and Henry Corry both voted with the minority against it.

Lady Louisa arranged for the previous governor, the Duke of Manchester, to meet Belmore at Hinchingbrooke to give him the benefit of his experience of Jamaica. His principal advice was that Belmore should not sail until at least the beginning of October, to avoid the hurricane season. This suited Belmore, for he had already asked Sir George Murray for more time to allow Juliana, who was to go with him, to complete their preparations. In reality, he also needed time to ease his cash flow by selling Hamilton Place (for which he got £30,000) and the valuable living of the village of Clogherny (which brought in a further £14,000).[2]

Belmore left lengthy pencilled instructions for his son Armar in a notebook about matters needing attention at Castle Coole. He attempted to have Captain Corry appointed as captain of the *Herald*, the vessel that was to take him to Jamaica, but this was refused because a captain was already in post. Belmore who, not unsurprisingly, had wanted to be taken in a navy warship, was persuaded that the *Herald* would be more comfortable than a frigate and that guns, in any case, were not necessary 'in the present state of the world'.

Belmore was still in England on 29 December 1828 because westerly winds prevented a departure. The *Herald* finally set sail in January and was nearly lost in an accident on the way. Twiss of the Colonial Office wrote to Belmore on 5 March 1829:

'I am very much obliged to you for your note detailing the particulars of your accident and escape. It was particularly welcome intelligence after the alarming reports which we had heard of your having been actually lost'.

Belmore arrived in Jamaica on 20 February 1829.

The perils of the journey were not the only difficulties attending such an appointment. Others included the long lapses of time in communications between the Governor and the Colonial Office in London and, for a new governor, his enforced detachment from normal society in view of what his private secretary, William Bullock, described as his 'high and delicate' situation as the King's representative. This detachment and his inexperience meant that Belmore necessarily had to rely heavily on the advice and guidance given to him by Bullock until, at least, he was able to get a feel for how things worked there. Belmore's isolation was intensified by the remoteness of the first living quarters found for him, a private house in the mountains at Phoenix Park. It needed alterations to suit his family but was still not ready by the end of March. Wind and heavy rain battered the house and he commented ironically, 'the climate is certainly very refreshing'; but the food was not, for he had no cook.

His gloom was added to by the lack of male company and he wrote to Bullock, 'if you do not come to see me I must soon desert for never before have I found myself without one of my own sex to converse with'. The isolation seriously affected his ability to do his job. It was almost as if he had been deliberately sidelined. The Governor's official residence, King's House in Spanish Town, was not large enough to accommodate his family. To Bullock he wrote again:

'The want I feel at present is the assistance of someone through whom I could transmit directions and that I find it both disagreeable and inconvenient to stand alone – at present I am the Governor, private secretary, Militia secretary, but without the possible means of knowing, when I am visited, whether I am talking to a Proprietor or an Overseer, a Member of Assembly or the least among his constituents'.

Not only was Belmore a jack of all trades but he was seriously out of touch. The first he knew about disputes arising out of applications for exemption for service in the militia was when he saw the issues raised in the newspapers, before he heard from Bullock. These applications were to be a bone of contention for him later.

Bullock offered a solution to Belmore's lack of male company, no doubt meaning to be helpful, but this would also become another source of trouble for Belmore:

'I am very sorry to find that you feel so much the want of society at Phoenix Park – I wish you could draw the parson to you for I know him to be a most delightful companion and his tastes are very similar to your own'.

A View of the King's House and Public Offices at St. Jago de la Vega.
Published as the Act directs July 1, 1774.

The Governor's house on the right and the Court House on the left

The parson was the Reverend George Bridges, Anglican Rector of St Anne's parish – whose tastes, like Belmore's, included an interest in studying the stars and in navigation. They spent hours together making handwritten observations of the heavens for navigation and for setting a telescope and micrometer at a particular spot in Jamaica. Belmore had brought his own reflector there. He was very glad to make the acquaintance of Mr Bridges, but he had also become cautious about relying on the Rector's opinions about business: 'I have, however, learned reason enough since I have been here not all at once to desire to fix upon him as the person to supply these deficiencies'. Bridges became a frequent visitor, who often stayed overnight. In 1827, he dedicated his book, *The Annals of Jamaica*, to Belmore, no doubt attempting to impress on a sceptical Belmore his own extreme vision of the remedies for the problems of Jamaican life.

The three family members suffered, as many new arrivals to Jamaica did, from various ills through the spring and summer. Belmore was ill with 'feelings of indisposition and uneasy sensations in the head'. Juliana Brooke had a fever and needed the attention of two doctors but, by July, the Belmores were 'relieved from anxiety about Miss Brooke'. Belmore suffered so much from gout of the elbow that he was unable to write but was 'delighted to employ Lady Belmore's assistance'. To cap it all, he was twice injured by falling from his old grey horse, which he was advised not to trust again. Belmore's leg, with its old injury, was badly hurt and he suffered great pain for many weeks. Eventually, by the end of July, he was able to write to Bullock, 'with the aid of crutches I have just succeeded to get from my bedroom to the sofa in the Gallery and, on the whole, made a gallant walk of it'. The final insult was an invasion of the house by yellow snakes, 'which emit a pestilential stench', and were mostly in the apartments of the two Julianas. By the end of September they seemed to have recovered from the attacks of pests, but their ailments were sufficiently serious to give rise to rumours in the English papers that Belmore was to return early. Belmore did not give up that easily and in August he had acquired a new house, Highgate, which had been substantially remodelled for the family.

Belmore's personal affairs were the background to a much more troubled public situation which clamoured for his attention as soon as he arrived. Lieutenant General Sir John Keane, who had been acting governor, summed up the problems in a report he wrote at the end of January to bring Belmore up to speed. The assembly was being extremely difficult. It had attempted to have the right to appoint public officers removed from the Governor and council to its own appointee. When Keane rejected the proposal the assembly revived it by making it an integral part of a finance bill, intended to raise money for the administration. When Keane rejected it again, as they knew he would, the whole bill failed, with the result that there was no money to pay creditors of the public service.

These difficulties reflected the resistance of white settlers to having their affairs regulated from London. Those particular issues, however, were minor compared with the tensions and difficulties caused by what were obviously the major sources of friction – slavery and the treatment of slaves. There were some 300,000 slaves on the island owned by a relatively small white population. The British government were intent on ameliorating the conditions of the slaves, especially in achieving greater toleration of their religious beliefs, and had also begun to respond to the growing movement for emancipation spearheaded by many Christian organisations – some of whom, Baptists and Methodists in particular, had missions in Jamaica. The Anglican Church, jealous of the possible effects on its own congregations, watched with concern the increasing influence of sectarian missionaries. George Bridges's future behaviour was to reflect this concern to an unfortunate degree.

Successive slave bills passed in the Jamaican assembly were the means by which the British government sought to improve the lot of slaves. Sir John Keane had previously presented a slave bill to that same restless assembly for its approval, but the assembly would only pass a version containing provisions that had already been disallowed by the Colonial Office in 1826. Keane rejected it. In a fit of pique, the assembly, awkward as ever, then refused to pay for iron bedsteads that Keane had already purchased for the troops in Jamaica. It proposed also to discontinue their subsistence allowances. These moves were also rejected by Keane. Not to be put down, they then passed a bill in favour of Jews, which the Colonial Office had already ruled unnecessary. Keane prevented it coming into effect by a formal suspension clause. Exasperated, frustrated and unable to get its own way, the assembly angrily departed and refused to reassemble when called upon to do so in the King's name.

Such was the state of affairs when Belmore arrived. He now had the unenviable and pressing task of getting an acceptable version of the Slave Bill passed and the finances of government restored, but had no assembly through which to work.

Underlying all the difficulties of any administration at that time was the determination of the plantation owners and other European settlers to maintain control over their privileges and way of life. The white population was becoming increasingly defensive and, by the same token, aggressive towards proposals to improve the conditions of slaves. One member of the assembly suggested that a despatch on the subject from England should be burnt by the common hangman. They blamed missionaries for instilling ideas of freedom and self-worth into slaves in the name of Christianity. Bullock said 'the inhabitants continually "tread on volcanic matter" and circumstances excite alarm and anxiety here' which go unnoticed in England.

Such anxieties, crystallised in the assembly debates, also simmered, and occasionally boiled over, in the countryside where slaves were often too harshly treated by those who feared the consequences if they were to slip out of control and rebel. The sheer size of the slave population was enough to frighten the settlers. There were laws protecting slaves, including special courts of protection, but since they were administered by members of a population that included slave owners, abuse was frequent. In his time as governor, Belmore had to deal with abuses by high-handed slave owners, magistrates who supported them rather than doing their legal duty to protect slaves, missionaries who insisted on special rights (such as exemption from the general requirement to do militia duty) and those whose preaching caused unrest.

Militia duty, in the absence of a police force and any large military establishment, was an important obligation of all eligible males. White settlers carried their prejudices with them as officers of the militia. If they showed leniency to slaves they could incur the displeasure of their commanding officers. Prejudice, however, was much harsher in its effects on slaves. All too often it was found deeply embedded in the very system that was meant to protect them: the magistracy and the Courts of Protection.

This, then, was the context in which Belmore had to exercise the authority delegated to him by the English government in the name of the King. Written instructions, rather like standing orders, were included with the documents appointing him, but they could not be expected to fit all situations. If they did not do so, he could write for specific instructions or use his discretion. In either case, he might well need the understanding and support of his chief, the Colonial Secretary. He certainly had to rely on the advice and experience of his private secretary, Bullock. At the beginning of his term these two elements worked in his favour; but from the moment of Lord Goderich's appointment in November 1830 everything changed.

Bullock was an influential attorney who acted for a number of absentee landowners and held public offices besides those of governor's secretary and island secretary. While his tactical and practical advice about relations with the assembly and the Colonial Office were usually sound, he himself shared many of the attitudes of the white settlers and plantation owners. In May 1831 he joked about colour prejudice:

> 'to remove all distinction of *colour* Mr Lynch has set a most patriotic example by
> marrying the amiable and accomplished Miss Nancy Speight with whom he has

corresponded … so long that one should have thought his pen had almost been worn out – and this he has done without changing colour!! Mr Williams, the attorney, emulating Mr Lynch's bright example has also married his squaw'.

Bullock marked this letter 'most private', which reveals another of Belmore's problems – leaks from Government House. Bullock warned against quoting his remarks in front of Captain Ramsay, Belmore's *aide-de-camp* and a notorious gossip, who was certain to repeat the story and the identity of its author. In August, he had to warn Belmore again that Ramsay had leaked a dinner-table remark of Belmore's about elections in Kingston. In that closed coterie Bullock was probably jealous of Ramsay's closeness to Belmore.

Happily, though, life was not all politics, even if politics was the business that had brought Belmore to Jamaica. Keane's soldierly humour hinted at the pleasures of social life and, as it happens, Belmore's coterie and style of life were recorded by none other than Captain Corry.[3]

He had sailed from Falmouth on 30 October 1830 in a schooner, the *Dolphin* (217 tons), with a crew of only two men. He arrived just before Christmas and stayed until 14 March 1831.

On Christmas day he went to church and was 'much struck by finding a Congregation almost entirely black', and had already begun to use his eye for the ladies, remarking particularly in what 'fine clothes the Sable Ladies were decorated, white cambric and fine muslin being the favourite ingredients'. In the evening they all 'took a drive (a daily custom) through some of the prettiest grounds in the neighbourhood' and a large party assembled for dinner. The carriage was brought to the door of the house at 4.45 p.m. every day for a drive. Belmore went about in his own curricle and Captain Corry usually went with him: 'All the population are keeping their New Year holiday, drums, music and dancing at every corner … a mass of discordant sounds'.

During the drive, the Captain happened to remark on what seemed to him the happiness and contentment of the slaves he had seen. Belmore replied with an anecdote which the Captain was sure would not be believed in England. A negro had just applied to him for work as a mason but because the work had already been contracted for there was none for him to do. The man then urgently pressed Belmore to get him a good master 'whose slave he was willing to become in order to be taken care of, as slaves usually are in this country'. The man said that although he had been a slave, had worked out and purchased his freedom, he had suffered more from unemployment and other causes since he became free than he had ever done as a slave. The anecdote illustrates the thinking behind Belmore's speeches later in the House of Lords about the condition of slaves if they were to be emancipated without careful planning.

On Sunday morning there were the usual prayers before everyone went to their rooms to write letters to England in time for the packet boat which was to sail the following morning. On Boxing Day the Captain encountered the next set of irresistible ladies:

> 'At this season the slaves have regular Christmas Holydays, and at this moment there is a set of girls, 12 in number, dancing in the large ballroom. It is a privilege which

Red Set – Girls and Jack-in-the-Green dancing by Isaac Mendes Belisario

their owners neither can nor wish to interfere with, and it is amusing to see *slaves*, which some well meaning people in England imagine to be very ill off – dressed in costly garments doing just what they like … I hear that some of them during this week will lay out from £20 to £30 upon their costumes'.

In fact, the dancers were organised into sets, one of whom was elected as mother of the set. She collected a few dollars from each to put towards the dresses. There were three sets, all dressed differently and none of whom wore the same dresses from one day to the next. 'The prettiest girls I hear are adverse to marriage although not to its consequences'. They were saved from the Captain because he thought none of them remotely pretty but, 'I never saw what appeared to me a happier population notwithstanding they are but slaves'. Unlike Belmore, who accepted without question the moral case for emancipation, Captain Corry allowed himself to be beguiled by superficial attractions.

After dinner one evening later in January, the ladies retired, as was usual, but when they all went downstairs to the ballroom they found it brilliantly lit. There were three sets of dancers, each with their own musicians, ready to perform. One set wore white muslin dresses with three tiers of roses, white necklaces and turbans; another wore red muslin picked out in black and turbans; and the third wore orange dresses with black lines curving around them and turbans:

> 'First, one set commenced a slow march to "God save the King" which, however, was soon changed to one more lively and purely native. There was no resisting this and in an instant every foot was in motion'.

Belmore's party, finding the music served equally well for a reel, danced together behind the columns at the end of the room, until their 'sable friends' retired, after which tea was served. The tables and chairs were pushed back 'as in some English Houses' and they danced a quadrille. The party ended a few minutes before midnight with a waltz.

A few days later, on 7 January, they set off in carriages at three o'clock to go to Highgate, the Belmores' private house up in the mountains.

They had to leave the carriages and proceed on saddle horses through a ravine, creeper-covered rocks rising high above them, and then through the cool shade of 'orange trees loaded with ripe fruit. The Pomela (the forbidden fruit), cedars, cabbage trees, bamboo … no words could describe the beauty of the landscape'. The assembly was building a new road to make the Governor's access easier. Later in the month the weather turned extremely cold and they all huddled around the fire, while outside a stiff north wind blew.

Captain Corry spent much of his time sailing around the island, often accompanied by Belmore. On one occasion they visited HMS *Blanche* which had recently arrived. The yards were all manned, the officers in full dress uniform, and as they left a 19-gun salute was fired. It was something of a come-down for Captain Corry when he learned that the crew of the *Dolphin* had been fighting amongst themselves. He had to discipline them, sacking the most unruly, William Downing. He seems to have left the *Dolphin* behind – on 14 March, he left for England as a passenger on HMS *Victor*, Captain Keane. Captain the Honourable Cavendish, recently made post, was a fellow passenger. Captain Corry arrived at Spithead on 27 April after a stormy voyage.

French Set – Girls with a 'shaka' (a rattle) and men with a drum made from barrels and goatskin
by Isaac Mendes Belisario

Shortly before he left, writing about a breakfast he had eaten at Highgate, he was impressed by the abundance of natural food in the countryside:

> 'I, this morning, ate some breadfruit for breakfast, and I may note it down that in this country rolls grow on trees – cabbages are 20 years old, some say fifty, the cabbage stalks are 40-50 and 60 feet high and oysters grow on trees – and you can buy three fine pineapples for twopence'.

The Captain was once again inadvertently reflecting views held by Belmore in the emancipation debates later in the House of Lords: his experience of the natural abundance of Jamaica led him to worry that it could provide freed slaves with food without the need for work, thus undercutting any government scheme for a system of contracts of employment.

Belmore's difficulties with the assembly and the Colonial Office really began with the appointment in November of Lord Goderich as colonial secretary. He had become used to dealing with Sir George Murray, an old soldier possessing sound judgement and common sense, who could accept that distance and local conditions required Belmore to exercise some discretion – even though he advised him, in case of doubt, to follow his written instructions. Besides, they had been political allies. Goderich, on the other hand, whose letter announcing his appointment arrived on 21 January 1831, was a weak administrator, afraid to delegate. He had failed in a short spell of less than six months as Tory prime minister and had then switched his allegiance to the Whig party of Earl Grey, resulting in his appointment as colonial secretary. Two of his nicknames encapsulated the nature of the man – 'the Blubberer' and 'the Duke of fuss and bustle'. Personally and politically Belmore and Goderich were antagonists.

The 'fuss and bustle' in Goderich's despatches began almost immediately and, as the months went by, such was his carping criticism that it became quite clear to Belmore that his time as governor was coming to an end. From the moment he knew of Goderich's appointment Belmore was paying careful attention in his official despatches to study how far it was 'necessary or prudent for me to couple myself with Lord Goderich in his Colonial policy'. By March he was instructing Bullock that Goderich 'evidently writes under an impression that I have adopted a temporising policy, and I wish to repel it'. He emphasised to Bullock that his despatches should be:

> 'ably and argumentatively replied to, totally devoid of sarcasm or anything which could betray personal feeling, because, if the period of my administration be drawing to a close, I must feel desirous not to lose … the means now afforded to me of justifying a course I have pursued'.

What was that course? Belmore was determined to resist what he thought to be Goderich's enthusiasm for overriding the legal structures of Jamaica in the name of protecting and improving the conditions of the slave population. The respect for established constitutional arrangements, which he had learned from his old tutor Townshend and to which he had appealed so strongly in the union debates, now came to the fore once again.

Goderich, writing under the intense pressure of the anti-slavery movement, was impatient to be seen getting on with the removal of all abuses, but was faced with what he saw as Belmore's stonewalling. Belmore admitted the truth of this when he told Bullock that he intended 'to check a line of policy which appears to be not only uncongenial, but inconsistent with the principles of the British Constitution'. Goderich wanted Belmore to override the Courts of Protection and, in Belmore's words, 'supply the place of a protector of Slaves, and war with the magistracy and planters in all directions'. It was Belmore's old favourite argument, the supremacy of constitutional principles.

In any case, Belmore was against Whig policies, in particular the administration's proposal to reform the franchise. He was not alone, for both Armar and Henry were to oppose Lord Grey's Reform Bill. Belmore took the view that reform was 'no gradual improvement in the constitution, conforming to any change in time or circumstance. It is a revolution'. He was about to face the reality of revolution nearer home.

Slaves in the west of the island believed that the British government had granted emancipation but that their owners were hindering its implementation. They rebelled in December 1831. It was the most dangerous and destructive rebellion in the history of the island.

Belmore declared martial law and by 1 February General Sir Willoughby Cotton was able to report that the army and militia had the situation under control, with most slaves returning peaceably to work. To secure the situation further, Belmore issued an amnesty on 3 February to all those who would come in within ten days, provided they were innocent of serious offences. The assembly, on the other hand, shocked by the dangers, resolved not to consider any proposals for improvement of the conditions of the slaves in the current session.

Settlers, too, began to take revenge against Baptist and Methodist ministers whom they accused of inciting slaves to violence. Baptist ministers petitioned Belmore, saying they had been seriously threatened and had to seek refuge in HMS *North Star* for protection. Their dwellings had been entered and their possessions destroyed or plundered and their chapels were destroyed – under the countenance, and with the aid, of magistrates and the militia. Belmore issued a proclamation against these attacks in February 1832 but, in spite of this, other magistrates ordered the closure of Methodist chapels, using the excuse that Belmore's proclamation required them to restore order. Mr Bleby, a Wesleyan missionary, was attacked by overseers and townspeople. He was tarred and feathered and an attempt was made to set him on fire.

Belmore attempted to restrain such excesses. He expressed concern about the punishment of rebel slaves because extreme measures, especially the death sentence, resulted in mistakes becoming irreversible. In a letter of 23 February 1832 he regarded six out of ten executions as 'a terrible average' and, if that continued, the consequence would be that 144 out of 240 slaves 'still must suffer'. He was convinced that 'so sanguinary a proceeding cannot be permitted'. He was anxious to show mercy to those who were not so active in the rebellion and in April 1832, to prevent summary executions, he ordered that all proposals for execution were to come before him for prior approval.

In April, even though Belmore could claim that his measures had at last resulted in calming the island, he was aware that he was to be recalled. In an early case of government leaking its intentions to prepare the ground, missionaries on the island had been informed of Belmore's forthcoming recall and had spread the news among their slave congregations. Ironically, even Goderich had been forced to acknowledge Belmore's success in dealing with the rebellion. But Belmore was fed up with being the government's scapegoat and wanted out, as he explained on 21 April 1832 to Sir Willoughby Cotton:

'I have received long communications approving of my conduct and it is not a little flattering to me to know that the order for my recall at this moment even Lord Goderich thinks unfortunate, but no intimation either of recall or a desire that I should remain here has arrived – I shall await the arrival of the next packet, when, if nothing more be said I shall expedite my departure as soon as possible on the supposition that the communication I have received is understood as a recall and I shall so inform Lord Goderich by the next packet. Nothing but a command shall keep me here'.

By the end of the month Goderich's detailed charges against Belmore's administration arrived. The fact that they had taken two of the worst months in Jamaica's history to get there reflected an abiding problem of colonial administration, the delays and hazards of communications.

From the beginning of his ministry Goderich could and would see nothing but resistance to his policies by Belmore. He expressed the case against him in formal and gentlemanly language, but it was at the same time deadly – calculated to destroy Belmore's reputation and protect his own.

Allowing for some grouping together of similar allegations, Belmore was accused of some 14 serious breaches of duty. The government, asserted Goderich, needed 'zealous and cordial cooperation' for achieving their aims but had found that:

'[Belmore's] views and sentiments on the most important questions involved in the government of Jamaica, so far as they can be judged from your measures, are so much at variance with their own, as to have tended to frustrate their intentions on matters of great moment, and to impede their efforts for what they have deemed to be evils and abuses'.

He accused Belmore of ignoring standing instructions requiring him to control the assembly's attempts to obstruct improvements in the lot of slaves. It is true that Belmore allowed the Slave Bill of 1829 to pass, but only because he could see a trade-off between its bad and its good clauses and because it would not take effect for seven months, giving the Privy Council in London ample time to disallow the bad clauses. What he could not have foreseen was that the King's illness prevented the Privy Council from meeting to consider the Bill, an accident of fate which Murray had understood, but which Goderich chose to ignore. Belmore commented:

'the answer I received from your Lordship's predecessor … gave me no reason to expect that my conduct on this occasion would expose me to future censure'.

Goderich cited four other cases of acts passed by Belmore which he considered 'highly injurious to the Slave Population'. He was mistaken, for they had been passed in accordance with instructions and without previous criticism. Belmore commented sardonically that his experience in the island had not, in any case, enabled him to discover how they could affect the slave population.

Goderich then wilfully linked two cases, which he acknowledged showed no personal animosity on Belmore's part towards missionaries, with a third, to attempt to prove exactly the opposite. The latter was one of a number of examples used by Goderich in which missionaries complained about the ill treatment of slaves – not to Belmore or to any of the authorities in Jamaica, but directly to the Colonial Office. Goderich's problem was that he tended to suppose the complaints were well founded. He had forgotten, or had chosen to overlook, that he had already written to Belmore conceding that 'I must entirely disavow any intention of attributing to you a deficiency of zeal for His Majesty's Service, or for the protection of the Slave Population of Jamaica'. Belmore pointed out that Goderich appeared simply to have changed his mind. Blithely ignoring his previous opinion, Goderich now sought to add an accusation that the complainant, Mr Whitehouse, had been left personally to take the risk of prosecuting the offender, a magistrate, with no help from Belmore and the authorities. This was untrue. Whitehouse had not provided sufficient corroboration of his allegations, was not prepared to swear to them on oath and had done nothing to protect the slave, a member of his own congregation. Given those facts, the Attorney General advised Belmore that there was no basis for a prosecution. Belmore had acted correctly and told Goderich so in no uncertain terms:

> 'Whilst your Lordship was inditing the fundamental and incurable difference between my sentiments and those of His Majesty's Government upon "subjects connected with the protection of slaves" and "the vindication of the principles of religious liberty" I stood between the Missionaries and popular clamour. I daily read their acknowledgements of the protection I afforded them in one part of the Public Press, and the calumnies levelled against me by those who sought their destruction in another'.

Wherever Goderich accused him of failing to act, Belmore was usually able to show it was because he could not know of problems until they were brought to his attention: the Governor was a remote figure.

One case, however, could have caused problems for Belmore. The Reverend George Bridges, the companion of his early days and frequent visitor to Highgate, was accused not only of cruelly mistreating a slave, Kitty Hilton, but also of overzealously criticising slaves who wished to leave his congregation to join one of the Baptist or Methodist chapels, to the point of persecution. Because of their friendship with him, Belmore and Bullock tried to help Bridges in formulating his account of the facts to the Colonial Office. It was a risky thing to do because Bridges got out of control, using increasingly intemperate language and attempting to have ill-conceived opinions published in the press. Goderich, mistakenly, simply criticised Belmore for failing to provide information about the case to the Colonial Office and for expressing support of Bridges. Belmore denied that he had ever intended to express any opinion in favour of Bridges but, in fact, described him as an indiscreet man who had, by his outspokenness, made himself unpopular in his parish.

Goderich accused Belmore of failing to ensure that owners who punished slaves too severely were prosecuted. Belmore pointed out that the law at the time had permitted such punishment but had since been repealed by his administration. He added, perceiving Goderich's weakness:

> 'Your Lordship will excuse me for offering an observation which may be found to apply to other parts of your correspondence, as well as the present, that I have never considered I have been sent here to make laws, but to administer them'.

It was a question, once again, of constitutional rights. Belmore was outraged by Goderich's complete disregard, in his pious zeal to remedy apparent abuses, for due legal process. A slave owner, Mrs Clarke, was accused of compelling her slaves to steal grass from the land of a Mr Taylor, but Taylor would not produce evidence or swear an affidavit to support his charge. The magistrates could not therefore proceed. Goderich, nonetheless, in his anxiety to have a public and open inquiry into the allegations, insisted she be brought before them. Belmore was:

> 'unable to conjecture on what principle of law, any individual can be put on trial, against whom no informations are laid, nor anyone willing to appear to prosecute, or that, on a simple statement, unsupported by affidavit, and which the informer refuses to substantiate by the production of witnesses, the Magistrates would have exercised a proper discretion by summoning a lady hitherto of unimpeachable character, in order to afford a chance of eliciting some evidence against her'.

Mrs Clarke was acquitted.

In truth, the real problem was that the Councils of Protection, set up to protect slaves, did not work because members of the Councils were drawn from the settler population, who could not be expected to sympathise with slaves. Actually, both men agreed about this, but they fell out because they could not cooperate to find a better system of protection. Because of their differences, it was easier for Goderich to blame Belmore for the problems than to propose a better way forward. He made too many mistakes in his despatch, which enabled Belmore to expose the prejudice behind it:

> 'Your Lordship has made an abstract of all the letters to be found in your office, which contains many imputations on my public conduct, or call for explanation, and my justification is founded on documents which are also in your Lordship's possession, but which have been strangely overlooked. I have pointed out much inaccuracy in these statements … illustrative, in no small degree, of the pains which have been taken to make out the case to which I have now replied'.

That was not the last Goderich would hear of the matter. He had taken on the wrong man and would have to answer for it. The assembly, meeting in May to pay its respects to Belmore on his forthcoming departure, declared that his local knowledge of the real condition of the slaves of Jamaica had given him the honest conviction of his own unbiased judgement. Belmore replied:

> 'The real condition of the slaves, it is true, must be seen to be known, and then it admits of various gradations. The real cause of your present distress results from the policy by which slavery was originally established and that fine Island can never develope [*sic*] the abundance of its resources whilst slavery continues. But it is obvious to everyone capable of forming an opinion on this important question, that any sudden measures produce consequences equally disastrous to the master and the Slave, to the UK and her Colonies'.

In June, Belmore and his family left on the *Sparrowhawk*, calling in at Havana on their way to New York.

Chapter Sixteen

Home, a Proud Victory and Family

By August, Belmore was back. Staying with Lady Louisa at her house in Dover Street, London, he lost no time in writing to and visiting ministers and friends to counter the unfavourable publicity that had surrounded his recall. He saw the Duke of Wellington first, who thoroughly disapproved of the recall:

> 'The King's Ministers may recall an officer who does not agree in opinion with them, if they should think proper. But they ought to be quite assured that the facts on which they found the censure of his conduct are true, and of a nature to have been avoided by him – quite inexcusably and highly injurious to the public service – before they bring them forward as the motive of his removal'.

Goderich delayed seeing Belmore as long as he could, but eventually had to give in. He tried to discourage Belmore from raising the matter in parliament, even though he had to admit it was natural and reasonable that Belmore wanted to. His reluctance did not surprise anyone – especially Wellington, who gave Goderich's excuses short shrift, feeling that it was important for the truth about Belmore's recall to be made known to the public.

In February the following year, Belmore had his day in the House of Lords, defending himself with complete success. Shortly afterwards, on 9 March 1833, his colleague in Jamaica, Sir John Keane, summed up the reactions of Belmore's friends in a letter to him. He remarked on the bigotry and lack of understanding of Antilles affairs and added:

> 'The like attack was never composed before. From its start to its finish it carries a fiery uncharitableness beyond example, but, my Lord, in my humble opinion you have in great force turned the enemy's flank and gained a *Proud Victory* and which has afforded me a sincere ecstasy – Viva, Hurrah, my dear and Noble Governor'.

There remained the debate in parliament on the bill to emancipate slaves. Given his experience as a governor, Belmore's views were important; given the unfair criticism he had suffered, he needed to justify his opinion that the moral drive for emancipation required a practical outcome.

In his speech in the House of Lords he said he would not prolong the existence of slavery:

> 'for a single hour beyond the period when, with safety and in justice, so uncongenial with our free institutions, it could be dispensed with … provided it could be effected on principles of justice as regards right of property, of safety to the commerce and

financial concerns of the country and contributed to produce ultimate advantage to the Negro population in our Colonies by promoting Industry, Civilization and Social Order among them'.

Belmore warmed to his theme. There were 301,723 slaves in the island – which provided a natural abundance of wholesome and nutritious fruits that the slaves could eat without the trouble of toil. Would Adam and Eve have toiled in paradise if they had not been thrown out for their offences? 26 days a year was sufficient for slaves to work for food for themselves. If laws were passed to make the slaves work they would have to be tyrannical and despotic, and even then were unlikely to be effective. He agreed that emancipation, which had already been approached slowly by previous administrations, should no longer be delayed – but should only come into effect if the Minister could show that his designs were practical in their execution and consistent with public property. The fact that compensation was to be paid afforded proof that injury would certainly follow. In any case the £20 million provided for compensation was inadequate to save the colonists from ruin. Nothing would actually be gained beyond the mere assertion of an abstract principle. If the measure did not maintain the value of trade with the colonies, it failed.

As it turned out, Belmore was not entirely wrong. Although emancipation was a moral victory it was a practical disaster, for neither slave nor planter prospered under its arrangements. The island's trade and prosperity declined.

A Season of Painful Uncertainty

The political career of Belmore's son, Armar Corry, ended after his election for a third term as MP for Fermanagh in 1830. He had previously had the support of the Enniskillen family because his cousin, Viscount Cole, had developed no interest in politics. That changed in 1831. Although the previous election had taken place as recently as 1830, parliament was dissolved by the death of George IV and a new election was called. Much to Belmore's chagrin Enniskillen wrote to him while he was still in Jamaica at the beginning of 1831:

> 'as there is nothing like openness between friends … unless the temper of the country and the general state of things alter greatly, I shall be obliged to set up Cole for this county'.[1]

Enniskillen's basic reason was that he would be losing the secure hold he had on 'his' borough under the proposed Reform Bill and that the county seat would be the only one available to his family. Belmore was furious. He accused Enniskillen of having had an unworthy motive in allowing Corry to fight the previous election against Brooke at great expense and trouble, 'in order that Cole might reap the fruits of victory' in the present one.

He had no doubt that Corry was being extremely badly treated and was angry that it removed the only place in life that Corry could take which would give him a useful future. Belmore's irritation was increased by the fact that he was so far away and had to leave the electioneering to Corry himself. He tried to put some of his own strength of feeling into Corry's attitude:

'The strongest manifestation of our resentment and displeasure becomes a duty. The chain is broken which linked our interest with Lord Enniskillen's'.

He reviewed the possibilities for Corry in the light of the Reform Act, which he thought would open up Enniskillen to Corry rather than to Cole since '*Castle Coole* is contiguous to Enniskillen and all the property around the town belongs to me'. His underlining of Castle Coole shows the importance he attached to its own influence. He even considered supporting the 'ultra' Brooke as long as it showed that the Corry interest was now separated from the Coles. But, knowing Corry's character, he fell back on two other suggestions, which would prevent expense and possible failure in a contested election.

Captain Corry had returned from Jamaica and had gone to see the Colonial Secretary, Goderich, who had 'touched on the politics of Fermanagh'. The Captain seized the chance to express the wish that Corry should be raised to the English peerage. Belmore (this was before he and Goderich had completely fallen out) thought this an admirable suggestion, especially as Corry seemed unlikely to marry:

> 'If, through Lord Goderich's interference, you were created a peer that would be best of all … I have strong claims on the government, such as I may fairly consider irresistible. I resign them to you. They will confer a great favour on me in creating you a peer, with descent, in case of your adhering to your *vows of celibacy*, to Henry and his issue, than by offering the dignity to myself'.

He urged Corry to acknowledge the obligation to Goderich and Goderich alone. Belmore was now engrossed by what he called 'the plot of his discourse', which 'will not be fully enacted without you, Henry and Armar to read your parts'. The peerage was one part. The other parts involved completing the purchase of the Bishop's leases of the Churchlands to increase their political clout and, finally, strengthening the Corry interest in Fermanagh by meetings with political friends and even by supporting Brooke so as to take credit for getting him elected. 'I would take my stand in politics, entirely opposed to what Lord Cole appears to have adopted for his rule of action'.

He accused Cole of attempting to gain popularity by 'vulgar and mischievous sentiments and emblems', leaving him 'to figure away in Orange placards and wear the laurels he may gain by retailing dull pot-house toasts at country dinners'. He advised Corry to put himself at the head of his own party of 'discretion and moderation', by means of which he would become powerful.

Corry himself called at Florence Court to see if a compromise was possible, but without success, for Enniskillen's view was that Belmore's 'political principles as to emancipation, together with the non-residence of any part of your family, have rendered it very problematical if Corry could carry the county again'. He asserted that Belmore knew that there would be difficulty in what he called 'again forcing Corry upon the county'.

Enniskillen's politics were certainly more 'ultra' than Belmore's, firmly planted in the Orange Order and set against emancipation. Enniskillen was right and Belmore's far-away plotting came to nothing – for Corry, still celibate and seemingly unsuited for political struggle, withdrew. In May 1831 Viscount Cole was elected for Fermanagh and by the year's end Belmore was out of favour with Goderich and the very government on which he had imagined he had irresistible claims.

In the meantime, it was, perhaps, some consolation that Corry was appointed high sheriff of the county for 1832. Otherwise, he was content to spend time at Cowes, sailing, or shooting and fishing on the Castle Coole demesne, where Belmore's planting schemes were taking effect and the present approach road from the Dublin Road to the house was laid out. In the summer of 1833, one particularly spectacular plant in one of the greenhouses in the walled garden, an *Agave Americana*, grew over 23 feet high and then, for three months, put on a show of 6,000 blossoms, all at once. During the short time that it remained in bloom crowds of visitors came to see it. 'The gardener (an intelligent old man) believes that it arrives at perfection in the course of 60 or 70 years'.[2]

Towards the end of the same year, Corry, like the agave, suddenly blossomed. He abandoned celibacy and announced that he intended to marry Miss Emily Louise Shepherd, the 20-year-old daughter of William and Anne Shepherd of Bradbourne, near Sevenoaks, Kent. Her older sister, Anna Maria, had been married to Richard Magenis of Finvoy, County Antrim for some 13 years, so it is likely Corry and Emily Louise had known each other for a while. Writing to Lady Louisa in January 1834, Belmore could not resist a bit of banter at Corry's expense:

> 'after a season of painful uncertainty, when he had shaken off reserve with any of his friends, there could be no uncertainty at all, he has at last "yielded to a burst of feeling" as Mama expresses it, and declared eternal devotion to Miss Shepherd, who (no doubt in a pathetic strain) expressed herself in terms to leave him "to desire nothing more"'.

The 'pathetic strain' was Belmore's way of saying she must have taken pity on Corry whose burst of feeling did not look as if it would produce what Belmore was really hoping for – a good financial outcome:

> 'The actual amount of Fortune to which she is now entitled falls far short of what report assigned to her – £40,000 in the Funds, subject however to a charge of £900 per annum to Mrs Shepherd is all I believe she can call her own, but if her sister has no children she will inherit other property the amount of which I do not yet know'.

To make matters worse as far as Belmore was concerned:

> 'I cannot speak of it by any means as certain, because for reasons which I need not now explain I know that difficulties may occur in arranging Settlements'.

The fact was that legal arrangements had to be made before Belmore's heavily encumbered estates could be cleared sufficiently to make way for a suitable financial settlement. By late May, all was completed and on 27 May 1834 Armar Corry and Emily Louise were married. They had eight children, four sons and four daughters. One of his sons, Somerset Richard (born in 1835), succeeded as fourth Earl; another son, Armar (born in 1836), followed his namesake into the navy and, ultimately, through his son Adrian, secured the succession to the title by the present Earl and his father.

Although Emily Louise was not the rich heiress Belmore had hoped for, she had a sufficient life interest under her father's will to give material help to the fourth Earl during the very difficult times which lay ahead. She and her sister shared the succession to the family estate at Bradbourne after their mother's death in 1864, and it went to her alone after her sister died in 1886. Her mother, Mrs Shepherd, left Edwardstone Hall in Suffolk to her grandson, Henry William Lowry Corry.

On 18 March 1830, while the Belmores were still in Jamaica, their younger son Henry had married Lady Harriet Ashley, second daughter of the Earl of Shaftesbury.

The marriages of Corry and Henry underscored the drawing power of England since the union and, possibly, its staying power. There would be a new direction for the Lowry Corry genes, away from Ireland and into English society. Their association with England, however, was less a union and more a federation, hence the description of their kind as 'Anglo-Irish'. Lady Louisa was an early and rather distinct example. She was already partly English and, in her teenage years, had been brought up under the aegis of the Castlereagh family in England.

Henry and Harriet had two sons, Armar Henry and Montagu William ('Montagu' was the family name of the Earls of Sandwich, Lady Louisa's family), and two daughters, Gertrude and Alice.

Henry began his successful parliamentary career in 1834 when he became comptroller of the household in the first ministry of Sir Robert Peel and, as a result, a privy councillor.

In 1835, after a lifetime of poor health, Juliana Brooke became seriously ill and Belmore and Juliana took her to stay with them in a house at Castleknock, on the edge of Phoenix Park, Dublin. There they had access to a spa and the best doctors in Dublin, but it was to no avail. An obituary in the *Clare Journal* for 14 January 1836 inaccurately recorded her parentage – 'at the Earl of Belmore's, Dublin, Juliana, daughter of Major General Brooke KCB'. But the *Belfast News Letter*, in its obituaries column, 5 January 1836, recorded correctly, 'December 31 1835 at Haymount, near Castleknock, where the Earl and Countess of Belmore were residing for the benefit of her health, Miss Julia Brooke, aged 22 years'. She was taken back to Enniskillen for the funeral, which was heavily attended, and buried in the family vault at Caledon.

For Belmore the 1830s ended with the final recognition that his income could no longer support his way of life. The marriages of Armar and Henry had further encumbered the estates, in Armar's case to the tune of £20,000 Irish. Belmore began to sell off land, starting at first with estates of least significance at Castle Coole. In October 1836 he agreed to sell Langfield in Tyrone to John and Ann Lowry of Drumsagh. Lowry recorded that Belmore 'had justly observed that in the course of time property must pass to different possessors'. This said much about Belmore's state of mind, but, sadly for him, the sale fell through.

In the following two years he attempted to sell the old Lowry family property, Aghenis, for almost £24,000. Lord Caledon was interested at first, but withdrew, remarking that it had been uninhabited for some time past and had become 'the abode of beggars'.

The pressure to raise capital and reduce his indebtedness increased in July 1837, when Auchenleck, his Tyrone agent, complained about his inability to meet Belmore's bills of exchange as they fell due for payment. Indeed, for one of them the only course he could suggest was that it should be renewed to avoid its being returned, protesting:

> '[it] would be a very unpleasant business … I told Mr Dane I could not pay it, having so many bills out here and demands to meet and it would be *rather hard to expect I could, by bills, pay off principal money in Fermanagh* when I am unable to pay that demand in Tyrone'.

Stewart advised Belmore not to try to raise one large loan, but rather a number of small ones so as to avoid the possible call for all his money by a single large lender. If that happened it might prove difficult to raise enough to pay him off and it was, in any case, difficult to raise large sums in Ireland. Whatever Belmore decided to do, said Stewart, at least £130,000 had to be raised. This inevitably meant selling more land than Belmore had hoped, but there was nothing for it. He put the Longford estate on the market.

In the meantime, until he could complete a major sale, he had to rely on a series of short-term borrowings to cover his spending. Though several purchasers seemed interested, Longford did not sell until 1839. After long and difficult negotiations, the Reverend John Grey Porter of Belle Isle bought it for £61,500. He was the son of that Bishop of Clogher who in the first Earl's time had so successfully increased the rents on the Churchlands and had established the basis of the Porter fortunes. The price was to be paid by instalments and most of it was to go directly to Belmore's creditors to clear the title. Porter also bought the Clabby, Loughside and Mountain parts of the Fermanagh estates for about £74,500, with the same condition that he paid off named creditors before Belmore received anything. Two years earlier, Belmore had managed to sell the Langfield estate for £14,200 to another reverend gentleman, Mr Thomas Hall Stack, with the same stipulation for using the proceeds to pay off encumbrances. Before the sales, his total capital debts amounted to £294,000, interest on which totalled not less than £12,500. Payments to family under settlements, added to his other outgoings, amounted to a further £10,500. Together they accounted for most of his annual income of about £25,600.

Even after the sales, within three or four years his debts charged on the Tyrone estates had increased to almost £160,000, so that interest payments still amounted to about £8,000 a year and annuities and rents to another £5,500 – a total of £13,500 taken out of a rental income which had had modest increases but was reduced by the sales to about £15,800. Similarly, his Fermanagh rental income of about £7,240 by 1841 was subject to interest and annuities of almost £5,000 and debt of £46,500. His total nominal income had therefore risen to about £23,000, but this allowed nothing for unpaid rent and rent abatements. The margin for his own expenses was a mere £4,600 or so but his annual expenditure ran at £17,000 to £20,000 a year.

In August 1837 there was a bit of light relief and a reminder of the happy days in the Mediterranean. A letter arrived from the Offices for Ordnance, Enniskillen:

'My Lord, I have the honor to inform you that two brass pieces of ordnance were received from Ballyshannon on 24th April 1833. Application must be made to the Hon'ble Board of Ordnance, London for their authority to enable me to issue them from my charge. M Jones ordnance storekeeper'.[3]

These were probably two of the *Osprey*'s guns, meant for decoration at Castle Coole. There is a tradition that Belmore lost a bet with his cousin, Lord Enniskillen, and to pay his debt gave him the two guns, which have since graced the front steps of Florence Court. In view of the state of Belmore's finances the story rings true.

A major expense, as always, was the business of politics and, in the summer of 1837, Belmore was politicking on behalf of Henry, who was up for re-election for Tyrone. There was now a distinct Conservative party, following the policies of Sir Robert Peel, and Henry was part of it.

Belmore's obvious concern was to ensure his son's re-election in the face of the ambitions of Lord Claud Hamilton and Lord Alexander, the Earl of Caledon's son, to be elected. Only one of them could succeed and then probably only if they had the support of Belmore's tenantry. They needed Belmore's consent for that but Belmore was unwilling to give it unless they both agreed to support Henry with their second votes, as they had done at the previous election. Even then, Belmore had been against the idea, and continued so, because he said it led 'his estate to be assailed by bribery'. Belmore was anxious to neutralise the negative effect the canvassing of the others could have on Henry's prospects. In the end he decided 'the only course the better to secure your election, is by my tenantry plumping in your favour'. Plump they did, arousing the anger of Lord Claud and the others. Henry was re-elected.

At the beginning of January 1839 the famous 'big wind' struck Ireland and Castle Coole did not escape. During the night the storm felled many trees, mostly in Drumcrin wood, which Belmore had finished planting in 1815. The fallen trees were cut for timber and sold. It was an ill omen – for, in the summer of that year, Belmore suffered a stroke while at dinner at Castle Coole. His cousin, John Cole, helped him onto a sofa in the drawing room where, as the fourth Earl later recorded with Victorian morbidity, 'he was bled, and where the stains remained on the silk for upwards of twenty years'. He never fully recovered but was reduced to using crutches or a wheelchair. Still, though, some of his old energy remained. He ordered replanting on the demesne, made a new walk through the woods at the top of the hill in front of the house and, in 1840, had the planting of Bonnybrook wood begun. He rented a house, 6 Clifford Street, in London for six months while receiving specialist medical attention. He continued to visit Cowes as he had done through the years.

On his way back to Castle Coole, on 18 April 1841, while staying with his sister-in-law, Mrs Georges at Leamington, he suffered another stroke and died. So ended perhaps the most colourful period in the story of Castle Coole. His body was taken back to Ireland and he was laid to rest at last in the family vault at Caledon.

Part Three

A Retiring Man: Armar, Third Earl Belmore, 1801–1845

Chapter Seventeen

'His Estate is his care and his tenantry, his family'

The only surviving picture of the third Earl is a silhouette, done when he was still Viscount Corry, which might be seen as a reflection of his fleeting influence on life at Castle Coole. He was 40 when his father died and in the words of the fourth Earl:

> 'did not survive to complete his forty fourth year. He went to reside at Castle Coole in October 1841, and he continued to make it his principal residence, going to Cowes (as he had regularly done for several summers before he succeeded his father), in 1842 and 1843, for the summer. He was very fond of yachting, although he did not own his own yacht. He was also a fisherman. In his day his own lake in the demesne was an excellent pike and perch lake; and occasionally he used to go a distance for salmon fishing. Although he did not hunt he rode regularly; he had for a good many years a very handsome chestnut horse, called Fairstar'.[1]

He suffered from severe attacks of gout – a term, like many medical terms, which described symptoms but did nothing to explain what was really wrong or to point to any cure. In 1844, he tried unsuccessfully to find relief in the waters and harsh treatments of the fashionable spa in Wiesbaden. If those treatments were harsh, the truth of his financial condition was even harsher.

Pressure for Money and Sales

During his short time in charge of the estates he faced nothing but bills and demands for payment and was constantly making endless, but inconclusive, calculations of income and expenditure. He became very distressed when he received a very large and long-overdue bill from Stewart, the Belmore agent in Tyrone, who asked for security to ensure it would be paid. Stewart explained that he had been constrained to postpone billing Belmore because of 'the pressure for money on other accounts, my knowledge of the intended sales and the health of your father'. There was almost £200,000 outstanding on bonds signed by the second Earl up to the time of his death, interest on which alone amounted to about £9,000. To this had to be added annuities of more than £6,000 a year to Lady Brooke, Mrs Shepherd, the dowager Lady Belmore, Lady Juliana Belmore and others.

In March 1841 his father had rented a house in Hill Street, Mayfair for a few months to arrange for the sale of those antiquities he had not already given to the British Museum. He had appointed R. and J. Newton of Soho Square, London, who held most of the

Silhouette of Viscount Corry, later Armar, 3rd Earl Belmore

Emily Louise, Countess of Belmore by Stephen Pearce

Egyptian antiquities in their storerooms, to exhibit them for sale in their Wardour Street premises. The British Museum was the principal bidder. The second Earl had died in April before the sale could be set up and the arrangements were taken over by the third Earl. The latter also had the Newtons sell a pipe of his father's Madeira wine from a storage cellar in London, which produced 213 dozen bottles of Madeira, most of which was taken by the Carlton Club. They raised nearly £640. Another 42 dozen bottles were sent to Castle Coole.

In May 1842 printed notices of the antiquities for exhibition and sale were distributed by the Newtons and their workmen fitted one of their storerooms with shelves for the exhibits. Henry Corry gave a hand in organising sets of lithographic drawings of the antiquities and the Newtons made a complete inventory. Lord and Lady Belmore stayed in London to see the work progressed. By February 1843 the Newtons were able to report to Belmore that the British Museum had agreed to buy the antiquities for £250, paying for them out of the first monies voted by parliament for the purpose. A considerable quantity of wearing apparel and other items were also sold at auction by Oxenhams. Later, in 1845, Belmore decided to see if he could raise a further sum from a sale of the remainder of his father's antiquities which were still at Castle Coole. Ten hampers of antiquities were sent to the Newtons between September and November 1845.[2]

To the Rt. Honourable the Earl of Belmore

The humble petition of Mary McWade of Knocknahorn
and parish of Dromore

Sheweth

That petitioner holds a farm of land under your
Lordship, in aforesaid place, and begs leave to lay before
you a narrative of her afflictions — Her husband fell
a victim to a lingering disease, in July last, leaving four
helpless children, her crop of potatoes was a miserable
failure and her stock consisting of a Mare & foal a cow
three hogs and two sheep were swept away by the
incessant attacks of Misfortune, leaving her unable to
maintain her family and procure seed for the land.

That petitioner puts forth her humble sup-
plication and most earnestly begs Your Lordship will
be graciously pleased to extend your beneficence in
relief of her distressed condition.

And petitioner as in duty bound
will ever pray

Mary McWade

Petition from a tenant for assistance

'His Estate is his care and his tenantry, his family'

Since his boyhood, Belmore had loved Castle Coole and, in spite of the financial constraints, planted a wood – the Killenure plantation – and made a walk out of part of the old Dublin approach to the house and the old public road of 1783, running alongside Lough Yoan. These alterations led to an auction of timber at Castle Coole in 1844.

Belmore showed kindness and understanding towards his tenants during difficulties they suffered in 1844 and 1845. He authorised payments to them in response to petitions they presented in 1844, seeking financial assistance for loss of cattle or for completing the building of their houses. Payments were made to 11 tenants on the Belmore estate whose land was flooded in April, August, September and October 1844 and May 1845. He also made allowances to tenants in 1845 for loss of cattle. 75 tenants in Tyrone presented similar petitions to Belmore in 1845, pleading losses and asking for compensation, which, in cases considered deserving (the majority), resulted in a payment. *The Impartial Reporter* newspaper in Enniskillen, even allowing for the fulsome language, supports a view of his character as a kindly man:

> 'Of the many excellent landlords resident in Fermanagh, we and the public, place this retiring nobleman FOREMOST AND THE BEST. His Estate is his care and his tenantry, his family. He regularly examines his rental and when necessary, reduces the amount – not for half a year – but permanently, although his lands are the cheapest let in Fermanagh. He is always at home to a tenant; and if illness or accident befall any of them, the early ride and familiar pad of his pony indicate the stolen message of mercy'.

Belmore was to have been the next Irish representative peer, but it was not to be:

> 'On 10th September, he took my brother … and myself to Mrs Peile's school, at Hatfield; we saw him there for the last time. He died, after a short illness, of gout, on 17th December, 1845, wanting a week to complete his forty-fourth year'.

So wrote the fourth Earl many years later, giving scarcely a hint of the feelings of loss of a ten-year-old boy. He and his eight-year-old brother Armar were staying at the house of their mother's family at Edwardstone in Suffolk but were taken to Castle Coole for their father's funeral. The procession left the house in the evening to make its way to the church at Caledon, where Belmore was buried in the family vault. The third Earl left eight children. It was first thought that Lady Belmore was pregnant again, but, wrote a relation, 'the report of her being in the family way was happily not true'. Each of the younger children was to receive a fortune of £4,000 to be invested until they were of age. Three of them, however, did not live to reach 21. Lady Belmore and their uncle Henry Corry were guardians of the remaining five – Somerset Richard, the new Earl, his brothers Armar and Henry William, and two sisters, Louisa and Florence. Uncle Henry and their Enniskillen cousin John Cole were trustees of their finances.

The third Earl's contemporaries, the two surviving illegitimate children of the first Earl, had overcome their difficulties with the second Earl about their financial support and had made their own way in life.

Admiral Armar Lowry Corry and his children at Ballinacourt, their home near Dublin

Maria Watson had twin children by Colonel Watson, Mary Anne Juliana, who died young, and Richard Luther, who married Louisa Anne Cole. They lived on the Grove Estate, Ecclerigg, Westmoreland, inherited from Richard Luther Watson's paternal grandfather, the Bishop of Llandaff. They had four daughters. After her husband's death, Maria married Christopher Salter, as already mentioned, and had two children.

Captain Armar Lowry Corry continued an active career in the navy. In April 1835 he took command of HMS *Barham*, a 50-gun frigate, and was sent as senior officer in command to the south-east coast of Spain. This was during an episode of the long-running Carlist wars of succession. The British government supported the regime of Queen Maria Cristina who faced another attempt at that time by the Carlists to take over the Spanish throne. Intending to advance on Madrid through Catalonia and Valencia, the Carlists had defeated the Queen's troops and were threatening the city of Valencia itself. Corry, at the urgent request of the Captain General of the Province, landed a body of seamen and marines on the coast, attacked and successfully dispersed the Carlists. For his sound judgement in taking prompt and decisive action he was thanked on behalf of the Queen for saving her throne and preserving Valencia and the city of Barcelona. The Spanish Queen herself, the British government and the Lords of the Admiralty all conveyed their thanks for his decisive action.

He remained in the *Barham* until 1839 and was then on half pay until 1844. While on half pay he at last laid to rest his sailor's reputation for philandering. On 10 December 1842, at Stillorgan, he married Elizabeth Rosetta, second daughter of James Hewitt Massey-Dawson and widow of Eyre Coote. They had three children – Juliana Benita, Mary Emma and Alvin Coote.

In September 1844 he was selected to command a steam frigate, the *Firebrand*, and an experimental squadron of brigs for a voyage of a few weeks and was then transferred as captain of the 80-gun HMS *Superb*, which he commanded in the Mediterranean during the civil war in Portugal. He received several commendations for the state of battle-readiness and his handling of the *Superb* and for the zeal and firmness of his command when carrying a large body of Portuguese prisoners.

From 1847 to 1852 he was *aide-de-camp* to Queen Victoria. He left the *Superb* in 1848 and in 1850 was additional captain of HMS *Victory* until in March 1852 he was promoted to rear admiral, when he commanded the Western Squadron. After that he hoisted his flag in HMS *Prince Regent* (90 guns), commanding the Channel Squadron. Finally, he transferred to the *Neptune* (120 guns), as second in command of the Baltic Fleet.

He retired owing to ill health in 1854 and went to live in Paris, where he died on 5 May 1855. He was buried in Montmartre cemetery but later removed to Bethnal Green. At the time of his death he was gazetted as a knight commander of the Order of the Bath.

Picture from the *Illustrated News* showing the *Neptune*, Rear Admiral Armar Lowry Corry, 1854

Part Four

A Practical Man: Somerset Richard,
Fourth Earl Belmore, 1835–1914

Chapter Eighteen

Youth and 'a dangerous situation'

The new Earl Belmore and his brother Armar remained for another three years at Mrs Peile's school in Hatfield, in the new Earl's opinion 'a very good school for general learning'. Their last school holidays at Castle Coole were in the summer of 1846.[1]

A year later, Henry Corry had to grapple with with the family's worsening financial situation. He had hoped that the settled property, charged with maintenance payments to members of the family, could be kept free from the demands of creditors, but he discovered that 'the entire debt' which at first he thought had risen to no less than £244,000 had risen yet again, but this time to almost £256,000. Even worse, the unsettled property, which should have provided income, was running an annual deficit of £2,000. The difference between their rental income from all their estates and their outgoings, including interest and payments to family, was a surplus of only £48 a year, and there were immediate demands from creditors for £20,000.

The obvious way out was to sell land to raise money, but they could not do so privately because they could not guarantee that a purchaser would not face claims from other creditors; and there were so many of those that more claims were expected than could possibly be satisfied. There was nothing for it but to put the estates under the protection of the Chancery Court. This would then prevent any single creditor from obtaining a judgement and enforcing it by bankruptcy proceedings. The Chancery Court had the power to hold off creditors while effecting partial sales of land to satisfy claims in an orderly fashion. Faced with what Henry Corry described as 'a dangerous situation' they had no alternative. To the Chancery Court they went.

In that same year, 1847, the effects of the potato blight and famine reached their height, with the workhouse in Enniskillen 'besieged by hundreds claiming admission'.[2] Inevitably, overcrowding led to outbreaks of fever and cholera. None of the family was at Castle Coole during this time, but Henry Corry kept in close touch with the Belmore agent, Auchenleck, about the subscriptions that the gentry of Fermanagh were organising for the relief of distress. Auchenleck at first reported that there was no very distressing case on the estate but Henry was afraid:

> 'our difficulties are only just beginning and there will be much suffering before they are over. The governess at Castle Coole wrote so melancholy an account to Lady

Belmore of the state of the poor about the place that I feared their condition must have greatly deteriorated during Paul Dane's absence'.

Dane, another of the Belmore agents, was also on the Board of Guardians of Enniskillen, responsible for the workhouse. Henry had written to Dane urging him to attend to the problems, if only because the usual charitable visits and gifts which had always been made at Castle Coole were not, in the absence of the family, available. He sent £50 of his own as a private charitable contribution towards the most urgent cases and suggested that preparations should be made for planting more grain instead of potatoes. He then secured the consent of the Chancery Master:

> 'to sanction whatever it may be right and proper to subscribe for the relief of the Poor, and he agrees with me in being surprised that larger amounts have not been required in some of the districts to the relief of which you have contributed'.

Dane had contributed £3 to Fintona, which Henry thought hardly sufficient, especially 'when many of our own people are to be supported'. £5 would be the minimum Castle Coole should contribute and:

> 'you who are on the spot know best what the amount of distress is, and what is necessary for its relief, but I think that good policy (notwithstanding our difficulties) as well as humanity ought to lead us to contribute in all cases with becoming liberality'.

He was also very concerned that only £10 had been the contribution in Beragh and Six Mile Cross:

> 'The smallness of these sums in the heart of the Property and in districts remote from the vicinity of any resident gentry, and where consequently nearly the whole burden must fall on the estate, appears to me difficult to understand. Is the amount of distress in these districts trifling? I trust this is the reason ... I am sure you will do what is right'.[3]

After 1847 the potato crop began to recover but the poorer population did not. The Enniskillen and other local workhouses remained overcrowded for some time.

In 1848 the Chancery Court appointed Richard Dane receiver of the Belmore settled estates and, in spite of the understandable concern and alarm of other creditors, Lady Belmore was given priority by the payment of her jointure of £8,000 and her annuity of £400. Henry Corry and Mrs Shepherd, Belmore's maternal grandmother, received payments totalling £2,800 a year, and rent due for the Churchlands was also paid. No interest was to be paid out of the unsettled estates without an order of the Court, but Dane pointed out the obvious fact that it would be hard to pay any interest on the outstanding debt of £230,000 without recourse to sales of land.

The importance to the young Belmore of the provision made for his mother and grandmother was soon to become apparent. In the meantime, in spite of Dane's opinion to the contrary, the family were forced to take advantage of the new Encumbered Estates

Early photograph of Great Court, Trinity College, Cambridge

Court Act of 1849, under which sales of land from the estate could be made, giving the purchaser a title clear of encumbrances, and paying off creditors. The Belmores were far from alone in selling land under the statute. In the next decade 3,000 estates, some 5,000,000 acres (more than a quarter of Ireland's total land area), were sold in the same way.

'Liking it pretty well': Education and Growing Up[4]

In the meantime, in September 1848, the 13-year-old Belmore was sent to Eton and placed in the lower fourth form as a pupil of the Reverend W. G. Cookesley. However, after taking his 'remove' examination in 1849, he stayed only until Christmas that year 'in consequence of deafness'. He rather damned the school with faint praise:

> 'At Eton I learnt very little, except to swim, and that I have not kept up. In fact, to bathing I attribute in a great measure, my deafness. I liked Eton pretty well, but was glad to leave it – I was fag to George Cayley, Lt Col Bathurst and Lt Col Rous'.

In February 1850 he was sent to a private tutor, the Reverend W. C. Roughton, Vicar of Great and Little Harrowden, Northamptonshire:

> 'I liked this place very much. After leaving Eton I lost my deafness very soon and here I learned to ride across country, principally with the Pychely [sic] hounds'.

As he was marked out for a career in the army he also learnt the elements of fortification.

He visited Castle Coole in 1852 and in the summer of 1853 when he noted in his diary:

> 'At Castle Coole 19th June via Castle Blayney walked out most days shooting rabbits. Shot a rabbit on "the new walk" (along Lough Yoan). 11th July, caught 21 perch, threw one back; 16th July caught about 30lb of pike. 26th July went to see farm and sailed on the *Wave*. [This must have been a small sailing boat kept on Lough Coole]. 9th July shooting – killed nothing. 3rd August with Lady B fished for perch. 7th August back to Harrowden via Dublin'.

In October 1853 he went up to Trinity College, Cambridge. He did not study for the tripos, an honours degree, but took a shorter two-year course known as 'the poll', which led to a pass degree and was commonly undertaken by noblemen. A poll man read a limited range of subjects – basic mathematics and some science (including hydrostatics), Greek texts, church history and moral philosophy. Belmore admitted he did not get much use out of his tutor's lectures and spent most of his time riding and playing tennis.

His Cambridge diary shows him leading a relaxed social life, typical of an undergraduate nobleman of the time. Particular friends were Lords Cavendish, Dunglass, Hervey, Leveson Gower and Sir Ivor Guest. Belmore was devoted to the Anglican faith for the whole of his life and it also played a most important role in the life of the College, where regular attendance in the College chapel was expected. A few of his diary entries give an impression of his university experience:

> 'Sat Nov 13th Went to morning chapel. Communicated. Read the prayers after. Breakfasted. Went to St Mary's. Dined in Hall. Pierce Butler and Dunlo took wine with me. Went to evening chapel. Went to Guest's room and to Leveson Gower's for tea.
>
> 'Mon Nov 14th Went to morning chapel. Ordered breakfast. Matriculated. Schrieber, Sir Ivor Guest. Lord Cavendish and Lord Hervey breakfasted with me. Went to the union and tennis court.
>
> 'Wed Nov 16th, Went to lectures. Breakfasted and went to Dunlo's room, who was getting up. Went to the union, looked at the papers and read some of the *Newcomes*, went to see the four oar race. St John's boat bumped 1st time. Dined in Hall. Went to Guest's room for a few minutes. Went to sleep. Read the *Bible* and the *Whole Duty of Man*. Prepared some *Oedipus Tyrannous*: wrote accounts and this.
>
> 'Th 17th. Went to chapel. I think read the Bible and Whole Duty of Man. Went to lectures. Went to Dunlo's rooms. Bought *The Young Duke* by Disraeli. Looked in at the tennis court. Dined in Hall. Guest took wine with me. Lost 1 shilling at whist'.

He took time out to go to Castle Coole and to visit friends and relations in Ireland:

> 'Tuesday. Went to Ireland via Preston & Fleetwood. Dined in refreshment room at Preston. Had a warm bath at Fleetwood. Passage rather over 12 hours.
>
> 'Wednesday. Went on deck about after 3 am. Went below again. Landed about 9 a.m. Breakfasted at the Donegal Arms Inn. Lord Gosford sent for me to Richill. Walked after luncheon.
>
> 'Thursday. At Castle Coole. Played cricket – walked after luncheon'.

Belmore played cricket in his short time at Eton and later, when he was in the Lake District with Sharpe's reading party. This is the first reference to cricket at Castle Coole but it was to become a regular event there later.

He spent much of his time there looking over the demesne with Hosegood, the head gardener. He went to the family church, Derryvullen:

'Sunday Sept 2nd. Talked to Hosegood. Went to church. Received the Holy Communion. Walked home. Walked with Lady Belmore.

'Monday. Arranged library books. Walked & talked with Hosegood.

'Tuesday. Saw Mr Dane. Walked with Mr Hosegood to Lough Erne.

'Thursday. Shot at Florencecourt. Brought home one bird.

'Saturday. Went over maps with Mr Dane.

'Tuesday. Went to the garden before breakfast. Saw whiskey uncorked. Walked with Lady B.

'Sunday. Sept 16. Went twice to church & to the farm.

'Tuesday. Walked into Enniskillen with Lady B & Lady Louisa [his sister]. Saw Capt Corry [his brother]. Some whiskey bottles were recorked.

'Wednesday 19th Sept. Went to shoot at Florencecourt. Saw Mr Cole.

'Thursday. Went to Omagh with Paul Dane by 6.20 train. Went over great part of Tyrone estate. Went to lunatic asylum and court house.

'Sunday Sept 23rd. Went to church. Mr Wilson officiated. Read the evening service two times'.

Back at university, he continued to spend most of his time on the approved physical exercises of a Victorian gentleman: walking, riding, hunting, fencing and gymnastics, but on Friday 11 November he records: 'Had a lecture-room examination'. It was a practice run for the real thing and a wake-up call to some hard studying.

He had already failed an earlier exam and had been ordered to attend freshmen's lectures for a further year but, taking his courage in both hands, he asked for an interview with the fearsome Master of Trinity, Dr Whewell, and managed to persuade him that he should be allowed to retake the exam at the beginning of the next academic year in October. 'I easily passed this time and then commenced to read for mathematical honours,' he wrote, but he found that course too difficult. He began to work more closely with his tutor, Sharpe, and during his last long vacation in the summer of 1856 he went on a reading party with Sharpe and a small group of fellow students. Reading parties had been encouraged by Whewell and had become a regular way of passing the summer vacation in the Lakes, Scotland, Ireland and Wales. The Victorians loved hillwalking and the growing railway network made their favourite places more accessible. The party read hard in the morning and walked hard in the afternoon. Sharpe thought their chances of passing were very mixed. One of them

William Whewell

Early photograph of Lough Coole

might be first class; Belmore and another 'had no chance'; yet another 'would be plucked'. Sharpe's opinion of his chances gave Belmore a sleepless week. He arrived late to hear the results read out and, as the second and later classes were reached, he had still not been mentioned. 'By no means comfortable', he walked slowly back to Trinity. Just arrived at the College gate, he heard his cousin shouting across the street that he had, in fact, passed first-class 'poll' – the equivalent of fourth class in an honours degree. This was the end of his formal education, but the public life he was ambitious to begin now invited.

Irish Representative Peer and 'the great confusion of the affairs of my property'
About a month after coming of age in April 1856 Belmore went on the first of several journeys abroad until the end of October, the customary addition to a Victorian gentleman's education. The tour took him through France, Belgium, Prussia, Austria and Bavaria. In the same year, in which he was appointed a deputy lieutenant for Tyrone and a magistrate for both Tyrone and Fermanagh, he wasted no time in applying to be entitled to vote in the House of Lords for the election of Irish representative peers, and then immediately began to canvass support for his own election. By the time he returned home in October he had succeeded and was formally gazetted a representative peer in January 1857. At such an early age, he was immensely proud of this result, writing in his diary at the time:

> 'Tuesday 13th January 1857 went from Castle Ward to Garvagh, via Belfast. I was this day declared duly elected as a Temporal Peer (for Ireland) to sit in the House of Lords of the United Kingdom, in the room of James, Earl of Bandon, deceased'.

He went hunting on his favourite horse, Finvoy, named after the village in Antrim where his relations, the Magenis family lived.[5]

However, whatever personal qualities fitted him for public life, if he was to succeed in it he desperately needed to resolve what he called 'the great confusion of the affairs of my property'. That he was able to do so was in no small measure due to the support he received from his mother and his grandmother, Juliana Belmore, as well as from Dane. They purchased land from the Court in or close to the Castle Coole demesne and later sold it back to Belmore at what he called 'a fair price'. He was able to pay £5,000 for the purchases, a fund accumulated for him out of family settlements the Court had protected from creditors.

Additionally, his other grandmother, Mrs Shepherd, made him a present of £7,000 – which he used, with loans of £1,500 each from Mrs Shepherd and his mother, to pay off a mortgage of £10,000 due to his uncle Henry. In fact, they effectively released him from capital and annual obligations due to them so that he had enough liquidity to save Castle Coole and its demesne and part of the Tyrone estate.

They went further, for they also ensured that he had enough money to support his parliamentary life and to complete his education by travelling abroad. While it was clearly in their own interest to see family settlements secured, the commitment of the women of the Belmore family at that difficult time, not just to the life of the family in the usual way, but also to the future of Castle Coole itself, cannot be underestimated. The pity is that no material for a record of their lives exists. Until Belmore married in 1862 they provided the support he needed to set him on his feet.

The role of Henry Corry, as trustee presiding over the legal but drastic disposal of the Belmore estates, was fundamental. He had, of course, grown up at Castle Coole during the heady years of his father's enrichment of the house and its grounds. After his marriage and because of his parliamentary career he lived in England but always had a close attachment to Castle Coole and to his nephew. He was a great help to Belmore in his career. In Peel's second ministry of the 1840s he was a junior lord of the Admiralty and then secretary of the Board of Admiralty.

The support of his family meant that Belmore had time to develop his own interests and also to stabilise life at Castle Coole. By 1861, he had managed to get possession of the whole of the Castle Coole demesne by an exchange of land with the then owner of Ballylucas. Parts of the Castle Coole demesne, such as Standingstone, Killenure, parts of Kedagh and Carrowmacmea, were also brought (or rather, bought) from family members back into the demesne by adjustments Belmore was able to make to provisions of his father's will in their favour. In Tyrone, in 1852 and 1853, substantial sales of land by the Court took place. Belmore was left with the townlands of Beragh, Letfern and Legacorry, most of the Manor of Finagh and the head rent of Moylagh. He also retained Swan Park in Monaghan.

The result of all these sales was to reduce Belmore's annual rental income from £23,000 before the Acts to about £9,000 afterwards. The gross rental sold in Fermanagh was about £6,000 and in Tyrone, about £8,000. His estates were, in his own words, 'reduced to a mere 20,000 acres' – about 14,400 acres in Tyrone and just over 5,000 acres in Fermanagh.

An account of Belmore's income in May 1857 shows a slight increase in his revenue: his rents from Fermanagh were just over £2,200 and his rents from Tyrone almost £8,000. Other receipts, including over £750 from the sale of old plate, took total income to just over £12,555. He included in his other receipts for that year, 'won at cards about £2-5-0'. This might be thought a ludicrously small amount to bring into an account amounting to thousands, but it illustrates an important trait in his character and his attitude towards money. It was, of course, necessary for him to be careful, but he was able to maintain a sensible level of expenditure over many years, which eventually enabled him to repay between £45,000 and £50,000 of his father's debts and substantially to reduce family charges on the settled estates. His own annual expenditure for many years was never more, and often less, than £2,500.

He was also able to carry out extensive land-drainage works on his estates with the help of loans from the Land Drainage Board, all of which he repaid by 1869. He was, as has been seen, helped very much by his mother and grandmothers, and later his finances would be transformed, if not necessarily improved, by sales to tenants under new legislation. Nevertheless, what underpinned the improvement in the financial stability of the family was his own sensible and measured approach to his finances. He was by nature a steady, sensible man.[6]

Belmore began an increasingly busy and productive life, at Castle Coole and in Tyrone, in London as a working peer and travelling in Ireland and abroad. He inevitably had to split his time between London and Castle Coole and to make room for travel.

At Castle Coole, during 1857, he began to plan to redecorate and, while in London 'chose some papers for rooms'. He had most of the house repainted and skylights reglazed. To raise some money towards the expense he sold some of the family's old plate and in October 1859 he noted: 'Lady Belmore gave me £115-5-0 to pay household bills and £200 towards painting the house'.

His major plan was to improve the main entrance to Castle Coole from the Dublin Road, which itself had been rerouted 25 years earlier. In late 1857 he had an engineer, Roderick Gray, lay out a new approach avenue to Castle Coole, and furnished it with a new gate lodge and main gates. James Wray gave an estimate on 24 June 1859 for the new gate lodge, 'a house of brick and stone' with five bedrooms and four principal rooms. Two years later, in 1859, a new 'Ornamental Wrought Iron Entrance' was designed and manufactured by Turner and Gibson of the Hammersmith Iron Works, Ballsbridge, Dublin, and was installed by men from the Strand Saw Mill of Londonderry – who took eight days 'at the railing', four days stonecutting and used a hundredweight of lead. The actual building of the gate lodge was done by William McClelland of Londonderry at a total cost of almost £600.[7]

In November 1857 Belmore also had Roderick Gray lay out a length of new road from Enniskillen to Tempo, between Breandrum and Garvary and Garvary and South Bridge. Extensive drainage work in the demesne also began and would be continued for many years as part of Belmore's many improvements to it. In fact, between 1856 and 1862 improved drainage was a major undertaking on both estates in Fermanagh and Tyrone. On the Castle Coole demesne, a new approach from Enniskillen and a new Enniskillen gate lodge were built. The bog road was made and the bog cottages were built.

By the time he went to parliament, party politics had evolved and political organisation, ministerial work and the civil service had become more businesslike. As a party man Belmore, like his Uncle Henry, was a Conservative. He saw his Uncle Henry return to a minority Conservative government for a short while in 1858–1859, once again as secretary of the Board of Admiralty.

As a young and ambitious politician, Belmore looked for work and was not long in finding it. Soon after he first took his seat in the House of Lords there was a general election and in the new parliament, after Easter 1857, he was appointed to the Standing Orders Committee and attended debates regularly, although in his first few years he did not speak in any of them. The parliamentary timetable was conveniently framed for the lives of gentlemen, most sessions starting at 4 p.m., leaving them plenty of time to spend on their estates and in travelling.

Chapter Nineteen

The 'skeletons of departed camels': Egypt and the Holy Land

In November, Belmore left a proxy for his vote in the House, intending to take some leave to go to the Pyrenees, San Sebastian and Paris. But on his way home to Castle Coole he was taken ill at Florence Court with an inflammation of his right lung and was laid up in bed there for three weeks. When he recovered, he collected his mother at Castle Coole and they went to Dublin, meaning to cross over to England after he had seen his doctor. Lady Belmore herself, however, fell ill with a fever and they were delayed for almost two weeks until she had recovered. Dr Stokes advised him to go abroad as soon as possible. He decided to go to Egypt and the Holy Land, attracted not just by the climate but also by the chance of following in the footsteps of his grandfather. The history of his family had already begun to preoccupy him and he had already this year begun to makes notes about it.

He had wanted his friend Pearce Butler to go with him, but Butler was unable to do so. He asked another friend instead, Richard Harrison, 'who was perhaps the most intimate friend I ever had and, except Lord Bangor, the only intimate one out of my own family'. Belmore received a letter to say that Harrison was dangerously ill with fever and, when he finally arrived in London in January, 'a letter from his father saying that he was dead'. The two had become close while Belmore had been at Ambleside with the reading party, and Harrison's family 'were very good natured to me – he had been a good deal at Castle Coole, and was with me during the worst of my illness at Castle Coole'. It was the third time that Belmore lost someone so close to him. A brother, Frederick, had died while at Rugby school in 1855, aged only 16.

Towards the end of the session, Belmore spoke in a debate on Irish endowed schools. Later in his career, education in Ireland would become one of his principal interests.

He left on 20 January 1859 in the P&O steamer *Pera* and arrived at Cairo after calling in at Gibraltar and Malta. He stayed for a week and chose to hire a boat himself to go up the Nile rather than use his local guide, Kaled. It was a mistake – the boat was too big to get up the river, 'a fact which Kaled took care not to let me forget'. He got as far as Thebes but, to his own subsequent regret, did not follow his grandfather's course up to Aswan. Besides Kaled, he had a cook, an English servant and an Arab boy, Hassan Mahmood. The crew of the boat were a captain (Reis) and 14 to 16 sailors. On his way back down

Honoria, Countess Belmore

Somerset Richard, 4th Earl Belmore

the Nile he saw the temple of Abu Simbel and the tombs of Beni Hassan. Because the Nile was low and the boat large it was continually running aground and they frequently had to ask the help of local villagers to refloat it. He did not enjoy himself: 'on the whole having a great deal of my own company I found the voyage very dull'. What his grandfather and Captain Corry would have made of it does not bear thinking about.

From Cairo he went by rail to Suez, 'a dreary enough place … the most striking objects in the environs being the skeletons of departed camels'.

Notwithstanding this note of Victorian melancholy he 'got over ten days at Cairo very pleasantly' and on 31 March set out for Jerusalem. Belmore and a companion, Hughes, a Welsh clergyman and fellow of Jesus College, Oxford, were provided with two old, lean mares, the latter's with a foal at its side. When they arrived in sight of their tents to camp for the night, Belmore gave his mare an over-eager kick, and it ran away with him. He lost his stirrups and then his hat; the mare swerved to avoid a camel and Belmore 'gradually slipped over on the off side'. He was not hurt but worse was to come. The cold and the dew at night, which Hester Stanhope had warned his grandfather to avoid at all costs, struck Belmore, who 'hardly slept and got a relaxed throat and cold'. A camp bed and a bernous (a long cloak with a hood) wrapped round his head and shoulders prevented any further chills.

Their practice was to get up at daybreak, breakfast, pack up the tents, load the camels and travel until noon, when they would stop in a shady place for a lunch, usually of hard-boiled eggs, bread and cheese and weak brandy and water with a slice of lemon, a quantity of brandy being lighter to carry than wine. After an afternoon's journey they would stop at about four o'clock and encamp, killing chickens or a sheep bought from the Bedouin for dinner.

On the following Sunday they wanted to catch up with another, larger party, but it was the Lord's Day and they needed time for worship. They solved the problem by reading their prayer books as they rode their horses and camels. There were more misadventures with the lean mares and Belmore concluded, 'I should advise anyone to put up with the inconvenience of the camel's jolt ... rather than try to ride a horse ... through the deep sand'. At Gaza they were resigned to being lodged in 'an exceptionally dirty quarantine house', but it turned out to be full and, much to their relief, they were allowed to sleep apart in their own tents.

Belmore's party eventually 'struck inland, across the country of the Philistines, and the hill country of Judea' but, on their second day, lost their way and then found that 'there was rather a disposition on the part of the natives to attack the baggage'. On the third day they arrived at Jerusalem, Belmore recording that 'arriving from the south it has a rather dreary appearance', but later in its crowded, narrow streets he found 'a wonderful collection of people of the Eastern European nations'.

Leaving Jerusalem, Belmore went on to Nazareth, staying the night in the convent on Mount Carmel, overlooking the sea just above Tyre, and eventually reached Damascus. He went on to Balbec but:

> 'did not go to the Cedars of Lebanon; it was not included in my agreement, and I should have had to pay extra for three persons, and did not feel very well when I got to Baalbec. I rather regret it'.

Two of the Ladies Lowry Corry

Captain John Neilson Gladstone
RN MP 1807–1863

Finally reaching Beirut, he boarded a Russian coastal steamer to Constantinople. After seeing the sights there he left on a French steamer for Marseilles and went home over land.

Belmore's experience of Egypt, the Holy Land and Syria contrasts sharply with that of his grandfather's party. His account, it is true, was written on board the ship taking him and his family to Australia in 1867, nearly 20 years later. For that very reason it is more revealing of his character, since he had the leisure to recall lasting impressions. What stands out is his wry recollection of accidents and misfortunes; his sense of loneliness and his particular interests as a Christian. Underneath the sociable, Christian gentleman lay a certain melancholy, especially if he was without company. All his diaries are notable for the names and family relations of people he met, but rarely did he have any comment on their lives or characters. An almost unique example was when he travelled home with a Mr Moore, whom he noted as the son of the Consul General in Syria and attaché in Constantinople. Belmore was intrigued by the fact that Moore 'had left England at 3 years old, and had never seen a train till he arrived at Marseilles'. Railways were to become something of a speciality for Belmore.

'Grateful for any favour conferred': Railways to the Rescue

Belmore was back in England by the summer but, as he felt there was nothing happening of political or Conservative party interest, he went in late August to Ireland and, after returning for the hunting season to England, he set off on another tour, this time to Spain and Portugal. While in Cadiz he heard of his eldest sister Louisa's approaching marriage with a cousin, Major Richard Magenis of Finvoy, County Antrim. The latter's father, also Major Richard Magenis, had married Belmore's aunt, but the connection between the families went much further back. Lady Elizabeth Cole, daughter of the first Earl's sister, Lady Enniskillen, had married their ancestor, Colonel Magenis.

In late 1859, Belmore had been approached by the Dungannon Railway Company, which wanted to buy some land at Beragh, Tyrone for their new railway line. Probably encouraged by this prospect, he had given notice to Louisa that he intended to pay off her fortune. The negotiations, however, dragged on and by the end of February 1860 he was pressing his solicitor, Robert Keys, for news. Belmore was in London, but expected to be in Ireland in the spring, by which time he hoped the Railway Company would have completed their purchase and paid. It was not until April that it was agreed he would be paid £2,600, and then partly in shares. Robert Keys appealed to the Railway Company's solicitors to expedite the matter, remarking that 'Lord Belmore is very capable of placing a just estimate on kindness – indeed, I don't know anyone more grateful for any favour conferred'.

The valuers for Belmore and the Railway Company could not agree so Belmore intervened personally, at Beragh, to resolve their differences and finally agreed to accept the £2,600 – £900 in shares and the balance of £1,700 in cash. This was some help towards paying Lady Louisa's fortune of £4,000, but each of his other siblings and his uncle were entitled to the same payment. However, the encounter with a railway company proved useful. In April 1859 Belmore, his mother and grandmother, his brother Captain Corry (then of HMS *Orion*), and Belmore's sister, Louisa Anne Corry, joined together to raise £10,000 by a mortgage from the Dundalk and Enniskillen Railway Company.

Some time later, Belmore again sold land to a railway company – the Great Northern Railway Company. It was a very small piece of land at Cooley, Tyrone, valued at £25. His agent Robert Brush thought it so high a valuation for such a small area that, at that price per acre, there would be no landlords left in Ireland. Railways were attracting investment and were spending huge sums on expansion. They were to feature prominently in Belmore's parliamentary career, for he was to become something of an expert on their financial operations when they came under intense parliamentary scrutiny from 1863 onwards.

Ave Atque Vale: Marriage, Politics and Employment

The early 1860s brought more deaths to the family. In July 1861 Juliana Belmore, who had lived at Greenbank, Rostrevor, County Down since the death of her husband, died. In April 1862 Lady Louisa, the Countess of Sandwich, died.

Belmore had originally been intended for the army but instead, probably influenced by his mother and grandmothers, opted for a parliamentary career and for bringing the family finances under control. Nevertheless, in September 1860 he gave a nod in the direction of a military life by accepting a commission as a lieutenant in the London Irish Rifle Volunteers. He was attached to a battalion of the Coldstream Guards for a month's drill and, during the following summer of 1861 did some spells of duty with the Rifles.

The early 1860s also brought a fundamental change in Belmore's life that would bring him into a relationship with the Gladstone family. He recorded the debates when Gladstone, then the Chancellor of the Exchequer, attempted unsuccessfully to abolish duties on paper; when the House of Lords rebelled against his finance bill – 'the radicals were frantic'; and Belmore himself made a short speech in the House 'on an unimportant bill'.

The one thing he does not mention in his diary is the event that was to change his life – he began to court Gladstone's niece. In fact, on 22 August 1861, he and Anne Elizabeth Honoria Gladstone, daughter of Captain John Neilson Gladstone RN, MP of Bowden Park, Wiltshire (William Ewart Gladstone's brother) were married. Honoria's mother was a daughter of Sir Robert Bateson of Belvoir Park, Belfast, later Baron Deramore. Honoria was deeply religious, very conventional and completely devoted to Belmore.

In his diary Belmore says nothing about her at that time or, indeed, at any other time, only noting, 'During the summer I resigned my commission and married in August'.

There is no record of Honoria's life before her marriage other than a brief reference in William Gladstone's diary for Thursday 20 June 1861: 'Dined with John to meet the Bride (Nora) & Bridegroom but was summoned away'.

After the marriage, they left in October for their honeymoon via Belgium, Germany and Switzerland into Italy. They stayed for three weeks in Florence, went to Rome for six weeks and then on to Naples for a week, returning to England in February 1862. On their return they went to Castle Coole. Belmore resumed his commission in the London Irish Rifles, promoted to captain, but actually spent very little time in London that year. There was no need, for while they were in Florence, Prince Albert died. Belmore noted that 'in consequence of the Queen's bereavement there was a general understanding that no attempt would be made to disturb the Government'. Belmore's affairs were seriously disturbed in July, however, when his agent Paul Dane 'resigned (or rather absconded) with a large balance against him for which he "confessed to judgement" in the Court of Exchequer'.

Castle Coole 1862–1867: Family Life

The big event of 1862 was the birth of the Belmores' first daughter, Theresa, on 24 October, at Molesworth Street, Dublin. Theresa was to be the first of ten children born in steady succession from 1862 to 1887. In the next five years, three more girls were born at Castle Coole – Florence in 1864, Madeline in 1865 and Mary in 1867. Honoria's life, not surprisingly, was therefore almost completely wrapped up in the rearing and education of their children. No doubt, four daughters meant trying again for a son and heir.

Belmore had intended to spend most of his time at Castle Coole after the birth of Theresa, but 1863 turned out to be another year of funerals. In February 1863 he and Honoria had to go hurriedly to England where her father was extremely ill. He died just two days after they arrived. In December 1863, Belmore's cousin and uncle, Major Richard Magenis, father-in-law of Belmore's sister Louisa, died. He was a real link with the origins of the Lowry Corrys, the grandson of Galbraith Lowry Corry, Belmore's great-great-grandfather, through Anna, Lady Enniskillen. Belmore's sister, Lady Emily, died in 1864 at the age of 20.

A Peer of Ability

While Honoria had to stay at Castle Coole, either looking after or expecting children and taking care of things generally, Belmore was becoming more involved in parliamentary business and was also being noticed as a useful politician.

Although his experience of speaking in the House was limited, his style was noticed and appreciated. On one occasion he made a speech against the appointment of Acheson Lyle as lord lieutenant of Londonderry, after which:

> 'Lord Carlisle, who probably expected a speech in the usual Irish style was kind enough
> … to compliment me on the moderation and taste of my observations'.

On another occasion he spoke against a proposed extension of the Dublin Metropolitan Railway, which would have cut across Westmoreland Street, 'one of the handsomest and most important streets of the city, by means of a bridge'. A senior member of the Lords audibly told his neighbour it was 'a very good speech'.

Later in his life, he commented that he did not like to write out speeches. It took time and did not allow for flexibility in debate. As for writing itself, he claimed, modestly perhaps, that he had little early experience of it, although he had published a correspondence he had had:

> 'with a belligerent North of Ireland clergyman, who, from his name of Flannagan, being probably of Celtic extraction was "more Orange than the Orangemen" … upon the subject of the clergy of the Irish Established Church accepting grants from the National Board of Education'.

This actually brought him to the attention of Lord Naas, the then Irish Conservative leader. Naas was a great supporter of the national system of education, a subject in which Belmore himself was later to become actively involved. Belmore 'found composition easiest when walking about the room, an hereditary habit in my family'. In these snippets of information about his political and literary beginnings Belmore reveals his gentle humour, courteous style and talent for anecdotes. It was later said that 'His wonderful memory seemed to be stored with an endless record of persons and events'.[1]

Belmore's increasing involvement in business in the House meant, inevitably, that Honoria saw less of him. They did manage to take a short break together in the summer when they went abroad to the Tyrol and Switzerland for a holiday, returning to Ireland in October. Belmore then took his brother, Henry William, then aged 18, to Trinity College, Cambridge where he was entered as a fellow commoner.

Belmore's work in parliament, which was to lead to his appointment as a junior minister, continued with a private bill providing for the amalgamation of the Great Western and West Midland Railway Companies and the London and North Western and Midland Railway Companies; and for the Manchester and Sheffield and the Lancashire and Yorkshire companies to share traffic arrangements, including standardising fares to make bookings easier. Competition between companies was making for inefficiency and expense at a time when all companies were increasingly hungry for capital investment. Their methods of inducing investors to provide capital, some of them bordering on the criminal, had led to a serious lack of public confidence. The problems were found to be deeper than at first thought and so a select committee of the House of Lords, which had been appointed to consider the Bill's proposals, was asked to widen its investigation into the financing and borrowing powers of railway companies generally. Belmore, due to the illness of the Chairman of the Committee, was asked to take the chair. He conducted the examination of all the witnesses, experts and otherwise and, as a result, acquired a detailed knowledge of the complexities of railway finance.

Photograph of HRH Prince Alfred, Duke of Edinburgh presented to the Earl of Belmore

He was then asked to bring in a bill to carry out the recommendations of the committee and had his cousin, John Corry Lowry, a Dublin lawyer, draft it. When he brought it to the House, 'as no one appeared to attend to what I was saying … I left off speaking'. The Bill passed. Belmore's main purpose was to secure more transparency in railway companies' financial affairs by requiring the publication of their borrowings. 'One or two of the railway companies had taken fright', so the Bill faced serious opposition in the Commons and the government withdrew it.

No further action was taken regarding the problem so, two years later, in 1866, Belmore asked the government if they intended to do anything. Lord Russell, the Prime Minister, gave a weak reply, as a result of which the *Times* and members of parliament called for Belmore's bill to be re-introduced. Conservatives and landowners were afraid it would increase their unpopularity and Belmore himself admitted, 'if this Bill passed which now there seemed nothing to prevent, the power and hopes of the party were irretrievably gone'. His fears were unfounded, for when in June the government was defeated on a vote the Queen asked Lord Derby to form a government. Unknown to Belmore at the time, he was to became responsible for his own bill again and, slightly modified, it was to pass into law.

In 1865 and 1866, Belmore had been appointed to three further committees – on land drainage in Ireland, on navigation on the Shannon waterway and on further aspects of railway financing. He also became very much involved in inquiries into the parlous condition of Irish railways. At the end of 1865, a new royal commission on railways became necessary and Gladstone asked Belmore to become one of its members.

At the first meeting of the Commission in January 1867 very few members were present and so Belmore, with his previous experience, was asked to take the chair. The Commission inquired firstly into Irish railways and then into English railways, going through some 16,000 questions and answers with witnesses, besides a mass of papers submitted to it. The inquiry was finally completed by Easter 1867 and it was Belmore who presented it formally to parliament. His work brought him recognition and office, for when he presented his bill and the Commission's report it was as a government minister – under secretary at the Home Office. Lord Granville later claimed that the Prime Minister, Lord Derby, 'reminded me … that I was the first person who had brought your ability as a peer to his notice'.

Owing to various unforeseen events, the formation of the new administration took a much longer time than usual. 'In fact, so long was it,' wrote Belmore, 'that I made up my mind that I should not be included in the Ministry and we left town'. As he could not be found, the note from Lord Derby confirming Belmore's appointment had gone to his mother's house in Eaton Place, from where she sent him a telegram announcing the news. Belmore, who had been told he would get an appointment, but had hoped for the vice presidency of the Board of Trade, was the first peer ever to fill the post of under secretary at the Home Office. It had, in fact, been offered to his uncle Henry, who had taken instead the vice presidency of the Council on Education.

On 9 March 1867, his birthday, Uncle Henry Corry was appointed first lord of the Admiralty – 'a very nice birthday present', he remarked to the Prime Minister, Lord Derby. He was an expert on the navy and naval service, a subject about which he frequently spoke in the House of Commons, and he wrote a pamphlet about naval pay. One of his most difficult tasks was to handle the delicate and expensive business of providing a new royal yacht for the Queen, who had definite views on the project. He was one of the longest-serving MPs of his day and became father of the House. He died in 1873.

Belmore began his work at the Home Office in July 1866. He was understandably pleased about the job and keen to do well – so keen, in fact, that he volunteered to take on extra duties. At first responsible for salmon fisheries, mines, burials and turnpikes and for Home Office business in the House of Lords, he assumed the additional responsibility for Board of Trade business in the House of Lords at the request of Sir Stafford Northcote. This recognised his abilities as a clear, capable speaker and organiser and was an indication that his career was promising. During that session he managed the Treasury and Irish Bills as well and, in all, passed some 31 bills through the House. The post also enabled him to pay off more inherited obligations: 'My official salary was a great help in that respect'. However, it seems likely that his commitment to business made it difficult for him to give his personal support to Honoria as much as she might have wanted, away in the north-west of Ireland.

When Belmore returned to London from Ireland in October 1866 he took on an extra load of work dealing with criminal cases, standing in for a colleague who was away on holiday. This kept him late at the Ministry and frequently meant he had to take work home. He had also to deal with increasing problems of unrest caused by trade-union disputes and increasing Fenian activity.

In Sheffield, the house of a former member of the union of sawgrinders was blown up, allegedly at the instigation of the union itself; and in Chester there was a suspected plot by Fenians to capture Chester Castle and its considerable quantity of weapons. Trainloads of men had arrived there during the night, encamped at the station and started to parade the following morning. Two other Fenian risings took place in Kerry and Dublin at about the same time, but all were unsuccessful. The rising in Dublin, noted Belmore:

'was suppressed by the police, who received gratuities afterwards amounting to £2,000 – the force was called the Royal Irish Constabulary in consequence of the distinction gained by its members on this occasion'.

Belmore came under more pressure when he was appointed chairman of a select committee inquiring into proposals to regulate London traffic just at a time when illness in his office meant a larger workload for him. Once again, he was working late at home. During his 12 months at the Home Office he was 'concerned actively in a rather unusual quantity of legislation', steering about 60 bills through parliament.

'Soon after Easter I requested my uncle to apply for a colonial government. He and I both wanted Canada'. The Colonial Secretary, the Duke of Buckingham, was a cousin of Honoria's and 'always very friendly' to Belmore. Even so, Henry Corry tried to persuade Belmore to remain in the administration, 'uncertain as its tenure of office was' – a point

The Derby Cabinet, 1867, including Henry Corry, by Henry Gales, 1868

no doubt weighing heavily in the balance for Belmore. He could foresee a bright future for Belmore in mainstream politics but, eventually, reluctantly consented to the idea even though it was 'rather against the grain'.

For Belmore, it was not just that the prospects for the government were bad, but he could not shake off his deeply pessimistic view of the prospects for his class if electoral reform, then being proposed, was completed. He could not have foreseen the resurgence after 1867 of the Conservatives under Disraeli; but his chief concerns were the constant separation from his wife and family and, in his own words, 'in the not very lucrative position of an Irish landlord', getting a job with longer-term prospects and a salary. Canada came with a salary of £10,000 and New South Wales with £7,000 – although, with expenses, that rose to about £9,000.

'The Duke of Buckingham asked if I would go to Australia. I told him I did not mind'. Lord Derby, the Prime Minister, did not like ministers resigning so insisted Belmore remain until the Reform Bill was under way through the Lords:

> 'Meeting him shortly afterwards at Lady Derby's evening party, he said shortly as I came in: "We shall be broken hearted at losing you" – a compliment which, being the only one he ever paid me, I duly appreciated'.

So it was that he was gazetted governor of New South Wales on 22 August 1867, succeeding Sir John Young, another Irishman, who had been chief secretary to the Lord Lieutenant of Ireland and MP for Cavan. 'I left the Home Office as soon as the Reform bill was through Committee in the Lords'.

He returned to Castle Coole and left there with the family on 16 September 1867, 'leaving things in good order', especially content that the new church and clergyman's house at Garvary, which he had paid for, was nearly finished. In Dublin, he was sworn in as a member of the Privy Council in Ireland and then went, via his Aunt Mrs Georges's house at Leamington, to see his mother, brothers and sisters and Richard Magenis at Edwardstone. They finally called at Honoria's old home at Bowden Park on their way to Plymouth where they embarked on the *Sobraon*, the regular sailing to New South Wales, and departed on 11 October with a fair wind. Buckingham had wanted them to leave in August on the P&O mail steamer but they were delayed. This was lucky for them, as it turned out – the steamer was wrecked in the Red Sea. It was not entirely surprising, therefore, that they found 'the sailing ship was much the most comfortable way of going'. Not only that, but it was a material consideration that Belmore's expense allowance for the journey of £800 covered the cost. He was, however, sailing into a dramatic start to his governorship.

Chapter Twenty

Complete Isolation and Dangerous Passion

His Royal Highness the Duke of Edinburgh, second son of Queen Victoria, a career naval officer and a skilful seaman, had arrived in South Australia at the end of October 1867. The Queen had given him permission to make a voyage round the world on the *Galatea*, a large steam-powered frigate, which he captained. He stayed for almost five months, visiting Adelaide, Melbourne, Sydney, Brisbane and Tasmania. It had been expected that by the time the *Sobraon* docked, the Duke would have been and gone, but he was enjoying himself immensely and decided to visit Sydney again.

Belmore may have been comfortable on the *Sobraon*, but travelling under leisurely sail, he and his party arrived at the climax of the preparations for the Duke's second visit. There were just two weeks before the 'jolly party' on the *Galatea*, with its 'excellent set of officers' would arrive. There were triumphal arches, transparencies and illuminations, a

The *Galatea*

naval reception, schoolchildren waving flags, a dramatic performance by students of Sydney University, exhibitions in Hyde Park, races at Randwick and a regatta.

Government House was in turmoil. The Governor's quarters upstairs had been taken over and were being furnished for the Duke and his party, in the middle of the cleaning and renovation work which had only recently started after the departure of the last governor in December. Belmore had to spend his first night on board and landed privately the next day to have a look at the house and to be rowed around Sydney bay in one of the *Sobraon*'s boats. The next day, he landed in formal dress, saluted by two navy ships and the 17 guns of Dawe's Battery, and was met by a guard of honour, the acting Governor and other dignitaries. He held a levée in the drawing room of Government House, remarking that 'as the morning had been wet the effect of some gentlemen carrying umbrellas through the room as they passed was peculiar'. It was only the slightest hint of the differences he might expect in the behaviour of the colonial society he would encounter – society where, in the words that same morning of the *Sydney Herald*:

> 'without hereditary position, or ascertained rank, the lines of demarcation are commonly arbitrary. Thus everything is possible to everyone, and in this eagerness for advancement there is often a ruinous competiton. It is fortunate when the good sense and good taste of those who are the head of our social system moderate by example this dangerous passion. We fear it would be found, if enquiry were made, that there are multitudes of families often in deep distress, sometimes in dishonour, through the facility of credit and the habit of exceeding their income'.

If local society was that undisciplined, the *Sydney Herald* thought its politicians worse. Belmore would require:

> 'no small degree of self-possession to escape the snares of faction ... The Earl of Belmore comes just as two parties, perhaps we should say twenty, are struggling for the possession of power'.

The paper concluded by hoping that his 'cultured mind and habits of business will enable him to master the difficulties of Colonial Government'.

Belmore found, like his grandfather before him in Jamaica, that 'the position of Governor was one of complete isolation'. Communication with the Home Office was no better, at intervals of six to ten weeks, than 40 years before, and he found almost the same type of thin-skinned politicians and unruly parliaments that had confronted the second Earl in Jamaica.

The Governor was by no means 'a mere figurehead'.[1] Belmore had often to judge whether he should take the advice of ministers or use his own discretion and hope for London's approval later – there was no one else for him to consult. In March, Buckingham had privately advised Belmore that he had nothing to say about Belmore's responsibilities 'except to hope that you will keep Sydney out of any mess similar to that now existing in Victoria'. Victoria's mess was constitutional and, in Sydney, Belmore would face some constitutional issues soon enough.

Portrait of the 4th Earl as Governor

He had already had experience, in February, of personal animosities between members of the New South Wales parliament. Insults exchanged between two of them resulted in scuffles and blows. For one of these men that was not enough – he hid a loaded horsewhip in the library and, when the session was adjourned, got hold of it and struck his opponent across the face with it. 'The scene that now ensued was more exciting than anything that had before taken place in the Parliament of New South Wales'. Others joined in and the melée continued in the reading room until they were all physically separated. The issue was payments out of government funds without the authority of a finance act, but in anticipation of it: 'The ever recurring difficulty of ministries was getting supply passed in proper time'. By 1870, Belmore had minuted ministers 'couched in as strong and plain language as I thought prudent', proposing changes which led to the Audit Act and a resolution of the difficulties. Even so, the treasurer thought this was interference by the British government with the principle of colonial independence.

In the absence of a clearly developed and mature party system, what should have been problems requiring parliamentary solutions were more likely to be driven by personal animosities. The Treasurer, a government minister, accused the Collector of Customs, an official, of insubordination, but the Collector refused to concede that the Minister had any control over customs. The real problem was bad feeling between the two and, although Belmore thought 'a full and ample' apology by the Collector should have ended the matter, the Minister was adamant and the Collector was dismissed.

In the meantime, Belmore's full attention had to be on the Duke's visit. 'It was a great scramble to settle down and get everything ready'. It was not until the day after the Duke's arrival that Belmore's belongings and everything necessary for his first full-dress official dinner that same evening were unloaded from the *Sobraon*. There was a further dinner the following day and then, a few days later, a ball that opened with a quadrille danced by the Duke with Honoria Belmore.

Entertainments followed in succession for several weeks, including a citizens' ball given by the Mayor of Sydney, Charles Moore, who had originally come from County Cavan. Belmore was constantly coming across fellow countrymen. During a visit to the Hunter river with the Duke a voice in the crowd called out 'Hurrah for Castle Coole!' It was the voice of a man who had been in a fight in Fermanagh on 13 July 1829, between Orangemen and Roman Catholics, known as the 'Macken fight'. Lead for the bullets had been stripped from the Belmore family vault under the church at Derryvullen. Some of the participants had been sent to Botany Bay.

The Duke and Belmore attended an agricultural show at Maitland and Nepean Towers, near which they shot rabbits: 'at that time the rabbit pest was not known and these were the only rabbits which I ever saw in the Colonies of Australia'. While the Duke visited Brisbane in Queensland, the Belmores went house-hunting for a summer residence, but only found an iron house which 'seemed to admit the rain very freely'.

On Thursday 12 March, continuing the celebrations, the Duke and his entourage with Belmore and his family and officials went by steamer to a public picnic on the shore at Middle Harbour, Clontarf. The fête, which was to raise funds for a charity, 'the Sailors' Home', was attended by about 1,500 people who came by water from Sydney and its neighbourhood. Lunch was in one of the tents that had been erected facing a large grassy, sandy space leading down to a fringe of gum trees along the shore. The area was crowded and a corroboree of some 300 aborigines was to take place there. The Duke left the tent in conversation with Sir William Manning, President of the charity, and Belmore supposed that he was to hand a cheque for the Home to Sir William.

'I did not, therefore, pay particular attention to the movements of his Royal Highness, but walked slowly in the same direction, engaged in conversation with the Chief Justice, for about sixty or eighty yards, when I believe I stopped and turned round towards the tent. Almost immediately I heard a cry from the other side of the clear space, near the belt of gum trees, and, on turning round saw a rush of people. I had heard no shots; and it at once occurred to me that some game, or the corrobboree [*sic*], was about to begin. Someone near me said "the Duke is shot"; and another person, "He is shot, and has fallen down dead."'

The Duke had been shot at close range in the back by a man called Henry James O'Farrell. O'Farrell tried to shoot a second time but the revolver had misfired; he then turned it on himself but a Mr Vial, a coachbuilder, jumped on his back and forced his hands down. The bullet struck a man who was running up to them in the ankle bone. The Duke was carried back to the tent and Belmore 'immediately saw that he was not killed, and the expression of his face struck me at once as not being that of a person mortally wounded'. The crowd were only just prevented by soldiers from getting hold of O'Farrell and lynching him. He was hurried away onto a steamer and taken to Sydney. A local writer, Elizabeth Rickets Hall, wrote:

> 'it would be impossible to describe how all felt and looked and the scene at Clontarf was terrible beyond everything – women and men fainted and sobbed and the criminal was nearly torn to pieces on the spot and with difficulty saved from lynch law'.

Several doctors were present to attend to the Duke's wounds and Honoria Belmore returned to Government House to prepare a ground-floor room for the Duke, complete with the services of 'two of the trained nurses selected by Miss Florence Nightingale for the Sydney Infirmary', who had only arrived the week before. The bullet had entered half an inch away from the Duke's spine and, after travelling downwards, lodged between his right nipple and navel. Because of the shock the bullet was not removed until two days later.

The immediate concern was how to let the government and the Queen know without delay and in secrecy what the Duke's condition really was. To prevent any likelihood that news of the attack would first reach the Queen unofficially by public telegraph, it was suggested a special fast steamer should be sent immediately. As the Duke had himself sent an open telegram to his mother, Belmore urgently needed to send a coded message to the Colonial Office. As the Office had no official cypher, he hit on the notion of using the current naval cypher and sending the telegraph via Henry Corry at the Admiralty. Even that was dogged by ill luck. The message arrived so mutilated it was not clear to the Colonial Secretary, Buckingham, that the Duke had survived. This 'caused the utmost alarm' and Buckingham had just steeled himself to break the news to the Queen and to say whatever he could to comfort her, when Belmore's own open telegram arrived. Buckingham went to Osborne, where the Queen bore the news well but, until she received Belmore's telegram explaining the whole situation, 'felt deeply a mother's anxiety'.

Shortly after the event, Belmore 'fully believed' that the task of killing the Duke had been allotted to O'Farrell and he dreaded another attempt. Government House became a barracks for the many sailors and police guarding it but the only creature they ever caught one night was one of the three emus that lived on the estate.

Belmore's official account was eventually published in the newspapers and it is apparent that even at that early stage he was careful not to give undue weight to allegations made about O'Farrell's motives. 'Although the prisoner has avowed himself to be a Fenian, his family have undertaken his defence on the ground of insanity'. Was O'Farrell a lone madman or part of a Fenian plot? The distinction became important, because politics kicked in and gave Belmore his first experience of the 'snares of faction'

The Earl of Belmore's 'punishment book' showing appeals from sentences of death

in local politicking. Henry Parkes, Colonial Secretary in the government of New South Wales, set out to turn the attempted assassination to his own political advantage, even to the extent of claiming foreknowledge of the conspiracy.

To gain public support, Parkes, who was strongly prejudiced against the Irish, immediately began his own, very personal, investigation, convinced in his own mind that the police force, mostly Irish, could not be trusted. He was supported, perhaps confirmed, in his views because Fenian terrorism in England was regularly reported in the local newspapers. As recently as 27 November, a crowd of Irish Catholics had stormed the Orange Lodge building in Melbourne, which the Prince was attending. Shots were fired and a youth was fatally wounded. There were rumours about an upsurge of sectarianism.

Parkes first personally interviewed O'Farrell on the evening of the shooting and then searched his hotel room in which he found some percussion caps, cartridges, wadding for revolvers, a Douay Bible and other religious books. At the interview he asked O'Farrell why he had committed such an outrage, to which O'Farrell replied, 'Come, come, it is not fair to ask such a question as that … it's only a side wound – I shall be hanged, but the Prince will live'.

Parkes convinced himself that a Fenian group and O'Farrell were all part of the conspiracy to kill Prince Alfred, but Belmore saw that Parkes had crossed over an

An Inspection Tour by the Viceroy on board the steamer *Agnes* – The villagers of McLean, Rocky Mouth bid farewell
to the viceregal party on its way to Grafton. Watercolour by G H Bruhn (geologist and amateur painter)
no date but possibly 1867

important line between lawful and unlawful behaviour when 'very irregularly on the part
of a cabinet Minister' he returned to the jail with a shorthand writer and cross-questioned
O'Farrell further. It was only then that O'Farrell actually said he was a Fenian who had
been chosen by lot to avenge three men who had been hanged at Manchester for the
murder of a police sergeant in 1867. Parkes had not cautioned O'Farrell but:

> 'believed all of this story, which in fact was so circumstantial, that, although it could
> not be made use of at the trial, the Prime Minister and his colleagues thought it
> desirable to take every precaution against a possible Fenian conspiracy'.

At the suggestion of the British Government, they speedily passed a Treason Felony Act,
even though, as Belmore observed, having plenty of parliamentary troubles of their own,
they would not, but for this event, have been very happy to introduce it.

O'Farrell was convicted of the then-capital offence of wounding with intent to murder.
Belmore had changed his earlier reaction and was, by now, so sceptical about the evidence
of a Fenian plot that he presented to his executive council a plea for clemency from the
Duke of Edinburgh himself and evidence of O'Farrell's mental state from the surgeon of
the jail. He also advised ministers to exercise caution in seeking to apply the unusual
powers of the new Treason Felony Act.

On the other hand, he was not impressed by O'Farrell's family and friends, of whom
he said in a letter to his sister, Louisa:

> 'With the exception of his sister Mrs Allan, who seemed to care more about the
> disgrace to herself than anything (and one man who goes in for the abolition of capital
> punishment) his friends have taken his case very coolly'.

The Roman Catholic Archbishop of Sydney took O'Farrell's dying confession, which was subsequently released and in which he said the shooting was that of his own doing and that what he had told Parkes was unfounded and there was no Fenian involvement. Parkes was then blamed for causing a Fenian scare after the shooting, especially since he had never really found any evidence. After exhaustive inquiries into the allegations of a Fenian conspiracy, Belmore thought that 'the balance of probabilities was in favour of O'Farrell's dying statement'. He thought that Fenianism in the colony went no further than sympathy. He had received one threatening letter 'in the regular old Irish style' but which was only 'a foolish attempt at a hoax on the part of a boy or a man in a shop'.

The fact that Belmore was himself Irish does not seem to have been a factor in the unrolling of the story. He kept troops discreetly out of sight when Roman Catholics held a meeting to express their loyalty and he refused to accept a loyal declaration from the Orange Order, because it was a political gesture. 'With public passions inflamed, the press on edge and his ministry alarmed, Belmore calmly and quickly helped to restore rationality'.[2]

Some time afterwards, Belmore heard from Buckingham, later confirmed by a lady-in-waiting, that the Queen had entirely approved of the way he had dealt with the attempted assassination and the events surrounding it.

During his tenure, Belmore presided at about 60 sittings of the Executive Council a year and made himself thoroughly familiar with government business and his ministers. He found that ministers were 'apt to act independently of their colleagues … Some ministers try also sometimes to keep the Governor in the dark as to what they intend doing'. In December 1868 he refused to dissolve parliament at the request of ministers who used it to sidetrack and undermine the Governor's authority, advising the Colonial Office that his practice of refusing dissolutions on request would stop ministers acting in departmental matters independently of the Governor and each other.

In spite of all these difficulties, Belmore, who became an acute observer of his ministers' friendships and animosities, felt he had much support from them and successfully got through a great deal of business. He also had to deal with matters outside the scope of New South Wales politics, for example: many cases of kidnapping in the Pacific by British subjects; keeping direct contact with the *de facto* ruler of Fiji; and the consequences of the Franco-Prussian war in 1870, including advice on the defence of Sydney. He felt that he had a special responsibility in criminal matters, especially in deciding whether death sentences should be confirmed or commuted. Each of his decisions was recorded in a book which is still at Castle Coole and suggests that he readily commuted death sentences although the alternative, a prison sentence with hard labour, was probably not much consolation for a prisoner.

His own personal enthusiasm for agriculture and railways sharpened his interest in their development in the colony and he made it his business to visit as many country areas as possible. In the frequent absence of railways at the time, he undertook these visits by steamer, by buggy and on horseback. He made 16 tours and, ironically, saw a great deal more than he would have done if railways had been built. He also visited Victoria,

Tasmania and Norfolk Island. He made several speeches about agriculture and railway development, describing his approach to them as 'a practical man of business' and 'a strong official'.

His experiences as an Irish landowner came into play in his speeches. He spoke especially about the vital need to raise finance for storing and distributing water to the interior, as one who had benefited from public loans in Ireland. While suggesting how results might be achieved, he ironically acknowledged that in Ireland the problem was not storing water but getting rid of it. He warned against the indiscriminate removal of too many trees, citing the example of Spain. As for railways, he had learned that the profitable way was to lay out main lines and avoid too many branch lines, which ran away with profits. He stressed the importance of winegrowing and coal and the dangers of allowing the soil to become exhausted, as had happened in Ireland. He demonstrated his commitment to the importance of these practical considerations by becoming an active member of the Agricultural Society and, in 1870, opened the first Intercolonial Exhibition in Prince Alfred Park. He presented £300 to Sydney University for a medal in agricultural chemistry and geology, later converted to a scholarship.

He developed these practical themes, especially about railway development, in great detail in other speeches, concluding in one saying that to the extent that railways increased free interaction between neighbours:

> 'nothing tends more to encourage the belief that those who differ from one another either in religion or politics may be actuated in their conduct by motives as disinterested, or as patriotic as one's own'.

This was more than a statement of worthy sentiment, for behind it lay Belmore's developing ideas for 'a closer bond of union' between the Australian colonies themselves and between the colonies and England; and increasing the number of visitors and immigrants. More even than that, it was only a short abstraction from his vision of 'a system of railways connecting the four continental capitals' to his proposal to the English government for an Australian federal government, presided over by a governor general, with a lieutenant governor for each colony. At the time, his idea was, as he himself said, abstract, but in the early twentieth century it was to become the reality.

Belmore's first year in office augured well for his future. He and Honoria Belmore, both tall, dark haired and good looking, made an impressive viceregal pair.

When Buckingham left office in December he wrote to say he had every reason to be satisfied with his choice of Belmore for the government of New South Wales and that he had no doubt that he would have a successful career.

Belmore, however, would soon be forced once again to choose between career and family. Their official residence, Government House, a Gothic-revival building, its north wall covered by a colourful bougainvillea, was in itself a pleasant place to live. It was set in beautifully laid-out grounds overlooking Sydney harbour. 'It was the fashion to call it too small,' but the Belmores found it large enough for all practical purposes.

The Belmore's house Throsby Park, Moss Vale, NSW

However, they were irritated by having to give in to snobbery about trifles – being criticised, for example, for sending out their invitation cards without envelopes. In London these had gone out of fashion but 'as the Stationary [*sic*] Department supplied them' Belmore brought them back into use, remarking, 'I must admit that I had not much patience with or time for trivialities of that kind'. He did not at all approve of the debt-ridden fashionable set of Sydney and felt that by setting a relatively frugal example he and Honoria 'very likely prevented a good deal of expenditure which could have been ill afforded, but which of course would have benefited a certain (shopkeeping) class'. For him, with a personal feeling of horror at the consequences of extravagance, the support of people whose good opinion he really appreciated was what mattered.

Nevertheless, the Belmores' social life was lively enough. It included the races, the theatre, public dinners and evening meetings (which he thought overdone, as they were scantily attended). That first year, 1868, meant a heavy list of dinners, about 50 in all (the usual number in a year was about 30) including four for members and officials of parliament. For the fashionable there was a season, beginning at about the time of Queen Victoria's birthday in May, when there was a birthday ball, which was 'considered the proper occasion for young ladies to "come out" at'. About 700 people were invited, including the Governor's principal tradesmen in Sydney, who considered themselves entitled to an invitation. Supper was contracted for by a well-known restaurateur, Compagnoni. Belmore always wore his Buckingham Palace uniform. There were other private balls to attend, some on men-of-war, including one on a French troop ship. There were about four dances a year with about 200 people and four evening parties with singing by very good amateurs.

The *Sobraon*

However, the hot summers of Sydney, the unrelenting social life and the many tours around the colony and elsewhere, affected Honoria Belmore's health. They had already tried to find a summer retreat and they were at last successful, renting Throsby Park House, built in 1836, in Moss Vale in the southern highlands, 124 kilometres south-west of Sydney, with a population of just 134. The district lies between two rivers, the Shoalhaven and Wollondilly, which have beautiful and dramatic gorges. The scenery and healthy climate made the place popular as a holiday resort – partly with the arrival of the Belmores, but especially with the coming of train travel from Sydney. The Falls, named after Belmore, are on a creek that flows into the Shoalhaven.

In 1869, they looked forward to the birth of their second child there. It was their first son, but he was stillborn. This made Honoria Belmore's condition worse and her sisters wrote from Bowden Park urging her to return home. The Belmores decided that they would not stay beyond March 1872. In the meantime she became pregnant again and had a son, Armar, Viscount Corry, born at Government House on 5 May 1870.

A year later, in June 1871, Belmore asked to be relieved of the government of the colony.[3] Although he said that he wanted to resume a parliamentary career and to give more time to his estates 'from the circumstances of recent Irish legislation' (the Land Acts), the real cause was Honoria's anxiety to return home to Castle Coole. She had now had six pregnancies in rather less than ten years, as well as the sadness of losing a child at birth, and was no longer able to support the pressures of life in New South Wales. The heat of another summer had settled the matter.

Belmore, anxious to get her and the children safely home again, proposed that his resignation should take effect in the following March so that they could sail in the *Sobraon*, a ship he particularly liked for its 'superior accommodation' (especially important with five small children) and 'a superior captain'. It was still cheaper than a steamer and, as he had resigned, he would have to pay his own passage money. He must have been disappointed not to have completed the normal five-year tour of duty, considering what a success he had been making of the job. The government in London certainly thought so. Kimberley, the Colonial Secretary, said:

> 'the affairs of New South Wales have gone on quietly and prosperously under your government, and your successful administration is fully appreciated here'.

The Belmores' departure from Sydney was accompanied by the usual ceremonies. Two parks were named after them – one in Goulburn, where the oak tree planted by Honoria Belmore still flourishes, and the other in Sydney.

On Belmore's return to England, the government expressed its gratitude for his services by awarding him the Order of Knight Commander of St Michael and St George, an honour, sixth at that time in the ranks of orders of chivalry, given to individuals who had rendered important colonial services. The Order's motto, 'Auspicium melioris aevi' (token of a better age), might well have appealed to Belmore as he looked forward to the next stage in his life.

Chapter Twenty-one

Marriage and Family Life at Castle Coole

When Belmore returned home with his family he found things there as he had left them, 'in good order', and the family quickly settled into a pattern of life at Castle Coole which had not changed greatly for many years, and which would continue fundamentally unchanged for very many years to come. It was to be very much a child-centred world for, by the summer of 1872, Honoria was pregnant again. She had already borne five living children and would have eight more in the next 15 years.

Honoria became the dominant influence in the family, a true matriarch, presiding over a quintessential Victorian regime of strict discipline, religious observance, schoolroom education and a social life typical of the upper classes of the time. The good condition in which the children's toys, games and books were handed down to later generations (who, according to a member of the present family, handled them less respectfully) is evidence of the influence of her authority.

Belmore himself liked a regular routine. He would, for example, when he was at home, go down to the grand yard each morning at a few minutes to ten, stand outside the entrance arch below the servants' tunnel, and, at precisely ten o'clock, enter the yard through the arch to inspect the work being done there, the horses and the carriages.

Honoria's bedroom at Castle Coole, known as the Victorian bedroom, is still dominated by her portrait on the far wall. Her eyes seem to follow a visitor to the room and this is the only room in the house in which guides and visitors have ever said they could feel a supernatural presence. However, as will be seen later, Victorian rules did not by any means prevent the children from enjoying themselves at Castle Coole, just as earlier children had.

In the wider Irish world, good order – the established order, as understood by Belmore's class – was increasingly being threatened by political change. As a committed Anglican, the disestablishment of the Church of Ireland in 1871 had been a major issue for Belmore, and for the rest of his life one of his chief interests was the life and work of the Church. In 1870 his practical administrative abilities had, while he was still in Sydney, already made a major contribution to the Church's organisation in Tyrone. He had secured the re-creation of a separate diocese for Clogher, which had been amalgamated with Armagh earlier in the century.

The position of landlords was about to become progressively 'disestablished' as well. Belmore was, at first, sublimely unconcerned at the protection given to tenants by the

Land Act of 1870, because tenants' rights had long been recognised on the Belmore estates. He had, some time before, abandoned attempts to impose a limit on what price a tenant could ask by 'Ulster Custom' on a sale and, instead, as he put it, 'merely retained the right to approve of a purchaser'. This arrangement, he thought, had worked so well that no claim was ever brought against him under the Act. Landlords elsewhere took a quite different view, seeing the Act as a cautious start by the government to conceding the principle of legislative interference in property rights: for them it was about to become a political line in the sand.

The issue was brought dramatically to life in early 1873 with the death of Belmore's uncle Henry Corry, after 47 years as member for Tyrone, resulting in a by-election, followed almost immediately by a general election in 1874. With no son old enough to contest the county, the Belmore interest seemed likely to lapse, and might never be recovered even when Armar came of age.[1]

At first, Belmore supported a strong candidate for the Conservatives, Stuart Knox, member for the borough of Dungannon, but immediately wrote to his brother, Henry William Lowry Corry, asking him to stand in Knox's place for Dungannon. Henry, who had inherited the old Shepherd home, Edwardstone Hall in Suffolk, was a captain in the army and had a real prospect of almost immediate promotion. Nevertheless, he answered the call to stand for Dungannon but, when Knox decided to stay put there, was thrown to the lions to contest the traditional family seat in Tyrone.

Political lions in the shape of the Tyrone Orangemen were real enough and were looking likely, in the absence of Knox, to support a barrister, Ellison Macartney. Macartney's extreme Orange supporters wanted unrestricted tenants' rights and he seemed to be collecting strong support. On tenants' rights, Henry reminded the farming constituency – 'the bone and sinew' of Tyrone – of 'the rights and privileges which have ever been ungrudgingly granted to the tenants on the estates of my ancestors' and promised 'to advance their interests'. This statement was too much for the fiery Knox and other Conservatives who thought it so vague as to establish no difference between them and Macartney and failed to make it clear that the provisions of the 1870 Act were, as far as they were concerned, a final settlement of the issue of tenants' rights.

Belmore and Henry had got into hot water right at the start. They were not helped by the existence of another Belmore family connection – thought by some, especially the Duke of Abercorn, to be the man most likely to beat Macartney to the Orange vote. This was Henry Corry's barrister son, Montagu William Lowry Corry. Montagu Corry had been Disraeli's private secretary since 1866 and this, added to his father's memory, was thought likely to influence voters in his favour. He would have been a formidable contestant as his subsequent career shows. He served Disraeli until 1881, and Disraeli recommended him for a peerage as Baron Rowton in 1880. He has been described as more than a private secretary; he was a surrogate son and Disraeli's 'true heir' – who, Queen Victoria remarked, had devoted himself to his chief 'as few sons ever do'. As if confirming this, Disraeli made him his literary executor.[2]

Montagu Corry, Lord Rowton by Violet Manners,
Duchess of Rutland 1888

When Disraeli had decided to buy the Suez Canal, it was Montagu Corry whom he sent to Baron Rothschild to ask for the loan of four million pounds:

> '"When" said Rothschild. "Tomorrow" replied Corry. Rothschild (*pausing to eat a muscatel grape and spit out the skin*) "What is your security?" "The British Government" said Corry. "You shall have it"'.[3]

In 1890, Montagu Corry helped to set up the Guinness Trust and, after surveying London's common lodging houses for it, decided to set up working men's hostels. He put up the initial £30,000 and the first Rowton House was opened at Bondway, Vauxhall in 1892. In the first year 140,105 beds were let at 6d a night. For this the customer received clean sheets, had the use of tiled washrooms, footbaths and washing troughs for clothes, all with ample hot water. There was also a lodgers' kitchen. Its success led to the formation of a company that constructed a number of similar establishments, known as Rowton houses.

Montagu Corry's loyalty to Disraeli was too strong to tempt him into frontline politics and, perhaps like Belmore, he saw himself more as a good administrator. Faced with criticism, differing advice and reports of the strength of Macartney's support, Belmore wavered, uncertain whether they should contest the county, and worried in case Henry succeeded only in splitting the Conservative vote and making them unpopular. He wrote anxiously to Knox, feeling that the Orangemen would not support any landlord's candidate. Knox would have none of it. Henry had to go on and fight it out: 'You are not standing against the Orangemen of the county, but against a clique of the Grand Orange Lodge,' who should not be allowed to dictate to the county 'even if you doubted'. Political in-fighting was not to Belmore's taste. He saw himself not as a politician, but as he had claimed in Australia, 'a practical man of business'. Besides, he was a rather shy man, who accepted that he 'carried reserve too far'. Nonetheless, he plucked up his courage and telegraphed Knox to confirm they would continue the fight. Knox, delighted, sketched the line they should take with 'a rap against Gladstone & Co' to support the Land Act as a final settlement of the problems of tenants' rights: 'I again say, I am certain of success, with boldness. Assert, without wavering that your brother will fight all comers'.

They fought on unhappily, in a campaign clouded by doubts and by continuing differences among their own supporters about Corry's policy on tenants' rights, and remaining uncertain as to whether to withdraw. After all the intense anxiety and the effort and expense of getting their voters to the poll, Corry was elected – but with a

Disraeli and Montagu Corry in a Spy cartoon Power and Place, Vanity Fair 16th December 1879

majority of only 47. It cost Corry over £4,000 and Belmore £1,000. Their agent John Corry Lowry wrote:

> 'It will be monstrous if the young man be left to meet this frightful expense out of his own private purse. The fight was not for himself but for the conservative cause'.

Nobody offered to help the young man and by January the following year they had to start all over again in the general election following the resignation of Gladstone's government.

The issues were the same but the prospects for both Conservative candidates, Corry and Lord Claud Hamilton, Abercorn's son, were not good. Disraeli himself, aware of what he called 'the critical, not to say perilous, state of affairs in your county', wrote to Belmore anticipating a Macartney victory – 'an example of triumph which may spread fatally'. He advised that Corry withdraw from the 'disastrous contest', offering to remember him and later to secure him 'a safe and honourable seat' in England. Belmore was by now somewhat more hardened to the political struggle and was determined that if one candidate had to retire it would be Hamilton and not Corry. He wrote in reply to Disraeli, having 'a strong feeling in the matter', and refused to suggest to Corry that he should retire, as it would seriously injure any prestige or political influence he had in the county.

Corry was unanimously endorsed at a meeting of his supporters, which embittered Hamilton, who alleged that Corry had broken a promise to retire. Belmore sold stock worth almost £1,000 as a contribution towards expenses. Macartney and Corry were elected. Hamilton, very angry, swore he would never set foot in Tyrone again. Nevertheless, he continued to press his claim for the next election.

By the time that took place in 1885 Henry Corry had already decided to bow out of politics. His reason, given to Belmore two years earlier, was that owing to the fall in the value of land his income in future would not be sufficient. In any case, with the coming of 'household suffrage' (extended voting rights) he would have no chance of success in either Fermanagh or Tyrone. To cap it all, he disliked the 'disgraceful way' in which Gladstone's government had carried out and manipulated the Land Act of 1881 and was not prepared to consider the question again. What Henry probably understood was that the Belmore political stake in Tyrone and Fermanagh was being eroded by fundamental social and economic changes signalled by the land wars, the extension of suffrage and the campaign for Home Rule. Their financial stake would also be reduced.

To begin with, in the early 1870s, John J. Benison, Belmore's Fermanagh agent, was able to report consistently that everything was going well in the demesne.[4] There was a lot of drainage work, tested by frequent floods; a new steward, Thomas Weir, was taken on – 'an intelligent but illiterate man' – with undoubted skill and knowledge about farming. He would remain for many years. There were careful judgements to be made with tenants when rearranging farm holdings. Widow Hurst, for example, facing the loss of her house when a new tenant took over her late husband's farm, found it impossible to find a small place to suit her and her four children. Belmore arranged to provide her with the cottage of a man he moved elsewhere and transferred her late husband's small pension to her, on condition that she continued to work on the farm and as caretaker.

The 14 or so men working about the demesne, on drainage, manuring, road maintenance and threshing made for a pastoral scene.

But, by the late 1870s the business of bringing on cattle, which had always been the main activity in demesne farming, was hit by a fall in prices. This pressure was set to continue for the next decade, owing to the competition from American imports and a demand for smaller cattle than were normally reared at Castle Coole. Benison reported in September 1879: 'I fear very much we are in the beginning of very bad times for farmers'. The result was the first sign of difficulty Benison experienced in getting in rents. Belmore began to receive reports from Benison which could have left him in no doubt about the increasing demands of his tenants for lower rents and more security. Belmore's Fermanagh and Tyrone tenants were late in paying but intended to pay.

It was otherwise for landlords in Leitrim, which was in a very disturbed state – 'the people coming down like Zulus from the hills'. That county was the scene of operations by the Land League, which was preventing landlords and their agents from access to their land, making it worthless. Benison had to take a police guard for haymaking.

In November 1880, notwithstanding speeches made at Enniskillen Fair by Parnell, Dillon and others, Benison had a good rent day. He felt nonetheless that 'the evil spirit of the Land League is rapidly extending and life and property will shortly be equally safe in Ireland as in Afghanistan'. In December he reported that 'the Land League combination is extending. Boycotting has now become very general … and Enniskillen has not escaped'. Donnelly, the local butcher, refused to join. His men were not allowed to work and his hayrick was burned down. Cattle continued to be difficult to sell and so was wool. The winter of 1880–1881 was very hard. Stored potatoes were lost in the frost and many people also lost their seeds.

Belmore became ill with what his Tyrone agent, Richard Brush, described as 'liver problems', and went on a short sea voyage in the hope of a cure. In Fermanagh the situation remained calm and Benison was able to collect rents without trouble in May, but by October the situation worsened. There was no doubt that many tenants had fallen on hard times. A petition to Belmore in November from Mrs Margaret Beatty is an example:

> 'Pardon me the liberty i take in laying before your Lordship my case first in the spring of the year 1879 i had two horses died within one week of each other which prevented me of getting in a crop in time that year and the same year i had a heifer died and also lost about 14 ricks of hay by being flooded rendering it quite useless and last year i had a cow died all these losses together with three bad seasons in succession presses me to make this application to your Lordship.
>
> 'In conclusion I hope your Lordship will kindly consider my case from the above facts which I have stated'.

The government brought in a further land act in 1881, recognising the 'three Fs' (fixity of tenure, fair rents and free sale) and provided a land commission to fix a 'fair rent'. Parliament also passed the Arrears Act, which meant that any tenant with a total annual rent of under £30 no longer had to pay rent arrears if they had any. Benison immediately encountered the result – tenants were asking for time to pay, and the first notice of an application to the Land Commission for a rent reduction in the demesne was served on him.

Mrs Beatty, notwithstanding her difficulties, was one of several tenants who did not claim reductions of rent before the Land Commission because they knew they held their farms at fair rents based on government valuations. Benison reported that rent reductions by the Commissioners were on the whole fair, at 15-25 per cent, but he did not expect that many of Belmore's tenants would go to the Commission. Their demeanour, compared with that of tenants in Cavan and Leitrim, was friendly. In any case, the Commission had so many cases, and moved so slowly, that even if there were cases involving the Belmore estates in Fermanagh, he did not expect them to be heard for another year. In the meantime, although there were delays in payment, most tenants did pay their rents.

The farm was never really profitable. As Benison explained:

> 'There is always a heavy loss on demesne lands when charged with the incidental expenses. If the land was worked by a farmer he would only employ four or five men on an average all the year to keep the place and after payment of their wages, rent and taxes, all was clear profit'.

Of course, the family at Castle Coole had the benefit of produce from the farm and a measure of expenses. There was trouble from time to time with workmen: Benison spotted McGarvey, responsible for the carriage horses and the phaeton, in Enniskillen in the custody of two policemen. He had taken to drink again after 18 months dry, following a warning from Benison. His fellow workers in the stable yard, the Robinsons, gave notice, hoping for an increase in wages, but Benison told them that 'they might pack up and go'. They stayed. During 1882 Belmore, to raise some money, was thinking of selling some land to speculative builders in the light of increasing demand for 'villa residences'.

During 1883, Benison found the Commission reducing rents by percentages up to 30 or 40 per cent:

> 'The question of 'fair rent' no longer exists, and a reduction in every instance has to be made and the landlord who adopted the live and thrive principle suffers for his generosity'.

He took the view that the Commission paid little regard to the valuations of land submitted to them but 'their object is to give a reduction, and, except in very rare cases, the applicant will get from 10 to 25 per cent'.

By April 1884 it was clear that Benison was succeeding in getting agreements for fair rents with Belmore's tenants and he was having no great difficulty in collecting rents in 1885. Delays in payment were usually caused by delays experienced by tenants in selling their cattle, but by November tenants of the Enniskillen school estate, led by their parish priest, faced Benison with a massive strike. Afraid of the priest, they refused to pay any rent even though they had it in their pockets. The tenants almost certainly knew there was to be a change in the law, this time making it possible for tenants to buy their farms. This was the effect of the Ashbourne Act of 1885, which provided a loan fund of many millions of pounds for tenants who wished to purchase their lands. Supplementary acts in 1887 and later effectively transferred the bulk of Irish landholdings away from large landowners to tenants. However, on Belmore's estates Benison was able to continue his tactic of meeting tenants to get agreed reductions and so avoid the delays and costs for both sides of resorting to the Commission. In September, he reported:

> 'I had a long interview on Saturday with several of your tenants, and parted with them on most friendly terms. I told them when they appeared with their rent I would then tell them what abatement they would get etc. They appeared quite satisfied … Many I think are anxious to buy. I believe every tenant in Garvary is prepared to purchase under Lord Ashbourne's Act, and will give twenty years purchase'.

Here, in the hopes of purchasing their holdings and an obvious feeling for the right valuation lay, no doubt, the satisfaction of the tenants. As a result of the Act, Belmore's satisfaction as a landlord hardly mattered. In the meantime, Benison had a tough winter with the tenants, all of whom were slow to pay their rents, pleading hard times, and all of whom were looking for substantial reductions, probably hoping to reduce the valuation for purchase later. If that was difficult for him, it was worse in Donegal, where 'people are striving to hold their land rent free'.

In 1886, Benison offered a general abatement of ten per cent to tenants who paid their rent promptly and, although his collection started slowly, later in the evening it improved. However, by June he had to report that tenants were setting their faces against paying, 'becoming sulky and hard to manage'. By the beginning of October, however, he reported that he had collected slightly more than the year before.

1887 was a very bad year for farmers, the worst since 1879. Benison thought a few of the tenants in the demesne might go to the Commission but expected that a ten per cent abatement would not be acceptable. He suggested that landlords and agents should meet to fix an agreed general abatement – 'uniform and not given at haphazard as in former years'. Though he continued to press for this it seems never to have happened. He continued to negotiate abatements on the Castle Coole demesne successfully, with an occasional exception when a tenant went to the Commission and to court. Even then the reductions were acceptably small.

However, by February 1888 Benison, faced with Land Commission reductions of 33 per cent, was disposed to settle with tenants 'if their terms are at all reasonable'. Rent arrears were being forgone under the Arrears Act and the police were inquiring into the behaviour of landlords over the collection of arrears. 'It is evident Landlords have few friends. The questions indicate a desire to wipe off all arrears without remuneration'.

Ten years later, as the process continued, Benison concluded:

> 'The report of the Land Commission is not pleasant reading. I gather Landlords are to expect a perpetual lessening of their income by revaluation. Taken as a whole the outlook is rather gloomy'.

The fact was that the pressure on Belmore's income was downward as government policy gradually turned him from a landlord with large estates to a rentier dependent on the value of the government and other stocks and shares with which the purchase price of the lands transferred was paid. No major work was carried out on the demesne during his later years: the building of the gatehouse and the new layout at the Dublin Road entrance, the erection of new cottages for workers, the extensive drainage works and other improvements to the demesne had all been long since completed. Even so, the demesne and the farm would have regularly employed 30 or more people – farm workers, a coachman and stable hands, gardeners, laundry maids and gatekeepers. There would be workers taken on for haymaking, bark stripping and other seasonal jobs.

Belmore's rental income, which had been about £9,000 a year after the sales under the Encumbered Estates Acts in the 1850s, was reduced over the period of the land legislation to an annual average of £6,396, but there were only four years (1876–1878 and 1884) in which this level was significantly exceeded. The fluctuations above and below the average reflected the bad years for farming and the effect of the abatements, both reflected in Benison's comments.

Many a paterfamilias would have been content to make his household his only concern, but Belmore had too much intellectual energy for that alone to satisfy him. He had put himself outside the mainstream of politics by going to Australia, as his late Uncle Henry had warned him he would. In any case, a political life was expensive so he tried the colonial service again, applying (unsuccessfully) for the governorship of Cape Colony. He had visited South Africa in 1872. He remained, however, one of the best debaters in the House of Lords at that time and, as in his earlier years, was in demand as a member of private bill committees and, notably, took part in an important joint committee of both houses set up to inquire into railway rating. His long-time interest in railway development (as important then as air travel now) was matched by his continuing interest in agricultural development and he took on the presidency of the Irish Agricultural Society.

In 1874, another son (Ernest) was born at Castle Coole and in 1876 another daughter followed (Lady Winifred, the eighth child to survive) also born at Castle Coole. In later life this daughter wrote a memoir, which gives an invaluable picture of life at Castle Coole and in London.[5] It opens:

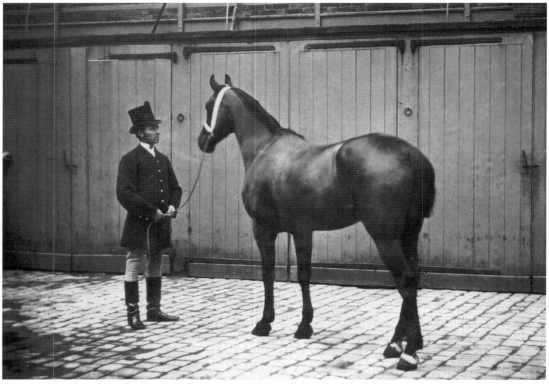

'Steersman' and William Yeates, Coachman

Photo of the Countess of Belmore's bedroom showing a selection of her children's toys

'I was born on August 19th 1876, the eighth child out of thirteen so no fuss was made over my arrival. I was a small baby – my mother having been ill with scarlet fever a short time before my birth and the doctor had told my mother that probably I would not live which made her very indignant and she was right'.

To house the children, the east wing of Castle Coole was turned into a nursery wing, including a schoolroom which (along with the corridor adjoining it) held a large collection of family books. Among them were many moral tales for young children produced annually by the Society for the Propagation of Christian Knowledge; a large collection of prayer books, Bibles and religious tracts (evidence of the intensity of the religious instruction and observance expected of the children); many storybooks for children of all ages; colourful scrapbooks; and many homeopathic and other medical guides for the treatment of children's ailments. The whole of this collection is now in the attics and some of the toys may occasionally still be seen in the Victorian bedroom at Castle Coole.

During the latter part of the nineteenth century, Castle Coole flourished again as a family home, as it had done in the second Earl's time. In July 1887 the last of the Belmores' 13 surviving children, Lady Katherine, was born.

Favourite pastimes of the girls were working in the walled garden and walking along their much loved paths in the beech walk and the woods on the hill above the front of the house. They planted hundreds of bluebells in the woods and each girl had her own seat in the beech walk.

Photo of the Ladies Lowry Corry in the walled garden

Inevitably, riding was both a necessity and a pleasure. Lady Winifred recorded:

'At Castle Coole my chief pleasure was riding. First, there was the donkey which when we were very small, I and my brother Ernest rode together in the double panniers – as he was much bigger than me a large stone was wedged in with me to make the weight right. We must have been a quaint sight – our "Nanna" as we called her carrying the small baby – the older baby in the pram – now in "the Museum",[6] the older ones on the donkey riding in turns led by a boy and the donkey's foal had to come too so the nursery maid led it by a red flannel string.

'I remember this cavalcade going on the high road – now we should all be killed by a car or lorry. I was delighted when I was promoted to riding a pony'.

Lady Theresa, who had literary ambitions, wrote many short stories which she sent off to publishers, but none was accepted; she was, however, probably the editor of the *Castle Coole Review*, handwritten and duplicated for circulation among family, friends and the people on the estate.

One of the constant worries the *Castle Coole Review* recorded was the danger of fire at a time when fire brigades were less efficient and had few means to cope with a large blaze. Letters in its correspondence column, signed by fiery names such as 'Salamander' made suggestions for improving fire alarms, water supply and firefighting. A few years later, in December 1902, fire did break out at Castle Coole, but was spotted and dealt with before it took hold. It was described as an escape from serious disaster.

Other concerns were lamps that did not smoke and gave better light in the schoolroom and in 'the gloomy tunnel' – suggested by 'petrolium spirit'. A major Fermanagh character in the *Review* was 'Jupiter Pluvius' who appeared regularly at events during the year, especially at cricket matches.

The *Review* also described the comings and goings of family members: 'During the first week of March the Head Quarters of the family were changed to Eaton House, 66a Eaton Square'. This was the home of the children's grandmother, Emily Louise, the dowager Countess, of whom it was said, 'her gracious and kindly ways made her a great favourite'.[7] Lady Winifred recollected their visits there as young children:

> 'Until I was eleven years old most of the year we children were at Castle Coole with trips to London where my parents used to rent houses for a few months at a time. My earliest recollection of London is curiously enough of being taken to church with my brother Ernest by our under nurse. We hit off [sic] a High Church with many lighted candles which I thought quite beautiful, like a Xmas tree.
>
> 'We children used to enjoy the journey to and from London and were a very large party when it included the schoolroom and nursery children's governess and nurses and domestic staff, butler, footmen, cook, kitchen maid, housemaids, schoolroom maid.
>
> 'We used to cross by the North Wall to the Holyhead boat and the meal of cold chicken and ham at Amiens St Station refreshment room was a high light of our journey. There were no refreshment cars in those days but we got to London in time for breakfast'.

The whole family would go to London for 'the season', when Belmore would rent a house in Mayfair or Belgravia. When they came of age, the girls had their 'coming out' during the London season and were presented to Queen Victoria at a 'drawing room'. For Belmore himself, politics, legal work or business meant spending time away from Castle Coole, perhaps in Dublin – where, like his ancestors, he stayed at the Sackville Street club. He was also sometimes in London where he would stay at the Carlton club, a centre of Conservative politics.

Ernest Lowry Corry with donkey

Photo of the family taken on the steps outside the saloon

It was especially during the 1880s that Belmore began to feel the pressure on his income. His own expenditure remained steady at about £2,500 a year but his household establishment, as Lady Winifred's memoir shows, was large and expensive.

He needed to reduce the sheer weight of such a costly establishment, so, at the end of October, Belmore took the whole family to Brussels for the winter, having taken advice on good lodgings, costing about £11 or £12 a week for full board, excluding wine. Lady Winifred recorded the experience:

> 'When I was eleven years old there was a great change as we all went abroad. My parents found that the only way to economise was to shut up Castle Coole for a time and reduce all round.
>
> 'We spent the winter and next spring in Brussels – and the following summer in the Ardennes where there were the most wonderful plum trees in the garden laden with plums. We shook the trees and ate the fruit. I never remember any of us being ill as a result!
>
> 'I made friends with (to my eyes) an old couple in a little villa next door and used to fish with the husband in the river Meuse and their little garden was full of rose trees and as the blossoms fell off the old couple put empty egg shells on each shoot which had a most peculiar effect'.

After Christmas 1887 Cecil and Ernest were sent to a school at 60 Rue de la Longue Haie, Avenue Louisa. They all stayed in Brussels until the end of summer 1888, returning to Castle Coole in September. Lady Winifred recalled:

'We returned to Castle Coole the next year to our joy and until I "came out" 5 years later I was busy with my lessons and except being very ill with diphtheria one summer in London and my sister Florence's wedding I lead [*sic*] the ordinary schoolroom life of that period'.

Letters in the archive suggest that the illnesses such as diphtheria tended to spread among the children and, necessarily, caused their parents great anxiety.

There was, naturally, huge excitement among the children whenever a ball was held in the house. A very special one was given for the twenty-first birthday of Armar, Viscount Corry. The *Castle Coole Review* for September 1891 recorded:

'The saloon was brilliantly lighted by many wax candles which saw themselves reflected in the long mirrors and polished floors over which … the dancers glided swiftly and easily … When wearied they rested in the library amid ferns and palms from the hothouses, bull rushes and reed maces which the shores of the lake gave as their share in the festivities, while all around were gaily coloured silks etc brought from the East by the 2nd Earl of Belmore. The "inner man" was refreshed with ices and sponge cakes and light beverages in the hall, while later in the evening a magnificent supper, prepared by Mrs Waspe, would have satisfied those who live "not wisely but too well"; and certainly rarely have such splendid fruits graced a board in this country, thanks to Mr Cox's care of the garden. Praise must be given to the musicians and to the choosers of the dance music. A new feature was the novel dance, the "Iolantha", the music being the well known "pas de quatre"'.

The youngest children were not allowed to go to the party but had a secret lookout into it. On the landing halfway up the servants' stairs in the nursery wing is a small half-moon window through which they could see all the comings and goings in the great hall. No doubt, they were able to give the *Review*'s reporters good copy. The *Review* did record a special visit to Tyrone in 1891:

'On Thursday October 8th Lord Belmore and Lord Corry visited the family property in Tyrone accompanied by Mr Brush, our courteous agent and were conveyed to Sixmilecross in a carriage drawn by two awful old horses. On entering the town they were received by a crowd of schoolchildren, cheering heartily who went with them to the Schoolhouse where Lord Corry was presented with a magnificent address'.

Ernest dressed for theatricals in clothes from the 2nd Earl's travels

Cricket match at Castle Coole

A certain Tony McManus wrote to the *Review* proposing that in return a dinner should be given for all the tenants and also the family's 'loyal and enthusiastic staff of employees, many of whom have been in our service a long time'.

Amateur dramatics were favourite pastime. Florence and Madeline performed in a play given by the officers of the King's Royal Rifles in Enniskillen in late 1889 but at Castle Coole everyone joined in.

In the summers of the late 1880s and early 1890s, the traditional outdoor pastimes – riding, fishing and shooting – gave way to cricket, introduced by Armar, Cecil and Ernest, who had picked up the enthusiasm for it at their schools (Armar at Winchester and the other two at Wellington). They formed the 'Castle Coole Cricket Club'. Belmore himself played cricket at Castle Coole, as an extract from his diary earlier shows. Rules were printed and distributed; attendance was regularly required at its committee meetings in a room in the grand yard; fixtures were arranged with local schools and with whatever regimental teams were in Enniskillen. The game brought everyone on the demesne together, whether as players or spectators, and brought in visitors to make it a real social occasion. The score cards suggest that cricketing skill was not an issue.

The pitch was on the site of the formal gardens of the Queen Anne house, where there was a small pavilion. An 'action' photograph of the time shows the ladies watching a game in progress, the bowler delivering a ball.

The teams were made up of family and friends and workers from the demesne. Some were very young.

The Castle Coole Review.

No. III.   1891.

The Weather

After a year whose weather has been as fickle as fortune is proverbially said to be, we again resume our editorial duties. January commenced the year with frost and snow. February however was wonderfully mild and bright. March on the contrary, signalized itself by its exceptionally snowy weather. April was as dull and showery as that month generally is. May came in as a lamb but went out as a ___. June was hot at first but very wet during the wet week. St July St Swithin although appearing on his own day in beautiful weather, turned on his old water taps a few days later. The summer as I could came in real earnest. September was changeable. It then brought a storms as well as pheasants. During November, Jupiter Pluvius was in great form in some parts of England, though we were not overly so much honoured by his presence. December began with rain and in its latter days varied between frost & thaw.

Sample page from a *Castle Coole Review*

One of the cricket team photographs showing Viscount Corry and Ernest Lowry Corry in the centre

Another great occasion was the marriage of Lady Florence to Lieutenant Colonel Eden on 12 October 1893. Lady Winifred reported:

'My sister Florence's wedding to John Eden was a great excitement locally as there had not been one at Castle Coole for many years. She was married at Derryvullen with 10 bridesmaids and a page and 2 Bishops and certainly two other clergymen.

'One Bishop was George Eden, the Bishop of Dover and he had never been in Ireland before. He brought over the brides and bridesmaids bouquets from London and was afraid of losing any of the boxes, and when he arrived at Amiens St Station he anxiously asked if he would make the connection all right at Dundalk and was told "Sure she will, she's a furious train" which I believe he never forgot.

'Castle Coole was absolutely packed out with family, guests and their retainers, maids and footmen and my mother must have had a job catering for all in the house, as well as the wedding breakfast and dinner parties.

'The bride wore a white satin dress and a full length Court train of brocade and the same Brussels lace veil my mother had been married in. We bridesmaids also wore white dresses with coloured short sashes and ecru lace hats. The church was packed out and the churchwardens had to keep the crowd from getting too near the bridal procession … I remember my father and sister walking up the church were described as "the splendid and handsome pair" ("as if we were carriage horses", he said) and the best man, it said, was "exceptionally good looking".[8]

The whole wedding party is shown in a photograph taken on the colonnade of the east wing.

Only one of the other girls, Kathleen, married. Her husband was Thomas Ward, an officer in the Second Dragoon Guards, the Queen's Bays, who rose to the rank of brigadier general and was awarded the Companion of the Order of St Michael and St

George. The other girls continued to live at Castle Coole for most of their lives but Madeline died in 1898, at only 33.

Belmore was an important figure in Irish government as one of its lords justices and general governors during the absence of the Lord Lieutenant in 1885, 1890, 1891, 1895 and 1896–1898. He was still an Irish privy councillor and frequently sat with the Judicial Committee. He eventually became the Senior Irish Representative Peer in the House of Lords, Senior Privy Councillor for Ireland and, in 1890, became a knight of the Grand Cross of St Michael and St George.

He continued to take a leading part in the affairs of the Church of Ireland, especially after its disestablishment, as a member of the Synods for Clogher, Armagh, Derry and Raphoe and the Representative Church Body. In 1877, he was the President of the Trinity College Commission, set up to consider reform of the divinity school jointly run by Trinity College and the University of Dublin. He introduced the reforms it recommended to parliament in a bill to transfer religious education from Trinity and the University to the Representative Body of the Church of Ireland. This seems to have antagonised the Trinity establishment, who were against the change and later refused to grant him an honorary degree.

Belmore's influence and standing in the Church of Ireland is shown by the last entry in Lady Winifred's memoir, an amusing account of an eminent visitor to Castle Coole, the Archbishop of Canterbury, with his wife and a chaplain. The Archbishop was on an official visit to the Irish Church and arrived at Castle Coole in September 1896:

Lady Florence Lowry Corry's wedding party photographed on the east colonnade

'There was a "house party" to meet him including the then Duke of Abercorn and his daughter (Lady Phyllis Hamilton) and I think they stayed three days and had the State bedrooms – the neighbourhood came to dinner and I remember the Duke of Abercorn wore his "Garter" ribbon and I told my father to go and put on his GCMG one, as they looked very smart. The silver gilt plate on the dinner table, candles all reflected in the looking glass "plateau". It certainly is a vanished age.

'Our housekeeper, Mrs Windrum, was very perplexed as to how to arrange the valets. She came to my mother to ask who should sit highest – the Duke's valet or the Archbishop's. She said of course Lady Phyllis' maid would come before Mrs Benson's. My mother told her to ask the Archbishop's man as soon as he arrived and he told her he always came first as he was the Archbishop's "Train bearer".

'The Bensons must have had a very good appetite as although a formal dinner party in those days would have had several courses, a tray of cold chickens and jelly had to be left in the bedroom every night.

'One of the lady guests made a great sensation on arriving for dinner with a diamond swan in the middle of her "Princess of Wales" fringe'.

Belmore became an expert in national educational issues, chairing the committee that produced a manual in 1897 on the way forward in technical education.

Closer to home, he was a member of the Irish Landlord's Convention and, no doubt using his personal experience, something of an expert in the thorny subject of land reform and tithe rent charges. From 1892 he was lord lieutenant of Tyrone and a justice of the peace for that county as well as Fermanagh, and was frequently chairman of the petty sessions. He was chairman of the Enniskillen Board of Guardians and also a member of the Omagh Board of Guardians (the Boards of Guardians were predecessors of local government bodies).

Even all these public offices were not enough to use up his capacity for work. A cynic, of course, might say he needed to find a peaceful corner in the house away from his large family. If so, he found it in the library, at his large desk, collecting the information to write the history of his family and many articles for the *Ulster Journal of Archaeology*. He had started his researches in the 1850s when still a young man.[9]

From November 1897 Belmore's health began to decline. He was diagnosed with neuralgia and in early 1898 went to England for treatment. He was missed, certainly by Benison, who wrote to Honoria at Castle Coole in July 1898:

'It is very sad to hear of Lord Belmore's long continued illness, and at a time when his guidance and counsel was most needed to protect the interests of the loyal minority from the radicalism of Mr Balfour'.

After a slight improvement he relapsed and during September he complained of lacking strength and energy. By the end of October he was improving. This became a pattern; slight improvements did not last long and he suffered long relapses all through the years to 1903. He made regular visits to Buxton in Derbyshire for treatment at the spa, but without any real success. He also went on voyages to Genoa and to Naples and Madeira in 1903–1904, no doubt for the beneficial effect of the warmer climates. None of these strategies helped and he gradually withdrew from all public life and remained an invalid, confined to his own rooms in the west wing at Castle Coole.

At the beginning of April 1899 Ernest set off to Argentina to start training as a ranch manager at Estancia Santa Teresa, Gualeguay, Entre Rios. He came back to visit Castle Coole in 1908 but left again in February 1909 from Southampton on the *Aragon*, this time bound for Buenos Aires. It was the last time that the family saw him. On 10 March 1912 he was shot and died the next day at Santa Teresa. At the time he had actually been negotiating to sell his interest in the ranch and return home. He had always been a great favourite and his death devastated the family. The records of dinner guests at Castle Coole during those years before the First World War, kept by the girls, end abruptly at that time. Belmore's health can only have been severely affected by the shock of Ernest's death. On Sunday morning, 6 April 1913, he died.

Another tragedy followed two years later when Edith was found drowned, lying at the edge of Lough Yoan. There was no explanation of how she came to die. Honoria lived for almost another six years, dying at Castle Coole on Sunday 5 October 1919.

During their father's last illness, Armar and Cecil took over Belmore's position as much as possible. Armar took a BA degree at Trinity Hall, Cambridge and qualified as a barrister; Cecil trained in estate management at the Cranborne estate in Dorset. They both became justices of the peace, high sheriffs for Fermanagh and Tyrone and prominent members of the Church of Ireland. Neither married.

Chapter Twenty-two

Epilogue

Against the background of Irish history and their own personal problems the Lowry Corrys' essential success was in establishing a family which, for over 200 years, through thick and thin, maintained itself at Castle Coole. Its direct political involvement lasted for 150 years until Conservatism itself moved away from them. The family included men of great administrative ability: Henry Corry, Somerset Richard (the fourth Earl) and Montagu Corry, behind whom stood Armar and his son Somerset, who each defied their own demons, took great risks in opposing the union and created the physical presence of Castle Coole and its demesne as their monument. The success of the surviving illegitimate children should not be overlooked: Rear Admiral Armar Lowry Corry and the Watson family of Cumbria.

By the time of the fourth Earl's death the Lowry Corrys had, in a sense, come full circle. Castle Coole and its demesne was, more or less, what they had built up in the seventeenth and eighteenth centuries, with the addition of the Churchlands by Margetson Armar. It was the estates in Tyrone and Longford that bore the brunt of debt and land reform.

It was inevitable that the fabric of Armar Lowry Corry's house would suffer with time. As a result of the Land Acts the family's income was exposed to poor returns from the investments which replaced their rental income. The *coup de grace* was the imposition of two lots of estate duty upon the death of the fifth and sixth Earls in 1948. But in 1951 the present Earl's father was able to arrest the decline by making an arrangement with the National Trust, resulting in the restoration of the house to a standard that the Trust, almost uniquely, has the skills and finances to achieve.

John, the present and eighth Earl, who owns all of the contents of the house, has also invested much time and energy in supporting the Trust's work and in ensuring, as far as possible, that the family touch remains at Castle Coole.

The second Earl's enterprise as a collector and connoisseur has recently made its mark in the international art market. One of the objects he negotiated to buy, probably when in Rome, possibly in Florence, was a bronze equestrian statue of Ferdinando de Medici by the seventeenth-century sculptor Giuseppe Piamontini. In late November 1820 it had arrived in his London house but subsequently found its way back to Castle Coole, where local circumstances and probably humour translated the Medici into Marshal Schomberg. It is easy to see why. Letters recently traced in the Belmore archive restored its true identity.[1]

The Belmore collection of Egyptian antiquities in the British Museum remains as evidence of the remarkable undertaking that was the voyage of the family in the *Osprey* and their uninhibited enterprise as collectors in the then-new competitive urge to uncover the treasures of ancient Egypt.

Life at Castle Coole, continuing well into the twentieth century in the slower manner of the nineteenth, is perfectly reflected in a memoir written recently by Brigadier G.W. Eden CBE, whose mother was Lady Florence Lowry Corry. His visits started before the First World War and continued at intervals up to the winter of 1938. The wagonette to which he refers was made for the fourth Earl in the 1860s and used by him in Sydney, at Throsby Park and on his return to Castle Coole.

Recollections of Visits to Castle Coole[2]

'On my earlier visits I cannot recall meeting my grandfather who was by then an invalid and kept to the wing beyond the drawing room – a part of the house I never remember going into as a child. My grandmother also had her bedroom there, as well as my eldest aunt, Theresa. Most of the rest of the house was fully occupied by the family, with aunts using the bedrooms and dressing rooms on the front staircase side of the Lobby and also the bedrooms along the passage in the (east) wing leading up to the schoolroom. Uncle Armar had a small bedroom (now a bathroom) at the top of the back stairs and Uncle Cecil had his bedroom on the attic floor (the Forest room, so called from the design of the wall paper). I think the servants all had rooms in the basement but some may have slept in the attics. The two big bedrooms (Blue room and Brown room) and their dressing rooms beyond the Lobby were used by guests and also the State Dressing room. The room on the Lobby was at one time my Grandmother's sitting room (the Bow room).

'Compared with the present day arrangement of rooms and furniture, the most striking change is the Drawing room which I remember being full of furniture in the Victorian style.

Quite a number of chairs were needed to seat all my Aunts (and occasionally my Uncles) at tea and after dinner. The Hall, Library Saloon and Dining room were much as they are at this time. The room (Breakfast/Morning room) on the right of the front door (now the family dining room) was a Billiard room, but, as I remember it, the Billiard table was always covered with books and my Aunts also used this room in which to "do" the flowers. The passage down to the School room was lined with bookshelves full of books and the School room, which was used by us when we stayed there as children, had its original furniture.

'We were always taken down to the basement to see the Cook and I remember the large kitchen with its well-scrubbed wooden table and lots of polished copper cooking utensils hanging on the walls. The basement was an intriguing area for children, especially beyond the kitchen where you could get out into a large tunnel, which led down towards the stables and was wide enough for carts to come up with deliveries to the basement back door.

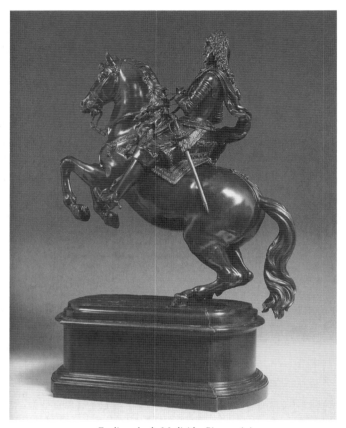

Ferdinando de Medici by Piamontini

'I am not certain what staff were employed before the wars but there was a butler and probably two footmen as well as Tommy, the handyman, probably two kitchen maids to help the cook and there must have been a number of housemaids as there were no bathrooms and all the water needed for the bedrooms for basins on washhand stands and for hip baths had to be carried upstairs. There were also fires to be lit in winter and lamps to be trimmed. I have an early recollection as a child of having a hip bath in front of a bedroom fire at night. The first bathroom was installed on the attic floor some time before the wars.

'Outside, there were horses in the stables used to draw carriages, a closed Wagonette and an Irish side car. Up to 1939 no motor vehicle was owned by the family though cars were hired for special trips from time to time. However, as late as the winter of 1938 when I wanted to bring over my car on a visit, I was told that my Uncle Armar would not approve of anyone coming to stay with a car! I am not sure what farm operations were carried out but I think the family solicitor, Mr Burke, acted as agent. None of the family were interested in the shooting which was left on the hands of the gamekeeper who was expected to supply game for the house and also to shoot or trap numbers of rabbits for which there was a good market. When I was old enough to learn to shoot on my holiday visits I was taken out by the keeper who was Mr Watts. Depending on the time of year, apart from rabbits, there would be wild duck on the loughs, pheasants (mostly wild but a few raised by the keeper), woodcock, snipe and a few grouse up on the moor. Apart from the actual estate, the family retained shooting rights over land that had been owned by them. Watts had some trouble from poachers from Enniskillen but he was allowed to organise small shoots and to invite the head of the local police as one of the guests – a move which was helpful in keeping down poaching. The garden and greenhouses were well kept by the Head Gardener – Maguire – who had two or three men working under him. Also my Aunts were mostly keen gardeners and liked to do some work in it from time to time. The garden supplied the house with all the fruit and vegetables needed. There were the domestic animals or pets apart from two collections of rather wild cats. One lot lived in the garden and the other lot in the kitchen and the area of the tunnel outside.

'There was a certain pattern to our visits. Arriving by train at Enniskillen Station we would be met by two of our Aunts and the coachman driving the Wagonette. When we arrived at the house the rest of the family would come into the Hall to greet us. On earlier visits as children we used the schoolroom a good deal but I think we had breakfast and lunch with the family in the dining room and later I remember teas in the drawing room when there were always lots of sandwiches, scones and cakes. At the dining room meals my grandmother, when she was alive, sat at the head of the table and was an expert at helping dishes so that they went round her large family. Every morning before breakfast, prayers were held in the saloon which were attended by the servants, After breakfast, my grandmother, and later one of my aunts, would go down to the kitchen to give orders to the cook.

The Belmore omnibus

259

The Drawing room furnished for the family in the 4th Earl's time

'Motorcars were frowned on and not encouraged onto the estate:

'The family gathered in the drawing room before dinner and when it was announced all trooped through the saloon. After my grandmother died, uncle Armar had the habit of coming into dinner late and then everyone had to wait till he caught up with whatever course we were eating. Otherwise he and Uncle Cecil seldom appeared at meals except at lunch on Sundays. In the evenings, after dinner, we would sit in the drawing room till it was time to go to bed, when on a table at the foot of the stairs there were candles which were lit for us to take to our rooms. After I was grown up I would sometimes sit in the Library for a while after dinner as I was allowed to smoke then.

'My aunts did a lot of visiting the people living in the cottages on the estate, sometimes taking food with them. We enjoyed going with them on these visits being much intrigued by the way in many cases their chickens etc seemed to have a free run of the living rooms. We would sit down for quite a long chat before moving on and the people were always very interested in family news. I remember visits to the coachman's cottage which was one of two cottages by Lough Coole, to the Watts, to a Miss James who lived in the Enniskillen gate lodge, to Maguire the gardener and to the

Cranstons who lived in one of the cottages near what is now the entrance leading to the Golf Club. There was one old lady we always liked to visit who lived in a cottage near the railway crossing. She seemed very old and always kept some kind of woollen hat or cap on her head and then put another on top of it as it wore out so that her headgear got higher and higher over the years.

'On Sundays we always went to Church at Derryvullen, being driven there in the Wagonette but Uncle Armar used to go to Church in Enniskillen, driven there in the Irish sidecar by Willie Cranston and being a very heavy man his weight always seemed to weigh down the car on one side. On Sunday afternoons some of the family always went for a walk in the grounds. On later visits we were usually taken on one or two expeditions in hired cars – sometimes to visit neighbours, sometimes to fêtes and on one occasion to Sports at a lunatic asylum at Omagh where Uncle Armar presented the prizes.

'My last visit before the Second World War was in the late autumn of 1938 when I was home on leave from India. As the years had passed the number in the family had contracted and staff had been reduced. Uncle Armar had been an invalid and now lived in a wing on the ground floor. I spent most days shooting with Watts and left with the memory of some lovely views of the estate and surrounding country on fine autumn days.'

The Lowry Corry Family and principal connections

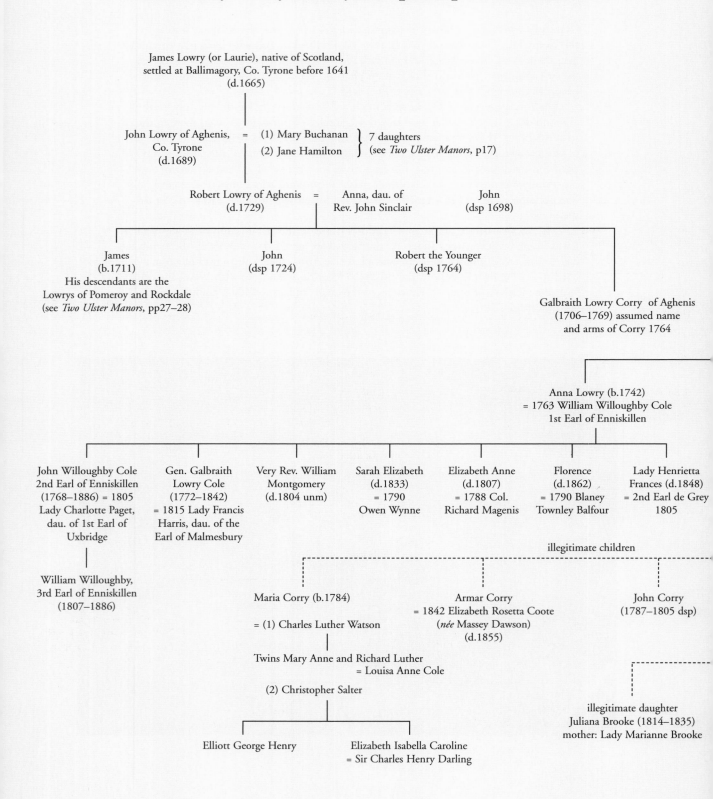

James Lowry (or Laurie), native of Scotland,
settled at Ballimagory, Co. Tyrone before 1641
(d.1665)

John Lowry of Aghenis,   =   (1) Mary Buchanan   } 7 daughters
Co. Tyrone   (2) Jane Hamilton   } (see *Two Ulster Manors*, p17)
(d.1689)

Robert Lowry of Aghenis   =   Anna, dau. of   John
(d.1729)   Rev. John Sinclair   (dsp 1698)

James   John   Robert the Younger
(b.1711)   (dsp 1724)   (dsp 1764)
His descendants are the
Lowrys of Pomeroy and Rockdale
(see *Two Ulster Manors*, pp27–28)

Galbraith Lowry Corry of Aghenis
(1706–1769) assumed name
and arms of Corry 1764

Anna Lowry (b.1742)
= 1763 William Willoughby Cole
1st Earl of Enniskillen

John Willoughby Cole   Gen. Galbraith   Very Rev. William   Sarah Elizabeth   Elizabeth Anne   Florence   Lady Henrietta
2nd Earl of Enniskillen   Lowry Cole   Montgomery   (d.1833)   (d.1807)   (d.1862)   Frances (d.1848)
(1768–1886) = 1805   (1772–1842)   (d.1804 unm)   = 1790   = 1788 Col.   = 1790 Blaney   = 2nd Earl de Grey
Lady Charlotte Paget,   = 1815 Lady Francis   Owen Wynne   Richard Magenis   Townley Balfour   1805
dau. of 1st Earl of   Harris, dau. of the
Uxbridge   Earl of Malmesbury

                                                                                                        illegitimate children

William Willoughby,
3rd Earl of Enniskillen
(1807–1886)

                          Maria Corry (b.1784)   Armar Corry   John Corry
                                                            = 1842 Elizabeth Rosetta Coote   (1787–1805 dsp)
                          = (1) Charles Luther Watson   (*née* Massey Dawson)
                                                             (d.1855)

                          Twins Mary Anne and Richard Luther
                                  = Louisa Anne Cole

                          (2) Christopher Salter
                                                                                                illegitimate daughter
                                                                                                Juliana Brooke (1814–1835)
                                                                                                mother: Lady Marianne Brooke

            Elliott George Henry   Elizabeth Isabella Caroline
                                            = Sir Charles Henry Darling

Names in bold indicate head of the family resident at Castle Coole

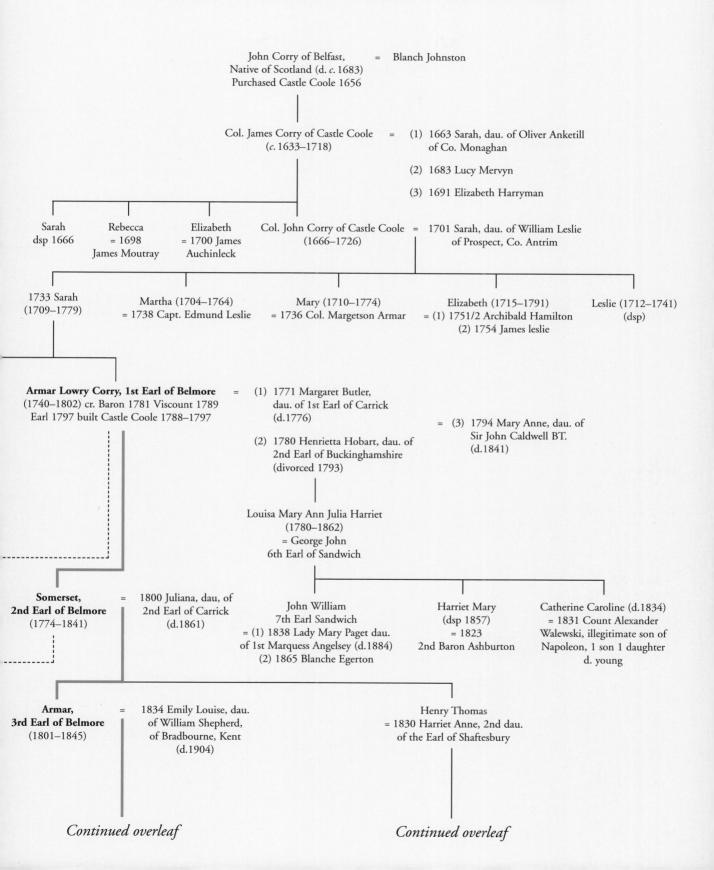

John Corry of Belfast, = Blanch Johnston
Native of Scotland (d. *c.*1683)
Purchased Castle Coole 1656

Col. James Corry of Castle Coole = (1) 1663 Sarah, dau. of Oliver Anketill
(*c.*1633–1718)   of Co. Monaghan

(2) 1683 Lucy Mervyn

(3) 1691 Elizabeth Harryman

Sarah   Rebecca   Elizabeth   Col. John Corry of Castle Coole = 1701 Sarah, dau. of William Leslie
dsp 1666   = 1698   = 1700 James   (1666–1726)   of Prospect, Co. Antrim
      James Moutray   Auchinleck

1733 Sarah   Martha (1704–1764)   Mary (1710–1774)   Elizabeth (1715–1791)   Leslie (1712–1741)
(1709–1779)   = 1738 Capt. Edmund Leslie   = 1736 Col. Margetson Armar   = (1) 1751/2 Archibald Hamilton   (dsp)
            (2) 1754 James leslie

Armar Lowry Corry, 1st Earl of Belmore = (1) 1771 Margaret Butler,
(1740–1802) cr. Baron 1781 Viscount 1789   dau. of 1st Earl of Carrick
Earl 1797 built Castle Coole 1788–1797   (d.1776)   = (3) 1794 Mary Anne, dau. of
                              Sir John Caldwell BT.
(2) 1780 Henrietta Hobart, dau. of   (d.1841)
2nd Earl of Buckinghamshire
(divorced 1793)

Louisa Mary Ann Julia Harriet
(1780–1862)
= George John
6th Earl of Sandwich

Somerset, = 1800 Juliana, dau, of   John William   Harriet Mary   Catherine Caroline (d.1834)
2nd Earl of Belmore   2nd Earl of Carrick   7th Earl Sandwich   (dsp 1857)   = 1831 Count Alexander
(1774–1841)   (d.1861)   = (1) 1838 Lady Mary Paget dau.   = 1823   Walewski, illegitimate son of
         of 1st Marquess Angelsey (d.1884)   2nd Baron Ashburton   Napoleon, 1 son 1 daughter
         (2) 1865 Blanche Egerton   d. young

Armar, = 1834 Emily Louise, dau.   Henry Thomas
3rd Earl of Belmore   of William Shepherd,   = 1830 Harriet Anne, 2nd dau.
(1801–1845)   of Bradbourne, Kent   of the Earl of Shaftesbury
      (d.1904)

Continued overleaf   *Continued overleaf*

The Lowry Corry Family and principal connections (cont'd)

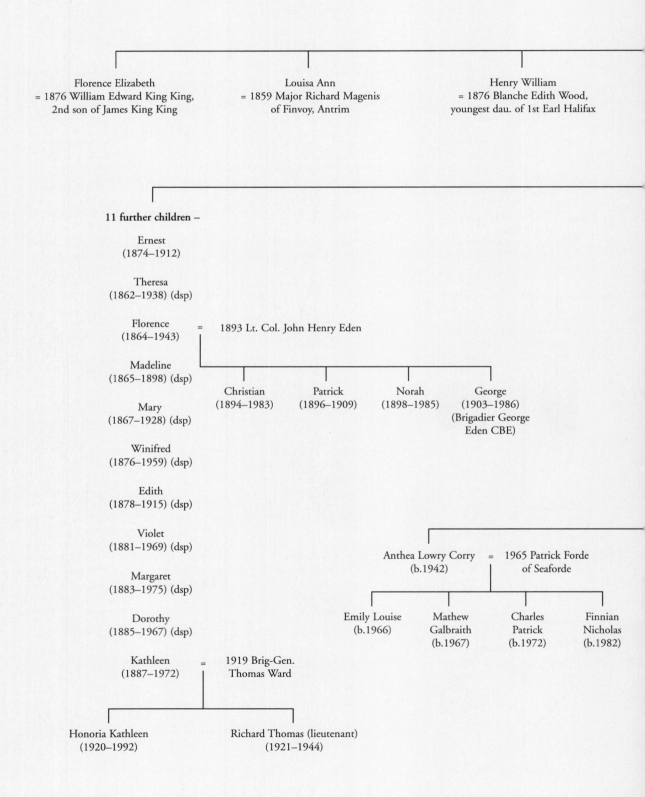

Florence Elizabeth
= 1876 William Edward King King,
2nd son of James King King

Louisa Ann
= 1859 Major Richard Magenis
of Finvoy, Antrim

Henry William
= 1876 Blanche Edith Wood,
youngest dau. of 1st Earl Halifax

11 further children –

Ernest
(1874–1912)

Theresa
(1862–1938) (dsp)

Florence
(1864–1943) = 1893 Lt. Col. John Henry Eden

Madeline
(1865–1898) (dsp)

Christian
(1894–1983)

Patrick
(1896–1909)

Norah
(1898–1985)

George
(1903–1986)
(Brigadier George
Eden CBE)

Mary
(1867–1928) (dsp)

Winifred
(1876–1959) (dsp)

Edith
(1878–1915) (dsp)

Violet
(1881–1969) (dsp)

Anthea Lowry Corry = 1965 Patrick Forde
(b.1942) of Seaforde

Margaret
(1883–1975) (dsp)

Emily Louise
(b.1966)

Mathew
Galbraith
(b.1967)

Charles
Patrick
(b.1972)

Finnian
Nicholas
(b.1982)

Dorothy
(1885–1967) (dsp)

Kathleen
(1887–1972) = 1919 Brig-Gen.
Thomas Ward

Honoria Kathleen
(1920–1992)

Richard Thomas (lieutenant)
(1921–1944)

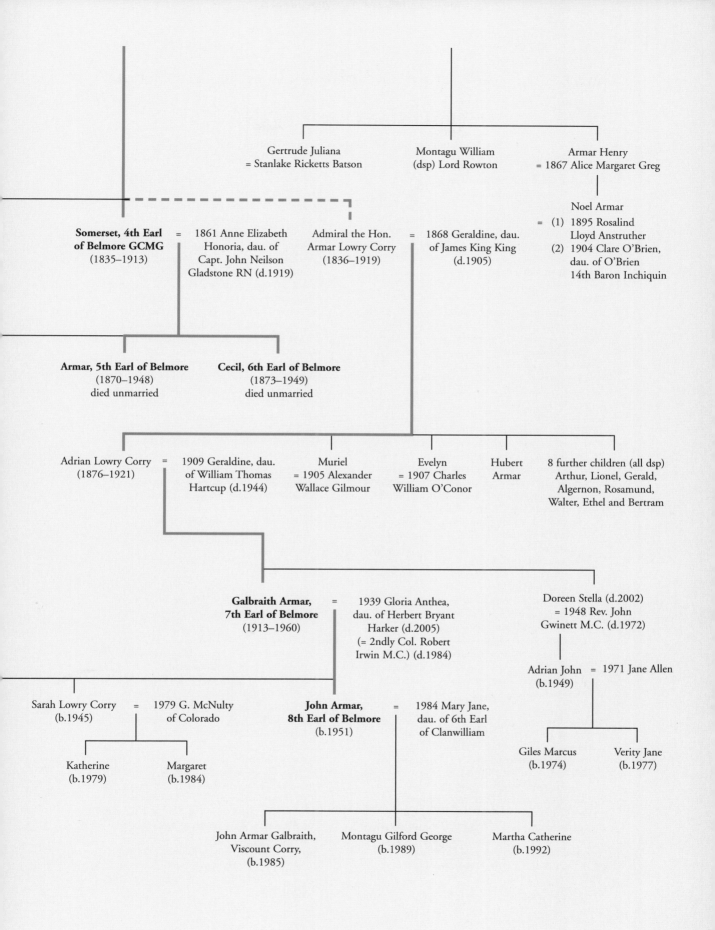

Gertrude Juliana
= Stanlake Ricketts Batson

Montagu William
(dsp) Lord Rowton

Armar Henry
= 1867 Alice Margaret Greg

Noel Armar
= (1) 1895 Rosalind
Lloyd Anstruther
(2) 1904 Clare O'Brien,
dau. of O'Brien
14th Baron Inchiquin

**Somerset, 4th Earl
of Belmore GCMG**
(1835–1913)

= 1861 Anne Elizabeth
Honoria, dau. of
Capt. John Neilson
Gladstone RN (d.1919)

Admiral the Hon.
Armar Lowry Corry
(1836–1919)

= 1868 Geraldine, dau.
of James King King
(d.1905)

Armar, 5th Earl of Belmore
(1870–1948)
died unmarried

Cecil, 6th Earl of Belmore
(1873–1949)
died unmarried

Adrian Lowry Corry
(1876–1921)

= 1909 Geraldine, dau.
of William Thomas
Hartcup (d.1944)

Muriel
= 1905 Alexander
Wallace Gilmour

Evelyn
= 1907 Charles
William O'Conor

Hubert
Armar

8 further children (all dsp)
Arthur, Lionel, Gerald,
Algernon, Rosamund,
Walter, Ethel and Bertram

**Galbraith Armar,
7th Earl of Belmore**
(1913–1960)

= 1939 Gloria Anthea,
dau. of Herbert Bryant
Harker (d.2005)
(= 2ndly Col. Robert
Irwin M.C.) (d.1984)

Doreen Stella (d.2002)
= 1948 Rev. John
Gwinett M.C. (d.1972)

Adrian John
(b.1949)

= 1971 Jane Allen

Sarah Lowry Corry
(b.1945)

= 1979 G. McNulty
of Colorado

**John Armar,
8th Earl of Belmore**
(b.1951)

= 1984 Mary Jane,
dau. of 6th Earl
of Clanwilliam

Katherine
(b.1979)

Margaret
(b.1984)

Giles Marcus
(b.1974)

Verity Jane
(b.1977)

John Armar Galbraith,
Viscount Corry,
(b.1985)

Montagu Gilford George
(b.1989)

Martha Catherine
(b.1992)

NOTES AND SOURCES

For full details of published works cited see bibliography.

Notes to Preface and Introduction

1   On the question of comparing costs and prices see *Inflation: The Value of the Pound 1750–1998*. A later Paper *03/82* November 2003 updates the tables to 2002 and higher multipliers could result but all need to be used with caution.

NOTES TO PART ONE

Chapter One

1   See Jean Agnew *Belfast Merchant Families* p. 35.
2   Much of the early history of Castle Coole is based on fourth Earl Belmore, *History of Two Ulster Manors*, part ii, chapters 6–9 and *History of the Corry Family*, chapter 2.
3   *Depositions of 1641*, p. 25; and fourth Earl Belmore, *History of Two Ulster Manors*, pp. 98–101.
4   The story of the 'Blue Sogers' is from an article entitled 'The Fermanagh Militia' in *The Impartial Reporter*, 27 December 1956.
5   The full will is in fourth Earl Belmore, *History of the Corry Family*, pp. 42–43. The church at Derryvullen has been the church of the Corrys since the time of John Corry, who is buried in the graveyard there. James, John and Leslie, Elizabeth Leslie Corry, John, the infant son of Edmund and Martha Leslie Corry, Margetson Armar and Mrs Armar are all buried in the vault. This church became Derryvullen South in 1874 when the parish of Derryvullen, which was very large, was split into two, the other being at Irvinestown. The parish can be traced back in records to the beginning of the fourteenth century. Incumbents have included Patrick Delany, husband of the well-known Mrs Delany and, during Armar Lowry Corry's lifetime, Thomas McDonnell, William Meade, Richard Godley, John Stack and George Miller, Master of Armagh School.

Chapter Two

1   Fourth Earl Belmore, *History of Two Ulster Manors*, pp. 194–195. For an interesting account of the social life of the gentry in Fermanagh in Mr Armar's time see fourth Earl Belmore, *History of the Corry Family*, p. 281.
2   Mr Armar's account book, the 'long brown book', PRONI D/3007/B/5/8/1 is the only source of information about his transactions at Castle Coole in the middle 18th century. It should be read together with D/3007/4/1/1. Francis Bindon (1698?–1765), well known wealthy painter and architect painted portraits of Swift, Richard Baldwin, and other eminent Irishmen. His designs for houses include Bessborough and Woodstock, Kilkenny and New Hall, Clare. He collaborated with Richard Cassels on Russborough, Wicklow.

    David Griffin has proposed that a design in the archive at Castle Coole was by Richard Cassels for a new house for Margetson Armar. Bindon seems to be a more likely candidate. In the period 1747 to the early 1750s, Mr Armar's improvements to the house, garden and the demesne were so extensive it seems unlikely he had a rebuild of his existing house in mind. It was not yet 40 years old and had been reslated some 20 years previously. Another factor militating against an extensive rebuild was that, by the 1750s Mr and Mrs Armar's health had declined. Francis Bindon was actually present at Castle Coole and worked on the improvements. The design is reminiscent of other designs by Bindon (see eg. M. Bence-Jones, *A Guide to Irish Country Houses*, London, 1988). There is no mention of any payment to Cassels in the otherwise meticulous accounts, indexed by Mr Armar himself. Mr Armar and Bindon were contemporaries and connected through a mutual friend, Dr Dunkin, headmaster of Enniskillen school.
3   Mr Armar's appointment as governor is at PRONI D/627/17.
4   The letter is in the correspondence of Sir James Caldwell in the Bagshawe muniments at the John Rylands Library 3/16/1–434.

Chapter Three

1   The fourth Earl's account of the Lowry ancestry in *History of Two Ulster Manors*, p. 16 and chapter 2 and in *History of the Corry Family*, pp. 144 ff is challenged by Joan Gladstone in *The Lauries of Maxwelton and Other Laurie Families*, p. 185. Lady Dorothy Lowry Corry spent some time attempting to clarify the Lowry ancestry but without success.
2   *Universal Advertiser*, 1754, quoted in fourth Earl Belmore, *History of the Corry Family*, p. 161.
3   His note is among the Belmore vouchers at PRONI D/3007/H/1/28–60. The New Style came into force in England in 1752 and dictated that Wednesday 2 September of that year was to be followed by Thursday 14 September, thus 'losing' 11 days. 'Give us back our 11 days!' was a popular cry. The point of the change was to

adopt the Gregorian calendar which was a more accurate measurement of the year than the old Julian calendar. Unfortunately, because the Roman Catholic Church had introduced the Gregorian calendar in 1582, many saw it as a popish trick.

4 The books are in the library at Castle Coole; Armar's notebook is at PRONI D/3007/F/2/1. Unless otherwise noted, the early history of Armar's family is to be found in the fourth Earl's works.

5 Fourth Earl Belmore, *The Parliamentary Memoirs of Fermanagh, County and Borough.*

6 PRONI D/3007/B/5/8/2B.

7 Stewart of Killymoon papers, PRONI D/3167/2/10.

8 Stewart of Killymoon papers, PRONI D/3167/2/14A.

9 Belmore papers, PRONI D/3007/B/5/8/2A and B.

10 The letter books of Sir James Caldwell in the Bagshawe muniments at the John Rylands Library 3/10/1–626 and 3/11/1–43.

Chapter Four

1 Memo by Shannon, late January or early February 1777, Shannon letters, National Library of Ireland 13205–13306.

2 Sir Richard Heron, letter to the lawyer Pollock, 20 February 1793, Lothian papers, National Archives of Scotland GD/40/9/188/1–92 and GD/40/198/1–46.

3 Buckinghamshire's memorandum book, Heron papers, National Library of Ireland 13061.

4 Shannon papers, PRONI D/2707.

5 Hobart papers, PRONI T/3110.

6 Hotham papers, PRONI T/3429/1/54 and quoted in fourth Earl Belmore, 'Parliamentary Memoranda of Bygone Days'.

7 Hotham papers, PRONI T/3429/1.

8 Letters of Lady Louisa Conolly, Heron papers, National Library of Ireland 13039, 13047–13056.

9 Shannon papers, PRONI D/2707/A/2/4/1–24.

10 Letters of Lady Moira to Henrietta Hobart are in the Lothian papers, National Archives of Scotland GD/40/9/186/1–58, and in volume one of the Granard papers, PRONI T/3765/M/3/14/1–34.

11 Peerage correspondence of Sir John Caldwell in the Bagshawe muniments, John Rylands Library 3/36/1–49.

12 Historical Manuscripts Commission, Stopford-Sackville MSS vol. i, 1904, pp. 268–269.

13 See David Large, *The Wealth of the Greater Irish Landlords, 1750–1815*, pp. 22, 34 and 39 ff.

14 Stewart of Killymoon papers, PRONI D/3167/20–23.

15 In Brian MacArthur (ed.), *The Penguin Book of Historic Speeches*, p. 387.

16 Hotham papers, PRONI T/3429/1/55.

17 Buckinghamshire to Lord George Germain on 22 April 1780 (during the passage of the Bill), Heron papers, National Library of Ireland 13034–39, 13047–56, 13061 and 1471.

18 Quoted in David Dickson, 'Coalition Under Stress', p. 165.

19 Heron papers, National Library of Ireland 13034–13039, 13047–13056, 13061 and 1471.

Chapter Five

1 The correspondence about the separation and divorce of the Belmores is in the Lothian papers, National Archive of Scotland GD/40/9/188/1–92 and GD/40/9/198/1–46. The original interrogatories are in the National Archives at Kew C/12/1262/3 and depositions were published at the time as *The Trial of Viscountess Belmore*, printed for T. Salisbury, London, a copy of which is in the Library at Castle Coole. The letters of Henrietta Hobart to Lady Enniskillen are in the archive of the Earl of Sandwich at Mapperton, Dorset. The letters to her father and the letters of Louisa Conolly are in the Heron papers, National Library of Ireland 13045.

2 Hotham papers, PRONI T/3429/1/62.

Chapter Six

1 PRONI D/3007/C/2/1–18.

2 Lady Moira to Henrietta Hobart in the Lothian papers, National Archive of Scotland GD/40/9/186/1–58 and in volume one of the Granard papers, PRONI M/3/14/1–34.

3 Letter to Grenville, 3 November 1789, Historic Manuscripts Commission Report 13, App. 3, 1892, pp. 536–537.

4 The sources for Belmore's three liaisons are in notes made by Lady Dorothy Lowry Corry in the archive at Castle Coole: for Emily Maria Corry, later Maria Watson, Belmore's will and Cumbria Record Office CR/57.144; for Armar Lowry Corry, (Captain Corry), correspondence at Castle Coole with his descendants, the Poore family, New Zealand and his naval record in the Admiralty papers, British Library; for John Corry, the cadet papers 1775–1860 in the East India Company archive and his will and other documents in the West Bengal Higher Education Archives, ref 765–C.

5 The marriage settlement is at PRONI D/3007/A/14/8 extended by PRONI D/3007/A/14/10.

6 In the Lothian papers (see note two).

7 The information about Buckinghamshire and Blickling Hall is in John Maddison *et al*, *Blickling Hall: A Guide*. Buckinghamshire invited Belmore in a letter of 14 May 1792 (see the Lothian papers).

8 For loans see the Belmore papers, PRONI D/3007/H/1/1–27, estate vouchers for Tyrone and Fermanagh, PRONI D/3007/C/1–2 and C/3/1–9; for the letter about Uncle Lowry and the mill see fourth Earl Belmore, *History of Two Ulster Manors*, pp. 260–261; the examples of daily business are from Samuel Galbraith's accounts, 1799 to 1811, Nov to Nov, PRONI D/3007/B/3/4/4; for additions to the landscape see fourth Earl Belmore, *History of Two Ulster Manors* pp. 260–263; for improvements to the Queen Anne house see PRONI D/3007/C/2/1–18; For Hood's surveys see PRONI D/624/1 (for the account book) and PRONI D/624/2 (for the maps); for the Lord Lieutenant's visit see PRONI D/3007/C/2/1–25. The reference to the knighthood was noted by Lady Dorothy Lowry Corry from William A. Shaw, *The Knights of England*, vol. ii, p. 300.

9 The new work on the demesne and its roads is described in fourth Earl Belmore, *History of Two Ulster Manors*, p. 262; Belmore's reasons for choosing the site at Castle Coole are described on p. 263.

Chapter Seven

1 Details of the building work and its progress from 1778 to 1798 are derived from Alexander Stewart's weekly accounts, PRONI D/3007/D/2/1–11. Stewart himself remains a shadowy character. He made his will at Castle Coole in 1796 and probate was granted in 1805, so by then he was dead (see PRONI T/700 – will abstracts in the Stewart Kennedy notebooks at Trinity College, Dublin). However, there is also an entry in Sir Arthur Vicars, *Index to the Prerogative Wills of Ireland 1536–1810*, describing Alexander Stewart as 'formerly of Co. Fermanagh and late of North Britain', and saying that his will was proved in 1808. The letters of Alexander Stewart are at PRONI D/3007/D/2/10 and those of Rose are at PRONI D/3007/D/2/17.

2 *The Dublin Gazette* is among the Dublin newspapers, PRONI MIC/457.

3 The rivalries between the architects were suggested by Dr McParland in a letter to the author; see also his introduction to a list of architects etc from Mary Colley, 'Wilson's Dublin Directory' and for Wyatt's work in Ireland see Maurice Craig, *The Architecture of Ireland: From the Earliest Times to 1880*, p. 244.

4 The reconciliation between sister and brother is mentioned by Henrietta Belmore in a letter to Lady Enniskillen in the Lothian papers, National Archives of Scotland; an account of the building of Florence Court is in *The National Trust Guide: Florence Court, County Fermanagh*.

5 For the building and design of Baronscourt see the introduction by A.P.W. Malcomson to the Abercorn papers, PRONI D/623, and Gervase Jackson-Stops, 'Castle Coole Co. Fermanagh', especially the illustrations on pp. 87–88. A bill of Wyatt's (now lost) suggests that he, in fact, produced designs for Mount Stewart, a house well known to the Belmores: see Anne Casement, *Mount Stewart Landscape Study*.

6 The quotations are from Edward McParland, *Guidebook to Castle Coole*; the original Wyatt drawings at Castle Coole are referred to here but there are copies at PRONI D/3007/D/2/20.

7 'It is a glorious thing to save an estate for a family, and eternize your name,' enthused Lord Delvin, writing to his son-in-law in July 1746: Nugent papers, PRONI D/552/A/2/6/8 and quoted in S.J. Connolly, *Religion, Law and Power: The Making of Protestant Ireland 1660–1760*, p. 59 and Francis G. James, *Lords of the Ascendancy: The House of Lords and its Members, 1600–1800*, p. 95.

8 The remarks of the Chevalier de la Tocnaye are in *Promenade d'un francais dans l'Irlande*.

9 PRONI D/3007/D/2/11/2, backsheet, 'Approximate cost of Castlecoole The Works begun May 1788 finished November 1798'. The heading to the bill is, 'Approximate cost of Castlecoole house, including the furniture made by the joiners on the spot, & some [work in the garden] not including Mr Wyatt (the Architect's fees)'. See also balance sheets from May 1788 to October 1793, PRONI D/3007/D/2/9 and D/2/11/1.

10 The work on the greenhouses is at PRONI D/3007/C/3/3; the seed list and ice house are at PRONI D/3007/C/3/5.

11 The letters are in the Lothian papers (see chapter five note one).

12 Rose's letters are at PRONI D/3007/D/2/17/1 and 3 and D/3007/D/18/2.

13 Mrs Hackett's inventories are at PRONI D/3007/C/5–6. The details of furnishing can be found at PRONI D/3007/D/2/1–9 and in a notebook by Lady Violet Lowry Corry, PRONI D/3007/D/2/19.

14 In Anna Walker, *A Colonel's Wife in Ireland 1802–1807: The Diary of Mrs Anna Walker*, PRONI T/1565, entry for Tuesday 2 July 1805.

15 C.J. Woods (ed.), *Journals and Memoirs of Thomas Russell*, entries for Sunday 24 March 1793 and Monday 25 November 1793, pp. 68, 137.

16 See the Pelham papers, PRONI T/755/4/69, T/755/4/1/132, T/755/4/2/217 and 229 and see PRONI D/572/19/197, Hertford to MacCartney. Stewart also reports the banking crisis to Abercorn in March 1797 in the Abercorn papers, PRONI D/623/A/140/6.

17 Both quotations are from a letter of 11 December 1797 in the correspondence of Sir John Caldwell in the Bagshawe muniments, John Rylands Library 3/35/1–44.

18 From Queen Ann (*sic*) Street East, 8 December 1797, PRONI D/3007/D/2/17/7.

Chapter Eight

1 This chapter is based principally on the Abercorn papers, PRONI D/623/A/2, A/77, A/109, A/136 and A/139, the introduction to the papers by Dr Malcomson and especially his 'A Lost Natural Leader: John James Abercorn'.

2 John Stewart to James Stewart, 27 May 1794, PRONI D/3167/2/103.

3 PRONI D/623 (introduction).

4 PRONI D/623 (introduction) and Malcomson 'A Lost Natural Leader: John James Abercorn', quoting the diaries of Sylvester Douglas.

5 Abercorn papers, PRONI D/623/A/77/29.

6 Fourth Earl Belmore, *History of Two Ulster Manors*, p. 266. The first part of Somerset's diary is at Castle Coole but the second part is lost.

7 The bill for Belmore's Omagh volunteers is at PRONI D/3007/C/2/1–18.

8 Abercorn papers, PRONI D/623/A/139/6.

9 PRONI D/3007/C/2/1–25.

10 John Stewart's view about registering enough votes to beat Belmore is in a letter to James Stewart, 27 May 1794, PRONI D/3167/2/103.

11 For the introduction of the Election Bill see PRONI D/623/A/139/23 and for the militia business see PRONI D/623/A/137/42 and 45; for the Montgomery Moore 'explanation' see PRONI D/3167/2/123.

12 See note four above for the general financial crisis.

13 Abercorn papers, PRONI D/623/A/140/34 ff.

14 In a letter to Henrietta Ancram in the Lothian papers, National Archives of Scotland.

15 Gosford papers, PRONI D/1606/1/1/201; Belmore's letter to Mary Anne's father is in the correspondence of Sir John Caldwell in the Bagshawe muniments, John Rylands Library 3/35/1–44.

16 Advertisements in the *Erne Packet*: for example, front page Saturday 22 April 1809, PRONI microfilm MIC/431/5.

17 'Mary Countess of Belmore' features in 'They Came to Bath' on the website www.bath.co.uk.

Chapter Nine

1 Corry seems to have had a series of tutors, perhaps specialists in different fields. In one of life's great missed opportunities, William Wordsworth himself applied to be Corry's tutor. On 12 July 1793 Dorothy Wordsworth commented in a letter to Miss Jane Pollard that 'the expectation which I mentioned that William had formed of being engaged as tutor to Lord Belmore's son is at an end. The place was engaged before his friend's application reached Ireland' (Dorothy Wordsworth, *Letters of William and Dorothy Wordsworth*).

2 Lady Dorothy Lowry Corry, having found at Castle Coole what she supposed were poles for cavalry standards, wrote to Mr T.G.F. Paterson of the Armagh County Museum about a possible cavalry commission of Corry's but, in his reply of 19 October 1943, he said he could find no such commission. There are now no poles or cavalry standards at Castle Coole. Mr Paterson's letter is in the archive at Castle Coole but there is no copy of Lady Dorothy's letter to Mr Paterson.

3 Letter to Martha McTier, Belfast, 22 February 1798, in Jean Agnew (ed.), The *Drennan-McTier Letters* 1794–1801, vol. ii, pp. 370, 393.

4 Letters to the second Earl Alexander and officers and other military papers, PRONI D/2433/C/3/20.

5 Fourth Earl Belmore, *History of Two Ulster Manors*, p. 288. There is a report of the trial at Enniskillen Assizes in the *Belfast News Letter* for 28 March–1 April 1796.

6 From John Maxwell's secret committee notebooks, 1797, ISPO 620/34/54, and Ker to Pelham, 9 April 1797, ISPO 620/29/201, quoted in R.B. McDowell, *Ireland in the Age of Imperialism and Revolution 1760–1801*, p. 547.

7 Fourth Earl Belmore, *History of Two Ulster Manors*, pp. 269–271 and E.M. Johnston-Liik, *History of the Irish Parliament 1692–1800*, p. 126.

8 *The Constitution or Anti-Union Evening Post*, 11 February 1800; fourth Earl Belmore, *History of Two Ulster Manors*, p. 277 and contemporary Dublin newspapers at PRONI. The union manoeuvres by government and opposition and the make-up of the latter, which forms the background to the positions adopted by Belmore and Corry, are fully reflected in Charles Derek Ross (ed.), *The Correspondence of Charles, First Marquis of Cornwallis*, vols ii and iii.

9 Letter of Charlemont to Stewart, 5 September 1799, PRONI D/3167/D/1/77.

10 Corry's full speeches were reported in The *Constitution or Anti-Union Evening Post*, 1800, bound copies of which are in the library at Castle Coole; corruption and allied activities are discussed fully by Patrick M. Geoghegan in *The Irish Act of Union: A Study in High Politics 1798–1801*, pp. 79, 294.

11 *Cornwallis Correspondence*, vol. iii and fourth Earl Belmore, *History of Two Ulster Manors*, p. 288.

12 Fourth Earl Belmore, *History of Two Ulster Manors*, pp. 272–273.

13 The firm was in Pond Street, London and the letter is in the Exchequer papers, miscellaneous correspondence etc. in the University of London Library; their intention to live in Aghenis is in fourth Earl Belmore, *History of Two Ulster Manors*, p. 19.

Chapter Ten

1 The correspondence showing the political manoeuvres is in the Abercorn papers, PRONI D/623/A/81 and A/141.

2 Babington's accounts, PRONI D/3007/B/5/8/3.

3 Fourth Earl Belmore, *History of Two Ulster Manors*, p. 274.

4 This narrative is based on Babington's accounts, 1798–1812, PRONI D/3007/B/5/8/3, and fourth Earl Belmore, *History of Two Ulster Manors*, chapter 18; Belmore's will of 10 December 1800 is at PRONI D/3007/A/14/2.

5 Unless otherwise referenced, the financial information in this chapter is taken from entries in Belmore's agents' books at PRONI: Alexander Gordon, D/3007/B/4/2/3B, D/3007/2/23B; Samuel Galbraith, D/3007/B/5/8/3C, D/3007/B/3/2/1, D/3007/B/4/1/1; and James Galbraith, D/3007/B/3/1/1–10. Captain Cole, as he was usually known, was a very important figure in the business and personal affairs of Belmore. It seems strange that such an active member of the Enniskillen family is not mentioned in anything so far found relating to the early Coles. A deed of 10 March 1780 shows that Lord Enniskillen and 'Henry Cole' of Clare Hall, Cambridge then resided at 10 Marlborough Buildings, Bath. Sir Richard Musgrave's *Memoirs of the Different Rebellions in Ireland from the Arrival of the English* has a Henry St George Cole, who was a magistrate in Waterford, 'most cruelly murdered' at Arruglin near Kilworth on 9 January 1798. Perhaps this explains his disappearance from records. Musgrave may, however, have been mistaken. The Reverend R.H. Ryland in *The History, Topography and Antiquities of the County and City of Waterford* gives details of unsuccessful attempts against the life of Cole and the Limerick *General Advertiser or Gazette* for 28 May 1819 has the following obituary:

> 'COLE Henry St George Esq Capt On 15th inst at Annstown in the Co Waterford, in the 74th year of his age Henry St George COLE Esq Capt in army & magistrate for several counties of Ireland and landwaiterr [*sic*] of the port of Waterford'.

An earlier report says, 'relation of the Earl of Enniskillen'.

6 'Extract taken from Mr Corry's Rentalls of the amount of his settled and unsettled Estates', National Archives of Scotland GD40/9/188/82.

7 The calculations of Belmore's indebtedness are based on: references in fourth Earl Belmore, *History of Two Ulster Manors*, chapters 18 and 19; an account of the Belmore finances, 1789–1893, PRONI D/300/B/1/1; the figures revealed by the agents' and stewards' accounts and the statement of Belmore's finances for the marriage treaty noted above. Farm income and expenditure are shown at PRONI D/3007/B/5/1–2.

The best indication of his borrowing from the early 1780s until the end of his life in 1802 is in a schedule of encumbrances prepared in 1852 for the Encumbered Estates Court, which shows a total borrowed during that time and still outstanding, of just over £54,000.

8 The figure of £70,000 is an estimate based on an average weekly cost, shown in the building accounts, from 1795 to 1798, when it can be said the major work was done. To this average cost has to be added suppliers' bills and an estimate made by Cole in a memorandum of 26 April 1793 of anticipated annual expenditure for the next five years of between £3,600 and £4,600 (the latter figure including £1,000 for 'foreign contingencies'), PRONI D/3007/D2/9/1. The estimate is also anecdotally confirmed by the assertion of the second Earl that the house cost a total of £100,000, a figure which would have included his outlay for furniture and furnishings (well over £20,000) and essential further work on the bare estate around the house.

9 Belmore's letters requesting money are among vouchers at PRONI D/3007/H/1/1–27.

10 The details are at PRONI D/3007/B/1/1.

11 In 1800 a paper entitled 'Dublin Will Lose by the Union', PRONI D/207/10/9, estimated Belmore's annual expenditure in the city at £4,000. It suggests an additional £3,000 would be lost by the sale of his house in Sackville Street. His annual expenditure is, with the Earl of Leitrim's, the highest figure on the list, suggesting that he was well known and a big spender in Dublin. As for his comment that the house could not hold his servants, it does seem that the houses in that street were not very large. Arthur Young commented that houses in Dublin were often not large enough to hold the numerous company squeezed into them – Arthur Young, *Arthur Young's Tour in Ireland*, quoted in S.J. Connolly, *Religion, Law and Power: The Making of Protestant Ireland 1660–1760*, p. 63.

12 PRONI D/3007/A/14/1–23.

13 The Abercorn papers, PRONI D/623/A/139/11–12.

NOTES TO PART TWO

Chapter Eleven

The early part of this chapter is based principally on the Abercorn papers, PRONI D/623A/2, A/77, A/109, A/136, A/139 and A/140.

1 Quoted in Jane A. Meredith, *Andrew Caldwell (1733–1808): A Study of a 'Guardian of Taste and Genius'* (M.Litt thesis: Trinity College Dublin, 2004).

2 The diary entries are from Anna Walker, *A Colonel's Wife in Ireland 1802–1807: The Diary of Mrs Anna Walker*, PRONI T/1565; the verse is in the archive at Castle Coole.

3 The complete accounts of Preston's work are at PRONI D/3007/D/2/13/1–2.

4 In the Wellington papers, PRONI T/2627/3/2/40.

5 Stewart to Abercorn, 8 March 1802, in the Abercorn papers, PRONI D/623.

6 PRONI D/3007/H/1/54–56, 59 and 60: affidavit and certificate of trees planted on the Bishop's land at Castle Coole and relevant statutory advertisements in the *London Gazette*.

7 There is no indication whether Mr Williams's school in Bangor was in Wales or the north of Ireland. The account of John's and Armar's setting out is based on Babington's accounts, PRONI D/3007/B/5/8/8 and their subsequent careers are in the PRO, Kew: Admiralty records ADM1, 9/26, 10, 12 and 196; War Office records WO4/515, WO25/748 and 3216, WO 31/18 and 332; army lists; India Office records and archives of the government of West Bengal, ref 475–SA: John Corry: His will is in the Supreme Court of Bengal records, ref L/AG/34/29/18. See also V.C.P. Hobson, *List of the Officers of the Bengal Army 1758–1834* (available in the British Library) and the supplement to the *Calcutta Gazette*, Thursday 11 December 1806.

8 Records for Lady Louisa, including her correspondence with Armar Corry and Juliana Belmore, are in the archive of the Earl of Sandwich, Mapperton, Dorset.

9 From Harriet Campbell, *Diary of Harriet Charlotte Beaujolais Campbell*, p. 42. Her presence in Brighton, noted by the diarist Lady Granville, is quoted in Margaret Barton and Osbert Sitwell, *Brighton*, p. 329.

10 Charles Luther Watson's will is in the Cumbria Record Office, as is the pedigree of Maria Watson's twin children by him and of her children by her second husband Christopher Salter. The twins were a boy (Richard Luther) and a girl (Mary Anne Juliana) who did not survive. Richard, the first Earl's grandson, married Louisa Anne Cole, with whom he had four daughters.

11 From Jonathan Binns, *The Miseries and Beauties of Ireland*, vol. i, pp. 281–282.

12 The vouchers that support the account of Belmore's activities including Salthill and the *Flying Fish* are at PRONI D/3007/C2/25–51 and D/3007/C/3/9/1–47; see also Babington's accounts for 1798–1815, PRONI D/3007/B/5/8/B–D; and John King Irwin's accounts, PRONI D/3007/B/5/8/4.

Chapter Twelve

1 For Seaview and the *Flying Fish* see PRONI D/3007C/2/26, an account book for 22 May 1813 to 22 November 1813 and a small account book rolled up inside it – 'Disbursements at Seaview Commencing June 1813'. For the purchase of Hamilton Place, London, see PRONI D/3007/C/6.

2 The acquisition, conversion and travels of the *Osprey* are at PRONI D/3007/C/4/1–2; D/3007/C/5 and C/6. The website www.wikipedia.org says, 'The first *Madison* (named after the President of the USA) was a 14-gun schooner launched in 1812 on Lake Ontario and used in the war of 1812'.

3 This is borne out by the account book at PRONI D/3007/B/1/1 and by the second Earl's later attempts to raise £120,000 from an insurance company (see PRONI D/3007/C/3/31/5).

4 Townshend's letter is at PRONI D/3007/H/6/4. In a later letter, also in May (PRONI D/3007/H/6/5), Townshend returned to an issue that had previously occupied him – the arrears of rent from Belmore's estates, which Townshend considered excessive. He thought Belmore could cut them down by changing the way in which he dealt with tenants, but the truth was that arrears were not the essential issue. They paled into insignificance in the bright light of Belmore's spending.

Chapter Thirteen

1 Marianne Brooke was the daughter of the Reverend William Sneyd of New Church Isle of Wight. The Sneyds and the Lowry Corrys were closely connected and had been for many years before Juliana's birth. The Sneyds were well-known Dublin wine merchants and neighbours of Belmore's in Sackville Street, Dublin.

According to the Brooke family memoir (Raymond F. Brooke, *The Brimming River*) the General, 'having retired, married – late in life – and settled down at Scribblestown, not far from Dublin, where he was much harrassed by his small son Arthur, known as Atty'. In other words, she did not marry General Brooke until after he had retired from the army in June 1814. Juliana was born in 1814 and so must have been conceived before the General reappeared in Ireland.

Brooke had been on continuous military service in the French and American wars from the 1790s until he retired. Whilst commanding the First Battalion of the Forty-fourth (East Essex) in Malta, apart from the day-to-day cares with the regiment, the then Lieutenant Colonel Arthur Brooke had a problem in his private life. His wife had been a passenger on board the frigate *Amphion* which was returning to England in July 1807 for repairs, under Captain William Hoste, who had been Nelson's protégé. During the voyage an attachment developed between the dashing 26-year-old Hoste and Mrs Brooke and, even after arriving at Portsmouth in early August, he continued to see her in England. Her husband insisted upon her returning to Malta promptly, which she did, but kept in correspondence with Hoste and met him occasionally when the *Amphion* called at Malta. By 1808 she was in Sicily with the regiment, and the liaison was ended.

This, surely, must have been Marianne Sneyd. There is no record of any other relevant Marianne. Drennan's reference to Miss Brooke should, perhaps, have been to Mrs Brooke. Among several of Juliana's books in the library at Castle Coole there is one, *A Cambridge Garden* by James Donn (1815) which is signed on the title page, 'Marianne Brooke May the 11th 1815' and 'Juliana Brooke April 27th 1834'.

Juliana suffered from poor health throughout her short life and died aged about 21. In his will of 7 March 1837 Somerset left a yearly rent charge of £100 to Marianne, Lady Brooke, wife of General Sir Arthur Brooke, plus a further sum of £100. He also left '£1,000 to Arthur, son of Lt General Brooke who is in the 23rd Regiment of Royal Welch Fusiliers to purchase a commission'.

2 For the travels for the period 1817–1820, see PRONI D/3007/C/28–29, C/4/1–2, C/4/5, H/5/1–79 and H/6/1–16. The letters of Lady Hester Stanhope and other travellers are in the archive at Castle Coole as are Mr de Keersmaeker's tracings of name carvings; see bibliography for M.D. Richardson, *Travels Along the Mediterranean in Company with the Earl of Belmore* and Belzoni's *Narrative of the Operations and Recent Discoveries in Egypt and Nubia*, which are in the in library at Castle Coole; Deborah Manley and Peta Rée, *Henry Salt: Artist, Traveller, Diplomat, Egyptologist*, which is invaluable; see also Jean Jacques Fiechter, *La moisson des dieux*, pp. 113–115, 120 and 131 for Belmore references.

3 A letter from a Mr P. Lee (Legh?) to Belmore, dated 13 October 1817, PRONI D/3007/H/5/1–79.

4 Sarah Belzoni, frequently left by her husband to fend for herself, gave a fascinating account of her experiences in *Mrs Belzoni's Trifling Account of the Women of Egypt, Nubia and Syria*. It was printed by John Murray in 1820 as an appendix to Belzoni's own narrative, but deserves reading for itself.

5 Episode described in letter four of Charles Irby and James Mangles, *Travels in Egypt and Nubia, Syria and Asia Minor* in the Castle Coole archive.

6 Letters between Belmore and Salt, 18 September 1818, from the Castle Coole archive.

7 From Campbell, 3 July 1821, from the Castle Coole archive.

8 Boxes at PRONI D/3007/C/4–5 which contain material about the travels are complemented by D/3007C/6 – several boxes relating to the purchase of Hamilton Place, London, residence there and then in Cowes, Portsmouth, the purchase of the *Osprey* and books of account for the period 1813–1821, during which the family were away from Castle Coole. See also letters and vouchers at PRONI D/3007/H/5.

9 The poem by Murphy is in the Castle Coole archive and two copies are also at PRONI D/3007/H/5/72–73.

Chapter Fourteen

1 The designs are at PRONI D/3007/D/2/20.

2 Letter from Robert Banks Jenkinson, second Earl of Liverpool (Prime Minister), of Fife House, London, to Arthur Wellesley, first Duke of Wellington in the Wellington papers, University of Southampton (accessible online).

3 PRONI D/3007/D/2/13/1.

4 Letters from Spiller, PRONI D/3007/B/5/1–5; B/6/1–5 and B/7/1–4; also C/2/28; H/5/46 and H/6.

5 Artemus Ward (Charles Farrar Browne), cited in *Oxford Dictionary of Quotations*.

6 The correspondence is at PRONI D/3007/H/14.

7 PRONI D/3007/C/3/26.

8 Sarah married Alexander Saunderson of Castle Saunderson in 1828. Her brothers became, successively, seventh, eighth and ninth Baron Farnham. Her sister Harriet married Edward Southwell, third Viscount Bangor in 1826 and was mother to the subsequent Viscount: see fourth Earl Belmore, *History of the Corry Family*, p. 178. The letters between Captain Corry and Lady Sandwich are at Mapperton in the private archive of the Earl of Sandwich. Lady Louisa's letter is in the Norwich Record Office Castlereagh Papers IV 1794–1827 ref MC 3/293

Chapter Fifteen

The narrative about the second Earl in Jamaica is, unless otherwise indicated, from PRONI D/3007/G.

1 Transcripts of the letters are available online from the Wellington papers, University of Southampton Docref WP1/936/21, Docref WP1/939/12, Docref WP1/940/16, Docref WP1/950/2.

2 Fourth Earl Belmore, *History of Two Ulster Manors*, p. 283.

3 PRONI D/3007/G/53 is a transcript by Lady Dorothy Lowry Corry of the original, which is referred to in PRONI D/3007/G/32/1, no. 19 ('Papers Relating to the *Dolphin*') but has a pencil note written and signed by the fourth Earl saying, 'Given to Captain Alvin Corry RN 23 Sep 1891 by me'.

Captain Alvin Corry was Alvin Coote Corry, the son of Captain Armar Lowry Corry, the first Earl's illegitimate son. Commander George S. Pearson OBE Royal Navy (retd) supplied the following information about him in a personal communication:

'He first features as a Sub Lieutenant of seniority 17 Nov 1868. He enjoyed steady promotion to Lieutenant (29 Dec 1871), Commander (30 Jun 1882), Captain (30 Jun 1890) and finally Rear Admiral (31 Aug 1903). As a Captain, he commanded the battleship HMS *Hood* in the Mediterranean in 1899. He died of pneumonia on 25 Jan 1907 in office as the Admiral Superintendent HM Dockyard Chatham. It is in his time in command of the Hood in 1899 that my particular interest lies. On 23 Sep 1891 when the fourth Earl wrote his note, Alvin had been on half pay since 31 Aug 1890. However, on 30 Sep 1891, he began a nine month period of study at the Royal Naval College, Greenwich.

'It is only fair that I declare my interest in Alvin's time in command of the *Hood*. It is clear that he and his Navigating Officer, Lieutenant Hughes Campbell Lockyer, did not see eye to eye. I have seen a letter dated May 1903 from Cam Lockyer to his father Sir Norman Lockyer the astronomer and discoverer of helium in which he refers back to the "row with friend Corry in the *Hood*". Lockyer clearly bore a lasting grudge because that year, three years after he and Alvin had parted company, a large correction based on a survey conducted by Lockyer was published to the British Admiralty chart of Mudros Bay in the Greek island Lemnos in which four hitherto anonymous hills were given the names Yam, Yrroc, Eb and Denmad: try saying those names backwards. The names stand on British Admiralty chart 1661 to this day!'

Chapter Sixteen

1 The political scene is at PRONI D/3007/H/14/1–32.

2 Angélique Day and Patrick McWilliams (eds), *Ordnance Survey Memoirs of Ireland Volume 14: Parishes of County Fermanagh II 1834–5*, Lower Lough Erne, p. 67.

3 PRONI D/3007/H/9/10.

NOTES TO PART THREE

Chapter Seventeen

1 Fourth Earl Belmore, *History of Two Ulster Manors*, p. 285 ff.

2 See Newton's accounts, PRONI D/3007/D/2/13/2. The Belmore collection of Egyptian antiquities can be seen in the British Museum, which also holds complete lists of the objects.

NOTES TO PART FOUR

Chapter Eighteen

1 The fourth Earl passed the time on the voyage to Sydney in the *Sobraon* by writing notes on his past life and career. The notes, sometimes referred to as the '*Sobraon* Diary', are at PRONI D/3007/K/1/1. In 1904, he also wrote an account of his time as governor, entitled *Four Years in New South Wales*, which was intended for publication but was never finished, either because of his failing health or because he could not justify paying the cost of publication. The proofs are at PRONI D/3007/L/1/620. The whole of that category has been used for this account. Newspaper accounts of his governorship can also be found at PRONI D/3007/S/5–9.

The fourth Earl's financial position and the steps he and his mother and the dowager Countesses took to stabilise the situation are to be found at PRONI D/3007/B/1/1, at D/3007/B/6/2–3 and in fourth Earl Belmore, *History of Two Ulster Manors*.

2 *Impartial Reporter* newspaper, quoted in Neil McAtamney, *The Great Famine* in County Fermanagh.

3 The correspondence is in the Auchenleck papers at PRONI D/674.

4 This section is based principally on the *Sobraon Diary* and Belmore's unpublished *Cambridge Diary* in the archive at Castle Coole.

5 *Punch's Pocket Book*, 1853.

6 For a list of the Churchlands sold in Fermanagh in 1851 see fourth Earl Belmore, *History of Two Ulster Manors*, Appendix N; for those outside the Churchlands sold in 1851 see Appendix X and for a list of the Tyrone lands sold in 1852 and 1853 see Appendix Y.

7   Designs for lodges and houses can be found at
    PRONI D/3007/D/2/18 and 20.

Chapter Nineteen

1   From C. F. D'Arcy, Archbishop of Armagh, *The
    Adventures of a Bishop*.

Chapter Twenty

1   Pike, Douglas (ed.), *Australian Dictionary of
    Biography Volume 3: 1851–1890*.
2   Pike, Douglas (ed.), *Australian Dictionary of
    Biography Volume 3: 1851–1890*.
3   The resignation letters and other correspondence
    with Lord Kimberley is in the Special Collections
    and Western Manuscripts Division of the
    Bodleian Library, Oxford.

Chapter Twenty-one

1   The political correspondence is at PRONI
    D/3007/P.
2   Stanley Weintraub, *Disraeli: A Biography*, p. 625
    and Robert Blake, *Disraeli*.
3   James Morris, *Heaven's Command: An Imperial
    Progress*, p. 420.
4   The long course of correspondence from

Belmore's land agent for Fermanagh, John J.
Benison, is at PRONI D/3007/U.

5   Lady Winifred wrote the memoir shortly before
    her death in 1959, especially for Lady Anthea
    Forde, the present Earl's sister, addressing it:
    'for Anthea I have written these oddments'.
6   This refers to the time when the Bow room was
    used to show various family objects to visitors.
    The pram is now one of the objects shown from
    time to time in Honoria's bedroom, now known
    as the Victorian bedroom.
7   When she died in December 1903 Belmore
    inherited the Bradbourne estate in Kent, which
    was sold in 1947.
8   In the local newspaper, the *Impartial Reporter*.
9   See bibliography for his published works
    and PRONI D/3007/T for a listing of his
    archaeological and antiquarian papers.

Chapter Twenty-two

1   Details of the statue's history, its acquisition
    by the second Earl and authentication are fully
    covered in Christie's sale catalogue for
    Thursday 7 July 2005.
2   The original is in the archive at Castle Coole.

BIBLIOGRAPHY

Unpublished Material

In the Public Record Office of Northern Ireland (PRONI) there are the following collections with connections to the Belmore or Lowry Corry names:

D/3007
The principal Belmore papers consisting of 36,400 documents in 278 volumes.

D/674
The Auchenleck Family Papers
Auchenlecks were land agents for the second Earl in Tyrone and the papers are mainly leases to tenants. However, there is important correspondence about the relief of distress of Belmore's tenants in Beragh and Six Mile Cross during the famine of 1846–1847. The fourth Earl had only recently succeeded and was a minor so his uncle, Henry Corry, conducted his affairs. The tenants were in great distress and funds were needed for relief.

D/624
Belmore Estates in Tyrone and Longford
A set of maps by Henry Hood of Longford, Granard and Clongesh, 1786, and rental of the Corry (Belmore) estate, Omagh, County Tyrone, 1777–1786 with a set of maps of the County Longford estate.

T/3668
Belmore Lands at Thomastown, Derryvullen
Map of Thomastown Farm, parish of Derryvullen, County Fermanagh, by J. Weaver, 1886 and a table setting out areas of constituent fields (*c.* 1890) let by the fourth Earl Belmore to James Whiteside Dane.

T/348
Family Wills
Extracts of wills dating 1624–1830 made by Lady Dorothy Lowry Corry.

Some of the Belmore papers have been copied onto microfilm:

MIC/671
This seems to be a general reel and consists of copies of the accounts and rentals in classification B. Since this was first written in March 2004 more categories have been microfilmed, particularly D/3007/G, the second Earl's Jamaican papers.

MIC/463
Copies of Australian papers relating to the fourth Earl's time as governor of New South Wales.

D/3850
29 and 30 September 1823, 1825 and 1835–1836 leases: Somerset, Earl of Belmore to tenants in Ballynahatty and County Tyrone.

The following unpublished memoirs are held in the archive in Castle Coole:

Eden, Brigadier G.W. CBE, *A Recollection of Visits to Castle Coole.*

The parliamentary careers of the Corrys will be found summarised in E.M. Johnston-Liik, *History of the Irish Parliament 1692–1800* (see below).

See the notes to each chapter for details of further unpublished material relating to the Belmore family at Castle Coole.

Published Material

Agnew, Jean, *Belfast Merchant Families in the 17th Century* (Dublin, 1996).
— (ed.), The *Drennan-McTier Letters* 1794–1801 (Dublin, 1999).
Belmore, fourth Earl, *History of the Corry Family* (London, 1891).
—, *History of the Manors of Finagh and Coole* (London, 1881), later revised as *History of Two Ulster Manors* (London, 1903).
—, 'Parliamentary Memoranda of Bygone Days', *Ulster Journal of Archaeology* 9, part ii (*c.* 1861).
—, *The Parliamentary Memoirs of Fermanagh, County and Borough* (Dublin, 1885).
D'Arcy, C.F., Archbishop of Armagh, *The Adventures of a Bishop* (London, 1934).
Johnston, Edith M., *Great Britain and Ireland, 1760–1800* (London, 1963).
Johnston-Liik, E.M., *History of the Irish Parliament 1692–1800* (Belfast, 2002).

Livingstone, Peadar, *The Fermanagh Story* (Enniskillen, 1969).

McDowell, R.B., *Ireland in the Age of Imperialism and Revolution 1760–1801* (Oxford, 1979).

Murphy, Eileen and William Roulston (eds), *Fermanagh History and Society* (Belfast, 2004).

Power, Patrick C., *The Courts Martial of 1798–99* (Kilkenny, 1997).

Richardson, M.D., *Travels Along the Mediterranean in Company with the Earl of Belmore* (London, 1822).

Background Reading (including bibliographies)

First Earl and Eighteenth Century

Barnard, Toby, *Making the Grand Figure: Lives and Possessions in Ireland, 1641–1770* (New Haven, 2004).

Black, Jeremy, *The British Abroad: The Grand Tour in the Eighteenth Century* (Stroud, 1992).

Carroll, Denis and Orla Davin, *Dublin in 1798: Three Illustrated Walks* (South Hill, 1997).

Dickson, David, *New Foundations: Ireland 1660–1800* (Dublin, 2000).

Geoghegan, Patrick M., *The Irish Act of Union: A Study in High Politics 1798–1801* (Dublin, 2001).

Kelly, James, *Prelude to Union: Anglo-Irish Politics in the 1780s* (Dublin, 1992).

Vickery, Amanda, *The Gentleman's Daughter: Women's Lives in Georgian England* (New Haven, 1998).

Second Earl

Belzoni, G.B., *Narrative of the Operations and Recent Discoveries in Egypt and Nubia* (London, 1820).

Fiechter, Jean Jacques, *La moisson des dieux* (Paris, 1994).

Gash, Norman (ed.), *Studies in the Military and Political Career of the First Duke of Wellington* (Manchester, 1990).

Irby, Charles and James Mangles, *Travels in Egypt and Nubia, Syria and Asia Minor* (London, 1823).

Keogh, Daire and Kevin Whelan (eds), *Acts of Union: The Causes, Contexts and Consequences of the Act of Union* (Dublin, 2001).

Manley, Deborah and Peta Rée, *Henry Salt: Artist, Traveller, Diplomat, Egyptologist* (London, 2001).

Murray, Venetia, *High Society in the Regency Period* (London, 1998).

Pakenham, Thomas, *The Year of Liberty: The Great Irish Rebellion of 1798* (New York, 1997).

Rodger, N.A.M., *The Command of the Ocean: A Naval History of Britain, 1649–1815* (London, 2004).

Rush, Richard, *Resident at the Court of London* (London, 1987).

Third Earl

Eagleton, Terry, *Heathcliff and the Great Hunger: Studies in Irish Culture* (London, 1995).

Johnson, Jack (ed.), *Workhouses of the North West* (Enniskillen, 1996).

McAtamney, Neil, 'The Great Famine in County Fermanagh', *Clogher Record* 15 (1994).

Fourth Earl

Blake, Robert, *Disraeli* (London, 1998).

Weintraub, Stanley, *Disraeli: A Biography* (London, 1993).

Lanigan Wood, Helen, *Enniskillen* (Belfast, 1990).

General

Bartlett, Thomas, 'Protestant Nationalism in Eighteenth Century Ireland' in Michael O'Dea and Kevin Whelan (eds), *Nations and Nationalisms: France, Britain and Ireland the Eighteenth-century Context* (Oxford, 1995).

Barton, Margaret and Osbert Sitwell, *Brighton* (London, 1935).

Binns, Jonathan, *The Miseries and Beauties of Ireland* (London, 1837).

Blackstock, Allan, *An Ascendancy Army: The Irish Yeomanry, 1796–1834* (Dublin, 1998).

Boyce, D. George and Alan O'Day (eds), *The Making of Modern Irish History: Revisionism and the Revisionist Controversy* (London and New York, 1996).

Brooke, Raymond F., *The Brimming River* (Dublin, 1961).

Campbell, Harriet, *Diary of Harriet Charlotte Beaujolais Campbell* (G.R. de Beer FRS, ed.) (London, 1951).

Colley, Mary, 'Wilson's Dublin Directory', *Bulletin of the Irish Georgian Society* 34 (1991).

Connolly, S.J., *Religion, Law and Power: The Making of Protestant Ireland 1660–1760* (Oxford, 1992).

Craig, Maurice, *The Architecture of Ireland: From the Earliest Times to 1880* (London and Dublin, 1982).

Cullen, L.M., *Economic History of Ireland Since 1660* (London, 1987).

Day, Angélique and Patrick McWilliams (eds), *Ordnance Survey Memoirs of Ireland Volume 14: Parishes of County Fermanagh II 1834–5, Lower Lough Erne* (Belfast, 1992).

Depositions of 1641, no. 31 (Fermanagh volume, Trinity College Library) (1641).

Dickson, David (ed.), *The Gorgeous Mask: Dublin 1700–1850* (Dublin, 1987).

—, 'Coalition Under Stress' in *New Foundations: Ireland 1660–1800* (Dublin, 1999).

Duffy, Sean *et al.* (eds), *Atlas of Irish History* (Dublin, 1997).

Ehrman, John, *The Younger Pitt* (London, 1969).

Fitzgerald, Emilia, *Correspondence of Emily Duchess of Leinster* (three vols) (Dublin, 1949).

Foster, R.F., *Modern Ireland 1600–1972* (London, 1989).

Gladstone, Joan, *The Lauries of Maxwelton and Other Laurie Families* (London, 1972).

Graham, B.J. and L.J. Proudfoot (eds), *An Historical Geography of Ireland* (London, 1993).

Grattan, Henry, speeches in Brian MacArthur (ed.), *The Penguin Book of Historic Speeches* (London, 1996).

Hobson, V.C.P., *List of the Officers of the Bengal Army 1758–1834* (London, 1947).

Honor, Hugh, *The Age of Neo-Classicism* (London, 1972).

Hussey, Christopher, 'Castle Coole, Co. Fermanagh', *Country Life* 78 (November 1935), 80 (December 1936).

Inflation: The Value of the Pound 1750–1998, House of Commons Research Paper 99/20, (1999).

Jackson-Stops, Gervase, 'Castle Coole Co. Fermanagh' in Gervase Jackson-Stops *et al.*, *The English Country House in Perspective* (London, 1990).

James, Francis G., *Lords of the Ascendancy: The House of Lords and its Members, 1600–1800* (Dublin, 1995).

Large, David, 'The Wealth of the Greater Irish Landlords 1750–1815', *Irish Historical Studies* 15 (1966/1967), pp. 21–45.

Maddison, John *et al.*, *Blickling Hall: A Guide* (London, 1987).

Malcomson, A.P.W., *John Foster: The Politics of the Anglo-Irish Ascendancy* (Oxford, 1978).

—, *The Pursuit of the Heiress: Aristocratic Marriage in Ireland 1750–1820* (Belfast, reprinted 2006).

—, 'The Irish Peerage and the Act of Union', Transactions of the Royal Historical Society 6/10 (2000).

—, 'A Lost Natural Leader: John James Abercorn', Proceedings of the Royal Irish Academy 88 (1988).

Maxwell, Constantia, *Dublin Under the Georges 1714–1830* (London, 1936, revised 1956).

McCracken, J.L., *The Irish Parliament in the Eighteenth Century* (Dundalk, 1971).

McParland, Edward, *Guidebook to Castle Coole* (London 1976).

Mitchison, R. and P. Roebuck, *Economy and Society in Scotland and Ireland*, 1500–1939 (Edinburgh, 1988).

Moody, T.W. *et al.* (eds), *A New History of Ireland* (Oxford, 1986).

Morris, James, *Heaven's Command: An Imperial Progress* (London, 1973).

Musgrave, Sir Richard, *Memoirs of the Different Rebellions in Ireland from the Arrival of the English* (fourth edition: Steven W. Myers and Delores E. McKnight, eds) (Fort Wayne, 1995).

Punch's Pocket Book (London, 1853).

Robb, C.J., 'The Fermanagh Militia', *The Impartial Reporter* (27 December 1956).

Ross, Charles Derek (ed.), *The Correspondence of Charles, First Marquis Cornwallis* (London, 1859).

Ryland, R.H., *The History, Topography and Antiquities of the County and City of Waterford* (London, 1924).

Shaw, William A., *The Knights of England*, vol. ii (London, 1906).

St Leonards, Lord, *A Handy Book on Property Law in a Series of Letters* (London, 1858).

Stone, Lawrence, *The Family, Sex and Marriage in England 1500–1800* (London, 1979).

The National Trust Guide: Florence Court, County Fermanagh (based on a text by Colin McMordie et al. (1979).

Tillyard, Stella, *Aristocrats: Caroline, Emily, Louisa and Sarah Lennox* (London, 1994).

Tocnaye, Chevalier de la, *Promenade d'un francais dans l'Irlande* (Paris, 1797).

Turnor, R., *James Wyatt* (London, 1950).

Vicars, Sir Arthur, *Index to the Prerogative Wills of Ireland, 1536–1810* (Dublin, 1897).

Westropp, M.S. Dudley, 'Notes on Irish Money Weights and Foreign Coins Current in Ireland', *Proceedings of the Royal Irish Academy* 33/C/3 (1916).

Williams, Joshua and T. Cyprian, *Principles of the Law of Real Property* (London, 1892).

Woods, C.J. (ed.), *Journals and Memoirs of Thomas Russell* (Dublin and Belfast, 1991).

Wordsworth, Dorothy, *Letters of William and Dorothy Wordsworth* (Ernest de Selincourt, ed.) (Oxford, 1967–1993).

Works on Demesnes, Landscapes and Gardens

Casement, Anne, *Mount Stewart Landscape Study* (1995).

Dale, Anthony, *James Wyatt, Architect, 1746–1813* (London, 1936).

McErlean, Thomas, *The Historical Development of the Park at Castle Coole* (Belfast, 1984).

Mitchell, Frank and Michael Ryan, *Reading the Irish Landscape* (Dublin, 1997).

Schama, Simon, *Landscape and Memory* (London, 1995).

Reference

Oxford Dictionary of Quotations (third edition) (Oxford, 1980).

Pike, Douglas (ed.), *Australian Dictionary of Biography Volume 3: 1851–1890* (Melbourne, 1969).

Walker, David M., *The Oxford Companion to Law* (Oxford, 1980).

INDEX